Language Intervention Series
Volume III

LANGUAGE INTERVENTION FROM APE TO CHILD

LANGUAGE INTERVENTION FROM APE TO CHILD, edited by Richard L. Schiefelbusch, Ph.D., and John H. Hollis, Ed.D., is the third volume in the **Language Intervention Series**—Richard L. Schiefelbusch, series editor. Other volumes in this series include:

Language Intervention Series
Volume III

LANGUAGE INTERVENTION FROM APE TO CHILD

Edited by

Richard L. Schiefelbusch, Ph.D.

University Professor
and
Director, Bureau of Child Research
University of Kansas

and

John H. Hollis, Ed.D.

Bureau of Child Research
University of Kansas
and
Kansas Neurological Institute

Technical Editors
Marilyn Barket
Robert Hoyt
Bureau of Child Research
University of Kansas

University Park Press
Baltimore

UNIVERSITY PARK PRESS
International Publishers in Science, Medicine, and Education
233 East Redwood Street
Baltimore, Maryland 21202

Typeset by American Graphic Arts Corporation.
Manufactured in the United States of America by
The Maple Press Company.

Jacket illustration by Myron Sahlberg.
Jacket design by Bob Christensen.

Library of Congress Cataloging in Publication Data

Main entry under title:

Language intervention from ape to child.
(Language intervention series; v. 3)
Based on material presented at a conference on
nonspeech language which was held at
Gulf Shores, Ala. in 1977.
Includes bibliographical references and index.
1. Animal communication—Congresses.   2. Handi-
capped children—Language—Congresses.   3. Primates—
Behavior—Congresses.   4. Nonverbal communication—
Congresses.   I. Schiefelbusch, Richard L.   II. Hollis,
John H.   III. Series.
QL776.L36   599'.8'0459   79-359
ISBN 0-8391-1413-3

contents

conference participants

*Joseph K. Carrier, Jr., Ph.D.
P. O. Box 21
Bellvue, Colorado 80512

John B. Carroll, Ph.D.
Keenan Professor of Psychology
   and Director, L. L. Thurstone
   Psychometric Laboratory
University of North Carolina
Chapel Hill, North Carolina 27514

Robin S. Chapman, Ph.D.
Associate Professor
Department of Communicative
   Disorders
University of Wisconsin
Madison, Wisconsin 53706

*Joseph B. Couch, Ph.D.
Department of Psychology
University of Oklahoma
Norman, Oklahoma 73069

*Ruth E. Deich, Ph.D.
Institute for Research in Human
   Growth
1737 Finecroft Drive
Claremont, California 91711

*Roger S. Fouts, Ph.D.
Research Associate
Department of Psychology
University of Oklahoma
Norman, Oklahoma 73069

Macalyne Fristoe, Ph.D.
Director, Speech Clinic
Associate Professor
Department of Audiology and Speech
   Sciences
Purdue University
West Lafayette, Indiana 47907

*Timothy V. Gill, Ph.D.
Georgia State University
Atlanta, Georgia 30303
and
Yerkes Regional Primate Research
   Center of Emory University
Atlanta, Georgia 30322

*Sam Glucksberg, Ph.D.
Professor and Chairman
·Department of Psychology
Princeton University
Princeton, New Jersey 08540

Deberah Harris, Ms.Ed.
Area Coordinator, Communication
   Research and Training
Trace Research and Development
   Center for the Severely
   Communicatively Handicapped
University of Wisconsin
Madison, Wisconsin 53706

*Patricia Hodges, Ph.D.
Institute for Research in Human
   Growth
1737 Finecroft Drive
Claremont, California 91711
and
Department of Psychology
California State University
Los Angeles, California 90032

*John H. Hollis, Ed.D.
Research Associate
Bureau of Child Research
University of Kansas
Lawrence, Kansas 66045
and
Kansas Neurological Institute
3107 West 21st Street
Topeka, Kansas 66604

*Robert M. Krauss, Ph.D.
Professor and Chairman of
   Psychology
Columbia University
New York, New York 10027

Lyle L. Lloyd, Ph.D.
Chairman and Professor of Special
  Education
Professor of Audiology and Speech
  Sciences
Purdue University
West Lafayette, Indiana 47907

Linda McCormick, Ph.D.
Department of Special Education
School of Education
University of Alabama
Birmingham, Alabama 35294

Eugene McDonald, Ed.D.
Research Professor Emeritus
Speech Pathology and Audiology
  Program
Speech and Hearing Clinic
Pennsylvania State University
University Park, Pennsylvania 16802

Shirley McNaughton, Ms.Ed.
Blissymbolics Communication
  Foundation
Toronto, Ontario
Canada

Donald F. Moores, Ph.D.
Head, Division of Special Education
Pennsylvania State University
University Park, Pennsylvania 16802

D. Kimbrough Oller, Ph.D.
P. O. Box 520006
Biscayne Annex
Mailman Center for Child
  Development
University of Miami
Miami, Florida 33152

*Charity R. O'Neil, M.S.
Parsons Research Center
Parsons State Hospital
  and Training Center
Parsons, Kansas 67357

*Dorothy A. Parkel, Ph.D.
Georgia Retardation Center
4770 North Peachtree Road
Atlanta, Georgia 30341
and
Georgia State University
Atlanta, Georgia 30303

*Duane M. Rumbaugh, Ph.D.
Chairman and Professor
Department of Psychology
Georgia State University
Atlanta, Georgia 30303
and
Yerkes Regional Primate Research
  Center of Emory University
Atlanta, Georgia 30322

*E. Sue Savage-Rumbaugh, Ph.D.
Georgia State University
Atlanta, Georgia 30303
and
Yerkes Regional Primate Research
  Center of Emory University
Atlanta, Georgia 30303

Benson Schaeffer, Ph.D.
Associate Professor of Psychology
University of Oregon
Eugene, Oregon 97403

*Richard L. Schiefelbusch, Ph.D.
University Professor and Director,
  Bureau of Child Research
University of Kansas
Lawrence, Kansas 66045

*S. Tom Smith, Jr., M.A.
Georgia State University
Atlanta, Georgia 30303
and
Georgia Retardation Center
Atlanta, Georgia 30341

*Herbert F. W. Stahlke, Ph.D.
Georgia State University
Atlanta, Georgia 30303
and
Yerkes Regional Primate Research
    Center of Emory University
Atlanta, Georgia 30322

Paula Tallal, Ph.D.
John F. Kennedy Institute
Hearing and Speech Division
The Johns Hopkins University
Baltimore, Maryland 21218

Gregg E. Vanderheiden, M.S.
Director, Trace Research and
    Development Center for the
    Severely Communicatively
    Handicapped
University of Wisconsin
Madison, Wisconsin 53706

*Harold Warner, B.E.E.
Yerkes Regional Primate Research
    Center of Emory University
Atlanta, Georgia 30322

Ronnie Bring Wilbur, Ph.D.
School of Education
Department of Special Education
Boston University
Boston, Massachusetts 02215

*S. Vanost Wulz, M.A.
Bureau of Child Research
University of Kansas
Lawrence, Kansas 66045
and
Kansas Neurological Institute
3107 West 21st Street
Topeka, Kansas 66604

David E. Yoder, Ph.D.
Chairman
Department of Communicative
    Disorders
University of Wisconsin
Madison, Wisconsin 53706

---

* Denotes contributing authors to this volume.

preface

In March, 1977 the editors arranged and participated in a conference on Nonspeech Language at Gulf Shores, Alabama. A primary purpose of the conference was to produce a book on nonspeech language and communication. The conference and the book were prompted by recent developments in language theory and by the efforts of language researchers who were designing nonspeech language intervention programs.

In viewing the experimental work on language interventions, the editors were intrigued by the work of Fouts and Goodin, 1974; Premack, 1976; Rumbaugh, 1977; Patterson, 1978 (see Chapter 16, this volume); and others who have designed language systems for apes. We were also excited by the range of work devoted to teaching nonspeech symbol systems to children. Perhaps we were most of all interested in the adaptations and the extrapolations being made from the research with great apes to programs for children.

We were taken by the possibility of integrating the nonspeech language intervention material (which has originated from a number of sources, including the work with apes) into a common design on which language specialists could build further designs for nonspeech work.

The objective of the editors was to establish an integration. We never intended to do more than select, compile, and interpret, but once into the project we were compelled to also look at the integrity of work with communication boards, which has emerged primarily from work with cerebral palsied children. The editors attempted to create a system for describing language and communication functions, including all of the channels, modes, and symbolization functions and processes built into the prominent nonspeech strategies in the literature. This was a formidable task.

At the time of the Gulf Shores Conference in March, 1977, our plan was formed and discussed. The plan appeared to have several weaknesses (as do most models that attempt to encompass a large amount of detail). Nevertheless, the resulting discussion verified the preconference views of a number of the participants, namely, that professionals from a wide range of research and clinical roles could find a common ground in nonspeech approaches to teaching language.

The manuscripts discussed at the conference provided a rich basis for a comprehensive book. As the editors began to put the material into final form for the book, however, several problems of omission and interpretation developed. The most salient, perhaps, was the incomplete and piecemeal way in which the source material for the important areas was represented. The unmet demands of children with special problems that call for special designs were not clearly represented. Finally, the theme of Ape to Child (the impact of nonhuman primate research upon language strategies with handicapped children) was not adequately highlighted.

Consequently the editors requested the authors' permission to rearrange the manuscripts and to add other materials in order to create two books: the first, *Language Intervention from Ape to Child*, and the second, *Nonspeech Language and Communication: Analysis and Intervention*.

Thus, the Gulf Shores Conference has produced two closely related books, each of which attempts to fulfill an important purpose. There is a great deal of cross-referencing and editorial interpretation. Nevertheless, each book can stand alone in representing the themes in the titles. The editors are pleased with the content of each book and with the implied future of work in nonspeech language teaching. The original plan for a single, unified design for nonspeech language and communication is still a challenge and, at some point, we feel, a reasonable expectation.

The participants in the Gulf Shores Conference will recognize many excerpts from the conference discussion in each of the books. Nevertheless, the zeitgeist of that intellectual happening is not completely reflected in either of the books. To atone in part for deliberate alterations, the editors have provided a summary at the conclusion of the second book. The result is a presentation that tries to do justice to an enthusiastic group of language scientists, who were assembled largely as strangers and who became professional colleagues. It is our hope that the spirit of cooperation will continue to cross fields and professional areas and that the relevance of work in previously unexplored realms will attract all of us to future projects.

The editors wish to commend each participant for sustaining enthusiasm during moments of ambiguity and confusion and for exercising restraint during peak moments of spirited communication. The efforts of scientists and clinicians somehow came together during moments of conceptualization when the purposes to be served were clearly acknowledged. We hope that the reader will sense this vitality and validity in the discussion.

We wish to offer special acknowledgment to Don Moores, Roger Fouts, Lyle Lloyd, and Joe Carrier for their assistance in the planning of the project. There was also the buoyant, creative presence of Linda McCormick during the conference and preconference events. Without her conference arrangements the discussion would have remained incomplete. We commend Duane Rumbaugh and his enthusiastic staff. Their contribution is apparent in the Ape to Child theme advanced in the first of the two books.

The editors would like to acknowledge the funding contribution of the Office of Maternal and Child Health, Bureau of Community Health Services, Health Services Administration. This office provided the funds for the Gulf Shores Conference. Also, we would like to thank Dr. Donald Harrington, formerly Chief of the Hearing and Speech Section, who discussed the plan in detail with the first editor and who encouraged him to submit the application for funding. Without Don's guidance and support the conference would not have been held and the books would not have been written.

The editors also wish to commend all of the listed conference participants who engaged in four days of productive discussion. Unfortunately the thinking of all did not find expression in the text of the book. We wish, too, to thank Winthrop N. Kellogg, Robert M. Yerkes, Henry W. Nissen, Keith J. Hayes and Catherine Hayes, R. Allen Gardner and Beatrice T. Gardner, David Premack, Emil W. Menzel, Marcia K. Johnson, and Francine Patterson for permission to include their landmark publications in appropriate contexts of the book.

Finally, the editors wish to thank Ms. Marilyn Barket and Mr. Robert K. Hoyt, Jr., who have given the manuscripts additional luster, Myron Sahlberg and associates at Parsons for illustrations and other artistic assistance, and Mr. Thomas Wheat, who recorded a clear transcript of the entire conference discussion. Finally, Ms. Mary Beth Johnston and Ms. Thelma Dillion gave more than full measure to the critical junctures of book preparations.

R. L. S.
J. H. H.

REFERENCES

Fouts, R. S., and Goodin, L. 1974. Acquisition of signs in chimpanzees: A comparison of training methods. Paper presented at the Psychonomic Society meeting, November, Boston.

Patterson, F. 1978. Linguistic capabilities of a lowland gorilla. *In* Fred C. C. Peng (ed.), Sign Language and Language Acquisition—New Dimensions in Comparative Pedolinguistics, pp. 161–201. Westview Press, Boulder, Col.

Premack, D. 1976. Intelligence in Ape and Man. John Wiley & Sons, New York.

Rumbaugh, D. M. 1977. Language Learning by a Chimpanzee: The LANA Project. Academic Press, New York.

Section

I

Introduction

chapter
1

A General System
for Language Analysis

Ape and Child

John H. Hollis

Bureau of Child Research
Lawrence, Kansas
and
Kansas Neurological Institute
Topeka, Kansas

Richard L. Schiefelbusch

Bureau of Child Research
University of Kansas
Lawrence, Kansas

contents

This book emphasizes the value of experimentally designed language models for clinical applications. For instance, the work with chimpanzees has revealed that, if language tasks are designed for the task performance capabilities of young apes, learning can be managed under experimental control. Some primates can learn to *sign*, while other primates cannot learn to *speak*. The primary issue is one of matching the topography of the task with the performance capabilities of the primate. As this pertains to research, the statement might more appropriately be as follows: Dispositions of the organism should be analyzed to enable the experimenter to choose functions that can be taught operationally. For instance, assuming that primates are capable of performing symbolic tasks, the researcher should select a symbol mode that the primate can be taught to perform. The Gardners obviously decided that Washoe was capable of symbolic behavior and that the symbol mode should be American Sign Language (ASL). As a result, Washoe learned to use signs to express symbolic relationships. Subsequent to the work with Washoe, the Premacks demonstrated that another young chimpanzee named Sarah could perform symbolic tasks with plastic symbols and referent objects. Likewise, Lana, a chimpanzee under the management of Rumbaugh at the Yerkes Laboratory, learned to perform symbolic tasks using a computerized communication board.

The sophistication of the "language" research with Washoe, Sarah, and Lana, to name only three famous pongids, demonstrated the power of careful experimental designs. Language designs, of course, are not without controversy. The controversial issues are discussed in this Chapter and in Chapters 2, 4, and 5 of Section II. As important as these controversies may be to a philosophy of language, several applied researchers have set them aside and extrapolated from the experimental designs to develop plans for teaching human children. It is apparent that Carrier (1974 [Chapter 17, this volume]), Hodges and Deich (Chapter 18, this volume), Parkel and Smith (Chapter 19, this volume), and others have found feasible language applications from apes to children. Consequently, they have demonstrated the potential value of the nonhuman primate models now in the literature.

A revolution in thinking about systems for nonspeech language teaching has been precipitated by nonhuman primate research. The chimps have taught us that experimentally viable language models can include alternative symbol sets characterized by flexible receptive and expressive modes, variable tasks functions, individualized behavioral topographies, and highly specialized pragmatic outcomes. The practical result may be the creation of new strategies and perhaps new models for teaching language to human children.

Preparation of this chapter was supported by Grants HD00870 and HD07339 from the National Institute of Child Health and Human Development.

We should not overlook the work of other researchers, including teachers and clinicians, who pioneered work with nonspeaking children. The oldest and most extensive activities have been with deaf children. This work is examined in considerable detail in the next Language Intervention Series volume, *Nonspeech Language and Communication: Analysis and Intervention.* Other important work has been done with cerebral palsied children, with autistic children, and with severely retarded children. These developments are also reported in the next volume. The important point is that research with the great apes has emphasized further the importance of operational designs to meet the language-training needs of nonspeaking human children.

ENVIRONMENT AND CHIMPANZEE LANGUAGE DEVELOPMENT[1]

Four decades have passed since Kellogg (1931, [Chapter 6, this volume]) discussed humanizing the ape. At the time it was hypothesized that the anatomy and vocal mechanism of the ape were suitable for human speech. Although Kellogg and Kellogg (1933) and Hayes and Hayes (1954) reported limited success in human speech development in the chimpanzee (i.e., three or four words), for the most part the hypothesis is untenable today. Nevertheless, their early work has made significant contributions to current language intervention issues.

Kellogg's 1931 paper presents a design for carrying out an experiment to compare the effects of the environment on the development of an anthropoid ape and a human child. Particularly concerned with whether human speech would develop in the ape, Kellogg stated, ". . . it is to me not entirely inconceivable that under the genetic process outlined, systematized language responses—at least in rudimentary form—would be found to develop." The experiment, reported in the book *The Ape and the Child,* compared the development of his child, Donald, and that of a chimp named Gua. The two were treated as equals with no special program devised to teach Gua to speak. Donald learned to speak in the normal fashion, but Gua never produced any distinctly human speech sounds.

The Hayeses at Yerkes Laboratories, Orange Park, Florida, two decades later, made a serious attempt to teach a home-reared chimpanzee named Viki to speak (Hayes, 1951). Viki learned to produce a few vocal utterances that approximated and could be identified as spoken "words." She learned to speak and use the words *papa, mama,* and *cup*

---

[1] A substantial portion of this section appeared in Hollis, J. H., and Carrier, J. K. 1974. Communication deficiencies from chimp to child. Educ. Considerations 1:6–11.

(Hayes, 1951). Moreover, she developed some receptive language and engaged in some appropriate "human-like" behavior.

The limited results of these two studies suggest that the speech response mode for chimpanzees will not provide an adequate assessment of their ability to learn language (Hollis and Carrier, 1975). As Menzel and Johnson (1976) have pointed out:

> The Hayes and Kellogg chimps and other home-raised chimps were not, in my opinion, "total failures" at learning verbal language. They failed only in producing words. All of these animals were reported to understand many (up to 100) words when the words were spoken by the trainer or parent surrogate, and they could "answer" with nonverbal signals (p. 758).

There appears to be a clear demarcation between receptive and expressive components of language. This is especially true when the animal (cf. Mason and Hollis, 1962) or child (cf. Hollis, 1966) has to create the expressive component.

Researchers working with chimpanzees in the laboratory setting over many decades have reported the use of gestural signs (e.g., Yerkes, 1943) and the development of prelinguistic sign behavior (Yerkes and Nissen, 1939 [Chapter 7, this volume]). It should also be noted that, in a social interaction involving chimpanzees and humans, chimpanzees have discriminated between different social roles played by the humans (Mason, Hollis, and Sharpe, 1962). With respect to the use and communicating function of signs by primates, von Glasersfeld (1977a) states:

> . . . it should be remembered that several years before the various communication studies with chimpanzees began, Mason and Hollis (1962) demonstrated that nonhuman primates cannot only communicate but also create artificial communicatory signs for the cooperative solution of a problem (p. 67).

This has also been demonstrated for severely retarded, nonspeech children (Hollis, 1966).

Approximately four decades after Kellogg's (1931 [Chapter 6, this volume]) initial proposal the Gardners (1969 [Chapter 9, this volume]) abandoned the speech response mode and succeeded in teaching the chimpanzee Washoe ASL (American Sign Language). Thus, substituting manual signs (motor movements with arm, hand, and finger) for the speech response mode, the program was similar to some developed for teaching language and communication to deaf humans (also see Fouts, Couch, and O'Neil, Chapter 15, this volume).

Following this initial breakthrough in teaching language to the chimpanzee, Premack (1970 [Chapter 12, this volume]) used plastic chips as word units, and Rumbaugh (1977) automated language training for the chimpanzee, using a computer instrumentation system (see Savage-Rumbaugh and Rumbaugh, Chapter 14, this volume), and the work of Patterson (1978 [Chapter 16, this volume]).

SYNTHESIZING CHIMPANZEE SPEECH

Disease or injury may damage the vocal, articulatory, or auditory system, requiring prosthetic devices to compensate for handicaps. Several artificial larynges have been developed for laryngectomees, and hearing aids are helpful for many auditorily impaired individuals. Except for the very young, most persons who use prosthetic devices have developed speech and language prior to the necessity for the prosthetic device.

Moderate auditory handicaps may also severely impair the development of speech and language. Although there is little remedial assistance for phonological problems (perhaps because in most cases language has developed before the trauma to the larynx), there is at least one report of teaching speech and language to a child laryngectomized at 20 months (Peterson, 1973). The training goals were to teach esophageal sound production, articulation, and training in expressive language.

The problem in working with animal models is how to circumvent the anatomical deficiencies that inhibit the production of human speech. The chimpanzee has frequently been selected as the "drawing board" for the study of higher mental processes. This is because the chimpanzee ranks high on the phylogenetic scale with respect to sociability and intellectual potential (Yerkes, 1943).

Although the chimpanzee is capable of producing a few human vocal responses, a review of the literature (Bryan, 1963) suggests that the vocal apparatus of the chimpanzee differs from that of man in ways that militate against the development of human speech (a phonological deficiency). However, there is sufficient evidence to prove the ability of the chimpanzee to learn to respond to human speech (receptive-auditory mode), that is, to complex auditory stimuli (Kellogg and Kellogg, 1933; Hayes, 1951). The chimpanzee's handicap in language development (speech) appears to be phonological in nature.

Premack and Schwartz (1966), believing that the chimpanzee's major deficiency lies in the expressive (productive) area of speech, embarked on a project to develop a synthetic (mechanical) device to produce complex audible stimuli. Although this device would not require the chimpanzee to vocalize, it would require a complex set of motor movements and the ability to make complex auditory discriminations. Most importantly, this approach to the problem forced Premack and Schwartz to make a comprehensive review of language development, grammar, and syntax (see Premack, 1970 [Chapter 12, this volume]; Stahlke et al., Chapter 4, this volume).

The study of the continuity problem between man and chimpanzee was continued by Premack and Schwartz in an experimental fashion. What they proposed to teach the chimpanzee was a five-dimensional code in which the auditory dimensions were correlated with the motor dimensions. The production of auditory signals was to be controlled by a joystick apparatus, with the sound produced by a device similar to an electric organ. It was proposed that the chimpanzee would be taught a phrase-structure grammar.

In contrast to the work of the Kelloggs and Hayeses, the most important question was: Would this study reveal something about language development? Premack (1970 [Chapter 12, this volume]) subsequently stated that "not only human phonology but quite possibly human syntax may be unique to man." However, there was still an assumption that, irrespective of higher cortical functions (e.g., Pribram, 1971), semantics, which form the basis for language, are present at the subhuman level. Therefore, Premack and Schwartz (1966) decided to circumvent the larynx problem with a synthetic device capable of stimulating vocalizations.

It is the authors' opinion that this multidimensional system is much too complex for the young child or ape. This system was eventually discarded, perhaps because of that complexity. However, there may still be good reason to use the chimpanzee as a "drawing board" for delineating strategies and tactics relevant to communication problems (see Rumbaugh et al., Chapter 3, this volume). Premack (1970 [Chapter 12, this volume]) was successful in establishing a continuity between human language and animal communication. For starters, with respect to language and speech, primates may be functionally limited, even with respect to the expressive aspects of speech and language development. In this regard we should beware of *the fallacy of equating speech with language.*

MANUAL SIGNING LANGUAGE WITH CHIMPANZEE

Now, consider the chimpanzee as another type of "drawing board." There is little doubt that laboratory and home-reared chimpanzees still display many of the characteristics of wild animals (Hayes, 1951). However, chimpanzees are highly social animals and do respond differentially to social roles, even those played by a human (Mason, Hollis, and Sharpe, 1962). Moreover, chimpanzees solve manipulatory mechanical problems, and even laboratory chimps gesture spontaneously (Yerkes, 1943).

Fingerspelling and American Sign Language (ASL) are standard systems for two-way communication by deaf or retarded children. Training a chimpanzee to use ASL would provide a linguistic environment analogous to that of a deaf child with deaf parents. In one situation, the Gardners undertook the task of training Washoe, a chimpanzee, to use ASL (Gardner and Gardner, 1969 [Chapter 9, this volume]). The strategy was to take advantage of two chimpanzee characteristics: 1) the ability to make complex hand movements, and 2) the frequency with which chimpanzees have been observed to imitate human acts. The tactic for training was to provide an environment conducive to the development of chimpanzee-human social interactions, while applying shaping and operant conditioning techniques to develop sign language in the chimpanzee.

Washoe (Gardner and Gardner, 1969 [Chapter 9, this volume])

The Gardners maintained records on Washoe's daily signing behavior. By the 22nd training month of the experiment, they were able to list 30 signs that met criterion; for example: COME-GIMME, UP, OPEN, DRINK, YOU, SMELL, CLEAN, and HEAR-LISTEN. The criterion for acquisition consisted of at least one appropriate and spontaneous occurrence each day over a period of 15 consecutive days. The results showed a median of 29 signs per day, with a range of 23 to 28 different signs out of a total of 34 signs. Reliability consisted of the agreement between three observers that the sign was actually in Washoe's repertoire. The chimp's rate of acquisition for the 21-month period shows the phenomenon of "learning to learn" or "learning sets" (Harlow, 1949). The Gardners acknowledged a language context problem and viewed it in terms of sign transfer, i.e., from a very specific referent in initial training to new members of each class of referents. Thus, after Washoe learned, in initial training, OPEN for a specific door and HAT for a specific hat, she was able to transfer her learnings to new members of each class of referents. The Gardners cited several examples of this class of behavior (Gardner and Gardner, 1969 [Chapter 9, this volume]). For example, they pointed out in their discussion of key use (to open locks) that Washoe learned to ask for keys (emitted key sign) when no key was in sight. In addition, Washoe was observed to use signs (i.e., two or more signs) in strings apparently spontaneously (i.e., without specific stimuli).

Did Washoe develop a functional language? The results of the experiment show that Washoe demonstrated: 1) spontaneous naming, 2) spontaneous transfer to new referents, and 3) spontaneous combinations and recombinations of signs. Fouts (1973) has replicated the Gardners' ASL study, using four young chimpanzees. Thus the learning of ASL in the chimpanzee population is not unique, and it can be concluded that Washoe was not an exceptional chimpanzee in her ability to acquire signs. This can also apply to retarded, deaf children, as Berger (1972) found in a clinical program using similar procedures. Schaeffer (1979) has demonstrated that instruction in signed speech may promote spontaneous speech in children with severe language deficits.

Bruno (Fouts, 1973)

Bruno's language training was an extension of the language training given Washoe by the Gardners (1969 [Chapter 9, this volume]). His verbal communication was in a modified form of ASL (American Sign Language). During training he had considerable social interaction with humans and was given as much exposure as possible to humans (trainers) using ASL. Figure 1 shows some examples of Bruno making the appropriate sign to environmental objects presented by his trainer (for example, making the sign EAT when shown a banana, making the sign BRUSH when presented a toothbrush, and so forth).

PLASTIC WORD LANGUAGE WITH CHIMPANZEE

We have noted the contribution of linguistics, programming, and logic to teaching language to the chimpanzee. The limiting factor for language development by the chimpanzee or language-deficient child may not be language per se, but the complexity of the response, i.e., its topography. For example, as Carrier noted, the response mode most commonly associated with language is oral speech, which can be defined as various phonemic responses arranged to create morphemes, which, in turn, are arranged to create grammatical utterances (Carrier, 1974 [Chapter 17, this volume]). Several years ago, Premack (1970 [Chapter 12, this volume]) reversed his earlier experimental direction and moved from the complex topography required by a mechanical device for phonological prosthesis to a simple synthetic (plastic word) system using abstract "words" on movable, metal-backed plastic pieces. Again, Premack was asking, "Would this teach us something about language?" The fundamental question was "What is language?" First, Premack provided a list of exemplars, things the chimp (or child) must be able to do in order to demonstrate functional language. Second, he stated that a method of training must be provided to teach the chimp the exemplars in question. For starters, Premack suggested the following exemplars: 1) words, 2) sentences, 3) questions, 4) metalinguistics (using language to teach language), 5) class concepts, 6) the copula (verb link), 7) quantifiers, and 8) the logical connective, e.g., *if-then*. The word stimuli in this system are pieces of plastic backed with metal so they will adhere to a magnetized

Figure 1.   Chimpanzee Bruno manual signing. Redrawn from the cover of *Psychology Today*, January, 1974.

slate. The plastic words are abstract configurations analogous to Chinese characters. The placing of the plastic words on the slate requires only gross motor movements, much simpler than the complex motor behavior and auditory discriminations required for spoken and gestural communication. A second advantage is that the sentence made by the chimp is permanent; thus, memory problems are avoided. Third, the experimenter can modulate the difficulty of any task by controlling the words available to the subject at a given time. It should be evident that the phonological problem has been circumvented and that the basic unit is the word (Premack, 1970 [Chapter 12, this volume]).

Sarah (Premack, 1970 [Chapter 12, this volume])

Sarah, Premack's chimpanzee, was able to read and write with more than 130 plastic words. But, more importantly, she learned 1) use of the interrogative, 2) metalinguistics, 3) class concepts, 4) use of simple and compound sentences, 5) pluralization, 6) quantifiers, 7) use of the logical connective *if-then*, and 8) use of the conjunctive *and*. Premack provided a functional analysis of language. This approach to analyzing and teaching language has reduced the cognitive parameters of language to discrete events that can be defined and manipulated. This strategy, coupled with the tactic of a simple-response topography, provides a powerful technique for training language-deficient children.

Sarah's language was restricted to a laboratory where she was programmed on a sequence of language-related tasks. The semantic units of her language were "words" made from plastic cut into abstract forms. Sarah was taught to "write" sentences vertically on the board. Figure 2 shows Sarah with two sentences (left, CHOCOLATE IS BROWN, and right, BROWN COLOR OF CHOCOLATE), which she must read in order to determine if the meanings are the same.

COMPUTER LEXIGRAM LANGUAGE WITH CHIMPANZEE

Lana (Rumbaugh, 1977)

Lana's language-training program differed markedly from the programs developed by the Gardners, Fouts, and Premack. First, language training took place in an experimental chamber and was programmed and monitored by a computer. Perhaps most importantly, her language behavior "functioned" to control her experimental environment. That is, if she "wrote" the sentence PLEASE MACHINE MAKE WINDOW OPEN PERIOD, by pressing the appropriate sequence of keys on the keyboard,

Figure 2.   Chimpanzee Sarah learning language, using a plastic chip system. Redrawn from the cover of *Scientific American*, October, 1972.

the window in the chamber would automatically open. Thus, by "writing" out the appropriate sentence correctly she would receive M&Ms, play activities (with a human), music, and so forth.

A second difference in the LANA Project involved the development of the "Yerkish" language and subsequently a computerized language-training program. The Yerkish language includes a set or *lexicon* of artificial signs and a *grammar* that determines the sequences of the signs (von Glasersfeld, 1977b). The lexigrams (symbols) used in Yerkish were derived by compounding simple geometric elements (vertical and horizontal lines, circles, triangles, diamonds, and so forth) to produce complex figures (symbols) that could be back-projected onto small manipulable panels in the language keyboard (see Parkel and Smith, Chapter 19, this volume; Savage-Rumbaugh and Rumbaugh, Chapter 14, this volume). Von Glasersfeld (1977b) says of Yerkish grammar: "The grammar of Yerkish was derived from the 'correlational grammar implemented some years ago in the *Multistore Parser* for English sentences.' It is an *interpretive* grammar and lays no claim to being 'generative' or 'transformational' in the Chomskian sense of these terms" (p. 103) (see Stahlke et al., Chapter 4, this volume). It may also be interesting to note that von Glasersfeld developed functional lexigram classes for Yerkish (see Table 5, this chapter). Figure 3 shows Lana in the process of "writing" a sentence on the keyboard in her experimental chamber.

SIMULTANEOUS COMMUNICATION

Koko (Patterson, 1978 [Chapter 16, this volume])

Koko's program was influenced by the training developed by the Gardners' work with Washoe. Patterson was interested in determining if Koko, a young lowland gorilla, could be the peer of Washoe in sign language acquisition. This question was answered affirmatively when Koko's progress was compared with Washoe's over a comparable time frame and with similar criteria.

In addition to developing a sizable vocabulary, Koko combined words into meaningful and sometimes novel strings of two or more signs. Koko also made responses to spoken questions. Thus, speech was used as a secondary mode of communication. Speech-delivered information resulted in a speech input and a manual sign output. The use of both manual and speech modes allowed a study of the transfer of information between modes. The procedures also allowed a study of Koko's capacity for complex auditory analysis.

A number of innovations have marked Koko's progress over the past four and a half years: She has invented signs and names for novel objects; she

Figure 3. Chimpanzee Lana writing a sentence, using a computer lexigram system. Redrawn from the cover of *Yerkes Newsletter*, May, 1974.

talks to herself; she engages in imaginative play using sign; and she has used language to lie, to express her emotions, and to refer to things displaced in time and space. (Patterson, 1978, p. 191 [Chapter 16, this volume, p. 348]).

Most language studies with apes are of a functional nature; thus, it is possible to analyze the functional aspects to help develop a model or system for a framework for further analysis.

Premack (1970 [Chapter 12, this volume]) gives a discussion of language as a functional system wherein the functions are described in terms of perceptions that serve as prerequisites to the symbolic exchange. Such an analysis emphasizes the mapping of language response classes to highlight language acts as transactional events displaying cognitive functions. Thus, Premack's language system led him to an analysis of cognitive performance and eventually to his significant work *Intelligence in Ape and Man* (1976).

Functional language is also defined by Carrier (Chapter 17) Fouts, Couch, and O'Neil (Chapter 15) and Rumbaugh et al. (Chapter 3), and by Moores and others in the subsequent volume, *Nonspeech Language and Communication: Analysis and Intervention*. None of them presumes an auditory-vocal mode (except for the receptive language training described by Patterson (1978 [Chapter 16, this volume]). The need now is for a common general system of language and communication to encompass all models, strategies, and programs that the designers of language for apes and children have created. The plan for analyzing the nonstandard systems discussed in this chapter should go a long way toward bridging the different designs.

The objectives of this chapter are: 1) to describe a general language system compatible with both speech and nonspeech modes, and 2) to discuss functional issues in the language development of apes and children.

A GENERAL SYSTEM OF LANGUAGE

In developing a general system of language and communication the authors present a design that highlights the different modes of nonspeech language and communication. Several language and/or communication designs for conventional speech-delivered language are available. The most logical way to proceed now is to use an existing model (for example, Osgood's (1957) model) and to observe the alternative modes that might be superimposed or substituted to accommodate the nonspeech systems. The reader should also consult the dual structure language model (Hollis and Carrier, 1978, pp. 66–67). In presenting our information we extrapolate from Osgood's 1957 design and present it as a language channel model. The language channel model involves *sensory-input, integrative processes, and response-output*. A psycholinguistic analysis model can be congruently displayed with the channel model.

A LANGUAGE CHANNEL MODEL

Input: Sensory Modes

In "normal" language processing the input sensory modes are auditory, visual, tactual, and olfactory. Speech scientists also call attention to the kinesthetic sensory mode that enables the speaker to sense subtle movements and positioning of the speech articulators in "hearing" and interpreting meaning from speech inputs. In a channel model we can focus primarily on the auditory, visual, and tactual inputs. We can readily accept the issue of impaired sensory processing and can also perceive that deaf, blind, and motorically impaired children have alternatives in the effective range of sensory inputs.

The sensory input mode selected for the development of a communication channel, then, depends on the individual's type and severity of impairment. Four sensory input modes are: 1) visual, 2) auditory, 3) tactile, and 4) olfactory (see Figure 4).

Integration and Mediation Functions

A second step in the development of the language channel model is the delineation of integrative processes. These are cognitive functions attributed to neurophysiological processes. The four integrative processes (selected with respect to the development of language channels) form a hierarchy that can be defined and programmed. The four integrative processes include:

1. *Imitation.* The imitative level refers to imitative or identity matching (matching-to-sample). The sample (input) stimulus and the selected response (output) stimulus are the same (object matched to object, picture matched to picture, printed word matched to printed word, or dictated word matched by spoken word).
2. *Symbolization.* The symbolization level deals with a nonimitative match, a symbolic response, i.e., "X is the name of Y." This is Level II mapping using symbols to label environmental events. Thus, solution of the matching problem requires the selection of a response stimulus that differs from the sample stimulus (environmental event); for example, matching a symbol or printed word to an object or picture, selecting a printed word that matches a dictated word, or vocalizing the word(s) when presented a picture.
3. *Construction.* The constructive level of integration deals with the ability to arrange elements (e.g., objects, pictures, and words) in a sequence of specific configurations (e.g., a kernel sentence). For example, given the outline of a face and its elements (eyes, nose, and

mouth), a child can place them in their respective positions. Or in the case of the kernel sentence he[2] can arrange symbols or words in sequence to produce, for example, *The boy pushes the block.*
4. Transformation.   The transformative is the highest level of integration to be discussed. In transformation, changes occur either in ordered sequence of elements, or in replacement, additions, or subtraction of elements or both (Warren, 1968); for example, a change in the spatial arrangement of facial elements to produce a Picasso type picture or the change of words or order in a sentence (e.g., transformational-generative grammar).

Output: Response Modes

The output or response mode forms the third step in the language channel model. This step is necessary because many handicapped children are unable to make the complicated motor movements required for speech. Likewise, such impairments may preclude them from producing manual signs or writing. In such instances the functional response mode may be gross motor (see the next volume, *Nonspeech Language and Communication: Analysis and Intervention*). The response output modes selected for the terminal slot of the language channel model are: 1) gross motor movements, 2) sign, 3) writing, and 4) speech (see Figure 4).

The information just presented can be added to the language channel model so that the options are easily perceived.

It is the clinician's or the teacher's task to assess the child and select the language channel features that are functional for that child. For example, if a child is severely retarded and has an auditory impairment, it might be possible to establish the following functional language channel: 1) input—visual and/or tactile, 2) mediation/process level—imitation, and 3) output—gross motor. The selection of input, process, and response levels depends on the handicaps and the aptitudes of the child.

PSYCHOLINGUISTIC ANALYSIS MODEL

A psycholinguistic analysis of language provides a method for relating the linguist's rules for generating sentences with the psychologist's attempts to determine what variables are related to an individual's communication. That is, what factors are relevant to an individual communicating about a specific environmental event in a certain way at a certain time? The psycholinguistic analysis involves receptive functions, linguistic rules, and expressive functions.

---

[2] Masculine pronouns are used throughout the book for the sake of grammatical simplicity. They are not meant to be preferential or discriminatory.

Communication Channels

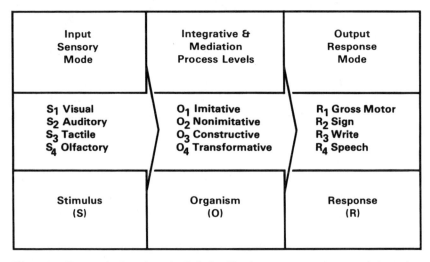

Figure 4.   Communication channels. Relationships between recepted sensory information (S), psycholinguistic processes (O), and expressed response (R). (From Hollis, Carrier, and Spradlin, 1976.)

Receptive Functions

The nonlanguage child's first map of his environment must be constructed from the salient stimulus characteristics. The normal child processes visual, auditory, tactile, olfactory, etc., stimuli from environmental events out of which he builds a cognitive map or schema of the environment. Table 1 provides a partial list of classes of environmental events that could be included in a child's knowledge of language. For the normal child, as language ability evolves, knowledge also changes and expands. This may not be true for the severely handicapped nonlanguage child. As a result of significant impairments in one or more of the sensory modalities, an incomplete map (or no map at all) of an environmental event may be formed (see Hollis and Carrier, 1978). An environmental event is defined as something happening with respect to objects or persons in a certain place (context) and during a particular interval of time.

Nonlinguistic Conceptualization

What does the nonlanguage child learn and know about his environment? What is his conceptual structure of the environment? Does the child discriminate among people, places, and things? How and what a child discriminates about his environment depends on sensory input (Figure 4).

Severe deficiencies in sensory input may significantly limit, modify, or distort the child's conceptual structure of environmental events. If language is viewed as a map of existing distinctions (Premack and Premack, 1974), then the child must have learned to distinguish between environmental events before labeling could become a functional part of language. (It is acknowledged that a child can learn a metalanguage that may be nonfunctional.) Thus, to learn that "X" is the name of "Y" it is necessary for a child to distinguish "Y" from other environmental events, for example, those outlined in Table 1. Language plays a significant role in conceptualizing the environment. In order to start the chain of events leading to functional language, it is assumed that the child has learned to discriminate between environmental events. For example, he should be able to discriminate between objects (dish versus spoon), persons (mother versus stranger), movement (car parked versus car in motion), and so forth (Figure 5). If a child is unable to make these environmental distinctions, it may be necessary to teach them. This is especially true with children who have sensory impairments and multiple handicaps (see "The Child's Archetypal Model," pp. 65–66, Hollis and Carrier, 1978).

Figure 5 presents a schema of an environmental event in which A (agent) pushes (action) B (object). This illustrative example of an environmental event is shown in Table 1 with respect to mapping and semantic relationships (items 9, 10, and 11).

What a child maps in the characteristics or attributes of an environmental event depends upon the adequacy or functioning level of his sensory modalities. A severe deficiency in one modality or multiple sensory deficiencies may severely impair mapping of environmental

Table 1.   Some mapping and semantic relationships in language

Item no.	Mapping archetype (environmental event)	Structural meaning		
		Semantic relations (function)	Construction (form)	Symbolization (example)
1	Specific object	nomination (label)	(that) + N	*car*
2	Objects part of a whole	perceptual halves	N + N	*eye face*
3	Episodic objects	recurrence	('nother) + N	*('nother) car*
4	Disappearance of object	nonexistence	(allgone) + N	*(allgone) milk*
5	Characteristics of object	attributive	Adjective + N	*big car*
6	Holder of object	possessive	N + N	*mommy drink*
7	Placement of object	locative (a)	N + N	*doll bedroom*
8	Movement place	locative (b)	V + N	*run outdoors*
9	Person movement (actor)	agent-action	N + V	*boy push*
10	Person object	agent-object	N + N	*boy block*
11	Movement of object	action-object	V + N	*push block*
12	Objects that go together	perceptual associates (conjunction)	N + N	*doll house*
13	Objects used together	functional associates	N + N	*hammer nail*

EVENT

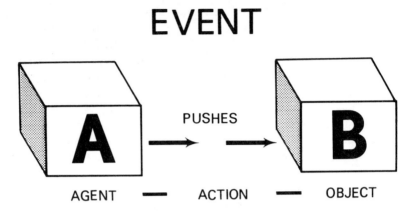

Figure 5. A semantic concept illustrated by three-term semantic relations (e.g., *Boy pushes block*).

events. For example, consider the mapping of an environmental event in which A pushes B with respect to sensory deficiencies. The *agent* and *object* in this situation could be two cars, people, blocks of wood, and so forth (Figure 5). For purposes of illustration, consider a blind child and a deaf child observing an environmental event in which one car (A, agent) pushes (action) another car (B, object). The blind child's mapping of the event would most likely consist of noise (sound-auditory input), generated by the spinning wheels and the two cars bumping together and possibly the smell of burning rubber. At best this child would have incomplete cues (stimulus input) to construct an adequate map of the event (also see Hollis, Carrier, and Spradlin, 1976).

The deaf child would be able to construct a more adequate, but still incomplete, map of the event from the visual and olfactory stimuli.

There is also a radical difference between the mapping by a developmentally deficient, sensory impaired child and the mapping of a child (over six years of age, for example) who becomes sensory impaired (i.e., visually or auditorially) after having developed a language.

Linguistic Conceptualization

Language is the mapping of environmental events (i.e., existing distinctions, Premack and Premack, 1974) with symbols. In this system the nonlinguistic conceptualization of environmental events forms the first conceptual level (level I, Figure 6) and the abstract representation of the events forms the second conceptual level (level II, Figure 6). That is, at level II the child learns that "X" is the name of "Y" and subsequently that "Xs" can be used by name or can label objects, actions, and so forth (Table 1). By learning basic linguistic rules, the child is then able to construct sentences and (by learning additional rules) perform transformations. In the following discussion of linguistic rules, illustrations are given of integrations and mediation functions.

Linguistic Rules

The development of lingustic rules is predicated on the following assumptions: 1) that the child has learned some basic nonlinguistic conceptualizations of environmental events (imitation), 2) that the child has

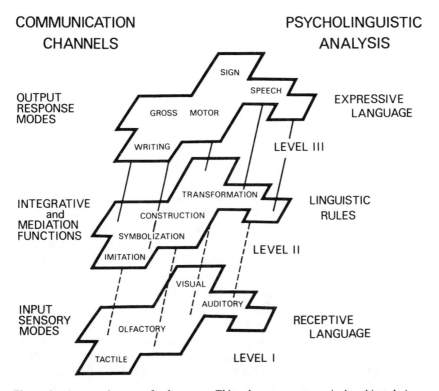

Figure 6. A general system for language. This schema presents a single-subject design, contrasting a communication channels approach (operant analysis) with a psycholinguistic analysis.

learned that "X" is the name of "Y" (symbolization), 3) that the child has learned to sequence symbols to form a sentence (construction), and 4) that the child's sentence forms demonstrate a knowledge of linguistic rules used in producing alterations in sentences (transformation).

Within the realm of linguistic conceptualization, mapping provides the first order base or phase. It is upon this base that the language map is overlaid or correlated. Thus, language rules are rooted in the child's nonlinguistic conceptualization of environmental events. The next phase in the development of language involves the process of *symbolization,* i.e., learning or teaching the child to use symbols to label environmental events. Following acquisition of symbolization, the child must learn the *construction* phase, the rules for sequencing symbols. At an abstract level, linguistic rules are a symbolic map that overlays or corresponds to the critical elements within the nonlinguistic conceptualization of the environment. In addition to the rules for symbol sequencing, the child must examine a range of intended meanings that fit the context. In matching the intended meanings to a linguistic expression, it may be necessary to transform the basic symbol sequence (the kernel sentence which specifies the grammatical relations of agent-action-object) into one that more accurately relates the intended meaning and the context.

For an illustration of transformational-generative grammar consider the following sentences:

1. *The boy pushes the block.*
2. *The block was pushed by the boy.*

Sentences 1 and 2 describe the same environmental event even though the symbols (words) are in different syntactic forms. Sentence 1 is *active;* sentence 2 is *passive.* Both sentences express in symbols the same environmental event. Thus, the passive sentence can be viewed as a transformation of the symbol structure represented by sentence 1. Therefore, sentences 1 and 2 are two possible symbol constructions. A significant feature of transformational-generative grammar is that the rules to generate sentences such as 1 and 2, above, can be applied and illustrated, using a notation that is independent of the symbol form, e.g., words, signing, rebus, Non-SLIP, braille, and Blissymbol, (see Hollis, Carrier, and Spradlin, 1976). Thus, independent of conceptual structure (semantics), the rules can be applied a priori to the development of a sentence whose components consist, for example, of a noun phrase (NP_1), a verb (V_t) and a second noun phrase (NP_2). Using this system of notation and transformational rules, an *active* sentence can be transformed into a *passive* sentence as illustrated below:

1. $NP_1 + V_t + NP_2$ can be rewritten as
2. $NP_2 + Aux. + V + Aff. + Prep(by) + NP_1$

The transformational rules interchange the subject (NP$_1$) and object (NP$_2$) noun phrases, add an auxiliary form of *be* (Aux.) and a participle affix (Aff.) to the verb (V), and identifies the agentive noun phrase (NP) by inserting the preposition (*by*) between the verb and the predicate noun phrase (NP$_1$).

The salient feature of this system is that the researcher, teacher, or clinician can apply the rules of transformational-generative grammar to developing sentence models independent of the response output mode—speech, writing, signing, or other symbols (Figure 4, and Hollis, Carrier, and Spradlin, 1976). This technique has been used by Carrier (1974 [Chapter 17, this volume]) to teach severely retarded children single sentences, using abstract plastic symbols (Non-SLIP, Carrier, and Peak, 1975). In an unpublished study, Sanders, Guess and Baer (personal communication) have demonstrated that they can teach transformational rules, active to passive and vice versa, to severely retarded children, using the speech response mode. These two research studies with developmentally deficient children and the language research with nonhuman primates (Rumbaugh et al., Chapter 3, this volume; Fouts et al., Chapter 15, this volume) attest to the potential of this approach for teaching linguistic rules to nonlanguage children and primates.

Expressive Functions

In the analysis of a child's language, the datum is the response, i.e., abstract sequence(s) of symbols that may be observed and studied as speech, writing, signs, or gross motor actions (level III, Figure 6). These symbol sequences in turn may be interpreted by phonological, morphographemic, or phrase-structure rules.

The first three common response modes, *gross motor actions*, *signing*, and *writing*, require an increasing refinement of hand movements and finger dexterity. The speech mode requires fine motor movements that involve quite different anatomical components, e.g., vocal cords, tongue, lips, etc. The various response modes can be adapted to a number of symbol and communication systems (see "Symbol Systems," this chapter; Hollis, Carrier, and Spradlin, 1976). The child's response modes are as follows:

1. *Gross motor actions.* The basic level of responding is represented by gross motor behavior such as grasping, pushing a button, etc., with the hands. This basic class of responding could also include such simple sequences as reach-grasp-pull-drop or reach-grasp-lift-phrase (e.g., Non-SLIP, Carrier and Peak, 1975). Even the most severely handicapped child (Hollis, 1967) with or without prosthetic devices, or a nonhuman primate (Premack, 1970 [Chapter 12, this volume]) can learn such simple motor responses.

2. *Signing.* At this level, the complexity of the motor response is increased to relatively fine movements of the fingers or arms, for example, the production of arm and finger movements required to produce the signs of SEE (Signing Exact English) or ASL (American Sign Language). (For nonhuman primates see Gardner and Gardner, 1969 [Chapter 9, this volume], and Fouts, 1973.) Fingerspelling requires even greater dexterity of finger movements.

3. *Writing.* A more complex level of motor behavior involves printing letters of the alphabet or words. Script writing and drawing (pictographs, etc.) are at this level.

4. *Speech.* This unique human response mode is the most difficult to learn and produce. Attempts to teach speech to nonhuman primates have met with failure. Speech or the phonological response mode requires very complex motor behavior to produce the required phonemes (Travis, 1957). Because a nonhuman primate or developmentally deficient child has not learned to speak does not mean that he has not developed language or does not have the ability to develop it (Premack, 1970 [Chapter 12, this volume]; Carrier, 1974 [Chapter 17, this volume]; Hollis and Carrier, 1975).

COMBINING LANGUAGE CHANNEL AND PSYCHOLINGUISTIC ANALYSIS MODELS

To combine language channels and psycholinguistic analysis we have only to match the process functions of the former with the psycholinguistic characteristics of the latter. For instance, the input sensory modes are the modalities that provide the child with (receptive) information about the world. This information is about object forms, colors, movements, relations, positions, distances, etc. To these are also added persons and identities. Initially there are no words for the agents, objects, and actions. When these function words are mapped onto the child's knowledge of the world, they, too, are received via the input sensory modes.

Both the knowledge of the world and the knowledge of words (symbols) are limited by the input modes. If one or more of the modes are impaired, the acquisition of knowledge will be impaired unless intensive provisions are made to increase the functional processing of the intact receptors. The extent of functional knowledge, of course, can be sampled prior to the time when the child projects this knowledge fluently through speech or other expressive language forms.

The relationship between receptive (level I) and expressive (level III) language functions is complex and difficult to analyze (Schlesinger, 1977;

Bowerman, 1978). The important factor in the current language design is that there is an apparent facilitation by both the receptive and expressive modes so that receptive functions enhance the expressive functions and vice versa. Logically, then, the child needs an active use of each mode. As is seen in subsequent chapters, if speech is not an active response form for the child, one or more of the other response forms should be developed.

Another area of comparative interest between language channels and psycholinguistic analysis is at level II, the relationship of integrative and mediation functions and linguistic rules. As explained in the previous sections, rules are not only apparent in the perceived form of receptive and expressive language, but also in the construction and modification processes that the individual exercises in integrating and mediating intended meaning. Any appropriate form of expressive language must allow flexible transformations and appropriate interpretation of rule and meaning adjustments on the part of the child (the nonspeaking child). Alternative modes of processing language and communicating the meaning of language must be considered in functional language development efforts.

FUNCTIONAL ISSUES IN LANGUAGE DEVELOPMENT

Language development involves interaction among a large number of variables. Some of these variables are relatively easy to define and manipulate, while others are difficult to pinpoint, much less manipulate. The development of functional language is more than programming and training specific aspects of language or the application of a general language system to remediate deficiencies.

Language, to be functional, must provide the individual (ape or child) with a communication tool and a means of controlling and manipulating the environment. This assumes that the child has acquired a knowledge of his physical, psychological, and social environment. It is this environmental surrounding that he must learn to map with symbols, i.e., language. For the nonlanguage organism to develop functional language it must have opportunities to interact with the environment and must have developed the cognitive capacity to learn and remember salient aspects of the environment.

Table 2 delineates and organizes some of the more obvious variables relevant to the development of functional language. The table relates these variables to the chimpanzee, gorilla, and retarded child studies presented in this volume.

Variables presented in Table 2 include: 1) physical and psychological environment, 2) social interaction, 3) cognitive development, 4) lexicon

Table 2. Comparison of functional language issues

	Chimpanzee			
Variables	Kellogg and Kellogg (1933) Gua	Hayes (1951) Hayes and Hayes (1954) [Chapter 8, this volume] Viki	Gardner and Gardner (1969) [Chapter 9, this volume] Washoe	Premack (1970) [Chapter 12, this volume] Sarah
Physical and psychological environment	Human household	Human household	House trailer	Laboratory cage
Social interaction	Human parents and human age-mate continuous	Human parents and visitors continuous	Several human companions during waking hours	Researchers and caregivers
Cognitive	At 18 months Gesell test showed development similar to normal human child	At age 2 years development (play, imitation, etc.) paralleled normal human child except no speech similar to human	Able to communicate with strings of two or more signs	Symbolization, construction (see Premack, 1970) transformation (see Premack, 1976)
Lexicon source	English language	English language	American Sign Language (ASL)	Plastic symbol word units, English derivation
Communication modes: Receptive language	Auditory—"comprehension vocabulary" 95 words and/or phrases CA = 16 mons.	Auditory—"comprehension vocabulary" similar to Gua	Visual—signs	Visual—plastic symbols
Communication modes: Expressive language[b]	No speech production	Speech—productive vocabulary of 3 words	Signing—productive vocabulary of 34 words and combinations	Plastic symbol selection, over 150 words; combines words

[a] Assessment of Children's Language Comprehension, Consulting Psychologists Press, Inc.
[b] *Words*, a gross estimate.

source, and 5) communication modes. Although the table presents only a gross analysis of the variables related to language development studies, there are striking differences between environmental and social variables. The genetic variable, although not listed, may play a significant role in language development (see Limber, 1977). This should be considered when making cross-species comparisons. The apes or human children may have predispositions to interact with their environments in different ways, thereby developing vastly different cognitive maps, even when

		Gorilla	Retarded children	
Fouts (1973) Lucy	Rumbaugh, Gill, and von Glasersfeld (1973) Lana	Patterson (1978) [Chapter 16, this volume] Koko	Hodges and Deich (Chapter 18, this volume)	Parkel and Smith (Chapter 19, this volume)
Outdoor compound	Laboratory cubicle with computer lexigram display panel	Zoo and house trailer room	Institution, sterile restricted	Institution, sterile restricted
Chimpanzees, researchers, and caregivers	Researchers, caregivers, and chimpanzees	Researchers, caregiver, and visitors (male gorilla)	Very limited, caregivers and peers	Very limited, caregivers and peers
Able to communicate with strings of two or more signs	Symbolization, construction, transformation (see Rumbaugh, 1977)	ACLC test[a] at norm for 5-year-old educationally handicapped child	IQ less than 30	IQ less than 30
American Sign Language (ASL)	Yerkish word units, English derivation	American Sign Language (ASL)	Plastic symbol word units, English derivation	Yerkish word units, English derivation
Visual—signs; and auditory— speech	Visual— computer lexigrams	Visual—signs; and auditory— speech	Visual— plastic symbols	Visual— computer lexigrams
Signing— productive vocabulary of over 80 words; combines words	Computer lexigrams selection; combines 250 words	Signing— productive vocabulary of 225 words	Plastic symbols selection; 39 words	Computer lexigrams selection 30 words

given the opportunity to interact within the same environment. The point is that although chimpanzees and gorillas are very social and intelligent they are still wild animals and become less tractable with increasing age.

The development of functional language depends on an unspecified interaction between heredity and environment or the *nature* and *nurture* forces. The nature forces are: 1) genetic biological variables, and 2) nongenetic biological variables (lack of oxygen at birth, visual and auditory impairments, and so forth). The nurture forces include: 1) past learning history, 2) immediate social and psychological environment, and 3) the general cultural milieu in which the organism develops. The remainder of this chapter provides a gross comparison of *nurture* variables across the ape and nonspeech child language studies presented in this volume.

PHYSICAL AND PSYCHOLOGICAL ENVIRONMENT

The chimpanzee's natural habitat is a broad band across equatorial Africa. This area includes woodlands, streams, hills, and rain forests. Although the range of the gorilla is more restricted than the chimpanzee, both animals inhabit the same forests in several parts of central and west Africa. The ecological niches occupied by apes may produce behavioral differences in group organization, food-foraging technique, and tool use. The data from field observations suggest that apes are capable of modifying their behavior to exercise a degree of control over the environment (DeVore, 1965). The environment provides ample food and shelter and is relatively secure with the exception of predators. Except for the social control exercised by their primitive communication, chimpanzees and gorillas have no need for a formal language system.

Kellogg (1931 [Chapter 6, this volume]), with respect to ape research, has stated, "The animal is never given a chance to learn human behavior." He therefore proposed to raise a chimpanzee in a human household. This experimental approach would provide maximum exposure to spoken English language and those variables that influence human behavior. For language to be functional it must serve to control an individual's (ape or child) behavior and in turn must provide a tool for controlling the social and physical environment.

Table 2 shows a great variability in the physical and psychological environments employed in the various ape and nonlanguage studies. The environments range from normal households to laboratory cages with varying degrees of confinement. In terms of cultural acquisition, there are profound differences in behavioral development. The chimpanzees Gua and Viki displayed behavioral repertoires similar to normal human children at a comparable age, with the exception of the element of speech. The conclusion is inescapable that the rearing environment, both physical and psychological, has a profound effect on the early development of home-raised apes.

In subsequent ape language studies the effects of the environment are difficult to assess, because this was not one of the variables manipulated and because developmental profiles were not established for the apes. A study of the available data suggests that the chimpanzees Washoe, Sarah, Lucy, and Lana and the gorilla Koko do not display the range of human-like behavior exhibited by Gua and Viki. Gua and Viki responded to spoken English (receptive language) but were totally deficient in speech (expressive language) (see Table 2). Apes trained in a nonspeech mode also learned both receptive and expressive language.

It is difficult to assess the effects of environment on language development. What is the function of environment in ape language development? Rumbaugh's (1977) research shows that Lana learned to use language to manipulate her environment; however, her environment and language context were limited to a laboratory cubicle. Those working with nonlanguage children in institutions are becoming aware of the importance of the environment in language development. Perhaps future ape language research will be directed toward the goals of the Kelloggs and Hayeses but at the same time will incorporate the language-training strategies derived from recent research. This approach, although difficult, could aid in delineating the function of environment in language development.

SOCIAL INTERACTION

The chimpanzee and perhaps the gorilla, in addition to displaying relatively intelligent behavior, are sociable. They form strong attachments to human beings. Ape language researchers are aware of the sociability of the ape and have used that sociability in teaching them language.

It is interesting to examine chimpanzee and gorilla social behavior in the wild (native habitat). The chimpanzee lives and travels in a loose and unstable group ranging from 10 to 23 animals and may share a 6 to 8 square-mile area with other groups. Although group composition may be highly variable, the typical group is a mixture of adult males, females, mothers with infants, and adolescents. Less frequent groups contain adults of both sexes, only adult males, or mothers with young (DeVore, 1965).

Chimpanzees are very noisy in the forest, frequently engaging in hooting, screaming, and drumming. Vocalizations often increase when food is found. In analyzing chimpanzees' social and communicative behavior, over ten distinct vocalizations have been recorded. Chimpanzees also produce four to five gestures and eight to nine facial expressions. Despite the looseness of the chimpanzee groups, it has been hypothesized that they have a highly organized social structure (DeVore, 1965).

The gorilla's social behavior and communication are slightly different from the chimpanzee's. Gorillas have been observed to form more cohesive groups than the chimpanzee, ranging from 5 to 27 animals. The group is led by a dominant male who determines the group's daily routine. Communication is through postures and gestures, vocalizations, and facial expressions. In general, however, social behavior and communication of the gorilla in the wild are similar to the chimpanzee (DeVore, 1965).

For the normal human, language develops as the result of direct social interaction during the first few years of life. Language is an integral part of social behavior. It functions to control the behavior of individuals and groups through the processes of communication. Normal human children are reared by language-competent parents in a human environment. Both the human child and the ape develop within a well defined social group, however different. In both cases the group serves a social function. In developmental language research with the ape, researchers have exercised great latitude with respect to type and degree of social interaction. These interactions take on many variations (see Table 2) and range from continuous access to human parents and agemates, to access to researchers and caregivers for brief periods. In some cases chimpanzees or gorillas have been permitted access to their own kind. Several researchers of ape language development have recognized the importance of social interactions and social transactions in the development of language (Savage-Rumbaugh, Rumbaugh, and Boysen, 1978; Fouts, Couch, and O'Neil, Chapter 15, this volume). However, the function of social interaction in language development has not been investigated systematically.

The initial studies of language development have depended, probably of necessity, upon human and ape social interactions. The language research involving human and ape interaction provides useful but limited information about the function of social interaction in the development of ape language. This point is especially important when the ape's natural habitat and social behavior are taken into account. In general, little attention has been paid to the function of ape social structure and organization in the development of language. However, there is at least one exception for captive chimpanzees. Fouts (see Fouts, Couch, and O'Neil, Chapter 15, this volume), in extending his chimpanzee language work, is attempting to develop a language-using chimp society. By rearing the chimpanzees in a large compound the effects of social interaction on language use and function can be studied. In this situation the chimpanzees still interact with researchers and caregivers.

This section has presented a brief overview of ape social interaction and communication modes in the native habitat to enable the reader to contrast the animal's natural social environment with the laboratory social environment provided by the ape language researcher. To say the least, the contrast is marked. Although researchers generally recognize the importance of social interactions in language development, its function has not been clearly delineated. However, recent attempts to develop a language-using chimpanzee society represent a move in this direction.

COGNITIVE DEVELOPMENT

The measurement of cognitive development is a difficult problem, especially across species. The problem of developing culture- and language-free tests has been formidable. As a result, there have been few studies in which standardized human tests have been applied to the assessment of chimpanzee cognitive and intellectual ability. Kellogg and Kellogg (1933) used the Gesell tests in evaluating Gua. Patterson (1978 [Chapter 16, this volume]) used the ACLC (Assessment of Children's Language Comprehension) test in evaluating Koko. A general overview of the home-raised chimpanzee data suggests that at least for the first two years of life the child and chimp closely parallel each other in cognitive development. It is possible to conclude that the linguistic differences are greater than the cognitive differences.

If we accept the premise that language learning is the mapping of preexisting cognitive structure with symbols, then establishing language use in the chimpanzee would require the development of a cognitive structure similar to that of a human child. The cognitive limitations on language for the chimpanzee have been discussed by Limber (1977), who suggests, "Those cognitive differences that emerge along with the development of language are as likely to be consequences of language as antecedents" (p. 291). Thus, there is an interaction between cognitive structure and linguistic development. When the physical and social environment is considered, this becomes a very complicated puzzle. Although there may not be a direct isomorphic relationship between conceptual structure and linguistic structure, the conceptual structure provides the basis for the development of cognitive-linguistic interactions. Premack and Premack (1974) state, "Language can be viewed as the mapping of existing distinctions" (p. 354). In this case the existing distinctions become the ape's cognitive map or environmental model. With respect to communication, Menzel and Johnson (1976 [Chapter 13 this volume]) sum up the problem as follows:

> Since successful communication depends on accurately assessing the available cognitive structures of other beings, and animals integrate information from various sources, it is misleading to think of communication as one individual transmitting information to another who knows absolutely nothing about the intended message. The more two individuals share common structures, assumptions, knowledge, and values, the more efficient their communication (pp. 133–134 [p. 266]).

Table 2 provides a gross comparison for cognitive development across the major chimpanzee language studies. This comparison is difficult because there are few instances of the use of standardized tests in the assessment of chimpanzees' cognitive ability. For the cases in which standard tests have not been employed, a gross analysis of the ape's linguistic ability has been presented, or the reader is referred to the original work.

Binet wrote of the intelligence of children who were retarded in school. These children were deficient in language and lacking in the areas of comprehension and judgment, among others. It was his contention that these mental functions are susceptible to development through educational processes. It appears that researchers currently teaching language to apes have adopted this approach. In their language research with apes, they have discovered that cognitive structures (concepts) *function* as a basis for the development of linguistic behavior (e.g., Premack 1970 [Chapter 12, this volume]). What are the ape's cognitive limitations with respect to language? Although this is a difficult question, the answer in part depends on the ingenuity of the researchers in educating apes. It seems that we are still far from defining the cognitive potential of the ape.

LEXICON SOURCE

The term *lexicon* refers to the number of linguistic signs (symbols, words, morphemes, and so forth) that exist in a given language. In general, the lexicon source for ape and nonspeech child language research has been of English derivation. However, the use of nonspeech language modes has placed certain restrictions on the form and size of the lexicon in language training. Table 2 provides a brief overview of the lexicon forms and their sources used in chimpanzee, gorilla, and retarded child language studies. Although the lexicon sources are substantially English, the lexicon forms vary across ape and child language studies. In the early ape research, spoken English was used for receptive language (Kellogg and Kellogg, 1933; Hayes and Hayes, 1954). Because of the failure of these apes to learn to speak, spoken English was abandoned in subsequent research. The ape language researchers adopted American Sign Language (ASL), plastic symbols, and computer lexigrams (Yerkish language) for teaching receptive and expressive language (see Hollis and Carrier, 1978).

These nonspeech language systems, although rooted in English (ASL is a variant of the French Sign Language), may, because of their form, place restrictions on the number of linguistic signs available. For example, manual signs (ASL, etc.) are restricted in number as a function of the ability to produce discriminable hand and arm configurations. In like manner, those systems involving plastic symbols (Premack, 1970 [Chapter 12, this volume]; Premack and Premack, 1974) and computer lexigrams (Rumbaugh, 1977) are restricted in lexicon size as a function of the ability of the experimenter to produce abstract symbols that can readily be discriminated by an ape or child. Thus, the size of the lexicon is dependent on the ability of the researcher to develop discriminable symbols. The lexicon functions to provide signs that have specified meanings. Therefore, the greater the number of restrictions on the size of the lexicon, the greater the limitations of a language and communication system.

One index of human intelligence or cognitive ability is vocabulary size. What is the size and content of the ape's and human child's lexicon? The child's lexicon in part is controlled by the maternal environment, whereas that of the ape is controlled by the experimenter. The initial vocabularies of the ape and very young child are comparable (e.g., Kellogg and Kellogg, 1933), although after the first two years of life the child acquires substantial linguistic superiority. Current ape research has reduced this difference somewhat, but, irrespective of the ape's ability, the size and form of the lexicon may be just another restricting force in language development for both ape and child.

Content Words

What do very young children talk about during the process of language acquisition? Or, in the case of teaching language to nonhuman primates, what does the experimenter provide the chimpanzee to "talk" about? As has been pointed out (Mahoney and Seely, 1976), there is a correlation between the content of the very young child's communication and the maternal environment.

In order to determine what very young children and language-acquiring chimpanzees "talk" about, a brief survey of the literature was undertaken. Table 3 presents a sample comparison of single-word content of normal children (Bowerman, 1973) and several chimpanzees (Gardner and Gardner, 1969 [Chapter 9, this volume]; Premack, 1970 [Chapter 12, this volume]; Fouts, 1973; and Rumbaugh et al., 1973) and Carrier's (1974 [Chapter 17, this volume]) language program for retarded children. The *content* words listed in Table 3, in most cases, are not complete lists of words in the individual's lexicon.

An overview of the various lexicons suggests that the comparisons would be facilitated by categorizing the *content* words. On a priori bases the words were sorted into 10 descriptive categories. As a result of sorting the content words into specific categories, some interesting similarities and differences emerged. First, the words for the normal child and the chimpanzee learning sign language (ASL) were similar. Although

Table 3.   Samples of single-word content

Persons	Animals	Objects	Food	Clothes	Toys	Actions	Mands	Concepts	Other
						Categories			
			(Child vocalizations, Bowerman, 1973)						
father	cow	car	coffee	hat	bicycle	sits	off		hi
cowboy	duck	tractor	food	shoe	ball	climbs	no		bye
man	monkey	truck	apple	shirt	doll	cooks	again		please
girl	dog	airplane	water	coat	swing	walks	more		naughty
baby	horse	train	sugar		book	sings	go		thank you
mother	cat	spoon	cookie		paint	turns	up		big
		(Chimpanzee Washoe—manual signs (ASL), Gardner and Gardner, 1969 [Chapter 9, this volume])							
you	cat	toothbrush	banana	blanket	baby	catch	come		please
me	dog	flower	berry	barrette		clean	hurry		sorry
Jack		brush	candy	coat		cry	go		in
Janet		napkin	drink	pants		kiss	enough		cold
Lucy		key	fruit	purse		listen	no		this
Maury		string	tea	shoe		look	out		there
Roger		spoon		clothes		open	want		funny
Steve		smoke				eat	more		
Sue						tickle	in		

(Chimpanzee Sarah—plastic symbols, Premack, 1970 [Chapter 12, this volume])

Sarah	dish	insert	give	same	is
Mary	pail	wash	take	different	
	chocolate			name-of	
	apple			no-not	
	banana			question (?)	
	apricot			if-then	
	raisin			color-of	

(Chimpanzee Lana—computer lexigrams, Rumbaugh et al., 1973)

Tim	window	open	give	piece	please
machine	room		come	(period)	into
	M&M		make		of
	juice				
	water				
	apple				
	banana				

(Retarded children—Non-SLIP, Carrier and Peak, 1975)

girl	tree	sitting	the
boy	car	playing	is
man	floor	running	are
lady	chair	laying	
baby	table	standing	
horse	sidewalk		
dog	grass		
cow	bed		
cat	box		
bird			

the chimpanzees in Premack's (1970 [Chapter 12, this volume]) and Rumbaugh's (1977) projects used similar categories, they were void of content words in three categories: animals, clothes, and toys. The program developed by Carrier (1974 [Chapter 17, this volume]) for retarded children was the most restricted with respect to the 10 categories. In his program there were no content words in the following categories: food, clothes, toys, mands, and concepts.

COMMUNICATION MODES

Language functions receptively and expressively with respect to communication. There is a "speaker" and "listener" in the functional communication system. This system may employ spoken English, manual signs, plastic symbols, computer lexigrams, and so forth. The stimuli may be auditory or visual, and may be productive or selective in form. Productive language systems require that the ape or child produce the symbol as in speech or manual signing (e.g., ASL). These systems are advantageous because of their speed and flexibility in transmission. However, apes and some children are unable to produce or use speech effectively. The chimpanzee does not learn to talk, and the deaf or severely auditory impaired child has great difficulty with speech, both receptively and expressively. The cerebral palsied child has problems with both speech and manual signing. Therefore, a symbol selection system can circumvent the productive problem. Symbol selection systems do not demand the fine motor movements required in productive systems. In these systems the symbols are prefabricated (e.g., preformed plastic chips or geometric figures on a computer display panel). In a selective system the ape or child need only pick up the symbol, press a computer lexigram, or engage in some other simple motor response. Much of the recent success in teaching receptive and expressive language to apes has come about as a result of abandoning speech.

Table 2 compares communication modes for receptive and expressive language across ape and child studies referred to in this volume. The table shows that the ape can learn functional receptive language through speech. However, apes do not learn to speak; therefore, they do not acquire expressive language. Those apes that have learned signing, manipulation of plastic symbols, and responding to computer lexigrams have acquired both receptive and expressive language.

The implementation of simple productive and selective symbol systems has provided the ape and nonspeech child with functional receptive and expressive communication modes. At this point it is difficult to evaluate the different systems in use; however, future research should provide data with respect to communication function (cf. Savage-Rumbaugh, Rumbaugh, and Boysen, 1978; Fouts, Couch, and O'Neil, Chapter 15, this volume).

SUMMARY

This chapter has presented an overview of the development of chimpanzee language research, presented a general language system, and discussed the functions of language-related variables. Thus, the chapter provides the reader with a frame of reference that will place the subsequent chapters in perspective.

Studies of language development in the chimpanzee have taken place over four decades, starting with the classic work of Kellogg and Kellogg (1933). The second section of this chapter summarized the chimpanzee language research from the Kelloggs (1933) through the Hayeses (1951, 1954), the Gardners (1969 [Chapter 9, this volume]), Premack (1970 [Chapter 12, this volume]), and Rumbaugh et al. (1973). This historical overview provides a synopsis of the evolution of strategies for teaching language to chimpanzees. Some of the original chimpanzee language research papers appear in Section III of this volume.

This chapter has delineated salient variables related to language acquisition and described a general system for language, with special emphasis on communication channels and the levels of psycholinguistic analysis. Both linguistic and nonlinguistic conceptualization are discussed. The system provides a perspective on alternative response modes—speech, lexical, and gross motor—that can be used to deliver language. Behavioral, linguistic, and cognitive issues are combined to form a functional design.

Linguistic rules, both semantic and syntactic, are considered in relation to existing nonspeech symbol systems, e.g., American Sign Language, plastic chips (Premack, 1970 [Chapter 12, this volume]), computer lexigrams (Rumbaugh, 1977), rebuses, Blissymbols, etc. This approach builds on work already published by Hollis, Carrier, and Spradlin (1976), and Hollis and Carrier (1978).

The pragmatics of language are considered in a functional language model. Thus, semantics, syntax, and symbols are discussed as they function within the communication context.

Finally, an analysis is presented on functional issues relevant to language development. These issues include physical and psychological environment, social interaction, cognitive development, lexicon sources, and communication modes. These issues should be given serious attention when analyzing ape language research and making comparisons between ape and child language development.

Subsequent sections of this volume cover: 1) language and communication models, 2) selected articles, in original form, to provide a historical perspective on primate language and communication development, 3) strategies for language and communication acquisition, and 4) application of nonhuman primate language strategies to language acquisition in handicapped children.

ACKNOWLEDGMENTS

The authors would like to express their appreciation to those individuals who contributed to the development of this chapter. Special thanks go to Barbara Horrocks and Susan Wulz, who contributed substantially to discussions of the general language system and the organization of figures and tables. The authors are indebted to Myron Sahlberg for the artwork.

REFERENCES

Berger, S. L. 1972. A clinical program for developing multimodal language responses with atypical deaf children. *In* J. E. McLean, D. E. Yoder, and R. L. Schiefelbusch (eds.), Language Intervention with the Retarded, pp. 212–235. University Park Press, Baltimore.

Bowerman, M. 1973. Early Syntactic Development: A Cross-linguistic Study with Special Reference to Finnish. Cambridge University Press, Cambridge, England.

Bowerman, M. 1978. Semantic and syntactic development: A review of what, when and how in language acquisition. *In* R. L. Schiefelbusch (ed.), Bases of Language Intervention, pp. 97–189. University Park Press, Baltimore.

Bryan, A. L. 1963. The essential basis for human culture. Curr. Anthropol. 4:297–306.

Carrier, J. K. 1974. Application of functional analysis and a nonspeech response mode to teaching language. ASHA Monogr. No. 18.

Carrier, J. K., and Peak, T. 1975. Non-speech Language Initiation Program. H & H Enterprises, Lawrence, Kan.

DeVore, I. (ed.). 1965. Primate Behavior: Field Studies of Monkeys and Apes. Holt, Rinehart & Winston, New York.

Fouts, R. S. 1973. Acquisition and testing of gestural signs in four young chimpanzees. Science 180:978–980.

Gardner, R. A., and Gardner, B. T. 1969. Teaching sign language to a chimpanzee. Science 165:664–672.

Harlow, H. F. 1949. The formation of learning sets. Psychol. Rev. 56:51–65.

Hayes, C. 1951. The Ape in Our House. Harper & Brothers, New York.

Hayes, K. J., and Hayes, C. 1951. The intellectual development of a home-raised chimpanzee. Proceed. Am. Philosoph. Soc. 95:105–109.

Hayes, K. J., and Hayes, C. 1954. The cultural capacity of chimpanzee. Hum. Biol. 26:288–303.

Hollis, J. H. 1966. Communication within dyads of severely retarded children. Am. J. Ment. Defic. 70:729–744.

Hollis, J. H. 1967. Development of perceptual motor skills in a profoundly retarded child: Part I—prosthesis. Am. J. Ment. Defic. 71:941–952.

Hollis, J. H., and Carrier, J. K. 1975. Research implications for communication deficiencies. Except. Child. 41:405–412.

Hollis, J. H., and Carrier, J. K. 1978. Intervention strategies for nonspeech children. *In* R. L. Schiefelbusch (ed.), Language Intervention Strategies, pp. 57–100. University Park Press, Baltimore.

Hollis, J. H., Carrier, J. K., and Spradlin, J. E. 1976. An approach to remediation of communication and learning deficiencies. *In* L. L. Lloyd (ed.), Communication Assessment and Intervention Strategies, pp. 265–294. University Park Press, Baltimore.

Kellogg, W. N. 1931. Humanizing the ape. Psycholog. Rev. 38:160–176.

Kellogg, W. N., and Kellogg, L. A. 1933. The Ape and the Child. McGraw-Hill Book Co., New York. [1967, Hafner, New York.]

Limber, J. 1977. Language in child and chimp? Am. Psychologist 32:280–295.

Mahoney, G. J., and Seely, P. B. 1976. The role of the social agent in language acquisition: Implications for language intervention. *In* N. R. Ellis (ed.), International Review of Research in Mental Retardation, Vol. 8, pp. 57–103. Academic Press, New York.

Mason, W. A., and Hollis, J. H. 1962. Communication between young rhesus monkeys. Anim. Behav. 10:211–221.

Mason, W. A., Hollis, J. H., and Sharpe, L. G. 1962. Differential responses of chimpanzees to social stimulation. J. Comp. Physiolog. Psychol. 55:1105–1110.

Menzel, E. W., and Johnson, M. K. 1976. Communication and cognitive organization in humans and other animals. *In* S. R. Harnad, H. D. Steklis, and J. Lancaster (eds.), Origins and Evolution of Language and Speech. The New York Academy of Sciences, New York.

Osgood, C. E. 1957. A behavioristic analysis of perception and language as cognitive phenomena. *In* J. S. Bruner et al. (eds.), Contemporary Approaches to Cognition. Harvard University Press, Cambridge, Mass.

Patterson, F. 1978. Linguistic capabilities of a lowland gorilla. *In* F. C. C. Peng (ed.), Sign Language and Language Acquisition—New Dimensions in Comparative Pedolinguistics, pp. 161–201. Westview Press, Boulder, Col.

Peterson, H. A. 1973. A case report of speech and language training for a two-year-old laryngectomized child. J. Speech Hear. Disord. 38:275–278.

Premack, A. J., and Premack, D. 1972. Teaching language to an ape. Sci. Am. 227:92–99.

Premack, D. 1970. A functional analysis of language. J. Exp. Anal. Behav. 14:107–125.

Premack, D. 1976. Intelligence in Ape and Man. John Wiley & Sons, New York.

Premack, D., and Premack, A. J. 1974. Teaching visual language to apes and language-deficient persons. *In* R. L. Schiefelbusch and L. L. Lloyd (eds.), Language Perspectives — Acquisition, Retardation, and Intervention, pp. 347–376. University Park Press, Baltimore.

Premack, D., and Schwartz, A. 1966. Preparations for discussing behaviorism with chimpanzee. *In* F. Smith and C. A. Miller (eds.), The Genesis of Language. The MIT Press, Cambridge, Mass.

Pribram, K. H. 1971. Languages of the Brain. Prentice-Hall, Englewood Cliffs, N.J.

Rumbaugh, D. M. 1977. Language Learning by a Chimpanzee: The LANA Project. Academic Press, New York.

Rumbaugh, D. M., Gill, T. V., and von Glasersfeld, E. 1973. Reading and sentence completion by a chimpanzee (*Pan*). Science 182:731–733.

Savage-Rumbaugh, E. S., Rumbaugh, D. M., and Boysen, S. 1978. Symbolic communication between two chimpanzees (*Pan troglodytes*). Science 201: 641–644.

Schaeffer, B. 1979. Spontaneous language through signed speech. *In* R. L. Schiefelbusch (ed.), Nonspeech Language and Communication: Analysis and Intervention. University Park Press, Baltimore. In press.

Schlesinger, I. M. 1977. The role of cognitive development and linguistic input in language acquisition. J. Child Lang. 4:153–169.

Travis, L. E. 1957. Handbook of Speech Pathology. Appleton-Century-Crofts, New York.

von Glasersfeld, E. 1977a. Linguistic communication: Theory and definition. *In* D. M. Rumbaugh (ed.), Language Learning by a Chimpanzee: The LANA Project. Academic Press, New York.

von Glasersfeld, E. 1977b. The Yerkish language and its automatic parser. *In* D. M. Rumbaugh (ed.), Language Learning by a Chimpanzee: The LANA Project. Academic Press, New York.

Warren, R. M. 1968. Verbal transformation effect and auditory perceptual mechanisms. Psycholog. Bull. 70:261–270.

Yerkes, R. M. 1943. Chimpanzees: A Laboratory Colon. Yale University Press, New Haven, Conn.

Yerkes, R. M., and Nissen, H. W. 1939. Pre-linguistic sign behavior in chimpanzee. Science 89:585–587.

Section

II

Language and Communication Models

Lana

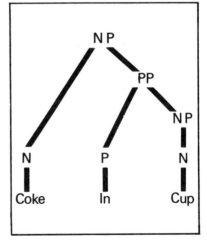

Grammar

Figure of chimpanzee Lana redrawn from *Yerkes Newsletter*, May, 1974 (Emory University, Vol. II, No. 1).

Editors' Introduction

Section II contains three main chapters and a summary. Each is an academic essay. To place the essays in an integrated perspective with the rest of the book, several issues should be examined.

THEORETICAL AND OPERATIONAL MODELS

Two of the chapters (those by Krauss and Glucksberg) do not focus primarily upon primate research or upon intervention applications. Yet each has much to say about both. Krauss and Glucksberg explain that there are theoretical models and operational models. Each model is frequently abused. They emphasize the abuses that have evolved from their own model of referential communication, abuses that happen when clinicians or scientists apply a referential model literally in teaching language and communication. Glucksberg is especially severe with clinicians for teaching referential "block stacking" while pretending they are teaching functional communication skills.

The cautions by both Krauss and Glucksberg are valuable because they come at an early point in a book that is devoted to the extrapolation of language procedures for apes to language work with human children. The message is that there are both advantages and dangers in the transfer of models designed for apes to applications with human children. Literalness, overgeneralization, and premature uses are dangers to be avoided. Krauss and Glucksberg, as scientists, understand the abuses to scientific validity that stem from poorly considered and poorly applied extrapolations. Both chapters should be read carefully for these insights.

The editors support their views. Nevertheless, there is also, at this point in the book, a good reason to point out how *models* of language instruction can be extrapolated to different subjects and under altered conditions. Rumbaugh et al. (Chapter 3) give considerable attention to models and their application and, later in the book, Fouts, Couch, and O'Neil (Chapter 15) and Carrier (Chapter 17) discuss these issues.

From the point of view of the clinician or the applied researcher who seeks better models for designing language activities with human children, application efforts are limited to the state of knowledge available from all sources, including research sources, and to the skills and technical information at the disposal of the clinicians. Clinicians are morally and professionally pressed to improve their teaching efforts, and they must continue to look for better models such as the referential model, the Language Analog (LANA) Project, the Non-speech Language Initiation Program (Non-SLIP), or others.

APPLICATION OF EXPERIMENTAL MODELS

There are three questions that might be raised in light of the information contained in this section.

First, what *conditions* predict successful application of an experimental model? The most pervasive answer is that the conditions, experimental and applied, should be similar so that appropriate adjustments in method and technology can be made. *Similar* means that the critical operations, including the response modes, symbol forms, lexicons, and social contexts, are similar or can be readily modified to be comparable. For instance, Rumbaugh and Parkel engaged in a number of planning sessions to determine if the Language Analog (LANA) Project could be installed in a training setting with retarded children. The concerns were related to the portability of the communication board, the availability of a functional computer, the feasibility of the training program for symbolization learning, possible alterations of the symbolic operations, and the anticipated alterations of the training contexts. As a result of these and other considerations, the decision to install the training model in the Georgia Retardation Center was reached. The decision was based on an affirmative answer to the question: "Are the conditions at GRC favorable for the application of the LANA Project to that setting?"

Second, does the application agent have the *skills* required for applying an intervention program from an explicit model? The skills involve planning, designing, and implementation and are central to good applied research or good clinical programming. However, a special issue in the ape to child theme pertains to operational adjustments that must be made. As is pointed out in the editors' introduction to Section V, a *literal* application is not likely to succeed because of the cognitive and social differences between the two species.

Third, what are the *common features* of the experimental model and the clinical model? Researchers who have undertaken to teach language to apes have asked, "Can we design a language program that can be taught to apes in the contexts available?" This is actually two questions. First, "What is the form and the content of the language to be taught?" Second, "What operations and contexts will be necessary to teach it?" Application specialists must answer the same questions in planning a language program for a nonvocal child. Consequently, the topography of the symbol system, the lexicon of symbols, the transactional functions to be categorized, the instructional program to be designed, and the maintenance features to be managed have comparable features; thus, the tasks faced by the designers include common features because the *functions* and the *operations* are comparable.

Each question includes issues that extend beyond the points just discussed.

We must also acknowledge that the questions may not be answerable in light of the current state of language research and clinical knowledge. Nevertheless, it is better to try to answer them than to ignore them. It is better also for professionals from several relevant fields to share information and to work together than for them to compartmentalize their data in specialized journals that isolate their efforts.

It is fortunate that Premack, Fouts, Rumbaugh, Krauss, Glucksberg, and other experimental psychologists are now concerned about how experimental formulations are being adapted and what the data look like when their models are applied in other contexts, with other clients, for other purposes, and by other persons. Perhaps the purposes of science and the purposes of clinical services can benefit from improvements in language models and improvements in our ability to alter and apply them in selective ways to serve valid purposes.

Krauss also makes the point that the referential model of communication, which he developed with Glucksberg, is limited because it does not include the pragmatic features that determine the patterns of human communication. Without using *pragmatics* to identify his topic, and without using the terminology of academic linguistics (pragmatics), Krauss artfully develops the social issues necessary for a system of language. The implication from his essay is that, unless the pragmatic functions are delineated and included in the language system to be taught, functional communication will not be realized. Referential language is thus only a limited part of a functional language system.

This point is also discussed in Chapter 1. However, Krauss' statement is especially cogent and is in close agreement with Bates (1976), Rees (1978), and other writers who have presented pragmatic issues to applied linguistic audiences.

NONHUMAN PRIMATE MODELS FOR LANGUAGE RESEARCH

Stahlke et al. (Chapter 4) analyze an issue of special interest to language specialists. The issue is often heralded by the question "Do apes actually learn to use a *true* language?" The implication is that apes may use signs but they do not learn the conceptual basis of meaning—form relationships—nor transformational rules that are necessary to factor the relationships. Stahlke et al. report that the language learned by the chimpanzee Lana is qualitatively similar to natural language. "The disparity in linguistic ability between ape and human must then lie in the area of cognition and intelligence" (p. 104). The authors also point out that apes use language for immediate gratification of some physical need or in direct response to human-initiated stimuli. The range of human language use is, of course, much greater.

The point stressed by Rumbaugh et al. (Chapter 3) is that the chimpanzee can serve as an animal model for language research. Chapter 4 certainly supports this view. Nevertheless, it is clear that language issues for which the ape is a relevant model have been limited primarily to referential features. The work of Patterson (1978 [Chapter 16, this volume]) and Fouts, Couch, and O'Neil (Chapter 15, this volume), however, strongly suggests that apes are capable of pragmatic functions of surprising complexity. Perhaps future research will extend the social possibilities of ape to ape and ape to human language so that further delineations will be possible.

REFERENCES

Bates, E. 1976. Pragmatics and sociolinguistics and child language. *In* D. Morehead and A. Morehead (eds.), Normal and Deficient Child Language, pp. 411–463. University Park Press, Baltimore.

Patterson, F. 1978. Linguistic capabilities of a lowland gorilla. *In* F. C. C. Peng (ed.), Sign Language and Language Acquisition—New Dimensions in Comparative Pedolinguistics, pp. 161–201. Westview Press, Boulder, Col.

Rees, N. S. 1978. Pragmatics of language: Applications to normal and disordered language development. *In* R. L. Schiefelbusch (ed.), Bases of Language Intervention, pp. 191–268. University Park Press, Baltimore.

chapter 2

Communication Models
and
Communicative Behavior

Robert M. Krauss

Columbia University
New York, New York

contents

Buried deep within our psyches there must exist a pleasure center responsive to the knowledge that someone who purports to be an expert has come a cropper. How else can one explain the exquisite joy we experience upon learning that Julia Child's omelet has stuck to the pan or that a famous psychiatrist has been arrested for exposing himself in the subway? In this connection, it may be of some interest to note that a psychologist who has spent the last dozen or so years researching and theorizing about human communication, namely, this author, prepared his conference[1] paper under a misapprehension about the topic he was to discuss. Not surprisingly, in the manner of all self-styled experts, I have managed to convince myself that my error reflects a profound truth.

THE MEANING OF THE WORD *MODEL*

The primary source of my confusion, I believe, is an ambiguity in the meaning of the word *model*. There are at least two senses that *model* may take in the present context. One sense is that intended in phrases like "the mouse as an animal model for cancer research." The meaning of this sense is close to "a paradigm or procedure for studying a particular phenomenon." I refer to it as M_1. A second meaning is the one we encounter in such phrases as "a stochastic model for paired-associate learning." Here the meaning is closer to "theory." As I have understood it, this sense of *model* refers to a formalization or particularization of a more general theoretical approach. I refer to this sense as M_2.

The paper I had originally prepared was directed to models (sense M_2) of communicative behavior. But gradually, during the last few weeks before the conference, it dawned on me that I had been invited to discuss referential communication tasks as a model (sense M_1) for human communication. Having acknowledged my confusion, like any good obsessive, it then occurred to me that the two meanings of *model* are not unrelated. That is to say, in order to develop a useful model (M_1) for human communication, a reasonably good model (M_2) of human communication is necessary. This is the burden of this chapter.

Referential Communication

By referential communication I mean the use of language to refer to (i.e., to distinguish by verbal means) elements of one's environment. As such it constitutes one of the simplest and most fundamental social uses of language. A referential communication task is simply a procedure designed to tap an individual's ability to use language to communicate referentially. Sam Glucksberg and I developed such a task that was

---

[1] The Gulf Shores (Alabama) Conference on Nonspeech Language, held in March, 1977, the proceedings of which provided the basis for this volume.

suitable for use with children some 10 years ago.[2] The task requires the presence of two subjects, one of whom functions in the role of sender (source, encoder, speaker, etc.), while the other functions as receiver (destination, decoder, listener, etc.). Apparatus consist of two duplicate sets of six blocks, a pair of stacking pegs on which the blocks (which have holes drilled through their vertical centers) can be stacked, a dispenser that dispenses the blocks one at a time, and an opaque screen that separates sender and receiver. Such a setup is illustrated in Figure 1. The task requires that the sender remove a block from the dispenser, place it on the stacking peg, and at the same time instruct the receiver which of the six blocks, randomly laid out before him, to place on the receiver's stacking peg. This having been done, the sender then removes another block from the dispenser, places it on the stacking peg, instructs the receiver which block to put on his stacking peg, and so on, until all six blocks are stacked.

The object of the task, from the subjects' point of view, is to construct two identical stacks of blocks. The task seems trivially easy even for quite young children, and so it would be except for one complicating factor. Each block in the sender's and receiver's sets is imprinted on its four vertical facets with one of six novel graphic designs. The six designs are shown in Figure 2. It is these designs that make it possible for subjects to discriminate among the otherwise identical blocks. But it is also these designs that create difficulties for subjects in our task. For, while the designs are easily discriminated visually from one another, they all share the quality of not resembling anything in particular, and therefore they become quite difficult to communicate verbally. The designs were, of course, chosen for this very quality, and the referential communication task (which has come to be called "Stack the Blocks") was designed as a convenient format for investigating the factors that affect children's ability to apply their linguistic competence to a set of novel referents. Glucksberg and I have used this task in a number of studies (Glucksberg, Krauss, and Weisberg, 1966; Glucksberg and Krauss, 1967; Krauss and Glucksberg, 1969) and have found that it possesses several useful features.

First, unlike many of the tasks that have been reported in the literature, the Stack the Blocks game permits subjects to use natural language to communicate. It is unnecessary to teach subjects a special language or to restrict their utterances in any way—something that is especially advantageous when working with children.

---

[2] This discussion should not be understood to suggest that the task Glucksberg and I developed was the first such task reported in the literature (which it was not) or that it is in some important way superior to other, similar tasks other investigators have employed. It is used in this discussion illustratively, largely because it is the one with which I am most familiar.

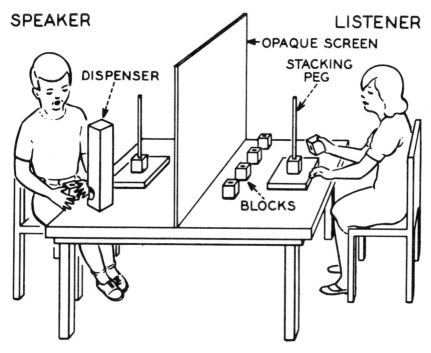

Figure 1.   Equipment setup for the Stack the Blocks game.

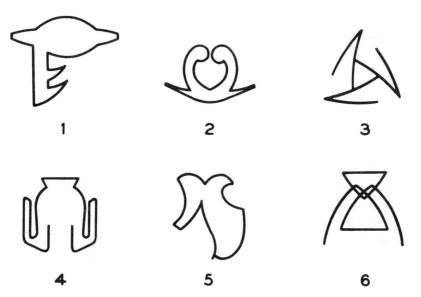

Figure 2.   The novel designs used in the Stack the Blocks game.

Second, the task gives subjects a common focus about which to talk, allowing us to make meaningful comparisons across subjects. A difficulty frequently encountered in the analysis of naturally occurring conversations is that topic accounts for so large a share of the variance across conversations that it is difficult to make sensible comparisons of, for example, the communicative effectivenesss of different speakers or dyads. The essence of a referential communication task is to pose a problem that subjects can solve only by communicating. To the extent that subjects are motivated to perform on the referential communication task, it is reasonable to regard their performance as reflecting an underlying communication competence, and, similarly, it is reasonable to examine attributes of their speech (or other communication modalities, for that matter) as strategies adopted to achieve the task-imposed goal. For example, Glucksberg and I analyzed the distributional properties of the conceptual elements incorporated into messages in the Stack the Blocks game by fifth-grade and eighth-grade speakers. We found that fifth graders and eighth graders did not differ in the total number of conceptual elements they used. Subjects from the two grades did differ, however, in the proportion of conceptual elements that were unique, i.e., used by only one sender. Eighth graders tended to use fewer unique elements than did fifth graders. Had we simply recorded conversations between pairs of fifth graders and pairs of eighth graders, allowing topic to vary freely, there is no way that such a comparison could have been made (Krauss, 1971).

Third, perhaps the most advantageous feature of referential communication tasks is that they provide an objective, nonlinguistic criterion by which the effectiveness of communication can be evaluated. Again, the communication task provides a nonlinguistic problem that can be solved only by communicating. The effectiveness of that communication can be gauged by how well it enables subjects to solve the nonlinguistic problem. In Stack the Blocks the effectivness of communication is typically measured in terms of the number of errors subjects make on each trial in their attempt to construct identical stacks of blocks. For example, Figure 3 shows increases of primary-school children's ability to communicate as a function of school grade in terms of the decrease in errors over trials. Of course, such scores are a composite of the sending ability of the speaker and the receiving ability of the listener. A high error rate can result from inadequate performance on the part of either or both subjects. However, the same tasks can be used to obtain independent assessments of subjects' sending and receiving ability. For example, subjects can be provided with messages of known effectiveness, as was done in Glucksberg, Krauss, and Weisberg (1966, experiment 2). Under such circumstances, the accuracy with which subjects select referents from

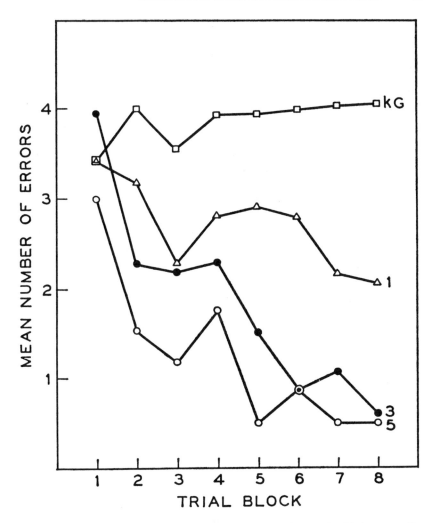

Figure 3. Mean errors over trials for matched-age pairs in four grades, kindergarten, first grade, third grade, and fifth grade. (From Krauss and Glucksberg, 1969; reprinted by permission.)

messages can reasonably be assumed to reflect their receptive competence. Conversely, the messages produced by one or more subjects can be presented to a large number of competent "listeners" who are asked to select the referent to which the message refers, as was done in Krauss and Glucksberg (1969, experiment 2). In such circumstances, the accuracy with which a message permits competent others to select the correct referent can reasonably be taken as an index of that message's effectiveness and, hence, an indication of the competence of the speaker who produced it.

Although this particular feature of referential communication tasks may seem obvious, its value should not be minimized. There are few situations indeed in which we can make assessments of relative ability among speakers or listeners whose competence exceeds some minimal level. Of course, one may evaluate a message (and by extension the speaker who produced it) in terms of a number of structural characteristics. One may, for example, characterize a message in terms of its length, its grammatical correctness, the distributional properties of its lexical elements, and so forth. But it is difficult to formulate a relationship between these attributes of a message and how well it communicates in a functional sense. Similarly, we can characterize in a reasonably objective and straightforward way an individual's ability to produce speech sounds, his mastery of the language's grammatical system, and the precision and extensiveness of his lexical knowledge. But we cannot assume that, because an individual demonstrates competence in each of these areas, he will be able to combine these elements to communicate effectively. To be more specific, I am suggesting that there is a competence in the functional utilization of communicative systems (language among them) that exists apart from the mastery of the systems themselves. In the past, Glucksberg and I, along with others, have referred to this ability as "communicative competence." It was our hope that, by studying the performance of children (who are less than fully competent communicators) developmentally on the referential communication task and by examining the circumstances under which they were likely to perform ineffectively and the nature of their ineffective performance, we could learn a good deal about our subjects' understanding of the communicative process.

Some of the same considerations must have motivated workers in the area of language intervention to adapt referential communication tasks for the purpose of training and assessment. I have been surprised to discover that the work Glucksberg and I did nearly a decade ago is better known by specialists in the area of communicative disorders than it is among our fellow psychologists. But, despite the apparent utility of referential communication tasks (Stack the Blocks among them) as a *model* (M_1) for language intervention and for understanding the nature of human communication more generally, I think we have now come to appreciate that such tasks have features that limit in quite important ways what we can infer from them.

Factors Limiting Referential Communication

There are a number of reasons for this, only a few of which are mentioned here. In the first place, tasks like Stack the Blocks and others that have been reported in the literature incorporate a component that, at least early on, was seldom given much consideration. I am referring to the perceptual-cognitive skills that are necessary to process the referent before it can be encoded verbally. For example, consider what a subject in the Stack the Blocks game must do. The referents about which he must communicate are not familiar objects for which names are readily available. Before the child can decide what to call them, he must first decide what it is they look like—and that is not an easy matter because these stimuli have been painstakingly designed to look like nothing in particular. Therefore, to be successful at this task, i.e., to communicate effectively, a subject must *first* perform a perceptual analysis of a fairly high order. Children not do fare particularly well on imbedded figures tests, and there is no reason to believe that they are substantially better at the somewhat similar perceptual task the Stack the Blocks game imposes on them. Yet their failures to perform well on the communication task have tended to be attributed to their ability to communicate rather than to their ability to process perceptual information. If an adult with color-defective vision consistently encoded objects incorrectly in terms of their hue, we would be well advised to test him for color blindness before we gave him low marks for communication competence. In rather general terms this is the criticism leveled by Shatz and Gelman (1973) against the early studies of referential communication by Glucksberg and myself, and to a considerable extent such criticisms are well taken. Experimental evidence supporting this position is provided by Longhurst and Turnure (1971).

But, even apart from this problem, which is primarily methodological, there is another more practical difficulty with referential communication tasks. We employ such tasks because they provide us with a communicative microcosm that is more readily controlled than the real world. That is, we are interested in children's performance on the Stack the Blocks task because we assume we can generalize from this situation to other communicative interactions. In recent years this assumption has become more difficult to maintain. If we look at the literature, meager though it may be, there is little to justify confidence in the generalizability of results obtained from referential communication tasks. The evidence is reviewed in Glucksberg, Krauss, and Higgins (1975). More recently, a doctoral dissertation done by Robert Strickler (Strickler, 1975) raises additional questions as to the usefulness of referential communication tasks as a measure of an underlying communication competence. Strickler found no relationship between a subject's ability to encode messages and to decode messages in the Stack the Blocks task, a finding that runs counter to the notion of a general communication competence. More important, perhaps, Strickler found that performance on the Stack the Blocks task was not a good predictor of performance on a different but conceptually similar communication task, the word association task developed by Rosenberg and Cohen (1966). If performance on one referential communication task does not even predict performance on another similar task, it is difficult to believe that it will tell us much about an individual's ability to function in the real world, which is to say that there is no persuasive evidence to support the notion that referential communication tasks are useful models (sense M_1) for such purposes as language intervention.

Often the ideas that most directly and importantly shape the nature of our work are not the ones we delineate explicitly in the introductions to our writings or purport to test in our ingeniously designed experiments. Underlying our conceptualization of a phenomenon is a set of assumptions that reflects our implicit understanding of how the thing works, what effects it has, and what makes it different from other, related things. These ideas are seldom stated explicitly, and, as a result, they can have an effect that is quite pernicious, because they may lead us to overlook the possibility that our notion of how a thing works is not at all the way it works and that, by defining the phenomenon in the way we have, we have excluded some critical aspect.

THE WAY PEOPLE COMMUNICATE

In the remainder of this chapter we shall pursue the possibility that referential communication tasks have turned out to be so disappointing a model (sense M_1) for the study of human communication because they have been based on a defective model (sense M_2) of human communication. Stated more generally, the models of communication, particularly models of linguistic communication, tend to ignore some fundamental facts about the way people communicate. One consequence of this is that we have completely overlooked some elements of the communication process and distorted quite beyond recognition our view of others. Let me quickly point out that none of the ideas I offer is completely my own. Some are old and familiar, while others have emerged from the inquiries of (mainly) philosophers interested in natural language. If I have a contribution to make beyond that of a mere reporter, it is to bring these ideas together and to try to put them in a more psychologically oriented framework.

It seems to me that when psychologists (and others) talk about verbal communication, they implicitly are thinking of a process something like the following: The communicative act begins as an idea in the mind of one person, an idea that person wishes to make accessible to another. To do so, the idea is encoded. That is to say, it is translated (by means which we do not presently understand) into a set of symbols.

These symbols, which may be thought of as words or morphemes, or what have you, may properly be called symbols by virtue of the fact that they stand for something and the something they stand for is what we ordinarily term their meaning. Most messages, of course, consist of more than one symbol. Symbols are strung together, and the stringing together is not random or haphazard. Rather, strings are constructed in accordance with a set of rules that details how the elements of the string are functionally related to one another. A message consists of one or more strings, each having a definable structure that accords with the rules for string construction. The meaning of a string is a function of the meaning of its elements (the symbols) as they are organized by the string construction rules. The meaning of a message can be derived from the meaning of the strings that comprise it.

When we understand the message of another, we apply this same process in reverse. From our knowledge of string construction rules and symbol meanings we can, again by means unknown, translate back into the ideas that generated the message. When the idea derived from the message is approximately the same as the idea that generated the message, we say that communication (or perhaps good or effective communication) has taken place.

If this description is vague, it is at least partly so by design. At this point, I want to avoid involvement in matters of particular detail— whether syntactic or semantic analysis is prior, whether the symbols are words or morphemes, whether meaning is to be understood as semantic features or propositions, etc. Not that these are unimportant issues; they surely are not. But they are largely irrelevant to my argument. The view sketched above does, I believe, capture the implicit understanding we have of communication, regardless of the specific detail in which that understanding is framed.

Such a point of view has certain consequences for the way we think about (and study) communication. For example, it implies that when we understand (or think we understand) someone, it is because we understand the idea or ideas that generated his message. It also implies that the elements of strings have meaning and that the meaning of strings (and messages) can be constructed from these meanings along with the rules by which they are combined. It also seems to imply that the meaning of a message somehow exists apart from the context in which it is uttered. What I want to argue is that each of these implications is in some sense true, but that, in another and rather important sense, each is quite false. At the limit, the view I put forth holds that the relationships between what people mean and the words they use to say what they mean, and between what they say and what they are understood to mean, are almost entirely plastic. That is, there is no *necessary* relationship between the words I use and what I intend to be understood as meaning by using them, and, moreover, this fact is acknowledged to be so by my listeners. Additionally, I contend that, if this were not so, we could scarcely be understood at all.

The argument can be made on narrow and rather conventional psycholinguistic grounds. Consider, for example, the case of semantic ambiguity. A good many of the sentences we hear are, by whatever linguistic canon one wishes to apply, ambiguous, although it is not often that they strike us as such. Of course, many are disambiguated by things that have previously been said. If I described how I once mistakenly measured out two tablespoons of cayenne pepper when the recipe called for a half teaspoon, you would probably understand the sentence "The chili was too hot to eat" as referring to an excess of spice rather than an excess of heat.

The Psycholinguistic Model

Even without such context we are often able to clarify potentially ambiguous sentences on the basis of things we know about the world. My favorite illustration is the pair of sentences "He saw the man eating chicken" and "He saw the man eating tiger." Despite the fact that these two sentences are structurally ambiguous in identical ways, they are apprehended unambiguously because, one must assume, of what we know about which animals people are likely to eat and which animals are likely to eat people. A psycholinguistic model for the processing of such a sentence would have the listener extracting the multiple senses in which the sentence can be understood and then making a decision between them on the basis of what is called "extrasentential information." This is a plausible view, but I do not think it is a correct one. In the first place, it simply does not accord with my everyday experience as a language user. When I hear "He saw the man eating chicken," the possibility that the chicken is doing the eating never occurs to me.[3]

But appeals to intuition are unconvincing, so I should mention that there is more acceptable evidence on which to base my rejection of the psycholinguistic model. If a subject is shown a sentence and then, after a brief interval, is shown a single word and asked whether or not the word had been contained in the original sentence, it will take him longer to say no if the word is a synonym of a word in the sentence than if it is unrelated in meaning to any of the words in the sentence. Robert Strickler and I have done this experiment and found a quite reliable difference in

---

[3] Were this not so, such puns as the Groucho Marx classic, "Last night I got up and shot an elephant in my pajamas. How it got in my pajamas, I'll never know," would not be at all funny.

response latency averaging about 100 msec. Strickler and I wondered what would happen if we did the same experiment using sentences that were semantically ambiguous. For example, the subject of the sentence "The yarn was long and colorful" could be taken in context as roughly synonymous with either *wool* or *tale* and the sentence would have quite different meanings depending on which of these senses of *yarn* was understood. Do *wool* and *tale* increase response latency equally if they are used as probe words? The answer is they do not. We established, on an independent sample, subjects' expectations of what our ambiguous sentences were likely to have been intended to mean. From these judgments, we were able to determine for each ambiguous sentence a more likely and a less likely interpretation. For example, in the sentence given above, subjects perceived as more likely the interpretation in which "yarn" meant *wool*, although virtually all acknowledged the possibility of the other interpretation. Strickler and I found an interference effect of about 100 msec for the synonym of the more likely interpretation. It is difficult to reconcile these results with a processing model that has a subject.entertaining alternative interpretations and then deciding between them on extrasentential grounds. Clearly, in understanding a sentence, even under such rarified conditions, we go beyond the semantic and syntactic elements with which we are presented.

These experiments, whatever they say about semantic information processing, are set in the framework of the standard psycholinguistic paradigm. I would like to propose an alternative point of view that leads us, I hope, to a more useful conceptualization of communicative phenomena.

WHY COMMUNICATE

This view begins with the question of why we bother to communicate at all. Except for some small number of us who are seriously disturbed, and the rest of us during those infrequent times when we talk to ourselves, we communicate—speak, but also gesture, grimace, etc.—in order to affect the behavior of others.[4] And it is fair to say that much communicative behavior, of which speech is but one element, does have the effect we intend it to have.

At this point a distinction is necessary, one first drawn by the British philosopher, J. L. Austin. Austin pointed out that our utterances may be thought of as having two rather different effects. If I say to someone

---

[4] Some cynic has suggested that psycholinguists think people speak in order to generate grammatical strings. I do not think psycholinguists really believe this, although it may not be an unreasonable inference to draw from their research.

"Isn't it uncomfortably warm in here?" two consequences may ensue. First, my auditor may understand that I feel uncomfortably warm and, moreover, that I intend him to understand that that is how I feel. The second sort of consequence might be for my auditor to turn on an air conditioner or electric fan, open a window, turn down the heat, or take some other action designed to reduce my discomfort. Austin designated the latter of these effects the "perlocutionary force" of a message, i.e., the consequences that, under certain motivational conditions, could reasonably be expected to follow from it. The former effect of a message, the auditor's understanding of what it is I intended him to understand, Austin called the message's "illocutionary force."

Functions of Language in Communication

Specification of a message's perlocutionary force is not a matter we will consider here. Whether my auditor chooses to turn on the air conditioner or otherwise lower the room temperature, or to tell me that he finds the room quite comfortable, or to throw another log on the fire, will be complexly determined by a number of factors, some having little to do with my communication. But the illocutionary force of the message has very much to do with my communication. Indeed, I find myself in agreement with John Searle's assertion that ". . . meaning something [i.e., communicating] is a matter of intending to produce certain illocutionary effects in the hearer, and on the hearer's side understanding the utterance consists in recognizing these intentions and thereby achieving their intended effect" (Searle, 1967, p. 126).

At this point it might be well to pause and inquire why it is necessary for us to consider something so vague and epistemologically shaky as "a speaker's intentions." Why cannot the communicated meaning simply consist of a decoding of the encoded message? The brief answer is that to do so (i.e., to regard the meaning of a message as its decoding) simply will not work. I will try to demonstrate the truth of that assertion. But first, let me address the epistemological considerations involved in the use of intention. I am fully aware that talking about intentions as determinants of behavior is a perilous venture, and I would like to stress that that is not what I am doing. It is not necessary from this point of view to assume that a person's intentions affect his behavior or even that people have intentions. What I am arguing is 1) that people perceive themselves and others as having intentions, 2) that, except in special circumstances, they perceive others as having intended to say the things they say, and 3) that one's understanding of the meaning of what another has said consists of his understanding of what it is the other intended to mean by what he said.[5] It is these assumptions that I am making.

Let me return to the question I put off above, why cannot one simply regard the meaning of a message as its decoding. The argument against this approach can be made in a number of ways, but they all focus on the same point, namely, there is no *necessary* relationship between the formal properties of an utterance (that is, its syntactic and semantic form) and what it will be understood, correctly, to mean.[6] Consider first the matter of syntax. We readily understand syntactic forms to have semantic (or, if you prefer, pragmatic) force. The interrogative form is used to ask questions, the imperative to give commands, the declarative to make assertions, and so forth. But, as Searle has pointed out, the illocutionary force of the utterance "Can you pass the salt?" is certainly not that of a question. The speaker is not asking whether the hearer is able to pass the salt. Rather the illocutionary act is a request, a polite one, to be sure, but clearly understood as a request and not a question. Similarly, one can use imperatives to ask questions ("Tell me why you think I'm wrong"), interrogatives to make assertions ("Did you hear that I was nominated for the Nobel Prize?"), declaratives to make requests ("I'd be grateful if you'd give me a lift"), and so forth. The point of these mundane examples is that a literal interpretation of these sentences would yield an understanding of them quite contrary to what the speaker can reasonably be presumed to have intended us to understand.

One way of dealing with these examples is to say that they are "figures of speech," idioms employed to achieve particular nonlinguistic effects. "Can you hand me the salt?" is after all a polite way to say "Hand me the salt," even more polite perhaps than "Please hand me the salt." It avoids the pejorative implications of imperative use, namely, the sense that one has a right to give an order to some other person. The problem with such an explanation is that it is no explanation at all. If I ask someone, "Can you complete the revision by Friday?" or "Can you meet me in a half hour?" the chances are that I am not making a request, but rather asking for information. There is no particular marking by which I indicate whether or not my utterance is to be taken literally. How, then, does my listener know what I mean?

---

[5] Somehow, I feel that I ought to add here that in my heart of hearts I do believe that I (and others) really do have intentions and that these intentions really do affect my (and their) behavior. But the argument above can be made independently of this belief.

[6] By "understand correctly" I mean that the understanding of the hearer is the understanding intended by the speaker, so that if the speaker were asked, "Did you mean x?" the speaker's answer would be, "Yes."

Utterance Meaning

Let us put this question aside for a moment and address a related phenomenon. It may not be very impressive that one grammatical form can yield the function of another. Perhaps it will be more impressive to show that the conversationally understood meaning of an utterance can be the precise opposite of its literal meaning. Grice (1975) gives the example of a man describing to another the perfidious behavior of his business partner. He finishes his narration by saying, "He's a fine friend." Now, even with the minimal context I've given, it is obvious that the sentence is intended to be taken as an instance of irony, that is to say, the speaker intended us to understand "He's a fine friend" to mean "He's a *terrible* friend." This strikes me as remarkable. Again, there is no marking to indicate that the specimen sentence is to be understood in other than its literal form. How, then, do we know? Irony of course, is not the only instance in which literal meaning is transformed. Meiosis ("Rockefeller isn't exactly a pauper") and hyperbole ("It's so cold out that I saw a politician with his hands in his own pockets") are but two other rhetorical forms in which the literal meaning of our words is not the meaning we intend to convey.

It is, of course, possible to dismiss such instances as highly specialized uses of language, special cases so different from ordinary usage that they tell us little of how communication is accomplished. One could pursue such a tack, but to do so would, in my judgment, be a serious error. Indeed, rather than regard such instances as an exotic and arcane form of usage, I want to argue that they constitute the prototype of communicative behavior.

To demonstrate this, let me take an example offered by Searle (1975). It consists of a brief exchange between two students:

Student X: "Let's go to the movies tonight."
Student Y: "I have to study for an exam."

As Searle points out, the first utterance constitutes a proposal by virtue of its literal meaning and particularly because of its use of *Let's*. That is to say, sentences of the form *Let's* plus some action will generally be understood literally as a proposal that the speaker and his listener(s) engage in that action (e.g., "Let's have a drink," "Let's take tap dancing lessons," etc.).[7]

On the other hand, the second utterance ("I have to study for an exam") *in the context of the conversation* constitutes a rejection of that

---

[7] I am aware that there is also an indirect use of this form which has imperative force (as when the teacher says "Let's put our crayons away"), but this is not what I am talking about here.

proposal. But that fact cannot be derived from its literal meaning, which is simply a statement about Student Y. As Searle (1975) points out:

> Statements of this form do not, in general, constitute rejections of a proposal, even in cases in which they are made in response to a proposal. Thus if Y had said: "I have to eat popcorn tonight" or "I have to tie my shoes" in a normal context, neither of these utterances would have been a rejection of the proposal. The question then arises, How does X know that the utterance is a rejection of the proposal? and that question is part of the question, How is it possible for Y to intend or mean the utterance . . . as a rejection of the proposal? (p. 62).

Searle attempts to reconstruct hypothetically the steps necessary for X to extract the intended meaning (the "primary illocution") from the literal meaning. Briefly they are (1) that Y has responded to a proposal with a statement that he must study for an exam. (2) Assuming that Y is cooperating in the conversation (i.e., not attempting to mislead or embarrass or to be facetious), and knowing (3) that a relevant response to a proposal must be acceptance, rejection, counterproposal, discussion, etc., and also knowing (4) that the *literal* utterance was not one of these, X must assume (5) that the primary locutionary point is different from the literal one. (6) Knowing that studying for an exam and seeing a movie are both time-consuming activities, it is likely (7) that both cannot be done in a single evening. And since (8) any acceptance of a proposal is predicated generally upon the ability to perform the act proposed, it seems reasonable to conclude (9) that Y has said something about his inability to accept the proposal and, therefore, he has (10) rejected the proposal.

Now I have no commitment to this particular chain of reasoning and neither, I am sure, does Searle. The point is that, since the conversationally understood meaning of Y's response transcends its literal meaning, it is necessary to explain how X understands it to mean what it was intended to mean. And since Y can dependably expect X to extract his intended meaning, there must be some common set of understandings that permits him to accomplish this. Note that the 10 steps that Searle hypothesizes call for a variety of different kinds of knowledge, both linguistic and nonlinguistic. Step 1 calls upon X's linguistic competence to derive the literal meaning of Y's utterance. Step 2 requires a judgment that Y is cooperating in the conversation. Steps 3 and 8 call for an understanding of speech acts, what sorts of statements may be considered relevant responses to an utterance. Step 6 calls for knowledge of the world, concerning the amount of time it takes to study for an exam or to see a movie. And, while it may seem that each of these necessary bits of information is elementary, let me point out that each (or something like it) is necessary to construct the conversational meaning of the utterance. For example, if X had mistakenly assumed that Y was serious when Y was in fact being face-tious (step 2), he might have taken seriously what was intended as humor. The point is that this mundane act—the immediate understanding of what Searle terms an indirect speech act—begs for a principled explanation. It is clear what we, as speakers, are capable of doing. What is not clear is how we manage to do it.

A VIEW OF COMMUNICATIVE BEHAVIOR

I would like to propose a way of looking at communicative behavior that is not really very different from the approach that underlies Searle's explanation of how "I have to study for an exam tonight" is understood. But it does attempt to cast the problem in a set of behavioral rather than logical terms and to develop a notion of conversational meaning as an emergent of social interaction.

It may be helpful to begin by drawing an analogy with the study of perception. One view of perception, a view that was quite influential early in the history of psychology, conceptualizes perception as essentially a passive, receptive act. Stimulus energies impinge upon the receptors and are processed in what can be described as a linear fashion. That is to say, there is a one-to-one correspondence between the pattern of energies fall-ing on, say, the retina and perceptual experience. Most contemporary students of perception would acknowledge that this view is, to a greater or lesser degree, inadequate. It is, for example, incapable of explaining such commonplace perceptual phenomena as size constancy. As a person walks toward us he does not appear to grow larger, although it is demonstrable that the image he projects on our retina does. Clearly "something more" is necessary to explain perceptual experience, and defining the nature of that "something more" has been a major preoccu-pation of the psychology of perception.

Perceptual Experience as a Hypothesis

Another way of thinking about the process of perception is to regard per-ceptual experience as a hypothesis. I am using the term *hypothesis* here in much the same way one does in talking about a hypothesis advanced to explain a set of scientific data. One is confronted by a number of data points, and the hypothesis is an attempt to make those data "under-standable" by referring them to the process that generated them. The hypothesis is based upon a set of assumptions, and when the hypothesis is verified—when it seems to fit (i.e., to explain) the available data—we are likely to take this as evidence that our assumptions were reasonable.

The formulation of a scientific hypothesis is often a matter of lengthy and conscious rumination, and I do not mean to suggest that we formulate our perceptual hypotheses in the same fashion. But it does seem to me useful to think of perceptual experience as an attempt (albeit quite unconsciously) to understand or make sense of the sensations we experience by hypothesizing the nature of the process (i.e., the stimulus) that has produced them. Like the scientific hypothesis, the perceptual hypothesis incorporates a number of assumptions, and, again like the scientific hypothesis, it sometimes is the case that one or more of these assumptions is unwarranted. When that happens, our perceptual experience is not an accurate reflection of the physical reality that gave rise to it. Particularly striking examples of this are often termed illusions.

A Visual Illusion

The familiar visual illusion called the distorted room or the Ames room (after its inventor, Adelbert Ames) illustrates this point nicely. Figure 4, which is taken from Ittelson (1952), presents the illusion from the vantage point of an observer. It is, of course, the disparity in size between the two women that is illusory, the product of some assumptions we make about the room's geometry that happen to be incorrect. Essentially we see the woman on the right as so much larger than the one on the left because we assume that the two far corners of the room are equidistant

Figure 4.   The Ames distorted room illusion. (From Ittelson, 1952; reprinted by permission.)

from our vantage point. We are lead to believe this because of our experience with rooms in general and also because this particular distorted room was carefully constructed to be geometrically consistent with such an assumption. Actually, the room is trapezoidal in shape, and the right far corner is much closer to our vantage point than the left far corner; this fact alone accounts for the apparent disparity in size between the occupants of the two corners. Because we assume them to be equidistant from us, we can only conclude that the size of the image each woman projects on our retinas accurately reflects her true size. Illusions, or at least some illusions, work because they lead us to make assumptions that are incorrect and, therefore, to interpret our data incorrectly.

The view I am proposing here is that conversational meaning, i.e., what we understand another person to mean by what he says, may usefully be regarded as a hypothesis we advance to explain, i.e., to make coherent, the data presented to us. These data are of several kinds: They include the verbal content of speech, the paralinguistic variations to which we can attribute significance, and such visible behaviors as gesture, facial expression, posture, etc. But they also include things we know about the world and about the person who is speaking, what we know about what he knows about us, what we know about conversation as a form of social interaction, and so on. The quantity of data we must take into account is very large, and our ability to fit a meaning hypothesis to so much data is remarkable indeed.

There is, however, one important way in which a meaning hypothesis differs from both a scientific hypothesis and a perceptual hypothesis: in the case of the latter two the data flow is unidirectional. The data points are there to be observed and, if possible, to be understood. But they do not tell us whether our hypothesis is right or wrong. They cannot aid us in formulating a correct hypothesis; nor will they deliberately mislead us. All of this is to say, in less metaphoric language, that, when the signal source is another person (as it is in conversation) and when the goal of the conversants is to understand and to be understood (as typically is the case in conversation), each party has a vested interest in ensuring that the hypotheses formulated by the other with respect to his utterance are consistent with the meaning he intended to convey.

Communication—The Back Channel

One device used by interactants to accomplish this is what has been termed "back-channel responses" (Yngve, 1970). Back-channel responses are vocal and visible behaviors emitted by a nominal listener during his conversational partner's utterance. They can be differentiated on formal grounds from interruptions (Duncan, 1975). Vocal back channels typically consist of such utterances as "m-hm," "yeah," "yes," "I see," and the like. In addition, they may include sentence completions, restatements, and similar brief utterances.[8] Visible back channels typically consist of head nods and shakes and, perhaps less frequently, facial expressions and expressive gestures.

Dittmann and Llewellyn (1967) found that listeners' vocal back-channel responses (which they termed "listener responses") are uttered almost exclusively in the junctures surrounding speakers' phonemic clauses. Visual back-channel responses tend to be found in the same location, and the two types of signals, vocal and visual, co-occur more often than would be expected by chance (Dittmann and Llewellyn, 1968). Duncan's meticulous analysis of back-channel responses in conversational interaction (Duncan, 1975) has demonstrated the involvement of back channels in "interaction units," i.e., segmentations within the speaker's turn. Roughly speaking, at frequent intervals during his speaking turn, the speaker will elicit such responses and monitor them, using them to guide his subsequent transmission. As Duncan (1975) puts it, "Through the back channel [the listener] may acknowledge the receipt and understanding—or lack thereof—of the speaker's message" (p. 177).

Research by Krauss and Bricker (1967) has shown that when communication channels do not permit the transmission of back channels, or substantially delay them, communication becomes less efficient, i.e., a greater number of words is used to communicate a standard informational content. Understandably, when it is difficult for a speaker to determine whether his message is being correctly understood, he will tend to increase its redundancy. In a more recent study, Krauss et al. (1977) have shown that the opportunity to transmit visible back channels will reduce this redundancy, even when vocal back channels are unavailable.

I am suggesting that the back-channel response plays an important role in the process by which the speaker's intended meaning is apprehended. In the course of the speaker's utterance, the listener formulates a hypothesis about the meaning that is intended.[9] In part, the data on which this hypothesis is based come from the verbal content of the speaker's message. Other data come from the speaker's concurrent non-

---

[8] It is important to note that back-channel responses are not differentiated from other communicative behaviors (e.g., attempted interruptions, changes of speaker turn, etc.) on the basis of content. As Duncan (1975) has quite elegantly shown, back channels are not responded to by speakers as interruptions or attempts to take the conversational floor, nor are they typically accompanied by other signs that the listener is attempting to negotiate a change of speaker state.

[9] There is an additional problem to which I will not address myself apart from this brief comment. Although many utterances in conversations are brief, a good number of them are likely to be quite lengthy. It would be unwieldy to fit a meaning hypothesis to so large a body of data, and it seems likely, therefore, that some means must exist for segmenting long utterances into shorter and more manageable units. It's my guess that the "interaction units" proposed by Duncan (1975), or something very much like them, represent just such segmentations.

verbal behaviors. And still other data are derived from information that each party knows and, equally important, knows that the other knows. The hypothesis constitutes a meaning—an interpretation of what it was the speaker wanted to be understood as having said. It is through the medium of the back-channel response that the listener displays evidence of the nature of his understanding, and it is this evidence, in large part, that the speaker employs to determine whether he has been correctly understood.

Precisely how this system operates is not yet well understood. Duncan (1975) suggests that the timing of the back channel with respect to the interaction unit is important:

> . . . an early auditor back channel may indicate, not only that the auditor is following the speaker's message, but also that the auditor is ahead of it. . . .
> In contrast, a between-unit auditor back channel would indicate that the auditor is following the speaker's message as it is developing. . . .
> By the same logic, a late auditor back channel would indicate some auditor acknowledgment, but also that he is not quite following the speaker's message (p. 179).

But it also seems clear that in addition to their placement in time many, perhaps most, back channels have semantic force as well. And this is true both of vocalizations and gestures. A smile in response to what was intended to be a description of a shocking occurrence may inform a speaker that his listener has understood an utterance literally when it was not intended to be so understood. An expression of mock disbelief may inform the speaker that his listener has understood, as he was intended to understand, that what was said was difficult to believe.

SUMMARY

The point of view proposed here is, of course, highly speculative. Surely it does not lead to a neat and rigorous conceptual model that can be tested readily. Nor is it immediately clear to what sort of investigative paradigm (or model M_1, if you prefer) it will lead. Its only value is that it compels us to take into account some of the capacities people employ when they communicate. This is something that the conceptualizations underlying our use of referential communication tasks fail to do. I believe that this is why such tasks have turned out to be less useful, both as research devices and as practical training tools, than we had initially hoped.

The late Hans-Lukas Teuber used to call the Skinner box a device that functionally decorticated both subject and experimenter. There is a sense in which much the same thing can be said about referential communication tasks. To the extent that they prevent our subjects from fully using their capacity to communicate, they lead us to making inappropriate assessments of communicative competence.

ACKNOWLEDGMENTS

I have discussed the ideas in this chapter with a number of individuals and have benefited greatly from their comments. I would especially like to thank Sam Glucksberg, Clifford Hill, and E. Tory Higgins, all of whom made numerous helpful suggestions, some of which I was not wise enough to heed. I am also grateful to the convener of the Gulf Shores Conference, Richard Schiefelbusch, for his suggestions, encouragement, patience, and good humor.

REFERENCES

Dittmann, A., and Llewellyn, L. G. 1967. The phonemic clause as a unit of speech decoding. J. Personal. Soc. Psychol. 6:341–349.
Dittmann, A., and Llewellyn, L. G. 1968. Relationship between vocalizations and head nods as listener responses. J. Personal. Soc. Psychol. 9:79–84.
Duncan, S. 1975. On the structure of speaker-auditor interaction during speaking turns. Lang. Soc. 2:161–180.
Glucksberg, S., and Krauss, R. M. 1967. What do people say after they have learned how to talk? Studies of the development of referential communication. Merrill-Palmer Q. 13:309–316.
Glucksberg, S., Krauss, R. M., and Higgins, E. T. 1975. The development of referential communication skills. In F. D. Horowitz (ed.), Child Development Research, Vol. 4. University of Chicago Press, Chicago.
Glucksberg, S., Krauss, R. M., and Weisberg, R. 1966. Referential communication in nursery school children: Method and some preliminary findings. J. Exp. Child Psychol. 3:333–342.
Grice, H. P. 1975. Logic and conversation. In P. Cole and J. L. Morgan (eds.), Syntax and Semantics, Vol. 3: Speech acts, pp. 41–58. Academic Press, New York.
Ittelson, W. H. 1952. The Ames Demonstrations: A Guide to Their Use. Princeton University Press, Princeton, N.J.
Krauss, R. M. 1971. The interpersonal regulation of behavior. In D. N. Walcher and D. L. Peters (eds.), Early Childhood: The Development of Self-Regulatory Mechanisms. Academic Press, New York.
Krauss, R. M., and Bricker, P. D. 1967. Effects of transmission delay and access delay on the efficiency of verbal communication. J. Acoust. Soc. Am. 41:286–292.
Krauss, R. M., Garlock, C., Bricker, P. D., and McMahon, L. E. 1977. The role of audible and visible back channel responses in interpersonal communication. J. Personal. Soc. Psychol. 35:523–529.
Krauss, R. M., and Glucksberg, S. 1969. The development of communication: Competence as a function of age. Child Dev. 40:255–266.
Longhurst, T. M., and Turnure, J. E. 1971. Perceptual inadequacy and communication ineffectiveness in interpersonal communication. Child Dev. 42:2084–2088.
Rosenberg, S., and Cohen, B. D. 1966. Referential processes of speakers and listeners. Psycholog. Rev. 73:208–231.

Searle, J. R. 1967. Human communication theory and the philosophy of language: Some remarks. *In* F. X. Dance (ed.), Human Communication Theory, pp. 116–129. Holt, Rinehart & Winston, New York.

Searle, J. 1975. Indirect speech acts. *In* P. Cole and J. L. Morgan (eds.), Syntax and Semantics: Vol. 3, Speech Acts. Academic Press, New York.

Shatz, M., and Gelman, R. 1973. The development of communication skills: Modifications in the speech of young children as a function of listener. Child Dev. Monogr. 38(Monogr. No. 152).

Strickler, R. D. 1975. A developmental study of the relationship between speaker and listener abilities in referential communication. Unpublished doctoral dissertation, Columbia University, New York.

Yngve, V. H. 1970. On getting a word in edgewise. *In* Papers from the Sixth Regional Meeting of the Chicago Linguistic Society. Chicago Linguistic Society, Chicago.

chapter

3

The Chimpanzee
as an Animal Model
in Language Research

Duane M. Rumbaugh

E. Sue Savage-Rumbaugh

Timothy V. Gill

Georgia State University
Atlanta, Georgia
and
Yerkes Regional Primate Research Center
of Emory University
Atlanta, Georgia

Harold Warner

Yerkes Regional Primate Research Center
of Emory University
Atlanta, Georgia

contents

LANGUAGE RESEARCH AND THE ANIMAL MODEL

Animal Models and Behavioral Research

The animal model concept is familiar in the field of biomedical research. Researchers working on problems of human health have for many years searched out specific forms of animal and plant life for specific experiments, the results of which sometimes lead directly to either a better understanding of a problem or, optimally, its solution. In contrast, the animal model concept is relatively new to psychology. Psychologists have studied animal behavior to gain a better understanding of man and his behavior; however, only in recent years have investigators focused upon single, carefully selected species to study a relatively narrow class of behaviors that might, if understood, have implications for the understanding of, and eventual solution for, some human health and welfare problems. Perhaps no such research program is better known than that of Harry Harlow (1971), formerly of the University of Wisconsin. His program, which is still being pursued by his students, concerns the parameters of complex learning processes in relation to brain function and in relation to social behaviors. The research has been justified not only for its scientific interest, but also because the research paradigms and the specific results obtained from the rhesus monkey studies have sharpened the thinking of theoreticians who are concerned primarily with analogs of those processes in humans.

Among other major contributions, Harlow's program has illustrated the importance of mother-infant interactions and peer experiences in the development of a socially and sexually competent primate. Another major finding is that the enriched rearing experience of the nuclear family group, in which animals are reared by their parents and have continued access to peers in a playpen situation, is associated with superior learning capabilities, as evidenced in the learning of oddity-concept tasks.

Primatology and Communication

There has been a recent surge of interest in comparative studies of the behavior of nonhuman primates. The research literature is replete with reports from field and laboratory studies that are affording us a better understanding of the species variable and how behavior has been selectively shaped in accordance with various ecological factors and resources. The studies also give us a better understanding of the forces that have led to the evolution of human social nature.

Notable in the evolution of man has been the evolution of his skills in the fabrication and use of tools and his ability to cooperate to optimize

---

Research reported in this chapter is supported by NIH grants HD-06016 and RR-00155.

success in hunting, food gathering, protection, child care, and securing shelter from the elements. Studies of human evolution indicate that it was man's ability to communicate through language that has made him effective in many cooperative efforts. While it is true that all animals have effective channels of communication, which allow for reproduction, at a minimum, and, at a maximum, for the complexities of social behavior, those communication systems are relatively stereotyped or closed. They do not appear, in the main, to have the characteristic of *openness* that is the hallmark of human language. Just what the relationship is between language and communication in general, just what the proper definition of language is, just what the basic requisites of language are, and what weights should be given to linguistic processes in the definition of man, are questions that are currently foremost in the thinking and research efforts of scientists from a variety of disciplines, ranging from comparative psychology to archeology, anthropology, and linguistics.

Apes and Language: Early and Recent Perspectives

Hewes (1977), in a comprehensive review of theories pertaining to language origins, notes that the idea that apes might be capable of at least rudiments of human language dates back as far as La Mettrie, who in 1748 conjectured that the ape might be able to speak, and that, if it did so, it would have a language that would serve to sharpen its mind. La Mettrie (1912) saw language as a requisite to human law, culture, and society. He held that, if the ape were able to learn language, it would then be no longer either an incomplete nor a defective man but would, instead, be a "gentleman."

Witmer (1909) and Furness (1916) made attempts early in the twentieth century to teach apes to speak. Their efforts met with only a modicum of success. Robert M. Yerkes, a pivotal figure in the field of comparative primate research of all types, with Learned held open the possibility that apes might learn to speak, although he was not overly optimistic about it (Yerkes and Learned, 1925). He did anticipate that apes might be able to learn a manual sign or gestural language.

Kellogg (1968) provided a comprehensive review of efforts to teach language skills to apes. His own work with a chimpanzee was not specifically designed to teach speech; however, he and his wife did nothing to discourage speech, should the animal have been so inclined to speak in the language-enriched home environment in which it was raised. It was Keith and Catherine Hayes (Hayes and Nissen, 1971) who, with their chimpanzee Viki made the first major effort to teach speech to a chimpanzee. Coupled with this effort were many research projects designed to trace the cognitive development of the chimpanzee. Despite long term, concentrated efforts, Viki failed to learn other than a few approximations of words as spoken by man. The Hayeses' research report is, nonetheless, rich and valuable, for it is replete with the details of their efforts, and equally replete with interesting results of psychological experiments designed to study Viki's problem-solving skills and related processes. The Hayeses' effort also served to discourage others from attempting to teach the impossible—human speech—to apes; in retrospect, a significant contribution.

Washoe   The first significant demonstration of the ape's ability to achieve two-way communication with man was accomplished by Beatrice and Allen Gardner (1971) of the University of Nevada. Their work with the chimpanzee Washoe commenced in the mid-1960s and provided findings that stimulated others to study the ape's linguistic skills, using modalities other than speech and hearing. The Gardners selected the American Sign Language for the Deaf (Ameslan) in recognition of the probability that Washoe would not be able to master human speech.

Sarah   Concurrent with the Gardners' work was that of David and Ann Premack (1971), then of the University of California, Santa Barbara. They used plastic symbols of random shapes and colors; each plastic unit served as the functional equivalent of a word. The work by the Premacks differed in many ways from that of the Gardners, but perhaps the most notable difference was that the Premacks were more specifically concerned with grammaticality than were the Gardners. The research efforts by the Gardners and the Premacks produced a valuable data base, which stimulated still others to either sustain efforts of similar types or to innovate new approaches to the study of ape language skills. The efforts and contributions of the Gardners and the Premacks were sufficient to jar the notion that language skills are specific to man, to bring into clearer focus questions pertaining to the nature of communication and language, and (in a broader sense) to examine man's relationship to the chimpanzee and other apes and monkeys.

THE LANA PROJECT

Research efforts initiated by Rumbaugh and Warner in 1971 have come to be known as the LANA Project. LANA is both an abbreviation for LANguage Analog Project and the name of the first chimpanzee subject, whose name had been assigned at the time of her birth, long before she was selected as our first subject. The LANA Project differs from those of the Gardners and Premacks in a variety of ways, the main ones being that the approach entails a computer-based language-training situation and automatic recording of all linguistic events in a manner that allows computer analysis. The computer makes many operations of language training much more objective as well as more reliable and efficient. The human experimenter has essentially no responsibility for determining what has been transmitted by the chimpanzee subject—that is the responsibility of the chimpanzee, the computer, and the recording systems it controls. As a rule, the human experimenter does not manually reward the chimpanzee subject for behaviors and performances deemed desirable or correct. That, too, is the responsibility of the computer, which controls the activation of a battery of vending devices for the dispensation of various foods, drinks, and entertainment in the form of music, slides, and motion pictures, and a view of the out-of-doors. The computer-based approach also permits around-the-clock operation, with the animal and the computer left to their own interactions through the hours of the evening and night and early morning when the experimenters are absent.

The LANA Project approach uses a keyboard. Each key is distinctively marked with a lexigram tantamount to a printed word. Each lexigram is a geometric figure that is reproducible on any of a number of projectors, where the projectors placed in rows produce the equivalent of written sentences. The locations of the keys are changeable to preclude location as a clue for the animal's selection of keys. Particularly in early training, the locations of the keys are changed frequently, thereby requiring the animal to attend to and discriminate keys on the basis of the lexigrams embossed on the surfaces. Details of the computer-based system can be found elsewhere Rumbaugh (1977). In particular, reports by Warner and Bell (1977) and by von Glasersfeld (1977) and Pisani (1977) describe the intricacies of the system and the Yerkish language designed specifically for the LANA Project. Other chapters in the book convey details of the training methods, results of various studies with Lana, and how the approach is now being extended in studies designed to better understand the problems of language acquisition by mentally retarded human subjects at the Georgia Retardation Center (Savage-Rumbaugh and Rumbaugh, Chapter 14, this volume; Parkel and Smith, Chapter 19, this volume).

Goals The first goal of the LANA Project was to determine if electronics and computer science could facilitate research efforts regarding the ape's abilities to learn the rudiments of human language. As a result of the initial success, attention has now shifted to studies to assess the suitability of the chimpanzee as an animal model for more extensive and comprehensive language-relevant projects that cannot be conducted with humans because of ethical constraints. Attention is also being given to whether the basic approach of the LANA Project is a feasible one for investigating and alleviating language acquisition problems in mentally retarded children, and for extending to those children channels of two-way communication that might be used on a day-in day-out basis with attendants, peers, parents, and relatives.

Strategy and Results   The basic strategy was to reinforce Lana's readiness to engage herself with work at the keyboard to get the basic requisites and comforts of her daily life. It was intended that Lana learn, through this initial training, the *power* that language-type skills avail to her. At her whim she could eat and drink what was available in her dispensers, and at her choice she could ask whomever was present to come into her room to interact with her socially.

Initially every effort was made to define beforehand in a very careful step-like manner the specific training that the lead technician was to give to Lana throughout the course of each day. This approach emanated from a basic experimental psychological orientation. It did not succeed to our satisfaction, and with considerable reluctance and resignation it was concluded that the technician must be given latitude for interacting with the chimp, as one might interact with a child to teach him basic language skills.

It was both to our delight and our chagrin that this approach produced very rapid learning by Lana. Our delight was a reflection of our appreciation of the rich data that began to be generated by Lana. Our chagrin reflected the fact that it would not be possible for us to document in any unequivocal way the exact training whereby Lana came to learn each of a variety of skills. In response to this development, it was concluded that we must differentiate between *training* and *testing*. By *training* we mean the procedures through which a subject is *taught* a given skill or set of skills. By *testing* we mean a highly controlled experimental condition under which, or in which, the subject is given an opportunity to demonstrate what it can and cannot do.

The differentiation between these terms is somewhat analogous to the holding of classes in school, where learning proceeds on the basis of reading, discussion, and lecture, with interruptions programmed at times for the purpose of testing just what, if anything, students have learned. Since Lana was viewed as a pilot animal and the entire LANA Project viewed as a pilot study, we felt justified in proceeding as stated because our basic goal was to assess whether or not we could succeed in developing a computer-based system to facilitate objective and scientific inquiry into the language-type skills reported earlier by the Gardners and the Premacks. If the approach proved feasible, the future would surely provide an opportunity to assess systematically and on a well defined basis what influenced the chimpanzee's learning of each skill. (We are now working to determine whether or not we can conduct systematic research projects that bear upon the questions of initial language-skill learning with four young chimpanzees serving as subjects in different training programs. See Savage-Rumbaugh and Rumbaugh, Chapter 14, this volume.)

Lana's acquisition of various language-type skills, such as the learning of names for things, learning that things have names, learning the names of various colors and objects, etc., are all documented elsewhere (Rumbaugh, 1977). Basic unit language skills were emphasized for the first year of Lana's training. Then an important thing happened, and it happened because of what Lana did on her own initiative. First, Lana came to use her stock sentences for other than the originally intended purposes. Specifically, she came to ask people to MOVE BEHIND THE ROOM when the system was malfunctioning and not just when she wanted them to do so in order to be able to view them through the window as she had been taught to do. She would even request that the machine operate a certain vending device (as for bread) to draw the technician's attention to where the malfunction was. There was no doubt about it—Lana had developed a sophisticated understanding about how the system worked. The technician soon needed only to point to a given unit of the system (to the tape deck or to the slide projector) and Lana would formulate an appropriate request to activate it, such as, PLEASE MACHINE MAKE MUSIC or PLEASE MACHINE MAKE SLIDE. Perhaps it was this specific understanding of the system that allowed her to use her stock sentences in response to unplanned problem situations.

Very shortly after she started to use the stock sentences with versatility and appropriateness, she began to converse, first with the lead technician. We had intended to contrive situations that would encourage Lana to formulate new sentences to exchange in a meaningful way transmissions or statements with us. What we did not anticipate was that Lana would do this on her own initiative.

The first conversation took place on March 7, 1974, approximately 1¼ years into training. The conversation was initiated at about 4:00 p.m., when Tim Gill, the lead technician, was drinking a Coke outside of Lana's room, yet in her full view. Lana knew the word for Coke and had asked for it to be vended through the machine whenever it was placed in the appropriate liquid dispenser. Lana looked at Tim and formulated the new statement, ? LANA DRINK THIS OUT-OF ROOM PERIOD. At an earlier date, she had come to use the word THIS primarily to refer to things for which she had no formal name, that development taking place through the course of teaching her that things have names, when the question was posed to her repeatedly, ? WHAT NAME-OF THIS PERIOD. In response to Lana's request, Tim opened the door and let her out and shared his "this" with Lana "out-of room." The scenario was repeated in the interests of reliability. A conference then took place between Gill and Rumbaugh as to the possible significance of the event. It was concluded that we should check to see what the referent for "this" was, due to the fact that Lana did know the name for "Coke." Tim returned to Lana's view with another Coke in his hand and very shortly she once again said, PLEASE LANA DRINK COKE THIS ROOM PERIOD. This statement was not acceptable; perhaps she had intended to say OUT-OF ROOM instead of THIS ROOM, but she had not. She then came back with the original composition, ? LANA DRINK THIS OUT-OF ROOM PERIOD, to which Tim responded with the question as agreed to in conference, ? DRINK WHAT PERIOD. Lana answered, LANA DRINK *COKE* OUT-OF ROOM PERIOD. Tim said, YES, the doors opened, and Lana shared the Coke.

It bears reemphasizing that this conversation was initiated by Lana. From examination of it, we decided upon the following three criteria for a working definition for the term *conversation:* 1) it must be a linguistic type of exchange between two beings, 2) at least one of the communications transmitted by each party must be novel, and 3) the exchange must be relatively constant and coherent across time.

Further discussion of conversation as a phenomenon can be found in Rumbaugh and Gill (1977) and Gill (1977). This was the first of a series of conversations that has been held between Tim and Lana during the years the project has been underway. We believe that the phenomenon of conversation serves more clearly than any other to support the contention that the chimpanzee, and probably the great apes, have cognitive processes that can be brought to bear in thought processes focused upon goal achievement. It particular, Gill's analysis (1977) makes it clear that the conversation is goal oriented and that its course with Lana is contingent upon the experimenter's response to transmissions made by Lana. As the following conversation substantiates, the content and character of the conversations that transpire between Lana and Tim are so much like those we experience in everyday human life that it seems highly probable the homologous processes are functioning in both chimpanzee and man, insofar as many characteristics of language-relevant behavior are concerned.

The conversation for consideration occurred on June 12, 1975. The time was late afternoon, when Lana ordinarily obtained her ration of chow, and the experimental paradigm called for Tim to ask her what it was that she wanted to eat. The following conversation took place:

Tim: ? LANA WANT WHAT EAT.   16:23
Lana: LANA WANT CHOW.   16:23

But Tim put water into the milk dispenser at this point. This was done in accordance with the experimental paradigm, which required Tim on this occasion to substitute a less preferred liquid for the food of relatively high preference that had been requested.

Lana: PLEASE MACHINE GIVE MILK.   16:28
(This stock stentence was clearly a reflection of the fact that Lana had seen Tim put some liquid into the milk dispenser, and had to use the stock sentence, PLEASE MACHINE GIVE MILK PERIOD in order to sample it. That she did not ask for more of it is clear evidence that she correctly identified it as water, not milk.)

Tim walked around from behind the room.

Lana: ? YOU PUT CHOW IN MACHINE.   16:28
(Chow is a commercial primate food.)
Tim: CHOW IN MACHINE.   16:28
(This, too, was done in accordance with the experimental paradigm, which in this particular setting required that Tim lie to her to see whether she would or would not agree with him.)
Lana: ? YOU PUT CHOW IN MACHINE.
Tim: CHOW IN MACHINE.
Lana: ? YOU PUT CHOW IN MACHINE.
Tim: CHOW IN MACHINE.
(Lana seemingly kept questioning Tim's assertion that he had put chow in the machine.)
Lana: ? TIM PUT JUICE IN MACHINE.   16:31
(Since no chow had been made available, perhaps juice might be?)
Tim: JUICE IN MACHINE.   16:31
(Once again, lying.)
Lana: ? YOU PUT JUICE IN MACHINE.   16:31
Tim: JUICE IN MACHINE.   16:32
(Again, lying.)
Lana: NO JUICE.   16:32
(Here she was declaring, we believe, that Tim's statement was not true; there was *no* juice in the machine.)
Tim: ? WHAT IN MACHINE.   16:32
Tim: ? WHAT IN MACHINE.   16:33
Lana: WATER IN . . . MILK.   16:35
(She waited a long time and went to various keys such as "machine," "milk," and "room" before concluding . . . MILK. We believe that she was saying as best she could that water was in where the milk normally is.)

Lana: ? YOU WANT WATER IN MACHINE.   16:35
(Here we believe that Lana wanted to know if Tim really meant that water should be there.)
Tim: NO.   16:35
Lana: ? YOU MOVE WATER BEHIND ROOM.   16:36
Tim: WATER BEHIND ROOM.   16:37
(Which was true, and Tim was just declaring it so.)
Lana: ? YOU MOVE WATER OUT-OF MACHINE.   16:37
(A novel and totally appropriate request by Lana, given the context.)
Tim: YES.   16:41
(And he removed the water.)
Lana: ? YOU PUT JUICE.   16:45
Lana: ? YOU PUT JUICE IN MACHINE.   16:45
Tim: NO LANA DRINK.   16:45
(It was time for her to eat chow.)
Lana: ? YOU PUT MORE JUICE.   16:46
Tim: NO JUICE.   16:46
(You can't have any. He was not going to give her any juice.)
Lana: ? YOU PUT JUICE . . .
(Tim cut her off.)

Tim got annoyed with her at this point because he had declared that she could not have juice.

Tim: NO JUICE.   16:46
Lana: ? YOU PUT CHOW IN MACHINE   16:47
Tim: NO "IN" . . . "ON."   16:47
(The actual loading of the chow is to place it "on" a vending device.)
Lana: ? YOU PUT CHOW *ON* MACHINE.   16:48
(It should be noted that Lana changed the preposition in accordance with Tim's insistence.)
Tim: YES.   16:48
(And Tim loaded chow into the machine.)
Lana: PLEASE MACHINE GIVE PIECE-OF CHOW.   16:52
(repeatedly until supply exhausted)   and following

Of particular significance in this conversation is the fact that, upon seeing Tim put something into the milk dispenser, she used the appropriate stock sentence, PLEASE MACHINE GIVE MILK PERIOD, in order to sample it. It seems clear that she knew that it was not milk, because milk is a highly preferred liquid and she would have asked repeatedly for the machine to vend more. She then returned to her request for chow. Failing to get any, since there was none in the machine despite Tim's declaration to the contrary, she then shifted tactics and asked for juice. Failing to get juice, and in apparent response to Tim's lies to the contrary, she declared, NO JUICE. It just was not there, despite what Tim said. Subsequent alteration in her use of prepositions is additional evidence in support of the conclusion that Lana was tracking quite accurately the conversation as guided by Tim's statements, his lies, and his insistence that she be correct in word usage.

Other important conversations, of particular importance because they indicate significant advances in Lana's use of language, are to be found in Rumbaugh and Gill (1977) and Gill (1977). In brief, these conversations serve as examples of Lana coming to do (without the instigation of specific training to do so) such things as: 1) asking that MILK BE MOVED BEHIND THE ROOM, a requisite for its being loaded into the machine, 2) asking for the name of something for which she had no name—a box—and then asking, by name, that it be given to her, 3) coming to identify things by their salient characteristics and to use those descriptions as names—asking for a Fanta orange drink as THE COKE WHICH-IS ORANGE (COLORED), and an overly ripe banana as BANANA WHICH-IS BLACK, and 4) extending the use of words from the contexts of original training to be able to ask Tim to PUT things into the vending devices, and to move or take something OUT-OF the vending device and to put something more preferred in its stead, for example, to take cabbage out of the machine and to put chow in.

We also studied Lana's use of names in a cross-modal test situation to determine if such use enhanced the accuracy of her judgments of sameness and difference. Briefly, Lana was given a series of problems in which pairs of items were presented to her, with one member of each pair presented visually and the other haptically. Half of the pairs comprised identical objects, and the other half comprised nonidentical objects. Lana's task was to be sensitive to whether or not the members were identical, and she was to classify pairs comprised of identical members as SAME and pairs comprised of dissimilar or nonidentical members as NO-SAME. Our studies have indicated that, if objects had names, there was greater accuracy in her judgments of sameness and difference than if the objects were without names. Familiarity, apart from names per se, did contribute to accuracy; however, if the objects had names that Lana could use, there was an additional and significant enhancement of her performance accuracy. During tests in which only one member of each pair had a name, either the visually or the haptically presented one, Lana did somewhat better if the named member was the haptically presented one (84% versus 72% correct, although not statistically reliable). These observations suggest that, when only minimal cues are available for identifying an object, as when an object is being palpated, names facilitate identification relatively more than if the sampling of the object is relatively enriched and complete, as is the case when an object is inspected visually.

THE POTENTIAL OF THE CHIMPANZEE AS AN ANIMAL MODEL

Ethical constraints preclude the radical manipulations of the child's environment that would be necessary to discern the roles played by a variety of everyday experiences in the structuring of cognitions which undergird language and the acquisition of various processes and skills that are requisite to the emergence of the child's language. We recognize language as being extremely important to the social competency of the maturing child. If at all possible, we should try to find some way to define the requisites of language so that we might better help the child who, for various reasons, is having great difficulty in the mastery of initial skills. It is our view that the chimpanzee holds great promise as an animal model for serving as subject material in experiments that cannot be conducted with the human child, yet relate directly to the ultimate welfare of the human child and the development of his communication and social competencies. Promises are not always fulfilled, however, and critical work remains to be done to determine the degree to which the chimpanzee might be used in this manner.

Humans and chimpanzees are very closely related biologically. They have many proteins in common, so many in fact that they are no more disparate than are many species that belong to a single genus (King and Wilson, 1975). Even more important is that in many ways the chimpanzee's sensory and perceptual worlds are similar to man's. We also know that chimpanzees and other great apes are capable of conceptual learning. There is a strong suggestion that they are more given to abstract learning processes than are gibbons (lesser apes, *Hylobates*) and monkeys in general, both New and Old World (Rumbaugh and Gill, 1973). We share a common psychological world to a very significant degree. The chimpanzee's manual dexterity more closely approximates the human's than does that of monkeys in general. And it should be added that there is an unspoken kinship between man and ape, particularly the young ape. There are numerous accounts of human adults who have adopted chimpanzees and who have cared for them just as they would a human child, and there are other reports that testify to the unspoken kinship and camaraderie between the young ape and the young child. Given these similarities, the question is: Might the chimpanzee be used as a surrogate for the human child in linguistic-relevant research that is addressed to the emergence of and refinement of basic language skills? If the answer is affirmative, then a number of matters might be explored with greater precision.

First, we might better understand the relationship between cognition and learning and the acquisition of language skills. With animals as subjects, we can dictate with great accuracy what it is that they will and will not learn and what it is that they will and will not experience during the course of their everyday lives. The reflection of those experiences and the contribution of learning and cognition to the acquisition of specific language skills should be possible.

Several questions can be asked: To what degree does the social milieu stimulate the child to attend to language as something important to be mastered? What social contexts are necessary for the child to *want* to learn language skills of ever-increasing difficulty? Conversely, what kind of social contexts discourage language acquisition? To what degree does play with various materials contribute to the understanding of relationships that might be requisite to language acquisition? Can daily activities be programmed to facilitate language learning, as with the learning of colors and the meanings of various prepositions? To what degree might language be shaped by day-by-day experiences?

Critical tests of the Whorf (1940) hypothesis might be achieved, and the degree to which there are optimal examples that form the cores of concepts, as suggested by Rosch (1973), seems accessible if it proves to be the case that the chimpanzee is an adequate surrogate for the human child in language-relevant research.

The contributions of formal language skills to the solving of problems can, perhaps, be explored most definitively with the ape, which is typically without language skills. Do *learned* words facilitate thought processes more than symbols that are otherwise idiosyncratically generated and that remain totally private to the organism? Might the nonhuman primate be told through formal language communications how to solve problems of a conceptual type, thereby circumventing the tedium of discrete trial training?

Because the chimpanzee's rate of learning is considerably slower than that of the normal human child, it might be possible to achieve a finer-grain analysis of language learning, even of simple words. Seemingly, the semantics of words should be more precisely controlled with the chimpanzee than with the human child because of the greater degree of control that can be exerted over their lives.

Accepting the presumed close relationship between the chimpanzee and human as both true and meaningful, in the sense of using the chimpanzee as a stand-in for the human child in linguistic research, might we be able to learn more about the relationship between symbols and thought through the chimpanzee than through the human child? For instance, what is it that makes certain figures or patterns highly iconic representations? Are the principles of iconicity the same for chimpanzee and human? And, if the same set of principles do hold for the determination of iconicity, are there not important implications for the topics of primate intelligence and the basic cognitive processes that catalog, organize, integrate, and create from the input of efforts to adapt?

The neurological basis for certain aspects of language skills might be better ascertained through studies with the chimpanzee than with a human child. Great caution needs to be advanced on this point, however, because it must be remembered that the chimpanzee's brain is not identical with the child's brain: there are important differences in its organization and function, despite the many dimensions of similarity the chimpanzee's brain holds with the human's.

There are, of course, limitations inherent in the use of apes as animal models in language-relevant research. Not the least of the limitations is that apes are not humans. Consequently, the question of generalizability of findings will always be an issue. The number of subjects required for assessment of treatment effects and processes related thereto are not minor issues, but it is surely true that, if we *do* learn how to use the chimpanzee in a truly meaningful and productive way as subject material in language research, funds will be forthcoming to meet whatever costs prove necessary.

Chimpanzees, and all other primates for that matter, present great individual variabilities that are both intriguing and problematic when it comes to systematic research with them. The problems they pose are no different from those encountered when one uses a small number of children in a research project. But the individual variability factor with the chimpanzee does complicate questions in the selection of a limited number of subjects, and, more importantly, raises questions about the specific research projects that will be undertaken. Research projects with the chimpanzee as subject material must prove of real value by way of yielding data and insights to help us better understand human language, either directly or in a comparative evolutionary perspective.

To end this on a positive note, consider two additional advantages. The first is that the chimpanzee potentially allows for long term studies that might allow the relating of a number of factors, including genetics, to cognitive competence and language-learning skills. Second, systematic inquiry into the effects of early experience and social interactions upon language learning can be studied experimentally with critical controls. Research efforts to teach chimpanzees language have already served to underscore the importance of the social interaction between the chimpanzee and the language tutor. It is clear that it is extremely difficult, if not impossible, to teach the chimpanzee the complexities of even rudimentary language-type skills through use of discrete trial, highly prescribed training procedures that exclude social intercouse. Somehow these procedures keep the chimpanzee subject and the human tutor out of sync. Given that, progress is nil in efforts to teach the chimpanzee anything at all about the dynamics of language. These experiences cannot help but influence how we come to view language, its acquisition and application, by the human child.

Köhler (1925) taught us many years ago that the chimpanzee, without special instruction or training to do so, will see relationships between things in its environment, and will, for example, use sticks that it has joined together and stack boxes to get at food which is otherwise out of reach. The reader is also reminded of Birch's (1945) studies with chimpanzees. They illustrate the contribution of experience in handling sticks with the facility with which chimpanzees will learn to use them, both singly and in interaction, to solve problems. Experience of a general nature *does* provide a great deal of informational input regarding the attributes of things and events of the environment. Quite possibly these experiences are the grist, the fuel, the raw materials necessary for the basic processes of primate intelligence to be primed and functional.

Riesen's (1958) studies in sensory deprivation emphasize the importance of basic stimulation, such as light, to the normal development of sensory systems, i.e., vision. Even the development of the neural tracks and the branchings between cortical nerve cells are radically influenced by the stimulation of light on the retina. Most surely, appropriate stimulation is of equal importance to the development of the cognitive processes, which are requisites to language acquisition.

Biological proclivities and constraints in learning are logically necessary, else the organism would be totally at the mercy of chance-encountered stimuli and events as it strives for adaptation in a very demanding environment. We are hopeful, indeed optimistic, that these processes are similar enough in chimpanzee and man to make the chimpanzee a meaningful substitute for the child in language-relevant research.

REFERENCES

Birch, H. 1945. The relation of previous experience to insightful problem-solving. J. Comp. Physiolog. Psychol. 38:367–383.

Furness, W. H. 1916. Observations of the mentality of chimpanzees and orangutans. Proceed. Am. Philosoph. Soc. 55:281.

Gardner, B. T., and Gardner, R. A. 1971. Two-way communications with an infant chimpanzee. *In* A. M. Schrier and F. Stollnitz (eds.), Behavior of Non-human Primates, Vol. 4., pp. 117–184. Academic Press, New York.

Gill, T. V. 1977. Conversations with Lana. *In* D. M. Rumbaugh (ed.), Language Learning by a Chimpanzee: The LANA Project, pp. 225–246. Academic Press, New York.

Harlow, H. F. 1971. Learning to Love. Albion Publishing Co., San Francisco.

Hayes, K. J., and Nissen, C. H. 1971. Higher mental functions of a home-raised chimpanzee. *In* A. M. Schrier and F. Stollnitz (eds.), Behavior of Nonhuman Primates, Vol. 4, pp. 58–115. Academic Press, New York.

Hewes, G. 1977. Language origin theories. *In* D. M. Rumbaugh (ed.), Language Learning by a Chimpanzee: The LANA Project, pp. 3–53. Academic Press, New York.

Kellogg, W. N. 1968. Communication and language in a home-raised chimpanzee. Science 162:423–438.

King, J. E., and Wilson, A. C. 1975. Evolution at two levels in humans and chimpanzees. Science 186:107–116.

Köhler, W. 1925. The Mentality of Apes. Routledge and Kegan Paul, London.

La Mettrie, J. O. 1912. Man a Machine. Opencourt, Chicago.

Pisani, P. 1977. Design of the LANA project—Computer programs. *In* D. M. Rumbaugh (ed.), Language Learning by a Chimpanzee: The LANA Project, pp. 131–141. Academic Press, New York.

Premack, D. 1971. On the assessment of language competence in the chimpanzee. *In* A. M. Schrier and F. Stollnitz (eds.), Behavior of Nonhuman Primates, Vol. 4, pp. 185–228. Academic Press, New York.

Riesen, A. H. 1958. Plasticity of behavior: Psychological aspects. *In* H. F. Harlow and C. Woolsey (eds.), Biological and Biochemical Bases of Behavior. University of Wisconsin Press, Madison.

Rosch, E. H. 1973. On the internal structure of perceptual and semantic categories. *In* T. E. Moore (ed.), Cognitive Development and the Acquisition of Language. Academic Press, New York.

Rumbaugh, D. M. 1977. Language Learning by a Chimpanzee: The LANA Project, pp. 111–144. Academic Press, New York.

Rumbaugh, D. M., and Gill, T. V. 1973. The learning skills of great apes. J. Hum. Evolu. 2:171–179.

Rumbaugh, D. M., and Gill, T. V. 1977. Lana's acquisition of language skills. *In* D. M. Rumbaugh (ed.), Language Learning by a Chimpanzee: The LANA Project, pp. 165–192. Academic Press, New York.

von Glasersfeld, E. 1977. Linguistic communication: Theory and definition. *In* D. M. Rumbaugh (ed.), Language Learning by a Chimpanzee: The LANA Project, pp. 55–71. Academic Press, New York.

Warner, H., and Bell, C. 1977. Design of the LANA project—The system: Design and operation. *In* D. M. Rumbaugh (ed.), Language Learning by a Chimpanzee: The LANA Project, pp. 143–155. Academic Press, New York.

Whorf, B. L. 1940. Linguistics as an exact science. Technol. Rev. 43:61–63.

Witmer, L. 1909. A monkey with a mind. Psycholog. Clinic 3:179–205.

Yerkes, R. M., and Learned, B. W. 1925. Chimpanzee Intelligence and Its Vocal Expression. William & Wilkins, Baltimore.

chapter 4

The Linguistic Innateness Hypothesis in the Light of Chimpanzee Language Research

Herbert F. W. Stahlke

Duane M. Rumbaugh

Timothy V. Gill

Georgia State University
Atlanta, Georgia
and
Yerkes Regional Primate Research Center
of Emory University
Atlanta, Georgia

Harold Warner

Yerkes Regional Primate Research Center
of Emory University
Atlanta, Georgia

contents

THE INNATENESS HYPOTHESIS

Fodor, Bever, and Garrett (1974) offer one of the most thorough reviews of the innateness hypothesis (IH). They discuss both a weak and a strong form of the IH. The weak form, not characterized directly, holds that language acquisition and use is innate to the extent that cognition requires innate, genetic structures because language is a function of cognition and intelligence. The strong form claims that natural language requires genetically programmed, species- and task-specific structures in the human brain. It is this strong form of the innateness hypothesis that is normally referred to in the literature, and it is this form that is considered here.

LINGUISTIC UNIVERSALS

An important corollary of the innateness hypothesis is the claim, common among linguists, that there are linguistic universals that define what is a possible natural language. Some of these universals are substantive, such as Greenberg's (1963) universals of word order, Keenan's (1972) Hierarchy of Accessibility, and Ross' (1967) constraints on variable movement rules in syntax. Others are formal, such as the claim that a grammar makes explicit the relationships between meaning and form and that to do this a grammar must have formal devices such as context-free and context-sensitive phrase-structure rules and transformations. The discovery and description of substantive universals require extensive data from many languages and frequently entail argumentation of exceeding subtlety.

We are some time away from having the capacity to posit and define substantive universals of ape language analogs, if, indeed, such universals exist. Formal universals, however, are another matter. Formal linguistic universals can be developed by modeling the knowledge that makes rule-governed linguistic behavior possible. Given a sufficiently large and varied body of linguistic behavior, and the possibility of eliciting further data, it is possible to construct formal models of chimpanzee linguistic competence just as has been done for human linguistic competence. Having constructed such models, it is then possible to compare a model of chimpanzee linguistic competence with a model of human linguistic competence. Such a comparison may enable researchers to judge the formal similarity of the models to each other and hence of the competences of the two species to each other.

While the linguistic analysis and writing were the responsibility of the first author, this chapter would have been impossible without the basic theoretical and experimental background and contributions of the co-authors in developing the LANA Project and the collaboration of Timothy V. Gill in the experimental work directly underlying many parts of this chapter. This research was supported by NIH grants HD-06016 and RR-00155.

FORMAL PROPERTIES OF NATURAL LANGUAGE

An all-pervasive linguistic phenomenon that linguistic models attempt to treat is the duality of language, that is, the fact that the pairing of meaning and form is not isomorphic. Natural language allows meaning-form relationships such as ambiguity, in which a single form must be assigned more than one meaning, and paraphrase, in which several distinct forms are assigned the same or very similar meanings. This duality is represented in a model in natural language by two types of rule. One is a set of phrase-structure rules which defines the set of possible underlying representations that may be meanings (Lakoff, 1971) or that may be the basis for assigning meaning (Chomsky, 1965). The other is a set of transformational rules, each of which represents a factorization of some element in the meaning-form relationship and some proper subset of which, if one follows the approach of Lakoff (1971), mediates the relationship between meaning and form for a particular sentence in a natural language.

Various other linguistic models of weaker formal power have been shown to be insufficient for natural language (Postal, 1964). The weakest model one might reasonably propose is one in which sentences are composed of linear sequences of words so that for any word w_j, the choice of word w_{j+1} is governed by the transitional probability between w_j and w_{j+1}. A model of this sort is a type of finite state machine, such as a first-order Markov process. A more powerful model would be a context-free phrase-structure grammar (CFPSG), which generates a linear string, the elements of which are grouped and interrelated hierarchically. This grammar more closely approximates the formal power needed to describe natural language. It is possible in a CFPSG to describe substitutability not merely of words, but of groups of words, such as prepositional phrases or noun clauses. A third model, of somewhat greater formal power, is the context-sensitive phrase-structure grammar (CSPSG). A CSPSG differs from a CFPSG in that the insertion of some word or string may depend on or be conditioned by words or strings elsewhere in the sentence. Thus the words *slaughter* and *assassinate*, in their basic meanings, are inserted into English sentences by rules that are sensitive to whether the direct object is a quadruped used for food or a human in a position of high public prominence. Thus it is semantically well formed to slaughter a steer or assassinate a king, but not vice versa. A fourth model, of still greater formal power, is a transformational grammar (TG) containing a CSPSG. Such a TG can provide an explicit account of relations between noncontiguous elements in sentences, can explain the presence of conditioned markers in sentences that seem not to contain the conditioning element, and can explicate the relationship between sentences of different structure but identical propositional content. Chomsky (1957) demonstrated that natural language requires a grammar with at least the formal power of a TG.

FORMAL PROPERTIES OF CHIMPANZEE LANGUAGE

To compare the formal linguistic properties of chimpanzee language grammars with those of human language grammars, we shall first construct a model of a chimpanzee language grammar. Our construction is based on a computerized concordance of the second year of the Language Analog (LANA) Project, on approximately 110,000 lines of data produced by the chimpanzee Lana, and on the daily printout of the fourth year, the quantity of which has not been calculated but is quite large.

Demonstrating the formal insufficiency of a finite state grammar is not difficult. Yerkish contains a lexigram for "that's," which serves to identify a following lexigram or string as modifying the noun preceding THATS. Since THATS can only follow nouns and since all adjectives, such as the color words, must be preceded by THATS when they modify nouns, it follows: 1) that there will be fairly high transitional probability between certain nouns, especially names of inanimates, and THATS, 2) that there will be high transitional probability between THATS and a following color word, and 3) that the transitional probability between a noun and a color word will be very low. Two types of well formed strings used by Lana are illustrated in the following year 2 examples.

096966211   COLOR OF THIS BOWL RED.
063776126   CAN NAME THIS.

The former is in answer to the experimenter's question WHAT COLOR OF THIS and the latter to WHAT NAME THIS. Although the animal was taught to use these two patterns differentially, putting an adjective answering WHAT at the end and a noun answering WHAT at the beginning, she is clearly not responding to the position of WHAT in the question, and so her answer is not simply a repetition of the question with an appropriate substitution. What is particularly significant in the sentences of the first sort is that Lana almost never (7 times out of 7,000) used THATS in a COLOR OF expression during year 2.

FINITE STATE GRAMMARS

The distribution of THATS in the two types of sentence illustrated above could be handled by a fourth- or fifth-order Markov process, but such a grammar would approach being simply a list and would lose virtually all capacity for generalization, a capacity Lana has clearly demonstrated. A second argument against a finite state grammar has to do with some fourth-year developments. Lana now uses prepositional phrases to modify nouns, as in the following strings recorded on January 18, 1977.

LANA WANT EAT BANANA IN MACHINE.   11:51:23
LANA WANT EAT BREAD IN MACHINE.   11:54:25

In this situation, the desired food was in a dispenser and Lana was requesting that particular food. On the other hand, on November 12, 1976, Lana produced the following sentence in which an adnominal prepositional phrase is introduced by THATS.

YOU PUT CHOW IN MACHINE THATS BEHIND ROOM.
                                          16:31:25

This construction is decidedly rarer. The important point of these examples is that in a finite state grammar the transitional probability of THATS after a noun is much lower if THATS is followed by a preposition than if it is followed by an adjective. Finite state grammars are formally incapable of capturing such a generalization, since transitional probabilities are all left-to-right linear and this case involves a right-to-left linear dependency. Thus a finite state grammar is insufficiently powerful to generate Lana's language.

PHRASE-STRUCTURE GRAMMARS

We move naturally to the next more powerful class of grammars, the phrase-structure grammar. Phrase-structure grammars involve rewrite rules of the form XAY → XBY. If X and Y are both null, then the grammar is context-free. If either X or Y or both are non-null, then the grammar is context-sensitive. Rewrite rules generate branching diagrams, which define both linear and hierarchical relationships. Thus the sample grammar given below generates, that is, assigns structural descriptions to, the sentences given in the example. Parenthesized elements are considered optional.

Sample Grammar I

    A → BC
    B → D (E)
    C → (F) G

Sentences generated:

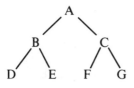

The strings DEFG, DEG, DFG, and DG are the well formed sentences of this artificial language. D and DE are strings which are *constituents* of type B, just as G and FG are constituents of type C. BC, and the four terminal strings given above are constituents of type A. While each terminal *node* is a constituent, EF, EG, and DF are not constituents because they are not uniquely and exhaustively *dominated* by a single node. Sample Grammar I is a CFPSG. If it were revised by the inclusion of a rule like that in Sample Grammar II, it would be a CSPSG.

Sample Grammar II

All rules as in Sample Grammar I
G → H I/F _____
(This rule is read: rewrite G as HI in the environment after F.)
Strings generated by Sample Grammar II but not by Sample Grammar I:

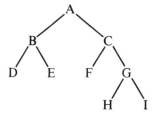 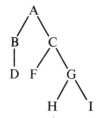

The strings DEFHI and DFHI are well formed in this artificial language, and HI is a constituent of type G.

To demonstrate that Yerkish requires a phrase-structure grammar, it is necessary to demonstrate that substrings of lexigrams function as constituents. Prepositional phrases appear to function in this way, as in the sentences below, recorded on December 25, 1976.

? YOU GIVE COKE TO LANA IN CUP.   13:50:36
? YOU PUT COKE IN CUP.   13:51:13
? YOU GIVE COKE IN CUP TO LANA.   13:52:54

The substring IN CUP occurs in different environments in this sample. In the first sentence, the cup is empty and Lana is making a double request, one she has used in such a situation repeatedly. One part of the request is stated in the second sentence, where IN CUP functions as a directional prepositional phrase. The third sentence is used when Lana sees that the Coke is in the cup. She can then use either this string or the string CUP OF COKE. In either case, the prepositional phrase modifies the noun COKE and is a structure analogous to the string MACHINE THATS BEHIND ROOM cited above. That is, these strings are examples of constituents containing a head noun and a prepositional phrase. Such a head noun is normally labeled as a Noun Phrase (NP) and seems to have the structure shown below, where the labels N, P, and PP mean noun, preposition, and prepositional phrase, respectively.

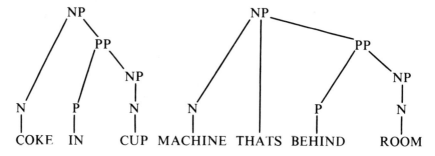

Strings such as ? YOU GIVE COKE TO LANA IN CUP, cited above, would require at least the structure below.

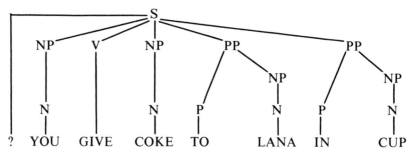

Whether any of the constituents are grouped together as a higher level constituent, such as a Verb Phrase (VP) containing GIVE . . . CUP, is not clear from the data. The label NP is used on even single-word nominal expressions because of the substitutability of multiword and pronominal expressions in those positions. That is, Lana could ask for THIS THATS IN CUP instead of COKE or she could simply use THIS, not naming the item she wants. The referential character of THIS is made explicit in Rumbaugh et al. (Chapter 3, this volume). Thus it is clear that Yerkish requires at least the power of a CFPSG and contains rules like the following:

Partial CFPSG of Yerkish

$$S \longrightarrow \left(\begin{Bmatrix} ? \\ PLEASE \end{Bmatrix}\right) \ NP \ V \ (NP) \ (PP) \ (PP)$$

$$PP \longrightarrow P \ NP$$

$$NP \longrightarrow (THIS) \ N \ \left(THATS \begin{Bmatrix} ADJ \\ PP \end{Bmatrix}\right)$$

Other phrase-structure rules will ultimately prove necessary but are not illustrated by the types of data presented above.

To show that a CFPSG is insufficient for Yerkish, all that is necessary is to show that some rule of Yerkish must be context-sensitive. Lana systematically avoids such strings as PLEASE MACHINE CARRY CHOW TO LANA or ? LANA GROOM M&M. That is, Lana selects lexigrams on the basis of the context in which they are to be used. Thus the lexigrams CARRY and GROOM are misused in the strings given above. They both require animate subjects and GROOM also requires an animate object. It follows then that Yerkish has rules of lexical insertion that are context-sensitive. If it is possible, as appears likely, to subclassify Yerkish nouns by their combinatory possibilities, then we could subclassify them as [±Animate], [±Ingestible], [±Concrete], etc. (cf. von Glasersfeld, 1975, for semantic categories used in Yerkish). With such a subclassification, we can then state context-sensitive rules for the insertion of verbs, such as the following.

$$V \rightarrow CARRY \ / \ [+ ANIMATE] _____ [\pm CONCRETE]$$
$$V \rightarrow GROOM \ / \ [+ ANIMATE] _____ [+ ANIMATE]$$

Other formalisms are possible for lexical insertion (Chomsky, 1965), but they will share the property of being context-sensitive.

TRANSFORMATIONAL GRAMMAR

Arguments that transformational power is needed in a grammar include arguments from simplicity of formulation and arguments from stylistic variation and paraphrase relationships. Admittedly, no single argument is compelling in itself, but the overall simplicity and generality provided by such a grammar suggest that it represents a hypothesis worth investigating. It must be stressed here that claiming that a linguistic model must have rules of a certain form is not tantamount to claiming that the language user operates such rules in sentence production. The model we are presenting is a generative grammar describing the knowledge of language which must be presupposed in an account of an individual's abililty to use language. A generative grammar is not a model of behavior.

THATS-Insertion

The first argument that Yerkish requires transformations involves the use of the lexigram THATS. In the data illustrated above there were two prepositional phrases modifying nouns, one introduced by THATS, the other not. The phrases were COKE IN CUP and MACHINE THATS BEHIND ROOM. Since adjectival modifiers normally use THATS, as in CUP THATS BLACK, one could account for the use of THATS, as we did above, with a phrase-structure rule. To account for the absence of THATS in COKE IN CUP, we could revise the rule by making THATS optional. However, the NP → (THIS) N ((THATS) $\left\{ \begin{array}{c} \text{ADJ} \\ \text{PP} \end{array} \right\}$) rule now says that THATS is optional before adjectives, which does not appear to be correct. Thus a phrase-structure description makes an incorrect claim. A simpler solution would be to revise the phrase-structure rule to exclude THATS and insert it transformationally, making the transformation obligatory before adjectives and optional before prepositional phrases. The rules needed are as follows.

$$ \text{NP} \rightarrow \text{(THIS) N} \left\{ \begin{array}{c} \text{ADJ} \\ \text{PP} \end{array} \right\} $$

Transformation: THATS-insertion

Structural Description	X	N	$\left\{ \begin{array}{c} \text{ADJ} \\ \text{PP} \end{array} \right\}$	Y
	1	2	3	4
Structural Change	1	2	THATS 3	4

Conditions: 1) 2 and 3 are dominated by the same NP
2) rule is optional with PP

OF-Insertion

Another possible transformation involves the lexigram for "of." OF is one of a very small set of lexigrams in Yerkish that seems not to have any semantic content. These lexigrams, including THATS, function purely as syntactic markers of certain types of relationship. OF is found between nouns under three different conditions. First, if N_1 is the lexigram PIECE and N_2 is some segmentable item, usually of food, OF will occur between N_1 and N_2. Second, if N_1 is the lexigram COLOR and N_2 is any object, OF will intervene. Third, if N_1 is a container, such as CUP, BOWL, BOX, or CAN, and N_2 is some substance, such as WATER, MILK, etc., then OF will be found. OF is not used after NAME, as in a sentence like ? WHAT NAME THIS. This last is an irregularity built into the language as originally taught Lana, and she has not deviated from it.

The lexigram OF has the black background common to prepositions, and so strings with OF look superficially like prepositional phrases. They are, however, unique among prepositional phrases for three reasons. First, the preposition is predictable from the semantic classes of the nouns around it. No other preposition, with the partial exception of TO, is in any way predictable. Second, prepositional phrases can ordinarily be either adverbial or adnominal in Yerkish. That is, Lana can ask, as she did on December 25, 1976,

? YOU PUT COKE IN CUP.   13:51:13

or

? YOU GIVE COKE IN CUP TO LANA.   13:52:54

using the prepositional phase to modify PUT in the former example and COKE in the latter. Prepositional phrases with OF, ⌄n the other hand, can occur only adnominally, never adverbially. Third, any adnominal prepositional phrase can be introduced by THATS, as in the example containing MACHINE THATS BEHIND ROOM, cited above. Prepositional phrases with OF are never preceded by THATS. The one apparent counter-example is in line 058260116. The example with its context is the following:

058257116   ? SHELLEY GIVE SHOE THATS RED.
058258116   SHUT.
058259116   ? SHELLEY GIVE THATS.
058260116   ? THATS OF THIS BLACK.
058261116   ? SHELLEY GIVE SHOE THATS BLUE.

The crucial line, line 058260116, is clearly a step in an attempt to ask for a shoe of a particular color. What suggests that this line is not a relevant counter-example is, first, that THATS is initial. There is no preceding noun and so its use is not clearly adnominal. Second, THATS seems simply to be out of place. If it were after THIS, giving OF THIS THATS BLACK, the string would be well formed. There seems little reason at all for OF to occur in this string. Finally, this is the only case of THATS OF in the approximately 7,900 uses of OF in the second year. Thus OF appears to be unique among prepositions.

   The problem for linguistic analysis is accounting for the distribution of OF and THATS so that they will never occur together. Both lexigrams are predictable from syntax or from semantic class, which makes them both unique among lexigrams in Yerkish. There is a general principle of linguistic analysis stating that what is not predictable in syntax is handled by the phrase-structure rules and lexicon, and that what is predictable is handled by transformation. If we follow this principle, then THATS and OF are clearly candidates for transformational analysis. The THATS-insertion rule has already been discussed. We can now state a transformation for OF-insertion as well. Such a rule presupposes that OF, like THATS, is not found in the phrase-structure rules. Rather, the phrase-structure grammar will generate NP of the type N

ADJ, N PP, and N NP. The rule given above, then, must be revised to read

$$NP \rightarrow (THIS)\ N\ \left\{ \begin{matrix} ADJ \\ PP \\ NP \end{matrix} \right\}$$

OF-insertion will then insert OF between two nouns just if they are in the same NP, and N_1 is not NAME. The rule can be stated as follows. OF-insertion:

Structural Description: X N_1 N_2 Y

                             1 2   3 4

Structural Change: 1 2 OF 3 4

Conditions: a) 2 and 3 are dominated by the same NP node
              b) 2 is not NAME

However, OF-insertion clearly generates something that looks very much like a prepositional phrase. Why then is THATS not inserted here as well? One appealing account is to order THATS-insertion before OF-insertion, as illustrated below.

Underlying string	MACHINE BEHIND ROOM.	CUP COKE
THATS-insertion	THATS	n.a.
OF-insertion	n.a.	OF
Surface string	MACHINE THATS BEHIND ROOM.	CUP OF COKE

In this analysis, at the time at which THATS-insertion applies, there are no prepositional phrases with OF, and so OF never occurs after THATS. A transformational analysis of this sort is possible only within a model of language that explicitly treats meaning and form as two separate levels of representation.

PARAPHRASE

Another indication that meaning and form are distinct in Lana's language comes from her use of paraphrase. A fairly typical example of paraphrase-like sentence sets can be found in the December 25, 1976 conversation quoted from above. The conversation is reproduced below.

Lana:	? YOU GIVE COKE IN CUP.	13:46:27
Lana:	? GIVE COKE.	13:47:08
Lana:	? YOU GIVE COKE IN CUP.	13:47:15
Lana:	? YOU COKE.	13:47:31
Lana:	? YOU GIVE COKE TO LANA.	13:47:40
Lana:	? YOU GIVE COKE IN CUP.	13:48:09
Lana:	? YOU GIVE COKE TO LANA.	13:48:20

Lana:	? YOU GIVE COKE TO LANA IN CUP.	13:48:37
Lana:	? YOU GIVE COKE TO LANA IN CUP.	13:49:13
Lana:	? YOU YOU GIVE.	13:49:27
Lana:	? YOU GIVE COKE TO LANA IN CUP.	13:49:39
Lana:	? YOU GIVE COKE TO LANA IN CUP.	13:50:00
Lana:	? YOU GIVE COKE TO LANA IN CUP.	13:50:36
Tim:	NO MORE COKE.	13:51:06
Lana:	? YOU PUT COKE IN CUP.	13:51:13
Tim:	NO MORE COKE TO LANA.	13:51:28
Lana:	? YOU GIVE COKE TO LANA IN IN CUP.	13:51:38
Lana:	? YOU GIVE COKE TO LANA IN CUP.	13:51:48
Tim:	NO MORE COKE TO LANA IN CUP.	13:52:16
Lana:	YES.	13:52:22
Lana:	NO.	13:52:24
Lana:	? YOU GIVE COKE IN CUP TO LANA.	13:52:54
Lana:	? YOU GIVE COKE IN MACHINE.	13:53:42
Lana:	? YOU GIVE COKE IN CUP.	13:54:00
Lana:	? YOU GIVE COKE TO LANA IN MACHINE.	13:54:22
Lana:	? YOU GIVE COKE TO LANA IN CUP.	13:55:11
Lana:	PLEASE MACHINE GIVE WATER.	13:55:29

Lana's initial question is ambiguous as to whether she wants Tim's cup of Coke or wants Tim to pour her a cup of Coke. At 13:48:37, she clarifies by inserting TO LANA between COKE and IN CUP, producing a structure which means that Tim is to pour Coke into a cup for her. Later, at 13:51:13, after Tim has refused her more Coke, she then produces a partial paraphrase in ? YOU PUT COKE IN CUP. This sentence is, in fact, presupposed by her sentence at 13:48:37.

A SUMMARY MODEL

It is clear that Lana has a grammar of a degree of formal power equivalent to a CSPSG with transformational rules. In principle it is possible to generate all of the well formed strings of Yerkish with a CSPSG without using transformations. However, such a grammar is inherently incapable of saying that two distinct strings have the same meaning. This could be done without using derivations, by allowing equivalence conditions on pairs of sentences stating that the two sentences mean the same thing. These equivalence conditions, which are what transformations originally were in the early work of Zellig Harris (1957), are formally and functionally almost the same as the transformations posited here in that they make explicit the claim that the meaning-form relationship is not isomorphic. Thus even if another model of grammar is appealed to, it will have to be equivalent in power to a transformational grammar and will probably be a notational variant of a transformational grammar.

IMPLICATIONS FOR INNATENESS HYPOTHESES

We have demonstrated that the linguistic competence of at least one ape language analog requires a set of formal devices including a CFPSG, a CSPSG, and a TG. Precisely these formal devices are among the formal universals of natural language. While both natural language and ape language may yet be shown to require some further formal devices, it is clear from those presented above that, formally, natural language and ape language are qualitatively very similar.

This is not to say that there are not striking differences between them. Apes, for example, do not learn language without extensive overt conditioning, including operant training methods. Apes have so far shown little evidence of using language, of the sort under discussion, among themselves, and it is not known if they might teach language to their offspring. Also, apes do not seem to use language for much beyond achieving immediate gratification of some physical need or in direct response to human-initiated stimuli, although there are on record some marked exceptions to this claim. These are, however, functional differences, not formal differences. The formal differences seem to be quantitative rather than qualitative. The respective grammars do not differ markedly in formal power. However, humans seem to be able to handle sentences of greater structural and perceptual complexity than apes, as yet, show evidence of handling. Humans are capable of a much larger vocabulary than apes, although the upper limits of apes' lexical storage have hardly been reached. Humans use modalities, tense and aspect, which seem at best to be rudimentary in ape language. These are not differences that require grammars of different formal power.

The strong IH claims that humans have a species- and task-specific preparedness for language learning and use. To the extent that apes are capable of grammars of the same formal power as humans are, preparedness for language learning and use can be neither species- nor task-specific, and the strong IH is falsified. The disparity in linguistic ability between ape and human must then lie in the areas of cognition and intelligence.

REFERENCES

Chomsky, N. A. 1957. Syntactic Structures. Mouton and Co., The Hague.
Chomsky, N. A. 1965. Aspects of the Theory of Syntax. The MIT Press, Cambridge, Mass.

Fodor, J. A., Bever, T. G., and Garrett, M. F. 1974. The Psychology of Language: An Introduction to Psycholinguistics and Generative Grammar. McGraw-Hill Book Co., New York.

Greenberg, J. H. (ed.). 1963. Universals of Language. The MIT Press, Cambridge, Mass.

Harris, Z. S. 1957. Co-occurrence and transformation in linguistic structure. Language 33:283–340.

Keenan, E. L. 1972. On semantically based grammar. Linguistic Inquiry 3:414–461.

Lakoff, G. 1971. On generative semantics. In D. D. Steinberg and L. A. Jakobovitz (eds.), Semantics: An Interdisciplinary Reader in Philosophy, Linguistics and Psychology, pp. 232–296. Cambridge University Press, London.

Postal, P. M. 1964. Constituent Structure. Indiana University Press, Bloomington.

Ross, J. R. 1967. Constraints on Variables in Syntax. MIT doctoral disseration, Cambridge, Mass.

von Glasersfeld, E. 1975. The Yerkish language for non-human primates. Am. J. Computation. Linguist. Microfiche 12.

chapter 5

Language and Communication Models

Summary Discussion

Sam Glucksberg

Department of Psychology
Princeton University
Princeton, New Jersey

contents

TYPES OF MODELS AND THEIR MISUSES

The chapters by Krauss, by Rumbaugh et al., and by Stahlke et al. deal with a central issue: What models are available for research and application in language and communication? Three types of models can be distinguished. The first is the experimental or training paradigm treated as a valid simulation of an important aspect of natural language or communication. The referential communication paradigm devised by Krauss and his colleagues (Glucksberg and Krauss, 1967; Krauss and Glucksberg, 1969; Krauss and Glucksberg, 1970) is an example of this type of model. Second are theoretical models. They are usually formalizations or explanations of specific phenomena or classes of phenomena. Chomsky's transformational-generative grammar is among the best known of this type within psycholinguistics. Finally, when a surrogate for human subjects is used for experimental purposes, that surrogate is often referred to as a "model." Such models are used when research with humans is either unethical or technically impossible. Pigeons, white rats, rhesus monkeys, and chimpanzees have served as models of human behavior.

Krauss' chapter concentrated upon specific misuses of the first two types of models. Krauss and Glucksberg's referential communication paradigm was originally designed for a specific, limited purpose—to describe the development of one, and only one, aspect of interpersonal communication. As Krauss points out, many of the characteristics of the experimental paradigm were well suited to that purpose, allowing him and others to discover a number of important facts about referential communication and how referential communication skills grow and change with age. Unfortunately, the specific referential communication task that had been designed explicitly as a discovery procedure was then woefully misapplied in at least two ways. First, investigators who were interested in the cognitive-developmental correlates of communication skills sought to find correlations between measures of communication performance and measures of cognitive development. Egocentrism in particular seemed a likely correlate, but the initial attempts to relate egocentrism to referential communication skills were uniformly negative (cf. Glucksberg, Krauss, and Higgins, 1975). How are we to resolve this apparent paradox? The intuitive plausibility of the argument that egocentrism was inherently involved in poor communication performance was apparently so compelling that a solution was finally found by using performance in a referential communication task as a measure of egocentrism (e.g., Rubin and Schneider, 1973). In other words, if you cannot find a relationship, redefine your measures to establish one. Science does indeed march on, sometimes in circles.

The second and far more serious misuse of the referential communication paradigm was to take it as a "model" for clinical use. The original version of the model, in the form of a set of experimental procedures, was designed neither as a diagnostic instrument for individual children, nor as a teaching device or program. Nevertheless, the paradigm was seized upon by some clinicians and therapists as if it were a panacea for all speech and communication ills. Versions of the two-person referential communication game were marketed commercially, to be used as diagnostic instruments and as teaching devices. David Yoder, during the conference on nonspeech language, acidly remarked that referential communication "therapy" metastasized throughout the field. The results of this could have been foreseen. Children who were given extensive practice and coaching in particular referential communication games generally learned to play those games quite well—and that is about all that they did learn. There were no good reasons to expect transfer from this type of game to other language behaviors, and no transfer occurred. If I may inject a personal observation, Robert Krauss and I were aghast to learn that children have been stacking blocks all over the country for some time now, apparently to no good end.

The moral to be drawn is fairly obvious. No single "model" of this sort can be taken intact from the context in which it was originally designed to serve and then applied blindly in quite different contexts. Advances in the laboratory and advances in theory rarely have direct practical application, but they can inform practitioners about some aspects of the behaviors with which they are concerned. A major purpose of the early work in referential communication was to draw attention to one aspect of language behavior that had, until then, been ignored. At the time, the major emphasis within psycholinguistics was upon syntax. The referential communication work seemed a necessary corrective to the overconcentration upon syntax to the exclusion of other important aspects of language behavior. On the other hand, referential communication itself is not the only, or even the most important, aspect of language behavior.

This is not the only model that can be misused, of course. Chomsky's seminal work on transformational-generative grammar provided a different kind of model, a theoretical model of the nature of language, but it led to similar misapplications. A *transformation*, as a formal theoretical concept, has been important and useful in formal linguistics, and has led to theoretical and empirical discoveries that have furthered our understanding of natural language. Transformations are not, however, things that humans actually do when they speak. Knowing how to transform one kind of sentence into another has nothing whatever to do with fluency in verbal communication. Nevertheless, some language teachers and speech therapists, who were appropriately impressed with the power and elegance of transformational-generative grammar, inappropriately had their pupils and clients practicing sentence transforms. While some children were practicing stacking blocks, others were practicing transforming active sentences into passive form and back, until they got to be quite good at it. Like the children who played referential communication games, these children got to be quite good at transforming sentences, but not at anything else. Here, as in the application of the referential "model," a useful and important concept was wrenched from its original context, misinterpreted, and then used to no avail. If there is a clear practical lesson here, it is that practitioners should avoid using new techniques or ideas before they are worked out, tested, and understood. Faddish devotion to techniques of the moment can easily take the place of sound practice and common sense.

These sentiments are directed primarily toward practitioners seeking more effective teaching and intervention strategies. They apply equally to those of us in the laboratory who are just as prone to latch on to new and potentially promising ideas, often prematurely. To those of us who are aware of the recent history of psycholinguistics, this lesson is a familiar one.

MEANINGS AND INTENTIONS

Partly in reaction to syntax-based approaches in linguistics and psycholinguistics, a number of linguists, including Searle (1969) and Grice (1975), argue that social-interactive processes and inferences must play a central role in natural language communication. Krauss (Chapter 2, this volume) points out that the linguistic content of utterances is but one of several sources of information used to arrive at the message intended by a speaker. Language comprehension is viewed not merely as a process involving the semantic and syntactic interpretation of linguistic strings, but rather as a hypothesis-generating and hypothesis-testing activity. Upon hearing a sentence, a skilled language user integrates the interpretation(s) of the sentence with the social and prior linguistic context, the nonverbal behavior of the speaker, and other information as well, and then arrives at an "intended" meaning—what it is that the speaker intended him to understand. This distinction between the intended meaning of an utterance and its literal or linguistic meaning can be seen in such indirect requests as "Is your mother home?" The literal meaning of this utterance is a question, demanding either a yes or a no answer. The most likely intended meaning is a request to speak to the mother. Many young children display linguistic but not conversational ability when they respond to such an utterance by simply answering yes. Krauss argues, along with many others, that the ability to go beyond the linguistic content of utterances is a necessary and central component of interpersonal communication.

Applications

How these ideas should or can be applied in nonspeech intervention programs is not clear. However, there are clear implications for what should *not* be done. Intervention programs should *not* concentrate on formal aspects of linguistic structure. They should *not* rely exclusively on linguistic or linguistic-like training procedures. They should *not* assume that sufficient knowledge and skill in the phonology, syntax, and semantics of a spoken language, or the analogous components of a nonvocal communication system, will automatically produce functional communication between the child and others. Functional communication is a complex social-interactive process that draws upon the knowledge we have about other people and of the world we live in, as well as of the communication systems we use. Any intervention program that ignores any one of these components could well be correspondingly deficient.

Two morals emerge from this: Practitioners should be trained to evaluate the ideas and research in fields relevant to their practice, and scientists should clearly point out both the assumptions and limitations of their techniques and theoretical models. If both of these morals are heeded, we will have fewer misapplications of theory to practice, both in the clinic and in the laboratory.

CHIMPANZEE AND CHILD

The third model is the human surrogate. Rumbaugh views the chimpanzee as a potentially useful "model" for language research and the development of intervention techniques in the same sense that pharmacologists view animal subjects as "models" of human reactions to new drugs. To the extent that a nonhuman species is similar to humans, to that extent can the species be used to circumvent some problems inherent in human research. There are many manipulations that cannot, for technical or ethical reasons, be performed with humans, but that could be done with nonhumans if an appropriate species were available. Thus, just as experimental drugs are first assessed by finding out their effects upon laboratory animals, so might research on language and cognition be done with chimpanzees provided, of course, that the chimpanzee is sufficiently similar to humans to be relevant to human language and cognition. Research on the effects of various early environments could be done with chimpanzees that could not be done with human infants. Explorations of brain structures could also be done with chimpanzees, but not with humans. Finally, research on the relationships among learning, language, and perception that would not be technically feasible with humans might be done with chimpanzees.

How similar are humans and chimpanzees in those characteristics relevant to language, cognition, and communication? The obvious similarities, biological, behavioral, and social, suggest that the chimpanzee might be a useful human surrogate for some theoretical questions. For example, we generally assume that there is an intimate relationship between language and cognition. This general assumption is virtually impossible to test with humans because it is difficult to imagine an intact human who has no language (vocal or otherwise) or who has nontrivial gaps in his language. Chimpanzees, however, can be systematically taught to have names for some things, and not to have names for others. Taking advantage of this, Rumbaugh and his colleagues have reported on a preliminary experiment on a relationship between language and cognition. Cross-modal matching is a difficult task for nonhuman primates. The chimpanzee Lana was tested in a cross-modal matching task in which she had to respond SAME or DIFFERENT when presented with two objects, one presented visually, the other haptically. Her performance was best when the two objects were ones for which she had "names," somewhat worse when the objects were familiar to her but had not been named for her, and worst of all when the objects were neither familiar nor named. This finding is intriguing and important in itself, and suggests that research of great theoretical interest—that cannot be done with humans—might well be done with chimpanzees.

Is the chimpanzee similar enough to human retardates, Down syndrome children, autistic children, or to any other diagnostic categories of speech-impaired humans to be a useful surrogate for clinical research? The issue of similarity in this context involves two separate questions. First, is the particular communication system acquired by a chimpanzee similar, in relevant ways, to the communication system to be acquired by one or more human target populations? Second, do chimpanzees and humans acquire that system in equivalent ways? Stahlke et al. (Chapter 4, this volume) address one aspect of the first question: to what extent is the communication system acquired by Lana "similar" to human language? Has she acquired a "true language" and not just a language-like set of behaviors? The answer to this question depends upon the criteria one selects for deciding whether a communication system is a "true language." Stahlke's criterion is formal in nature. Given the corpus of Lana's message productions, what kind of formal grammar is needed to account for that corpus? Stahlke argues that if the formal power of the grammar needed to account for Lana's productions is equivalent to that required for a grammar of English, then the two "languages," Lana's on the one hand and English on the other, are formally equivalent. The two languages might differ in degree or complexity but not in kind.

As in human languages, there is no one-to-one correspondence between form and meaning in Lana's communication system. This fact, plus the particular distribution of symbols functioning as "prepositions" in Lana's corpus, led Stahlke to conclude that a grammar describing Lana's productions must have at least the mathematical power of a transformational-generative grammar. During the conference, Oller pointed out, however, that this conclusion depended upon the arbitrary classification of symbols to grammatical classes, which in a sense prejudges the issue. If, for example, the symbol for "of" were not classified as a preposition, then a transformational grammar, or its formal equivalent, would not be required by the data. What are the justifications for classifying the lexigrams of Lana's communication system in terms of the grammatical classes of English? Indeed, what are the justifications for assigning English meanings to those lexigrams?

The issue seems simple enough when we consider lexigrams for such concrete objects as apple, or chow, or Coke. But what meanings should we assign to words like "please," which appear in such strings as PLEASE MACHINE GIVE PIECE OF CHOW? Does the lexigram PLEASE represents the word or the concept *please* or is it nothing more than an arbitrary start symbol which, when pressed, activates the computer program? Does the lexigram PIECE-OF represent the same conceptual meaning as the English words "piece of"? The difficulty of technical questions like these suggests that a formal grammatical approach to the problem of whether or not Lana has "language" may prove fruitless. In any case, such an approach also seems irrelevant for one of the central goals of the LANA Project—to develop intervention techniques for nonspeech children.

This last point concerns questions about the kinds of sentences Lana has and has not yet produced. Does Lana use her symbols for propositional conjoining? Does she use embedded constructions? Does she play with her language by punning or by rhyming? Does she ask Wh-questions? Answers to these questions would undoubtedly tell us something about the kind of animal Lana is, but these questions are rather off the point. The main issue is whether or not the LANA Project can develop anything that might be useful with handicapped persons. After all, some handicapped persons may not use embedded constructions, they may not conjoin propositions, and they may never play punning or rhyming games. At the same time, they may well be able to develop or acquire a functional communication system that accomplishes at least some of the things that natural spoken language does. The question of Lana chimpanzee having acquired a "really" human language, by whatever criteria, is tangential to these concerns.

What are the characteristics of Lana chimpanzee's communication system that are relevant to the development of effective clinical intervention programs? The most obvious, and possibly the most important, is the system's functional characteristics despite its being nonvocal. Lana is able to communicate her wants and desires and can control significant aspects of her environment. She can get the computer or people to deliver food, drink, and entertainment. She learned, apparently with no direct tutoring, to call people's attention to machine malfunctions or to mistakes that her trainers had made, like putting water into the milk dispenser. She has initiated dialogues with one of her trainers. When stock sentences that had been taught to her proved inadequate for novel communicative needs, she invented new ones. In brief, the system is instrumental and is useful to her, and functions in a complex, socially interactive manner. Finally, the system is open, or productive, enabling her to construct novel "sentences." In these important functional ways, the LANA system, if acquired by nonspeech people, could be a useful and reasonable substitute for spoken language.

The system can thus serve as a pragmatic experimental model for the development of alternative communication systems for handicapped persons, much as Premack's communication techniques, as developed for the chimpanzee Sarah, have so served (e.g., as in Non-SLIP). However, some caution is in order. Assume that the LANA system does all those things we might want a functional communication system to do. Assume also that there is a clinical population of handicapped children or adults who would be capable of using the system. Two additional questions arise. First, is the particular overt realization of the system—pushing illuminated lexigram keys on a computer or computer-like display console—either necessary or desirable? Recall that one of the original purposes for computerizing a chimpanzee communication system was to provide a complete experimental record for data analysis. Although a complete record of a child's learning may be useful for teaching purposes, such a record need not be a necessary component of a training or therapy program. Thus, even if a LANA communication apparatus could be miniaturized and made completely portable, it might still be preferable to consider alternative response modes, such as signing, which could retain the functional and formal characteristics of the system without the associated hardware. In other words, the external realization of the LANA communication system, be it via manual signs, plastic symbols, or electronic communication panels, need not be an inherent and indispensable feature of that system. If the system itself can be dissociated from the particular response mode used with the chimpanzee Lana, then those response modes most appropriate for each clinical group could be selected to meet the needs of the persons involved.

A second issue that is yet to be resolved concerns the ways the system may best be acquired. Will the techniques that work best with chimpanzees also work best with retarded children, or with autistic children, or with aphasic adults? For example, a central element in Lana's acquisition of her communication system is her close social relationship with humans around her. Will such a close relationship be necessary, or even desirable, for all types of handicapped persons, including the autistic? A second important aspect of Lana's development is the utility of the system for controlling her social and physical world. Will this be a necessary component of a human version of the system, or a desirable one? The hope, of course, is that the techniques that work best with chimpanzees will also work best with humans. If the chimpanzee is to serve as a human surrogate for research in developing nonspeech intervention programs, then this hope must be realized. At the moment, the question is open.

Perhaps we should hedge our bets and conduct research with handicapped adults and children as well as with chimpanzees in our search for effective training and therapeutic techniques. Those research questions that cannot be addressed by experimentation with humans should, if appropriate, use nonhuman surrogates. Those questions that can be investigated with humans should not, for obvious reasons, rely exclusively on such surrogates. The overwhelming bulk of clinical research will eventually have to be conducted with the specific clinical target populations. The techniques that might work best for chimpanzees might not be most effective for Down syndrome children, and what might work best for Down syndrome children might not work at all for autistic children.

The achievements and capabilities of chimpanzees like Washoe, Sarah, and Lana are impressive and have told us a great deal about the cognitive and linguistic capabilities of the chimpanzee. More important, the techniques developed for studying cognition and language in the chimpanzee promise to help us learn important things about the nature of the functional relationships between cognitive processes and symbol systems in general, be they "language" or not. There might, however, be one unforeseen development which could severely limit the use of the chimpanzee as an animal model in the sense intended by Rumbaugh. Should we ever get to the point where we must admit that the chimpanzee is too close to us for comfort, those very ethical considerations that led us to the chimpanzee in the first place might well constrain our actions in the future. The day that a chimpanzee "speaker" plaintively asks, "Why me?" may mark both the crowning achievement of the ape language workers and the end to some of that work.

REFERENCES

Glucksberg, S., and Krauss, R. M. 1967. What do people say after they have learned how to talk? Studies of the development of referential communication. Merrill-Palmer Q. 13:309–316.

Glucksberg, S., Krauss, R. M., and Higgins, E. T. 1975. The development of referential communication skills. *In* F. D. Horowitz (ed.), Review of Child Development Research, Vol. 4, pp. 305–346. University of Chicago Press, Chicago.

Grice, H. P. 1975. Logic and conversation. *In* P. Cole and J. C. Morgan (eds.), Syntax and Semantics, Vol. 3: Speech Acts, pp. 41–58. Seminar Press, New York.

Krauss, R. M., and Glucksberg, S. 1969. The development of communication: Competence as a function of age. Child Dev. 40:255–266.

Krauss, R. M., and Glucksberg, S. 1970. Socialization of communication skills: The development of competence as a communicator. *In* R. Hoppe, E. Simmel, and G. Z. Milton (eds.), Early Experiences and the Processes of Socialization, pp. 149–166. Academic Press, New York.

Rubin, K. H., and Schneider, F. W. 1973. The relationship between moral judgment, egocentrism, and altruistic behavior. Child Dev. 44:661–665.

Searle, J. R. 1969. Speech Acts. Cambridge University Press, Cambridge, England.

Section III

Historical Perspectives

Nonhuman Primate Language and Communication Development

Donald and Gua

Viki

Editors' Introduction

For centuries man has been intrigued by the human-like characteristics of the great apes (gibbon, orangutan, chimpanzee, and gorilla). From an evolutionary point of view, these primates are man's closest relatives. Although there are gaps in the evolutionary chain from the great apes to man, the biological and behavioral similarities are so striking that one is tempted to refer to them as prototypes or as sibling species to man.

In their study of the great apes, Yerkes and Yerkes (1929) discuss vocalization, speech, and language behavior. From a historical perspective there is some validity in the belief that chimpanzees can learn to understand human speech or its elements (receptive language). Although chimpanzees can produce a variety of sounds, the Yerkeses caution the reader not to infer that reports of speech (expressive language) in the chimpanzee are true. In fact the Yerkeses reported that their attempts to teach speech to a chimpanzee were discouraging. However, their observations of gesture and other forms of behavioral symbolism play an important role in the daily life of the chimpanzee. In this regard Yerkes and Yerkes (1929) state:

> We would especially emphasize the conspicuousness of such forms of behavior, their importance for our understanding of the mental life of chimpanzees, and the suggestion that if a language can be developed by them it is more likely to be constituted of visual or kinaesthetic than of auditory elements (p. 309).

From the work of the Yerkeses it appears that they believed the chimpanzee had the cognitive ability to develop language (i.e., form *associations* between gestures, or symbols, and environmental events), but that human speech was an inappropriate expressive mode for the chimpanzee. It took almost four decades for the Yerkes and Yerkes' (1929, p. 309) statement to bear fruit. In 1969 the Gardners (see Gardner and Gardner, 1969 [Chapter 9, this volume]) demonstrated language acquisition in the chimpanzee using a visual-kinesthetic system (manual signing).

J. R. Kantor (1933), in discussing experimental learning, lists six general conditions: 1) biological nature of the organism, i.e., what an organism can learn depends on its organization and evolutionary level, 2) normality of the organism, e.g., normal child versus deaf or retarded child, 3) reactional biography, i.e., an individual with a large behavioral repertoire is a more capable learner than one whose repertoire is small, 4) age, 5) learning material, i.e., the nature of the material to be learned, and 6) general surrounding condition, e.g., the opportunity to come into contact with objects, events, people, etc. It is the editors' contention that the work of Kantor had a profound effect on the direction of speech and language research with the chimpanzee.

In 1927 Winthrop N. Kellogg started to develop a comprehensive plan to study simultaneously the development of a normal human infant and an infant chimpanzee. It is J. R. Kantor to whom Kellogg gives much credit for stimulation, encouragement, and assistance in the development of the project (Kellogg, 1931 [Chapter 6, this volume]). Thus, with Kantor's learning conditions as a springboard, Kellogg (with the aid of his wife) undertook to rear an infant chimpanzee in a human environment with their son (Kellogg and Kellogg, 1933). They studied the development of the two infants in a manner similar to that of Gesell and published the results in the classic work *The Ape and the Child.*

HUMANIZING THE APE

The first chapter in this section is Kellogg's plan for studying the effect of environment on development of an infant chimpanzee. In discussing the effects of environment on the development of the human infant, Kellogg raises the issue of what would be the effects of rearing a child in the jungle or some similar situation, i.e., the reverse of rearing a chimpanzee in a human environment. We of course cannot thrust a child into a nonhuman environment for experimental purposes. However, as Kellogg points out, this is not necessary because there are a number of reported cases of feral children (those reared in the "wild" or by an alien species with little or no human contact). Today, 1979, we still find abused children who have been confined in dark closets for extended periods during the formative years.

Figure 1 is a matrix illustrating species by environmental interactions. Although one may question the authenticity of some of the reports on feral children, the reports suggest that the children had not developed normal human behavior and most especially were totally lacking in speech and language. When some of these children were transplanted to a human environment they failed to acquire desired behavior (cf. Itard, 1962). Kellogg said this was because they had advanced too far in age to reverse habits acquired at an earlier date.

In support of his research plan Kellogg points to the work of Yerkes and others who studied the similarities rather than the differences between man and the chimpanzee. In objecting to previous chimpanzee investigations, Kellogg notes that most research had been conducted after the most formative period in the animals' lives. In addition to being deprived of maternal care the chimpanzee had not been given a chance to learn human behavior. Even under the best of circumstances, Kellogg

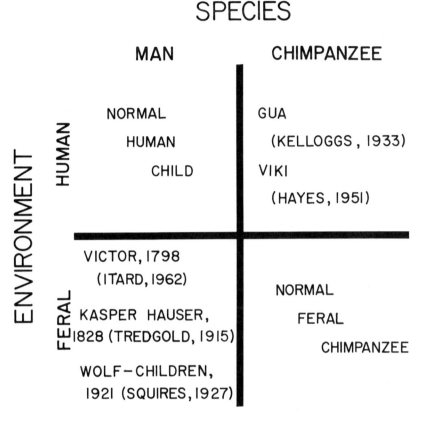

Figure 1.   Matrix showing species by environmental interactions.

(1931, [Chapter 6, this volume]) states, "At least seven-eighths of his waking life, therefore, is consumed in typically infrahuman surroundings" (p. 154 [p. 135]). This is not unlike some institutional conditions where retarded children are reared today.

Would human speech develop in an infant chimpanzee reared in a human environment? This was a question asked by Kellogg. It was believed that the vocal mechanism of the chimpanzee was sufficiently similar to that of humans to permit the development of speech. However, this hypothesis is no longer tenable (cf. Bryan, 1963).

On August 31, 1930, a son, Donald, was born to the Kelloggs, and subsequently Yerkes provided them with an infant female chimpanzee, Gua, born November 15, 1930. From June 26, 1931 until March 28, 1932 Donald and Gua were reared together in the Kelloggs' household. On developmental progress as measured by Gesell tests for preschool children Gua and Donald showed about equal progress. However, they differed significantly in the realm of language. Gua never mastered *expressive* language. Donald progressed normally.[1] With respect to *receptive* language (words spoken by humans) Gua initially surpassed Donald, and at approximately 16½ months Gua responded to 58 phrases (Kellogg and Kellogg, 1933, pp. 297–306). Although there appears to be no direct evidence of Gua forming *associations* between abstract symbols and environmental referents, her performance on some tests suggests that she had this ability. For example, when the phrase "Show me the shoe" was spoken, she pointed to the shoe on the Gesell test card.

PRELINGUISTIC SIGN BEHAVIOR IN THE CHIMPANZEE

To the linguist a sign is a visible symbol of an idea, i.e., a word symbol. As a function of interaction with the environment and through the educational processes the normal child learns to use symbols and to produce them as in speech and writing.

The study of the relationship between signs and their interpreters has been labeled *pragmatics* by Morris (1955), who states:

> The interpreter of a sign is an organism; the interpretant is the habit of the organism to respond, because of the sign vehicle, to absent objects which are relevant to a present problematic situation as if they were present (p. 109).

In view of Morris' *pragmatical dimension of semiosis*, Premack (1976, personal communication) suggests that *selective attention*, *representation*, and *displacement* are cognitive functions that provide a basis for the development of language and communication. These basic skills are defined as follows:

1. *Selective attention.* The ability to discriminate between attributes of persons, events, places, or things, and to classify or categorize by the use of these attributes.
2. *Representation.* The ability to develop iconic or noniconic associations (symbolization) to environmental referents (persons, places, things, etc.). Symbolization may be viewed as: a) *productive*, e.g., speech, writing, or manual signing, b) *selective*, e.g., pointing to a symbol or printed word, selecting a plastic symbol (Premack, 1970 [Chapter 12, this volume]); or c) *cognitive*, e.g., an unobservable response.

---

[1] There was no attempt on Gua's part to use her lips, tongue, teeth, and mouth cavity in the production of new utterances, whereas in the case of the human subject a continuous vocalized play was apparent from the earliest months (Kellogg and Kellogg, 1933, p. 281).

3. *Displacement.* The ability to respond to persons, objects, etc., not present in the organism's immediate environment or which have been obscured from the organism's sensory boundaries for variable periods of time (delayed response).

In their initial attempt to study prelinguistic sign behavior in the chimpanzee, Yerkes and Nissen (1939 [Chapter 7, this volume] elected to use the nonspatial delayed response technique. This task involved placing food in one of two different containers in the presence of the chimpanzee. The containers were then withdrawn from view, changed with respect to spatial orientation and after a predetermined period of time re-presented to the chimpanzee. The chimpanzee then had only to select the correct container and retrieve the food. Although some chimpanzees showed performance well above chance, overall performance for the group was only 56.7% correct (chance, 50%). Despite the poor showing on the nonspatial delayed response task, Yerkes and Nissen were convinced that "some cue or cues, unobservable directly by us were operative." This task involved the skills of selective attention, representation, and displacement. The behavior of Gua suggests that the chimpanzee has these abilities. It would appear that the problems of performance on the nonspatial delayed response task involves training technique rather than the chimpanzee's ability; subsequently, Finch (1942) demonstrated that chimpanzees can solve nonspatial delayed response problems employing a matching technique. Recent successes in teaching language to the chimpanzee have involved training derivations of the match-to-sample technique (see Rumbaugh et al., Chapter 3, this volume; Premack, 1970 [Chapter 12, this volume]; Fouts, Couch, and O'Neil, Chapter 15, this volume; Carrier, 1974 [Chapter 17, this volume]).

THE CULTURAL CAPACITY OF THE CHIMPANZEE

In 1947 the Hayeses, at Yerkes Laboratories of Primate Biology in Orange Park, Florida, undertook another home-raised chimpanzee project. The project had the encouragement, cooperation, and advice of Robert M. Yerkes, Karl S. Lashley, and Henry W. Nissen. The Hayeses were especially interested in studying (over an extended period) the development of social behavior and communication ability. They studied Viki, a female chimpanzee, from shortly after birth until approximately six years of age. A serious attempt was made to indoctrinate Viki with human culture although she did not have, as Gua did, a human age-mate.

The process of cultural indoctrination stressed the development of oral speech and specifically attempted to train it. It should be noted that

Viki's training took place before the advent of modern behavior modification techniques. However, in training Viki's speech, techniques such as reinforcing successive approximations of appropriate sounds were employed. Viki eventually learned to emit discriminable versions of the words "papa," "mama," and "cup." These words were learned only with great difficulty and were sometimes used incorrectly.

In her everyday behavior Viki is reputed to have made only limited use of gestures, but she appeared to engage in a kind of communication involving "iconic signs." She learned to convert such signs into "symbols," for example, going to the bathroom and returning with diapers, to indicate that she wanted to go for a ride in the car (see Hayes and Hayes, 1954 [Chapter 8, this volume]). Viki's behavior suggests that she responded to *receptive* language (words spoken by humans) and that she could form *associations*, e.g. between diapers and the event of riding in the car. Although she surpassed Gua in *expressive* language (speech), her three words were small reward for considerable effort. In retrospect Viki's ability to adapt to the human culture was impressive. Catherine Hayes (1951) published a delightful book entitled *The Ape in Our House*, which describes the Hayeses' trials and tribulations with Viki.

TEACHING SIGN LANGUAGE TO A CHIMPANZEE

Four decades have passed since the Kelloggs started their study of the ape and the child and the Yerkeses suggested that language development in the chimpanzee is more likely if a visual-kinesthetic approach is used. In June, 1966, Gardner and Gardner (1969 [Chapter 9, this volume]) began training an infant chimpanzee named Washoe to use gestural language (i.e., American Sign Language). After 22 months of training the Gardners were convinced that they were correct in selecting manual signing (ASL) to teach language. By the end of 22 months Washoe had acquired 30 signs that she could use spontaneously and appropriately. In addition, by the time she had acquired 10 signs she started to use them in strings of two or more. In terms of language and communication Washoe demonstrated *receptive, associative,* and *expressive* functions in the use of signs. She is reported to have engaged in spontaneous naming, spontaneous transfer to new referents, and spontaneous combinations and recombinations of signs (see Gardner and Gardner, 1969 [Chapter 9, this volume]).

COMMUNICATION AND LANGUAGE
IN THE HOME-RAISED CHIMPANZEE

The final chapter in this section is a review by Winthrop Kellogg of six comprehensive studies concerning civilizing influences on the development of chimpanzees. In general, home-raised chimpanzees adapt readily to the physical features of the household. In some respects they are comparable to human children. The greatest deficiency shown by young chimpanzees is in language ability. Thus, as the human child develops proficiency in language use he is able to use it in manipulating the environment and learning new behavior. It is at this point in development that the human child surpasses the chimpanzee. The rest of the story is yet to be written; with the abandonment of the speech mode and adoption of manual signing the chimpanzee is still in the language game. Furthermore, the development of a plastic symbol system (Premack, 1970 [Chapter 12, this volume]) and a computer lexigram system (Rumbaugh et al., Chapter 3, this volume; Stahlke et al., Chapter 4, this volume) provide unique methods for teaching language to chimpanzees and handicapped children.

REFERENCES

Bryan, A. L. 1963. The essential basis for human culture. Curr. Anthropol. 4:297–306.
Finch, G. 1942. Delayed matching-from-sample and non-spatial delayed response in chimpanzee. J. Comp. Psychol. 34:315–319.
Gardner, R. A., and Gardner, B. T. 1969. Teaching sign language to a chimpanzee. Science 165:664–672.
Hayes, C. 1951. The Ape in Our House. Harper & Brothers, New York.
Hayes, K. J., and Hayes, C. 1954. The cultural capacity of chimpanzee. Hum. Biol. 26:288–303.
Itard, I. M. G. 1962. The Wild Boy of Aveyron. Appleton-Century-Crofts, New York.
Kantor, J. R. 1933. A Survey of the Science of Psychology. The Principia Press, Bloomington, Ind. (Reprinted in 1949)
Kellogg, W. N. 1931. Humanizing the Ape. Psychol. Rev. 38:160–176.
Kellogg, W. N., and Kellogg, L. A. 1933. The Ape and the Child. McGraw-Hill Book Co., New York. [1967, Hafner, New York].
Morris, C. W. 1955. Foundations of the theory of signs. In O. Neurath, R. Carnap, and C. Morris (eds.), International Encyclopedia of Unified Science, Vol. 1. University of Chicago Press, Chicago.
Premack, D. 1970. A functional analysis of language. J. Exp. Anal. Behav. 14:107–125.
Squires, P. C. 1927. "Wolf-children" of India. Am. J. Psychol. 38:313–315.
Tredgold, A. F. 1915. Mental Deficiency. William Wood, New York.
Yerkes, R. M., and Nissen, H. W. 1939. Pre-linguistic sign behavior in chimpanzee. Science 89:585–587.
Yerkes, R. M., and Yerkes, A. W. 1929. The Great Apes: A Study of Anthropoid Life. Yale University Press, New Haven, Conn.

chapter 6

Humanizing
the Ape

Winthrop N. Kellogg*

Indiana University
Bloomington, Indiana

contents

The opinion seems to persist among certain contemporary psychologists that a sharp qualitative demarkation between the behavior of man on the one hand and the behavior of infrahumans including the anthropoid apes, on the other hand, is an established fact. The strength of this view is evidenced in part by the recent controversy involving the doctrine of instinct and the support which this conception continues to receive from some quarters, especially with reference to the interpretation of the activity of animals. It is the object of this paper 1) to point out in this connection an aspect of comparative work with higher primates which appears to have been thus far overlooked, and 2) to propose a technique of investigation which will take account of this new factor. Our general thesis is that despite the evidence which indicates that the anthropoid apes are inferior to man in behavioral potentialities, it is quite possible that a radical change in experimental procedure would definitely remove many of those qualitative distinctions that are frequently thought to exist.

THE EFFECT OF ENVIRONMENT

Without recourse to further introductory discussion, we may point the way to the initial arguments to be considered by the following question: What would be the outcome if a human infant, the child of civilized parents, were placed in the environment of the jungle or in some similar situation, and allowed to mature in these surroundings, without language, without clothes, and without the association of other humans? Fortunately it is not necessary to rely entirely upon speculation to answer this question, for a number of cases are on record of the discovery of "wild" children, who have been reared from an early age with little or no human contacts.[1] Although not all such instances are perfectly authenticated, the facts in some of them are established beyond a reasonable doubt.

One of the earliest of these children to attract scientific notice was "Itard's wild boy" who was found in 1798 by a group of French sportsmen (Murphy, 1929, p. 137). The child seemed to be fully ten years old, but he was unable to talk and had been living, so far as could be ascertained, on whatever provender he could find in the forest. He was taken to Paris and after a long period of relatively ineffectual training was pronounced mentally deficient.

The Kasper Hauser case, another notable example, is doubly important because there is no question of its authenticity. This boy, who has been variously regarded as a royal pretender or as an heir to some princely German house, was apparently put out of the way by political

From Kellogg, W. N. 1931. Humanizing the ape. Psychology. Rev. 38:160–176.

* Affiliation given reflects the author's affiliation at time of writing.

[1] According to Murphy (1929, p. 137) about a dozen such foundlings are known to history.

schemers of his time. He was confined alone in a dark cell so small that he could not stand upright till he was 17 years old and was fed on bread and water throughout this period. No one saw him except his keeper. When found in 1828 he could walk only with the greatest difficulty and scarcely knew how to use his hands and fingers. He could not understand what was said to him, was able to speak only one sentence, and was ignorant of the most elementary facts of everyday life. He possessed, however, a remarkably keen sense of smell and a capacity to see in the dark far surpassing that of the average person. Intensive educational training was only partially successful because, according to Tredgold (1915), "the prolonged isolation had wrought an effect upon the brain cells from which they could not completely recover" (p. 301).

Of a number of more recent instances, the "wolf children" of India are probably the most striking. Two of these children, one of whom is presumably still living, were found as recently as 1921 in a cave inhabited by wolves (Squires, 1927). Their ages were estimated at two and eight years respectively. When discovered, they had no language responses and could not walk upright, but instead crawled about on all fours. They ate and drank like dogs, making little or no use of their hands in these activities. The younger of the two died sometime after removal from the cave and the other, a girl, was kept in the household of a Christian missionary, who named her Kamala and who undertook with the assistance of his wife to provide her with a special course of education. At the completion of four years of this training Kamala could speak no more than 40 words and still uttered strange animal-like howls at night. Efforts to break her of the habit of pouncing upon and devouring small birds and mammals had not been successful. Although the child eventually learned to walk, she is reported never to have learned to run.

Instead of supposing that these children were congenitally feeble-minded as has usually been done, I submit that originally they probably possessed an entirely normal equipment of reactions—otherwise survival against the terrific environmental influences would have been impossible. On the strength of this view, it would seem that they had made natural and adequate adjustments to their surroundings. They seem, in fact, to have developed responses which were particularly suited to their immediate contacts. Those placed with wild animals *learned* themselves to be wild animals in a literal sense of the word. When suddenly trans-planted, therefore, to a highly organized society which was entirely foreign to them, they had no adequate responses available and were as a result stigmatized as feeble-minded.

Their inability to acquire the desired kind of behavior even with careful training is assignable to the fact that they had advanced to too mature an age to uproot the fundamental habits so basically entrenched by earlier experience. This explanation follows readily from the recognized importance of the very early years in psychological development. Watson, Kantor, and others have held, in fact, that the baby at birth represents virgin soil which can be cultivated by special training in any direction. Criminals and geniuses are made, therefore, by a genetic process, rather than born. One does not necessarily need, on the strength of this assumption, to conclude that all feeble-minded children, like criminals and geniuses, are feeble-minded as a result of deficiencies in training. Certainly congenital defects prohibit normal development in a great number of cases. With the perfection of efficient methods in clinical psychology, however, a large percentage of children previously diagnosed as feeble-minded have been proven to be sound in all respects except in equipment of acquired reactions. If discovered at an early enough age the "inherited" deficiencies of these individuals have been satisfactorily corrected through specialized education, although this has not been possible if they have persisted too long in their original habits. "Wild" children, according to this view, should be regarded as feeble-minded only to the extent that higher animals raised under like conditions might be expected so to be.

EXPERIMENTAL SUPPORT

Even if one accepts, however, the necessarily great influence of genetic factors, does not the mass of experimental data from animal psychology definitely *prove* the ape inferior to humans? Much of the available evidence appears, indeed, to have been interpreted in this direction. Yerkes, however, who has probably done more work with anthropoids than any other contemporary psychologist, has recently remarked: "It is indicated by current research . . . that behavioral adaptivity is qualitatively similar in man and in anthropoid ape . . ." (1927c, p. 191). Some few comparisons in which the environmental preparation of the humans has been no different from that of animal subjects (anthropoid or otherwise) point strongly as well to a similarity rather than a difference in the abilities studied. Thus Alpert (1928) has shown that young children behave much like Köhler's (1925) chimpanzees in solving similar problems. Hicks and Carr (1912) have demonstrated that man possesses little if any superiority over rats in learning to run a maze; Warden and Baar (1929) have found that birds as well as humans are subject to the Müller-Lyer illusion; and Gesell (1928, pp. 344 ff.), who tested an adult street monkey of the species *Cebus sapajous* with his standardized tests for infants, discovered many similarities to the behavior of young children. Witmer (1909), in fact, at one time examined a trained theatrical chimpanzee, Peter, in the Psychological Clinic of the University of Pennsylvania. The ape was not only able to perform many simple tests commonly employed with children, but even went so far as to imitate the tester in writing the letter "W" on the blackboard—a problem which so far as is known was in every aspect new to the animal. This anthropoid, whose age was probably not more than five or six years, was considered by Witmer to be equivalent on a human scale to a low or middle grade imbecile.

Evidence is indeed not entirely lacking to show that it is possible for primates under certain conditions to perform at least one elementary psychological test more proficiently than humans. A recent study by Tinklepaugh (1928), who worked with one *Macacus cynomologus* and three *Macacus rhesus* monkeys in a modification of the delayed reaction experiment, brought out the surprising fact that these animals were frequently superior to the experimenter and to various observers who entered the laboratory (p. 205). Comparative studies with two twin boys four years and nine months of age showed furthermore that the children exhibited behavior strikingly like that of the monkeys in similar problem situations.

OBJECTIONS TO PREVIOUS INVESTIGATIONS

There are two serious criticisms which may be brought to bear, it seems to me, against nearly all experiments upon the behavior of apes which have thus far been attempted:

1. Since these have been chiefly of the analytical type, e.g., concerned with the study of special abilities such as sensory discrimination, memory, insight, learning, etc., they have necessarily been undertaken with animals at least sufficiently mature to be independent of maternal care. It is doubtful, in fact, if anthropoids have ever been employed for genuine experimental purposes at ages much under two or three years. Hence the most formative period in these animals' lives has been spent with others of their kind in the acquisition of typically infrahuman modes of response. How could they ever be expected under these conditions to develop basic reactions which were not predominantly of an animal nature?

2. A much more significant and generally overlooked point, however, is that without exception the laboratory animal is treated by the experimenter, and by all others with whom he comes in contact, essentially as an animal. Although elaborate precautions are taken to eliminate "secondary cues" during the performance of the tests, *primary cues* of the most disturbing sort are entirely overlooked outside the test periods. The animal is never given a chance to learn human behavior. Everything is against him from the start. He is kept in a cage, in a characteristically animal environment, or he is led about on a chain or leash. He is fed like an animal, must sleep like an animal, and is gaped at

and teased by curious bystanders. He may even be poked with a stick to "see what he will do."

Under the most favorable circumstances he is seldom used for experimental purposes for more than two hours a day. At least seven-eighths of his waking life, therefore, is consumed in typically infrahuman surroundings. Yet all our psychological conclusions regarding his behavior are based upon the short interim of experimentation and fail utterly to take this longer period into account. If the animal can learn laboratory tricks in one-eighth of his time, must he not learn a very great deal in the other seven-eighths even though no specific effort is made to motivate him by hunger or punishment? A conservative inference would be that he is not only permitted to continue in his animal ways by such a procedure, but that he is forced by *environmental circumstances* to remain upon the animal level. Could one honestly anticipate anything different from normal human children reared under like conditions, experimented upon in the same manner, and similarly caged when not being tested?

Even those splendid experiments which have done more than any others to bring out the highest types of behavior in the highest types of animals, e.g., Hobhouse's (1901, pp. 235 ff.) and Köhler's (1925) studies of chimpanzees and Yerkes' work with chimpanzees, orangutan, and gorilla (1916, 1926, 1927a 1927b, 1928) are all subject to these specific criticisms. Considered in the light of their own limiting conditions, their results represent outstanding contributions to the investigation of anthropoid behavior, but as studies of the comparative psychology of humans and animals—and as such they are frequently interpreted—they seem to have ignored completely factors of vital importance. Indeed, the objections of the *Gestalt* psychologists to earlier experiments with animals (Koffka, 1925, pp. 167 ff.) may with some stretching be turned against their own work. Thus it may be said that although Köhler took account of the configural responses of the apes to his experimental situations, his findings are invalid for comparative purposes since he failed to consider the larger *Gestalt* of which the experiments themselves were only a minor figure.

By analogous arguments it can be shown that the anthropoids of Kohts (1924) and Cunningham (1921) which were primarily household pets, could never have risen above typical pet behavior, since the responses integrated by the environment and by the reactions of humans with whom they came in contact were essentially "pet" responses.

THE GENETIC METHOD OF APPROACH

The animal as well as the human must be definitely regarded as a product of its surroundings. There is no justification for ascribing to either a special immunity from environmental influences. Such meager evidence as we have, moreover, points decidedly to the fact that if the environment of an animal is changed sufficiently, *and changed at an early enough age*, entirely different behavioral characteristics will result. Thus Scott (1901) and Conradi (1905) have demonstrated that birds of various species reared with those of other species develop—not the song peculiar to their own kind—but a song like that of the foreign birds with whom they have been reared. The teaching of growing canaries to sing popular melodies has, in fact, since these classical experiments become a well established business (Monro-Wark, 1930). The young are kept from all musical sounds except those of the tune to be acquired, which is played to them several times a day—usually upon a phonograph. Most birds readily develop faithful reproductions of at least one melody which thereafter becomes their characteristic song.[2]

An example of similar type is afforded in the case of the pedigreed German police dog, Fellow, whose master made a point of treating him more like a human than an animal from earliest puppyhood. According to statements of Mr. Jacob Herbert of Detroit, owner of the dog,[3] Fellow was constantly with human companions who verbally directed, instructed, and encouraged him. Never was he whipped. His environment so far as was consistent with social propriety was that of a child instead of a dog.

Fellow was able to understand, as a result of this development, an astoundingly large number of words and to respond to them in such a way as to remove all doubt of his thorough comprehension. He appeared before the Galton Society and the American Psychological Association and was examined many times by competent animal psychologists. Several detailed reports of his activities have been published by Warden (1928a, 1928b) and Warden and Warner (1928). According to the view set forth in this paper, the dog himself is not to be regarded as inherently exceptional. It is his "education" which has been so.

Here then is an animal, lower in the phyletic scale than the anthropoid, which displays surprisingly human characteristics as an outgrowth

---

[2] Z. Y. Kuo has very recently reported a study (The genesis of the cat's responses to the rat, *J. Comp. Psychol.*, 1930, 11:1–35) in which he reared several groups of cats in different environments, some having rats as cage companions while others had only other cats. Of those which lived with the rats none ever killed a rat of the same species with which it was raised, although ample opportunity was afforded. On the other hand, the members of a group which lived only with cats but which were permitted to see their mothers kill rats, all themselves became rat-killers by the time they attained the age of four months. This author holds that if there exists therefore an "instinct" in cats to kill rats, there must also be an "instinct" to love them.

[3] Mr. Herbert is neither a psychologist nor a biologist, but a layman—and a great lover of dogs.

of its near-human environment and treatment. The apes, consequently, which are morphologically closest to the human species, should be capable of much more striking development. Their long period of infancy and their length of life are similar to those of man; their hands permit them to perform many human tasks; their nervous system is markedly superior to those of birds or dogs.

A PROPOSED EXPERIMENT

Suppose an anthropoid were taken into a typical human family at the day of birth and reared as a child. Suppose he were fed upon a bottle, clothed, washed, bathed, fondled, and given a characteristically human environment; that he were spoken to like the human infant from the moment of parturition; that he had an adopted human mother and an adopted human father. Suppose further that he were placed in a baby carriage and wheeled; that he were given selected playmates—young children who would be reared with him—who could be counted on to treat him as an equal and not as an inferior or as an animal; that he were taught to walk on his hind legs as the human child is taught; and similarly that his education and his environment were modified, as he grew, in accordance with the standards of human society.[4]

Under no circumstances should the subject of such an experiment be locked in a cage or led about on a leash. Under no circumstances should he be fed from a plate upon the floor. The criterion for his treatment should be without exception the same as that of a human. Throughout his upbringing his mistakes should be carefully and persistently corrected as are the mistakes of a child.

The experimental situation *par excellence* should indeed be attained if this technique were refined one step farther by adopting such a baby ape into a human family with one child of approximately the ape's age. Genetic case studies of the two individuals could then be undertaken, supplemented by such comparative tests as it seemed feasible to make throughout their development.[5]

Possible results to be achieved from this type of investigation can only be imagined. Theatrical apes have been taught remarkable performances. We know already that many of them eat like humans, dress and undress themselves, ride bicycles, skate on roller skates, smoke cigarettes

---

[4] The general plan for an experiment of this type is by no means original. As far back as 1909 Lightner Witmer wrote, "I venture to predict that within a few years chimpanzees will be taken early in life and subjected for purposes of scientific investigation to a course of procedure more closely resembling that which is accorded the human child" (p. 205).

[5] It would probably not be practicable, however, to continue such an experiment after the organisms had reached the age of five or six years.

(apparently with a relish), and understand a large number of human words. But these activities are learned as mere stunts which are performed only at stated intervals under very special conditions. They are not made integral and necessary parts of the apes' lives. The theatrical animals furthermore, like the experimental ones, are kept in cages or chained much of the time. Their respective environments, again, are predominantly those of an animal world.

WOULD HUMAN SPEECH DEVELOP?

Although the majority of investigators seems to regard human speech as quite beyond the capacity of the anthropoid ape,[6] it is to me not entirely inconceivable that under the genetic process outlined, systematized language responses—at least in rudimentary form—would be found to develop. Observations of chimpanzees have shown that they possess without special training a fairly well organized "emotional language" and that they employ in many cases sounds which appear to be specific to particular behavioral situations.[7] It has long been known furthermore that the anatomy of the vocal mechanism of the higher apes is enough like that of man to permit the possibility of human speech. In fact, the reports of careful investigators indicate that the cry of the newly born orangutan or chimpanzee is hardly distinguishable from that of the human infant.

If then during the process of uttering some infantile wail the ape baby in the human environment happened to close its lips, it would, quite by accident, pronounce the word "ma." Its adopted parents should, however, at this point markedly *increase the stimulation* as is done in the case of a human child. Their activity would be characterized by picking up the infant, hugging and fondling it, repeating the word "ma" to it many times with perhaps additional exclamations of "Baby's first word!" Ultimately this method, which is almost universally practiced with the young of the human species, might lead in the ape as it does in man to the voluntary use of the sound "ma" to indicate the female person who acts in that capacity. By various extensions of this procedure the word "da" and the names of simple objects could next be learned. The same painstaking effort and corrections which are directed toward the acquisition of language responses in the child would, of course, be necessary in the case of the anthropoid.

Unless the ape is lacking in a motor speech area, as some authorities contend, there is a reasonable possibility, it appears to me, that under the

---

[6] Cf. the many references to this topic in Yerkes (1929), Chaps. 13 and 24.

[7] Cf., e.g., Yerkes and Learned (1925).

proposed technique it might develop human speech in the same natural manner that it is integrated by the child. Witmer (1909), Garner (1896), and Furness (1916), in fact, have all reported cases of articulation accurately imitative of human speech in trained anthropoid apes. The latter investigator not only succeeded in getting an orangutan to utter the two words "papa" and "cup" but to say these words, so he believed, both intelligently and meaningfully. The progress in the speech training was, however, slow and laborious, but this again can be accounted for on theoretical grounds by the too-mature age of the animal at the time its education was undertaken.

A VALID BASIS OF COMPARISON

The present relative position of civilized man and the ape and the proposed plan for equating extraneous influences are schematically indicated in the accompanying diagram (Figure 1). M′ represents man as developed on the highest environmental level. M then indicates the original basic man evolved within the lower stratum of uncivilized surroundings. The point A on the parallellogram may serve for the ape who grows up in a situation similar to that of the man, M. The resulting organisms,

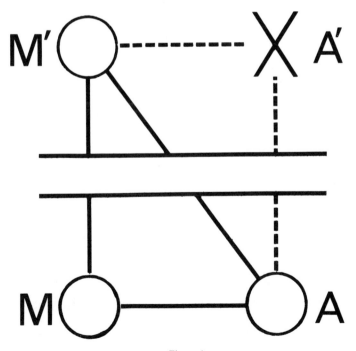

Figure 1.

whether M or A, apparently differ but little, as we have tried to show throughout this paper. That comparisons which have heretofore been made, namely, those between civilized man, M', and the ape, A, are spurious, however, should now appear from the diagonal M'A, since two variables, one of which has previously gone unconsidered, are present in such a comparison. The first of these variables is the difference in organisms, and the second is the difference in training or environment. It remains, however, to complete the figure by means of the experiment outlined. The resulting organism, A', reared upon the same environmental level with M' then becomes comparable to civilized man with the same degree of validity that A and M are comparable at the present time.

POSSIBILITY OF NEGATIVE RESULTS

There can be little doubt that the conceptions upon which the foregoing remarks are based are fundamental. It would be presumptuous, however, to attempt any theoretical interpretation of proposed results before those results, whether they be of value or not, have been attained. It may not be amiss therefore at this point to note that the writer subscribes to no particular theory as a possible explanation of the differences which are supposed to exist between the capacities of man and the infrahumans. Although it may appear from a perusal of these paragraphs that a defense for radical environmentalism has been propounded, such is by no means the object of this report. If undue emphasis seems in fact to have been placed upon environmental factors it is only because the project outlined is more favorably presented from such a position and because one of the chief desiderata has been to point out the importance of extraneous developmental influences.

I fully appreciate furthermore that in presenting arguments intended to emphasize what to me appears to be the importance of this proposed investigation I have subjected myself to possible criticism on the grounds of gross anthropomorphism. In order therefore to give adequate weight to the opposite side of the case we list below a few fairly obvious morphological and physiological distinctions which suggest possible differences in behavior between the ape and the child even though environmental factors are equated as completely as possible.

1.   The first and most significant of these is the considerably smaller brain size of the anthropoids.[8] Upon the assumption of a close cor-

---

[8] F. Tilney (1928, II, p. 567) reports that the chimpanzee brain occupies about one-fourth the volume of the human brain.

relation between neurological development and behavioral capacity, the ape might thus at the start be expected to be inferior to the human in tasks of any complexity.

2.   The relatively longer and stronger arms of the anthropoid, it may be supposed, would lead to greater aptitude in climbing than that possessed by the human. To the extent that it became necessary to curb this supposed tendency to climb more in one organism than in the other the upbringing of the two would necessarily differ.

3.   None of the anthropoid apes possesses the *opposable thumb*, with the power of bringing the thumb against each of the fingers, which is so well developed in man (Osborn, 1915). Probably this would result in differences in manual dexterity. The greater facility with which the ape manipulates objects with its feet could be readily eliminated, however, by the use of shoes.

4.   If the orangutan were selected for an experiment of this kind, a further structural distinction is to be pointed out, since this ape when walking erect steps on the outside of its feet, curling the toes inward. The chimpanzee and gorilla, however, tread on the soles of the feet like man.

5.   The somewhat more rapid rate at which the anthropoid infant begins to crawl and stand is also to be remarked. It has been maintained that an ape of one year is about equivalent in physiology and behavior to the human baby of twice that age. The period of adolescence and the growth of the permanent teeth, however, suggest that the ape during later childhood is in advance of the human by an interval variously estimated at from two to four years. Giving the human baby in this experiment a year's advantage in age would do much to balance this inequality.

6.   Other less apparent distinctions would doubtless appear when direct comparisons could be made.

It is entirely possible, therefore, that the findings of the proposed investigation would be predominantly negative in character. I cannot believe, however, that this would seriously vitiate its significance, since either negative or positive results should be of some importance not only to psychology and education, but to biology and sociology as well. Some light in addition should be thrown by this means upon the ancient controversy between the environmentalists and the hereditarians. If demonstrable differences in behavior existed at any given stage of training, and if the environmental factors had without question been held constant throughout that training, then the conclusion that the differences were due to native influences would be well-nigh unimpeachable. It could be maintained, should such results be secured, that the ape, given full opportunities to acquire a complete repertoire of human reactions, had progressed only part of the way.

SUMMARY

The chief points which we have endeavored to bring out in the preceding sections may be summarized briefly as follows:

1. There is some evidence which indicates that human children, if kept throughout the early impressionable years in surroundings similar to those of wild animals, develop permanent behavior traits which are more like those of animals than of humans.

2. Comparative psychology, however, seems largely to have overlooked the tremendous role played by environmental influences upon captive wild animals before they are captured and brought to the laboratory. It is probable in fact that anthropoid apes have rarely if ever been obtained for experimental purposes at young enough ages to preclude their already having acquired basic infrahuman modes of reaction.

3. A further criticism which may be levied against most experiments with the higher primates is that the experimenter and all others who observe captive specimens, although meticulous with reference to the elimination of "secondary cues" during laboratory tests, are likely to introduce unwittingly *primary cues* of a seriously disturbing nature when experiments are not in progress. The effect of this extra-experimental stimulation may be not only to stamp-in existing animal reactions, but even to integrate in the animals many additional responses of the same character. The current practices of confining anthropoids in cages most of the time and of leading them about on chains, must certainly be conducive as well to typical infrahuman activity.

4. We have suggested that procedures of this sort are at least partly responsible for the failure to elicit more human-like behavior from anthropoid apes. Such factors may therefore be regarded, it appears to us, as invalidating in large measure those conclusions which infer that the ape is *naturally* inferior in various capacities to man.

5. Since it is manifestly impossible to impress upon a human subject environmental influences identical to those of captive animals, we have proposed as a fair experiment which will permit a valid comparison of the behavior of these organisms that an infant ape be adopted *at birth* into a human family and be raised, not as a pet, but in all respects exactly as a child. It has been suggested furthermore that the ideal situation would be to bring up the anthropoid with a human baby of about the same age, so that genetic case studies of the two individuals would be possible.

6. How far the ape would develop in these surroundings is of course a matter of conjecture, but the possibility cannot be denied that if this animal is at all capable of acquiring human speech, it would probably do so in a situation of this kind.

7. We have also tried to consider at some length the opposite possibility, viz., that the outcome of this genetic investigation would be chiefly negative so far as the animal subject is concerned. In either event it has seemed to us that the results attained would adequately compensate for the difficulties to be encountered in such an undertaking, since the findings of an experiment of this nature, regardless of its outcome, should be of considerable scientific importance.

Arrangements for the carrying out of an experiment of the type outlined with an anthropoid ape and a human child are at present being formulated. If the plans can be satisfactorily consummated we hope to be able through later papers to report the progress of the work.

REFERENCES

Alpert, A. 1928. The solving of problem-situations by preschool children; an analysis. T. C. Contrib. Educ. No. 323.

Conradi, E. 1905. Song and call-notes of English sparrows when reared by canaries, Am. J. Psychol. 16:190–198.

Cunningham, A. 1921. A gorilla's life in civilization. Bull. Zool. Soc. N.Y. 24:118–124.

Furness, W. H. 1916. Observations upon the mentality of chimpanzees and orangutans. Proc. Am. Phil. Soc. Phila. 55:283–285.

Garner, R. L. 1896. Gorillas and chimpanzees. London.

Gesell, A. 1928. Infancy and Human Growth. Macmillan Publishing Co., New York.

Hicks, V. C., and Carr, H. A. 1912. Human reactions in a maze. J. Anim. Behav. 2:98–125.

Hobhouse, L. T. 1901. Mind in Evolution. Macmillan Publishing Co., New York.

Koffka, K. 1925. The Growth of the Mind. Harcourt, Brace, New York.

Köhler, W. 1925. The Mentality of Apes. Harcourt, Brace, New York.

Kohts, N. 1924. Untersuchungen über die Erkenntnisfähigkeiten des Schimpansen. Moscow. (Summarized by R. M. Yerkes and A. Petrunkevitch. 1925. J. Comp. Psychol. 5:98–108.)

Monro-Wark, P. 1930. Mrs. McCoy coaches feathered prima donnas. Am. Mag. 109:69–70.

Murphy, G. 1929. Historical Introduction to Modern Psychology. Harcourt, Brace, New York.

Osborn, H. F. 1915. Men of the Old Stone Age. Charles C. Scribners, New York.

Scott, W. E. D. 1901. Data on song in birds. Science. 14:522–526; 1902, 15:178–181.

Squires, P. C. 1927. "Wolf-children" of India. Am. J. Psychol. 38:313–315.

Tilney, F. 1928. The Brain from Ape to Man. Hoeber, New York.

Tinklepaugh, O. L. 1928. An experimental study of representative factors in monkeys. J. Comp. Psychol. 8:197–236.

Tredgold, A. F. 1915. Mental deficiency. William Wood, New York.

Warden, C. J. 1928a. The ability of "Fellow," famous German shepherd dog, to understand language. J. Genet. Psychol. 35:330–331.

Warden, C. J. 1928b. The sensory capacities and intelligence of dogs with a report on the ability of the noted dog "Fellow" to respond to verbal stimuli (Proc. Galton Soc.). Eug. News 13:2–6.

Warden, C. J. and Baar, J. 1929. The Müller-Lyer illusion in the ring dove, *Turtur risorius*. J. Comp. Psychol. 9:275–292.

Warden, C. J., and Warner, L. H. 1928. The sensory capacities and intelligence of dogs, with a report on the ability of the noted dog "Fellow" to respond to verbal stimuli. Q. Rev. Biol. 3:1–28.

Witmer, L. 1909. A monkey with a mind. Psychol. Clin. Phila. 3:179–205.

Yerkes, R. M. 1916. The mental life of monkeys and apes; a study of ideational behavior. Behav. Monogr. 3:No. 1.

Yerkes, R. M. 1926. Almost Human. Century, New York.

Yerkes, R. M. 1927a. The mind of a gorilla. Genet. Psychol. Monogr. 2:Nos. 1–2, 1–193.

Yerkes, R. M. 1927b. The mind of a gorilla: Part II. Mental development. Genet. Psychol. Monogr. 2:375–551.

Yerkes, R. M. 1927c. A program of anthropoid research. Am. J. Psychol. 39(Washburn Com. Vol.):181–199.

Yerkes, R. M. 1928. The mind of a gorilla: Part III. Memory. Comp. Psychol. Monogr. 5:No. 2.

Yerkes, R. M. 1929. The Great Apes. Yale University Press, New Haven, Conn.

Yerkes, R. M., and Learned, B. W. 1925. Chimpanzee Intelligence and Its Vocal Expressions. Williams & Wilkins, Baltimore.

chapter

7

Pre-Linguistic Sign Behavior
in Chimpanzee

Robert M. Yerkes*

Henry W. Nissen*

Laboratory of Primate Biology
Yale University
New Haven, Connecticut

The expression "symbolic behavior" has been used frequently for types of adaptation which resist explanation by accepted principles of "animal learning," or even as substitute for "insight" and "higher mental processes." It is true that some of the most impressive contrasts between the behavioral capacities of man and other primates may be attributed to linguistic process or neural mechanism which is present in the former and either absent or rudimentary in the latter. Thus the great difficulty of double alternation (Hunter, 1928) and temporal maze (Spragg, 1936) problems for animals other than man may be attributed to inability to count. Likewise, differences in ability to respond to complex, obscure, or novel relations, as in multiple-choice problems (Yerkes, 1934), in rate of acquiring simple discrimination habits and in various tests of "reasoning" and "insight," are subject to a similar anthropomorphic explanation.

Analysis reveals, however, that many of these manifestations of behavioral adaptivity can be accounted for, without the postulation of symbolic processes, in terms of innate and acquired perceptual organization, generalization, transfer, processes involved in delayed conditioning, and other relatively simple and widely applicable determinants of animal behavior. For example, performance in double alternation and temporal maze experiments might be explained as differential conditioning to two stimuli in a series of intraorganic stimulus-responses initiated by the external situation. Logically viewed, adaptive response to relations of varying degrees of complexity and unusualness, as widely exhibited in the animal kingdom, should not require the appearance of an entirely new process at some point in the series of events. Indeed, few if any of the attempts to account for tool using or construction and for other presumptively "insightful" problem solutions, occasionally exhibited by animals, have excluded the possibility that perceptual organization and transfer may suffice as principles of explanation.

Considerations, elsewhere discussed (Hunter, 1913, 1924; Nissen, Riesen, and Nowlis, 1938), which suggest the operation of symbolic processes in delayed response will be summarized briefly. In infrahuman animals the establishment of a discrimination habit *in the absence of spatial cues* commonly requires a large number of differential rewards and frustrations, whereas the establishment of a comparable habit in delayed response tests *when spatial cues are available* may occur in a single trial and with signified versus actual reinforcement (Cowles and Nissen, 1937). This contrast may be accounted for by the relative obtrusiveness and prepotency of the two varieties of cue or by the diversity of mechanism operative in the two cases. Man adapts as promptly to the delayed response type of situation without spatial cues as with them. It

From Yerkes, R. M., and Nissen, H. W. 1939. Pre-linguistic sign behavior in chimpanzee. Science 89:585–587. Reprinted by permission.

* Affiliation given reflects the authors' affiliation at time of writing.

seems probable that his success is due entirely to capacity for linguistic response—use of symbols for white-black or right-left, as the case may be. The diverse observations cited may be brought into relation by assuming 1) that delayed response requires the mediation of a symbolic process and 2) that some of the vertebrates are capable of symbolic response to spatial but not to nonspatial cues. The latter assumption is strongly supported by the relative frequency and evident significance of spatial factors in the lives of most animals.

For present purposes a symbolic process may be conceived of as a differential, and usually implicit, response established by previous training, whose "meaning," as exemplified by its positive or negative valence, is extremely labile. The sign response is differential in the sense and to the extent that it varies for different stimuli. It is especially significant that unambiguous differential delayed conditioning has been reported only for cases in which the stimuli were spatially differentiated. In discriminational behavior, including delayed response, lability of the consequences of sign response is manifest by the readiness with which approach and avoidance may replace one another. This feature of symbolic behavior distinguishes it from all instances of habit acquisition, including delayed conditioning, in which the nature or direction of the overt response is fixed only after many trials and can be changed or reversed with difficulty. This characterization of symbolic process differs to some extent from all the many definitions proposed. It is less limited than most of them, more specific than some. In common with other conceptions of symbol, it exhibits relationships to language, the outstanding difference in this respect appearing in what Morris (1938, pp. 29ff.) designates as the "pragmatical dimension of semiosis." We are interested in the experimental and systematic consequences of the concept of symbolic process, not in the problem of terminology.

Inasmuch as it has been demonstrated (Nissen, Riesen, and Nowlis, 1938) that delayed response in the absence of spatial cues is possible for young chimpanzees, but only after very extensive training, it seemed to us not improbable that mature individuals, with the advantage of more varied experience, might possess this ability in higher degree and consequently be capable of prompt adaptation. To test this possibility, a survey was made of the reactive capacities of members of the Yale chimpanzee colony.

Twenty-four individuals (19 adult, 5 adolescent, 4 male, 20 female) were tested in the summer of 1938 by the following procedure. After brief preliminary training of a subject, two rectangular wooden boxes, with hinged lids, the one painted white, the other black, were displayed before the animal and it was permitted to see a piece of apple placed in the box at its right. Thereupon the boxes were taken up by the experimenter and shifted in position relative to one another beyond the range of the subject's vision. They were then presented before the netting wall of the animal's cage in such manner that it could definitely indicate its choice by lifting the lid of one box. The food-containing or correct box might be at the right, left, above, or below a central point, and the white and black boxes were used with equal daily frequency and in irregular, predetermined order.

At the outset the experimenter shifted the boxes by turning his back upon the subject. At first two, and later 4, trials were given per day. Under these simple conditions most of the subjects were given 96 trials. (In 9 cases the trials varied between 45 and 95.) The interval during which a box was hidden from a subject was not more than 2 or 3 seconds.

During this phase of the investigation, individual differences in the pattern of response and degree of success were extreme. Thus some individuals tried to follow the boxes visually as they were being shifted; others did not. Some acted as if keenly interested, eager, and expectant of success; others as if relatively indifferent or lacking confidence in their ability to secure the food. The percentages of correct response for individuals ranged from 44% to 99%. The average for all individuals in a total of 2,183 trials is 65%. The subject who succeeded best made only one mistake in 96 trials, although she apparently made no effort to follow the boxes visually or to maintain direction of attention or bodily orientation during the brief interval of delay.

On the basis of the above results, the eight individuals with highest scores (99%, 94%, 90%, 86%, 81%, 72%, 72%, 69% correct) were selected for further use. Each subject was given a series of 10 trials daily, with predetermined order of use of the white and black boxes and of the presentational position and relation of the boxes. Shift of the boxes was effected behind an opaque screen, and they were invisible to the subject during this process for not more than 5 to 8 seconds.

In their first hundred trials these eight animals ranged from 44% to 58% correct choices. Success in daily series varied from 20% to 90%. Six subjects were above 50% correct, the chance score.

Once more the most successful subjects were selected and the experiment continued with five individuals. There was no immediate change in procedure. Success varied between 57% and 64% in the second hundred trials. For the third hundred, effort was made to attract the attention of the subject to the correct box by holding it up to view after it had been baited and by pointing to it as the subject watched box and experimenter.

At the end of the third hundred trials the experiment was discontinued because of evidence of diminishing success and varied behavioral indications of increasing discouragement and frustration. Witness the percentages for the last hundred trials, which range from 43% to

63% and also the results for the total series of 300 trials when percentages are figured by successive groups of 50 trials: 47.8%, 55.8%, 59.6%, 61.6%, 51.6%, 58.4%.

The accompanying condensed table (Table 1) presents data for the five subjects (two males and three females, ages 8 to 14 years) who were used in the preliminary stages of the investigation and throughout the 300 trials reported in the table.

Behavior in these tests indicated adequacy of motivation, and as a rule diligence of effort to choose the correct box in order to obtain the food. There were many daily series in which success exceeded chance by 20% to 40% but in no case was perfection of response achieved, even for a single daily series. The degree of success exhibited, together with the behavior of the subjects in making their choices, convince us that some cue or cues, unobservable directly by us, were operative. Among them may have appeared symbolic process representative of white box or black box. But, if this occurred, it is clear that it did not function readily and smoothly, for the subjects obviously worked very hard to adapt to a situation which for the normal human being is extremely easy, and, moreover, they often were much disturbed emotionally. It appears that, whereas the "thereness" of the correct box may readily be responded to by the chimpanzee, the "thatness"—as exemplified by a symbolic process equivalent to rectangular whiteness—is used with difficulty and uncertainty. Nevertheless, it is our opinion, based upon the results of varied and long-continued training experiments, that symbolic processes occasionally occur in the chimpanzee; that they are relatively rudimentary and ineffective; and that our experiments with subjects ranging in stage of development from early childhood to maturity have supplied no convincing evidence of the increase in frequency and functional value of symbolic response with increase in experience and age.

Table 1.

| Subjects | Average percent correct | | | | Range in per-cent |
	1–100 trials	101–200 trials	201–300 trials	Total	
Alpha	54.0	59.0	63.0	58.7	30–90
Bimba	54.0	57.0	61.0	57.3	30–80
Bokar	54.0	64.0	56.0	58.0	40–80
Frank	58.0	60.0	43.0	53.7	20–90
Lia	53.0	63.0	52.0	56.0	20–90
Total correct	54.6	60.6	55.0	56.7	
Total W correct	52.0	57.2	54.0	54.4	
Total B correct	57.2	64.0	56.0	59.1	

In our findings we consider most significant the evidence that delayed response, in the absence of spatial cues or with misleading cues, is either extremely difficult or impossible for most chimpanzees. This suggests that we may have happened upon an early phylogenetic stage in the evolution of symbolic process. There is abundant evidence that various other types of sign process than the symbolic (Esper, 1935, pp. 426ff.; Morris, 1938, pp. 17ff.) are of frequent occurrence and function effectively in the chimpanzee.

REFERENCES

Cowles, J. T., and Nissen, H. W. 1937. J. Comp. Psychol. 24:345–358.

Esper, E. A. 1935. Chapter 11 in A Handbook of Social Psychology. Clark University Press, Worcester, Mass.

Hunter, W. S. 1913. Behav. Monogr. 2:1.

Hunter, W. S. 1924. Psychol. Rev. 31:478–497.

Hunter, W. S. 1928. J. Genet. Psychol. 35:380ff.

Morris, C. W. 1938. Foundations of the Theory of Signs. University of Chicago Press, Chicago.

National Resources Committee. 1938 (December). Research—a National Resource. (1) Relation of the federal government to research.

Nissen, H. W., Riesen, A. H., and Nowlis, V. 1938. J. Comp. Psychol. 26:361–386.

Spragg, S. D. S. 1936. Comp. Psychol. Monogr. 13:2, 38ff.

Yerkes, R. M. 1934. Comp. Psychol. Monogr. 10:1, 89ff.

chapter 8

The Cultural Capacity of Chimpanzee[1]

Keith J. Hayes*

Catherine Hayes*

Yerkes Laboratories of Primate Biology, Inc.
Orange Park, Florida

contents

From Hayes, K. J., and Hayes, C. 1954. The Cultural Capacity of Chimpanzee. Hum. Biol. 26:288–303. Reprinted by permission of The Wayne State University Press. © 1954 The Wayne State University Press.

* Affiliation given reflects the authors' affiliation at time of writing.

The problem with which we are here concerned has been referred to by Kroeber (1948) as "the unknown organic basis of the faculty for culture" (p. 69).[2] What sequence of events in organic evolution was necessary to prepare our presumably anthropoid ancestors for the way of life that uniquely characterizes man?

We have approached this question by way of the assumption that man's ancestry includes, at some stage, a species which was physically and behaviorally similar to the modern chimpanzee—in a general way, if not in detail.[3] (This assumption is not entirely unreasonable, but its main virtue is convenience: chimpanzees are available for behavioral research.)

[1] The work reported here has been assisted by grants from the American Philosophical Society, The Samuel S. Fels Fund, and by research grant M669 from The National Institute of Mental Health, U. S. Public Health Service. Footnotes 2, 3, 4, and 6 have been added in response to comments made by W. L. Straus, Jr., in his "concluding remarks" on the symposium.

[2] We are surprised by Straus' comment that "culture" is virtually undefinable, especially in view of his recent statement (1953) that culture "implies social inheritance from one generation to another," and that "man, or the genus *Homo*, may then be defined as an animal possessing a culture, for it is this feature that particularly distinguishes him from all other animals" (p. 262). Others use the term in the same way, without making an issue of its definition (e.g., Kroeber, 1948, p. 8; Dobzhansky and Ashley Montagu, 1947, p. 587). Moore and Lewis (1952) have discussed the operational definition of culture at some length, but their product differs from others primarily in its unfortunate interaction with the definition of "hominid." Brief definitions are poor substitutes for thorough discussions, which are plentiful in the literature, and which indicate that most anthropologists use the term "culture" consistently, and know what it means.

[3] This is perhaps ambiguous. We do not assume that man's ancestry includes a form which resembled the chimpanzee more closely than it did the orangutan or gorilla. We merely assume an ancestor of broadly "anthropoid" type, which was enough like the modern chimpanzee to make our study of the latter relevant. The chimpanzee provides a good "model" for our purpose: it has many of the characteristics that man's ancestors are presumed to have had, and it is not highly specialized, in the sense of being irrevocably committed to a narrow adaptive zone. (The chimpanzee is capable of a variety of modes of locomotion, and can utilize a variety of foods obtained in a variety of ways (Yerkes, 1943, p. 15; Yerkes and Yerkes, 1929, pp. 213–216.)

It is generally agreed that man's ancestry passed through a 400 gram brain stage and a 50 kilogram body weight stage. Most, though not all students (Straus, 1949) consider it likely that man's ancestors were structurally adapted for brachiation, at one stage. One of the purposes of this investigation is to evaluate the possibility that an animal with these structural characteristics could have entered the human, or cultural, adaptive zone. If it could, we see no reason to doubt that it could subsequently have made whatever progressive adjustments this adaptive zone favored—even though such adjustments might involve reversal of earlier adjustments to other adaptive zones.

There is some reason to suppose that the African apes have already undergone considerable reversal of the brachiating specialization. Despite common belief (Straus, 1949; Hooton, 1942), the Hylobatidae are the only living apes that actually use brachiation as a usual or important mode of locomotion (Yerkes and Yerkes, 1929, p. 537; Nissen, 1931, p. 34). Although the other anthropoids, including chimpanzee, are "brachiators" in a structural sense, they show this adaptation in very attenuated form, as compared with the Hylobatidae. The large apes may reasonably be thought of as descendants of a siamang-like species, who have long since ceased to be selected for brachiation, and whose brachiating structure has been modified toward a more generally useful form. (This interpretaion is supported by consideration of the laryngeal air sac, which is prominent and possibly functional in the siamang, but small and almost certainly nonfunctional in the living African apes.)

We have attempted to estimate the extent to which characteristics essential for culture were already present in this hypothetical, chimpanzee-like ancestor.

Our procedure has involved the intensive study of Viki, a chimpanzee who has spent the first six years of her life in our home and has been treated as nearly as possible like a human child (Hayes, 1951; Hayes and Hayes, 1950). This approach is necessitated by the fact that the behavior of man or any other animal may be markedly influenced by experience—a fact which is seldom denied but which is, unfortunately, often overlooked in comparative psychology (Harlow, 1949; Hebb, 1949).

We have given special attention to our subject's social behavior, and particularly to her communicative ability—since communication is the primary prerequisite for culture. We have also been concerned with her use of implements, since tool using is a prominent feature of all known cultures.[4]

It seems conceivable, a priori, that cultural capacity might have developed through evolutionary changes of three general types: 1) changes in gross anatomy, 2) development of special mental abilities, and 3) changes in motivational makeup. We will examine each of these possibilities in some detail.

CHANGES IN GROSS ANATOMY

The Hand

It might be supposed that considerable modification of the anthropoid hand would be needed to make it adequate for skillful tool using. However, our data do not support this hypothesis; our subject uses a great variety of tools, and she uses them skillfully and easily enough to be of considerable practical value to her (Figures 1 and 2).[5] The relative shortness of her thumb does not, despite common belief, prevent her grasping small objects between thumb and forefinger (Figure 3). We suspect that another peculiarity of the chimapanzee hand, less often mentioned in the literature, may cause more difficulty. This is the lack of dorsiflexion of the wrist (Straus, 1940) which sometimes makes it hard to

---

[4] Invention and construction of tools are important too, of course; however, one of the prime functions of culture is to relieve the average individual of much of the burden of creation, by allowing him to utilize the products of his more capable fellows—as pointed out, e.g., by Hooton (1942, p. xxxix). In particular, six-year-old children need not, and normally do not, invent or construct tools to a practically significant extent. For this reason we are postponing a detailed account of Viki's creative activities to a later and more appropriate date.

[5] Viki's use of tools is illustrated extensively in a 16-mm silent film (Hayes and Hayes, 1953).

Figure 1.   Lighting a cigarette at six years.

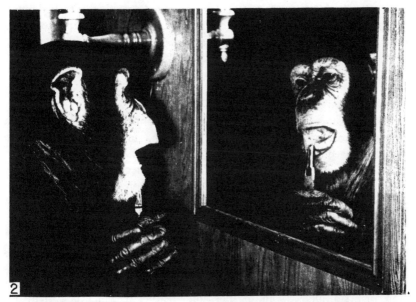

Figure 2.   Trying to pull a loose tooth with pliers and mirror (six years).

Figure 3.   Holding a cigarette with good thumb opposition (six years).

position a tool properly, after it has been grasped. However, this is not a really serious impediment to tool using. Functional plasticity tends to outweigh structural rigidity. If Viki's dexterity is greater than that observed in most other chimpanzees, the discrepancy is readily understandable in terms of the oft-neglected factor of experience. Most chimpanzees have much less opportunity to develop their manual skill than human children have. Also, it must be remembered that many of the tools we ask chimpanzees to use were designed specifically to fit human hands, and are ill-suited for use by chimpanzees. The chimpanzee hand performs rather poorly with our shears, for instance; but it would probably operate quite effectively with shears designed to fit it (Kroeber, 1948, p. 68).

Posture

It has been suggested that modification of the anthropoid posture was the first and most basic step in human evolution, since bipedal locomotion would be needed to free the hands for the use of tools (e.g., Washburn, 1950). However, if evolution operates by selection, rather than by foresight, tool using must have appeared first. Only then could the intrinsically inefficient, bipedal mode of locomotion be favored in selection (Bartholomew and Birdsell, 1953, p. 482). We seriously doubt that precultural tool using, on an individual basis, would be of sufficient importance to permit bipedalism, and we therefore suggest that cultural tool using appeared when posture was still of the anthropoid type. This seems entirely possible. Most of man's tool using occurs in a sitting position, or a stationary, standing position—neither of which is difficult for chimpanzees (Figure 5 and 6). So far as the transportation of implements

Figure 4.   Carrying a heavy box at four years.

is concerned, a chimpanzee can carry small objects in all four extremities while walking quadrupedally, and heavy objects can be carried in both arms, while walking upright—for short distances, at least (Figure 4).[6]

Speech Organs

The anthropoid lungs, larynx, and mouth have commonly been considered adequate for the production of speech sounds. However, Kelemen (1948) has recently ascribed the absence of speech in chimpanzee to its laryngeal structure. We are not prepared to evaluate Keleman's anatomical study as such, but we can say with confidence that he is mistaken about its functional significance. It may be true, as he reports, that the chimpanzee larynx is more complex than man's, but it is not true that chimpanzee voice production is more complex than man's, and therefore useless for speech. Chimpanzee vocalization does not differ appreciably from ours in its use of inspired breath or double tones, and the chimpanzee's air sac is not involved in vocalization. Chimpanzees can and do produce a variety of vowel and consonant sounds.

Brain Size

Controversy over the classification of extinct primates often centers around their cranial capacities. Unless the brain was large enough, the

---

[6] Contrary to Straus's interpretation, these two paragraphs have not denied "morphological and physiological changes in [non-neural] parts of the body an important role in the evolution of human behavior." We *do* deny that changes of this type were prerequisite to the transition from anthropoid behavior to cultural behavior. The omission of certain changes might have led to "men" whose behavior, while quite different from ours, would still be cultural, and in this sense "human."

Figure 5.   Digging with a spoon at five years.

Figure 6.   Throwing a toy to knock down a lure at three years.

creature presumably could not have been sufficiently "intelligent" to behave like a man, and must therefore have been an ape. We do not know of course, just how large a brain is "large enough," though Keith (1948, p. 206) has boldly drawn the line at 750 cc. The matter is obscured by the vague manner in which the term "intelligence" is often used. However, if this word is defined operationally in one of the various possible ways, we still have no definite information about its relation to the size of the brain or any of its parts. In the absence of data we venture to speculate as follows: Such processes as forming or retaining an association, perceiving a relationship, drawing an inference, or generalizing a principle, should be relatively independent of sheer mass of tissue. We consider it likely that the quantity of brain is primarily related to a quantitative aspect of its function—specifically to its information-handling capacity. One of the most distinctive tasks imposed upon the human brain by man's cultural way of life is the assimilation and storage of a tremendous amount of information. On the other hand, the chimpanzee's 400 gram brain seems to be fully capable of handling all the useful information likely to be encountered directly by the individual. From this point of view, an increase in the size of the anthropoid brain would be of no advantage to its possessor, so long as he continued to lead a non-cultural existence. We suggest the possibility that most of the fourfold increase in cranial capacity, from anthropoid to man, took place after the appearance of culture and language, and therefore after primate behavior had become essentially human.[7]

SPECIAL MENTAL ABILITIES

The second type of evolutionary change which may, conceivably, have led to the appearance of culture, is the development of complex patterning in the fine structure of the brain, which would provide special mental abilities not adequately developed at the anthropoid level. These micro-anatomical details would be inaccessible not only to paleontological methods, but also to present histological techniques, so this kind of structural evolution could be known only by inference from behavioral data (Lashley, 1947).

This brings us to the question of whether chimpanzees are deficient, as compared with man, in their neurological capacity for behavior which may be characterized as, for instance, abstract, symbolic, conceptual,

---

[7] Thorndike et al. (1927, p. 415) have suggested that the innate component of intelligence is nothing more than the number of potential associative bonds available in the brain. We have made one abortive attempt to deal with information capacity experimentally, but there is still considerable doubt whether this will ever be practical (Hayes, Thompson, and Hayes, 1953).

relational, insightful, or foresightful. These concepts appear to have their sources in the complex behavior (or introspection) of sophisticated humans. This may account for the difficulty of defining them in terms of experimental operations applicable to noncultural, nonlinguistic, and uneducated subjects (e. g., Seward, 1948, p. 280).

Man does not display these "higher mental functions" in a vacuum, but only in the context of skills and information which have been acquired through experience. A primate who has not acquired the same skills and information can hardly be expected to display these functions in the same form as man. If a primate's background of experience is sufficiently restricted, he may fail to display any "higher functions" in any form whatever—simply because of his lack of skills and information and regardless of the detailed structure of his brain. There have been only a few experimental studies which bear directly on this question, but they tend to support the hypothesis that "higher mental abilities" are acquired rather than inherited.

Tasks which involve the integration of events separated by an interval of time are sometimes said to require special "symbolic processes," and it is known that such tasks are extremely difficult for naive chimpanzees (Hallowell, 1950, p. 165; Yerkes, 1943, p. 188). Several studies have shown, however, that this difficulty may be eliminated by prior experience with simple, discrimination-learning problems (Harlow, 1944; Hayes and Thompson, 1953; Riesen, 1940).

It was once possible to suppose that learning by observation, as contrasted with direct experience, depended on some faculty which was confined primarily to man. Here again, however, an adequate background of experience has been found to make such learning very easy for other primates (Harlow, 1944; Hayes and Hayes, 1952).

In short, when the factor of experience is considered, there is no clear evidence that chimpanzees are deficient in any hypothetical, higher mental faculties. Furthermore, it may be questioned whether these special abilities actually exist, as such, even in man. We are inclined to favor Thorndike's hypothesis that "in their deeper nature the higher forms of intellectual operation are identical with mere association or connection forming, depending upon the same sort of physiological connections but requiring *many more of them*" (Thorndike et al., 1927, p. 415). We suggest that the "higher mental functions" observed in man are more nearly results of culture than causes of it.

MOTIVATIONAL MAKEUP

The third and last type of evolutionary development concerns the neural mechanisms which cause an animal to engage in various kinds of activity

(Harlow, 1953). These mechanisms are presumably microanatomical and inaccessible to direct observation but may be inferred from behavior. We are not particularly interested in the drives which cause an animal to eat, drink, and reproduce, but rather in the play drives—the innate tendencies toward behavior which serve no immediate, practical purpose. Such behavior has survival value because it provides opportunity for the acquisition of skills and information which may later be useful in the solution of practical problems. To avoid any irrelevant connotations of the word "play" (Beach, 1945; Schlosberg, 1947) and to indicate explicitly the significance of this phenomenon, we offer the alternative term "experience-producing drives."

Cultural living, as we know it, requires an adequate background of experience in at least two broad areas: mechanical and social. The first is essential to the technological aspect of culture and the second to communication and cooperative enterprise.

Mechanical Play

The chimpanzee resembles man very closely in mechanical interest. Our subject, Viki, spends a large part of her time playing with tools, toys, and household equipment, as well as with more primitive materials, such as sand, sticks, and water. This extensive mechanical play, coupled with the dexterity mentioned earlier, permits the chimpanzee to develop a very respectable amount of mechanical ability. It is our belief that no further evolution would be necessary to prepare the chimpanzee for the tool-using side of cultural life.

Social and Communicative Play

Chimpanzees also resemble man quite closely in preference for social play. Viki likes simple games which involve tickling, wrestling, chasing, and teasing; and it seems likely that such communicative ability as she has was acquired largely in the course of such play. However, she is markedly deficient in one type of drive which is very prominent in man—the drive toward specifically communicative and linguistic play.

This type of play appears as babbling in the human child, early in the first year of life, and provides extensive practice in the motor skills of producing and combining speech sounds. During the next few years, after the child has learned the elements of speech, he takes great interest in learning new words—most of which have no practical value for him at the time, though they may be useful later. For the rest of the child's life, a large proportion of his speech satisfies no more immediate, practical need than that for self expression.

In the infant chimpanzee, however, vocal play is almost completely absent. During her first five months, Viki babbled enough to show that her vocal apparatus was capable of producing a variety of vowel and consonant sounds; however, she did much less of this than human infants do, and the activity did not persist nearly so long (Hayes, 1951, p. 63).

After their first year, many chimpanzees engage in a type of sound-producing play which is somewhat similar to babbling; however, the sounds are produced by mouth movements only, without use of the larynx, and usually without use of the lungs. Some of these sounds closely resemble the "clicks" which form a part of certain human languages. Viki has produced only six of these sounds, and has shown no tendency to combine them in groups. They could thus provide only a very limited potential vocabulary.

Viki readily imitates our production of her mouth sounds and learns meanings which we assign to them. She can thus ask for a drink by saying "ch" (with the German pronunciation, as in *Ich*), or for a cigarette by saying "tsk," or for a ride in the car by clicking her teeth together. However, unlike the human child who has just begun to speak, Viki uses her words only for the practical purpose of getting what she wants. She does not engage in purely sociable conversation, or egocentric expression. She does not even use her words for practical purposes, if she can show us what she wants without them. When she wants a cup of cocoa, for instance, she silently leads us to the kitchen and hands us the ingredients. Only if we refuse to be led and stubbornly ask, "What do you want?" does she say, "ch."[8]

We suggest that the most important step in the evolution of modern man from an anthropoid ancestor was an increase in the experience-producing drives relevant to the skills of communication. Others have hypothesized that apes do not talk because they have nothing to say (Kroeber, 1928, p. 329). This seems to us like an inadequate reason—it does not keep people from talking. Furthermore, we have found that Viki often does have things to say. We contend that apes do not talk because unlike man, they have no inclination to talk when there is nothing to be said.

We have, in the past, suggested that chimpanzees may be innately deficient in some neurological mechanism which provides the capacity to learn language (Hayes, 1951, p. 66). We still consider it conceivable that if a chimpanzee and a human child both had the same language experience, the chimpanzee might learn much less language. However, we now recognize that such speculation is meaningless, so far as available operations are concerned. It is impossible to coerce a chimpanzee into the kind and amount of language practice that the human child gets

---

[8] Some of Viki's vocal behavior is illustrated in a 16-mm sound film (Hayes and Hayes, 1950).

spontaneously. Since the known difference in motivation accounts for the observed difference in attainment, there is no point in postulating an unknowable difference in capacity.

COMMUNICATION AND EARLY CULTURE

The simple beginnings of culture would require only a little skill in communication—perhaps about as much as chimpanzees already have (Kroeber, 1948, p. 223). It is important, in this connection, to note the difference between the invention and use of tools, on the one hand, and tool culture on the other. The importance of communication increases as the probability of an invention decreases. Invention of the wooden club, or the stone-used-as-a-missile, would probably occur in a large majority of isolated, individual chimpanzees, under appropriate circumstances, and would thus be independent of culture. The stone-tipped spear, however, would probably be invented very seldom, and would be available to a whole population, in successive generations, only if the methods of manufacture and use could be communicated. The chimpanzee's ability to learn by imitation would appear to make this possible—at least for simple tools and techniques.[9]

Another function of communication in culture is the facilitation of cooperative enterprise. Chimpanzees are capable of considerable communication which could serve for directing, instructing, commanding, or soliciting. Crawford (1937) has demonstrated cooperative behavior in the setting of a laboratory problem, and Viki commonly displays it spontaneously. She often requests our help with things which she cannot do, or is forbidden to do, or afraid to do, by herself.

The first method she used was the simple one of leading us where she wanted us to go. More recently, she places our hands on the objects she wants us to manipulate and often moves our hands in a manner suggesting the action to be performed. For instance, if she wants to go outside, she leads us to the drawer where the door key is kept and places our hand on the drawer pull. If we don't open it promptly, she gives our wrist a tug. When the drawer is open, she puts our hand to the key, and when we grasp it, she moves our hand to the key hole. If we continue to lag, she moves our hand till the key enters the key hole and finally twists our wrist to indicate the unlocking movement. (She knows how to unlock the door for herself, of course, but is not permitted to.)

Viki makes relatively little use of gestures of the hand alone, without contacting an object or person. She often points to things she wants, when they are near by and could be touched if that were allowed; but she

---

[9] Viki's imitative ability is illustrated in a 16-mm silent film (Hayes and Hayes, 1952a).

seldom points to the door across the room, for instance, though she responds appropriately when we do so. She uses movements of her own hands to indicate an activity only rarely—as in the case where she wanted to help with the ironing but was forbidden to touch the iron. She moved her empty hand back and forth above the ironing board, apparently to show what she wanted.

This kind of communication may be said to involve "iconic signs," whose meanings are related in an obvious and logical way to their physical character. We have observed some behavior in Viki which suggests that chimpanzees may readily convert such signs into "symbols," whose meanings have an essentially arbitrary relationship to their physical character. When Viki was very young, we never took her for a ride in the car without taking some spare diapers along. As a result, she invented the device of asking for a ride by bringing us a handful of diapers from the bathroom. Later, she no longer wore diapers, but there were still some in the bathroom, and she still brought them out when she wanted a ride. When we eventually disposed of the nonfunctional diaper supply, Viki asked for a ride by running into the bathroom and coming out with a handful of Kleenex tissues—which bore only a faint resemblance to diapers. These tissues had never had any direct connection with rides, and by this time Viki had quite likely forgotten how the whole thing started. Except for its history, this would now appear to be communication by means of an arbitrary convention developed by the chimpanzee.

Viki commonly employs a particular type of vocalization in combination with her nonlinguistic communication. This is a hoarse, "ah," which serves to attract attention, and to indicate "asking," in a very general sense. We have observed a few other chimpanzees using this sound in the same way, but there appear to be very large individual differences in the ease with which it is produced. Some seem to do it spontaneously, while others fail to do it even with extensive training. This sound, unlike the chimpanzee's vocal expressions of emotion, is produced at will (Hayes, 1951, p. 66) and could, conceivably, provide the starting point for development of spoken language.

We estimate that chimpanzees are capable of enough communication to permit several kinds of cooperative enterprise which might be typical of very primitive culture. An individual could go and get one or more others and bring them to a place where there was something to be done: a heavy load to be transported, a large animal to be attacked, or a good supply of fruit to be picked. If the nature of the task were not immediately apparent to the newcomer, he might be shown what was wanted. If he did not understand the technique to be used, he could ask for a demonstration. If he were reluctant to work, he might be coerced.

Chimpanzees could probably communicate well enough for some kinds of organized, group hunting: they might, for instance, be able to surround a herd of animals and stampede them over a cliff. We doubt, however, that they could arrange for certain individuals to wait in ambush while others drove the quarry to them. Their communication would probably be inadequate to deal with events remote in time or space.

If chimpanzees have this much cultural capacity, the question naturally arises, "Why don't they have culture?" There are several possible answers. One is that perhaps they do have some. We know relatively little about chimpanzee behavior in the wild (Nissen, 1931), and cultural factors may well be involved in some of it. Another possibility is that culture appears only in the presence of excess capacity. Or it may depend on some unrecognized factors which we have not considered.

However, we tend to prefer the hypothesis that chimpanzees lack culture because they are adequately adapted to their environment without it (Nissen, 1931, p. 104). Their mortality is probably due primarily to infectious disease (Schultz, 1950, p. 51) and would not be reduced by the techniques of a primitive culture. Food shortage, predators, or a rigorous climate could be combatted by simple cultural means, but these do not appear to be important factors in chimpanzee survival.

CONCLUSION

In summary, we hypothesize that modern man evolved from an anthropoid ancestor by way of the following sequence of events.

1. Due to migration or changing climate, a population of anthropoids encountered an environment in which cultural behavior had greater survival value than it has in the ecology of present anthropoid species. (This probably involved a shift from vegetable to animal food, which would present no serious difficulty. Viki eats a considerable amount of eggs, fish, and meat, including small lizards which she catches.)
2. In response to the new environmental pressure, a simple, nonlinguistic culture developed, which provided primitive tools and techniques for obtaining food, or protection from predators or climate.
3. In this cultural setting, language acquired a value it did not have before and began to develop on the foundation of a few sounds such as chimpanzees are able to use. With the appearance of language, selection occurred in favor of individuals with strong drives toward vocal and linguistic play, so that successive generations learned more language, and learned it more easily.

4. Finally, as the linguistic culture became more complex, larger information capacity became advantageous, and selection for large brains began. This selection probably operated on the growth pattern, producing a rather generalized fetalization (Keith, 1948, p. 197; Schultz, 1950, p. 46), with mature brain size as the basis of selection, and jaw size, head balance, etc., as incidental, correlated features.

It will be noted that the much discussed change in posture does not appear in this behaviorally oriented schema. The recent discovery of the pelves of South African ape-men (Broom and Robinson, 1950; Dart, 1949) suggests that bipedal locomotion preceded brain enlargement in the evolution of man. However, it does not follow that upright posture was the first or most basic step in human evolution (Washburn, 1950). The present analysis shows that it is a secondary character of only moderate importance. We agree with Kroeber's suggestion (1948, p. 68) that it could have been omitted completely, without seriously altering the basic outlines of human evolution.

REFERENCES

Bartholomew, G. A., Jr., and Birdsell, J. B. 1953. Ecology and the proto-hominids. Am. Anthropol. 55:481–498.
Beach, F. A. 1945. Current concepts of play in animals. Am. Nat. 79:523–541.
Broom, R., and Robinson, J. T. 1950. Notes on the pelves of the fossil ape-men. Am. J. Phys. Anthropol. n. s. 8:489–494.
Crawford, M. P. 1937. The cooperative solving of problems by young chimpanzees. Comp. Psychol. Monog. 14:No. 68.
Dart, R. A. 1949. Innominate fragments of *Australopithecus prometheus*. Am. J. Phys. Anthropol. n. s. 7:301–333.
Dobzhansky, T., and Ashley Montagu, M. F. 1947. Natural selection and the mental capacities of mankind. Science 105:587–590.
Hallowell, A. I. 1950. Personality structure and the evolution of man. Am. Anthropol. 52:159–173.
Harlow, H. F. 1944. Studies in discrimination learning by monkeys: II. Discrimination learning without primary reinforcement. J. Gen. Psychol. 30:13–21.
Harlow, H. F. 1949. The formation of learning sets. Psychol. Rev. 56:51–65.
Harlow, H. F. 1953. Mice, monkeys, men, and motives. Psychol. Rev. 60:23–32.
Hayes, C. 1951. The Ape in Our House. Harper & Brothers, New York.
Hayes, K. J., and Hayes, C. 1950. Vocalization and speech in chimpanzees (16-mm sound film). Psychological Cinema Register, State College, Pa.
Hayes, K., and Hayes, C. 1951. The intellectual development of a home-raised chimpanzee. Proc. Am. Phil. Soc. 95:105–109.
Hayes, K., and Hayes, C. 1952a. Imitation in a home-raised chimpanzee (16-mm silent film). Psychological Cinema Register, State College, Pa.
Hayes, K., and Hayes, C. 1952b. Imitation in a home-raised chimpanzee. J. Comp. Physiol. Psychol. 45:450–459.
Hayes, K., and Hayes, C. 1953. The mechanical interest and ability of a home-raised chimpanzee (16-mm silent film). Psychological Cinema Register, State College, Pa.

Hayes, K. J., and Thompson, R. 1953. Non-spatial delayed response to trial-unique stimuli in sophisticated chimpanzees. J. Comp. Physiol. Psychol. 46:498–500.

Hayes, K. J., Thompson, R., and Hayes, C. 1953. Concurrent discrimination learning in chimpanzees. J. Comp. Physiol. Psychol. 46:105–107.

Hebb, D. O. 1949. The Organization of Behavior. John Wiley & Sons, New York.

Hooton, E. 1942. Man's Poor Relations. Doubleday & Co., New York.

Keith, A. 1948. A New Theory of Human Evolution. Watts & Co., London.

Kelemen, G. 1948. The anatomical basis of phonation in the chimpanzee. J. Morphol. 82:229–256. (Reprinted in Yearbook Phys. Anthrop. 1948. 4:153:180.)

Kroeber, A. L. 1928. Sub-human cultural beginnings. Q. Rev. Biol. 3:325–342.

Kroeber, A. L. 1948. Anthropology. Harcourt, Brace, New York.

Lashley, K. S. 1947. Structural variation in the nervous system in relation to behavior. Psychol. Rev. 54:325–334.

Moore, O. K., and Lewis, D. J. 1952. Learning theory and culture. Psychol. Rev. 59:380–388.

Nissen, H. W. 1931. A field study of the chimpanzee. Comp. Psychol. Monogr. 8:No. 1.

Riesen, A. H. 1940. Delayed reward in discrimination learning by chimpanzees. Comp. Psychol. Monogr. 15:No. 5.

Schlosberg, H. 1947. The concept of play. Psychol. Rev. 54:229–231.

Schultz, A. H. 1950. The specializations of man and his place among the catarrhine primates. Cold Spring Harbor Symp. 15:37–53.

Seward, J. P. 1948. The sign of a symbol: A reply to Professor Allport. Psychol. Rev. 55:227–296.

Straus, W. L., Jr. 1940. The posture of the great ape hand in locomotion and its phylogentic implications. Am. J. Phys. Anthropol. 27:199–207.

Straus, W. L., Jr. 1949. The riddle of man's ancestry. Q. Rev. Biol. 24:200–223.

Straus, W. L., Jr. 1953. In S. Tax (ed.), An Appraisal of Anthropology Today. University of Chicago Press, Chicago.

Thorndike, E. L., Bregman, E., Cobb, M., and Woodyard, E. 1927. The Measurement of Intelligence. Bureau of Publications, Teacher's College, Columbia University, New York.

Washburn, S. L. 1950. The analysis of primate evolution with particular reference to the origin of man. Cold Spring Harbor Symp. 15:67–77.

Yerkes, R. M. 1943. Chimpanzees. Yale University Press, New Haven, Conn.

Yerkes, R. M., and Yerkes, A. 1929. The Great Apes. Yale University Press, New Haven, Conn.

chapter

9

Teaching Sign Language to a Chimpanzee

R. Allen Gardner*

Beatrice T. Gardner*

Department of Psychology
University of Nevada
Reno, Nevada

contents

The extent to which another species might be able to use human language is a classical problem in comparative psychology. One approach to this problem is to consider the nature of language, the processes of learning, the neural mechanisms of learning and of language, and the genetic basis of these mechanisms, and then, while recognizing certain gaps in what is known about these factors, to attempt to arrive at an answer by dint of careful scholarship (see, for example, Lenneberg, 1967). An alternative approach is to try to teach a form of human language to an animal. We chose the latter alternative and, in June 1966, began training an infant female chimpanzee, named Washoe, to use the gestural language of the deaf. Within the first 22 months of training it became evident that we had been correct in at least one major aspect of method, the use of a gestural language. Additional aspects of method have evolved in the course of the project. These and some implications of our early results can now be described in a way that may be useful in other studies of communicative behavior. Accordingly, in this article we discuss the considerations which led us to use the chimpanzee as a subject and American Sign Language (the language used by the deaf in North America) as a medium of communication; describe the general methods of training as they were initially conceived and as they developed in the course of the project; and summarize those results that could be reported with some degree of confidence by the end of the first phase of the project.

PRELIMINARY CONSIDERATIONS

The Chimpanzee as a Subject

Some discussion of the chimpanzee as an experimental subject is in order because this species is relatively uncommon in the psychological laboratory. Whether or not the chimpanzee is the most intelligent animal after man can be disputed; the gorilla, the orangutan, and even the dolphin have their loyal partisans in this debate. Nevertheless, it is generally conceded that chimpanzees are highly intelligent, and that members of this species might be intelligent enough for our purposes. Of equal or greater importance is their sociability and their capacity for forming strong attachments to human beings. We want to emphasize this trait of sociability; it seems highly likely that it is essential for the development of lan-

From Gardner, R. A., and Gardner, B. T. 1969. Teaching Sign Language to a Chimpanzee. Science 165:664–672. Reprinted by permission. Copyright 1969 by the American Association for the Advancement of Science.

* Affiliation given reflects the authors' affiliation at time of writing.

The research described in this article has been supported by National Institute of Mental Health Grants MH-12154 and MH-34953 (Research Scientist Development Award to B. T. Gardner) and by National Foundation Grant GB-7432.

guage in human beings, and it was a primary consideration in our choice of a chimpanzee as a subject.

Affectionate as chimpanzees are, they are still wild animals, and this is a serious disadvantage. Most psychologists are accustomed to working with animals that have been chosen, and sometimes bred, for docility and adaptability to laboratory procedures. The difficulties presented by the wild nature of an experimental animal must not be underestimated. Chimpanzees are also very strong animals; a full-grown specimen is likely to weigh more than 120 pounds (55 kilograms) and is estimated to be from three to five times as strong as a man, pound-for-pound. Coupled with the wildness, this great strength presents serious difficulties for a procedure that requires interaction at close quarters with a free-living animal. We have always had to reckon with the likelihood that at some point Washoe's physical maturity will make this procedure prohibitively dangerous.

A more serious disadvantage is that human speech sounds are unsuitable as a medium of communication for the chimpanzee. The vocal apparatus of the chimpanzee is very different from that of man (Bryan, 1963). More important, the vocal behavior of the chimpanzee is very different from that of man. Chimpanzees do make many different sounds, but generally vocalization occurs in situations of high excitement and tends to be specific to the exciting situations. Undisturbed, chimpanzees are usually silent. Thus, it is unlikely that a chimpanzee could be trained to make refined use of its vocalizations. Moreover, the intensive work of Hayes and Hayes (1951) with the chimpanzee Viki indicates that a vocal language is not appropriate for this species. The Hayeses used modern, sophisticated, psychological methods and seem to have spared no effort to teach Viki to make speech sounds. Yet in six years Viki learned only four sounds that approximated English words (K. J. Hayes, personal communication[1]).

Use of the hands, however, is a prominent feature of chimpanzee behavior; manipulatory mechanical problems are their forte. More to the point, even caged, laboratory chimpanzees develop begging and similar gestures spontaneously (Yerkes, 1943), while individuals that have had extensive contact with human beings have displayed an even wider variety of communicative gestures (Hayes and Hayes, 1955, p. 110; Kellogg and Kellogg, 1967; Kellogg, 1968). In our choice of sign language we were influenced more by the behavioral evidence that this medium of communication was appropriate to the species than by anatomical evidence of structural similarity between the hands of chim-

---

[1] Dr. Hayes also informed us that Viki used a few additional sounds, which, while not resembling English words, were used for specific requests.

panzees and of men. The Hayeses point out that human tools and mechanical devices are constructed to fit the human hand, yet chimpanzees have little difficulty in using these devices with great skill. Nevertheless, they seem unable to adapt their vocalizations to approximate human speech.

Psychologists who work extensively with the instrumental conditioning of animals become sensitive to the need to use responses that are suited to the species they wish to study. Lever-pressing in rats is not an arbitrary response invented by Skinner to confound the mentalists; it is a type of response commonly made by rats when they are first placed in a Skinner box. The exquisite control of instrumental behavior by schedules of reward is achieved only if the original responses are well chosen. We chose a language based on gestures because we reasoned that gestures for the chimpanzee should be analogous to bar-pressing for rats, key-pecking for pigeons, and babbling for humans.

American Sign Language

Two systems of manual communication are used by the deaf. One system is the manual alphabet, or fingerspelling, in which configurations of the hand correspond to letters of the alphabet. In this system the words of a spoken language, such as English, can be spelled out manually. The other system, sign language, consists of a set of manual configurations and gestures that correspond to particular words or concepts. Unlike fingerspelling, which is the direct encoding of a spoken language, sign languages have their own rules of usage. Word-for-sign translation between a spoken language and a sign language yields results that are similar to those of word-for-word translation between two spoken languages: the translation is often passable, though awkward, but it can also be ambiguous or quite nonsensical. Also, there are national and regional variations in sign languages that are comparable to those of spoken languages.

We chose for this project the American Sign Language (ASL), which, with certain regional variations, is used by the deaf in North America. This particular sign language has recently been the subject of formal analysis (McCall, 1965; Stokoe, Casterline, and Croneberg, 1965). The ASL can be compared to pictograph writing in which some symbols are quite arbitrary and some are quite representational or iconic, but all are arbitrary to some degree. For example, in ASL the sign for "always" is made by holding the hand in a fist, index finger extended (the pointing hand), while rotating the arm at the elbow. This is clearly an arbitrary representation of the concept "always." The sign for "flower," however, is highly iconic; it is made by holding the fingers of one hand extended, all five fingertips touching (the tapered hand), and touching the fingertips first to one nostril then to the other, as if sniffing a flower. While this is an iconic sign for "flower," it is only one of a number of conventions by which the concept "flower" could be iconically represented; it is thus arbitrary to some degree. Undoubtedly, many of the signs of ASL that seem quite arbitrary today once had an iconic origin that was lost through years of stylized usage. Thus, the signs of ASL are neither uniformly arbitrary nor uniformly iconic; rather the degree of abstraction varies from sign to sign over a wide range. This would seem to be a useful property of ASL for our research.

The literate deaf typically use a combination of ASL and finger-spelling; for purposes of this project we have avoided the use of finger-spelling as much as possible. A great range of expression is possible within the limits of ASL. We soon found that a good way to practice signing among ourselves was to render familiar songs and poetry into signs; as far as we can judge, there is no message that cannot be rendered faithfully (apart from the usual problems of translation from one language to another). Technical terms and proper names are a problem when first introduced, but within any community of signers it is easy to agree on a convention for any commonly used term. For example, among ourselves we do not fingerspell the words *psychologist* and *psychology*, but render them as THINK DOCTOR and THINK SCIENCE. Or, among users of ASL, "California" can be fingerspelled but is commonly rendered as GOLDEN PLAYLAND. (Incidentally, the sign for "gold" is made by plucking at the earlobe with thumb and forefinger, indicating an ear-ring—another example of an iconic sign that is at the same time arbitrary and stylized.)

The fact that ASL is in current use by human beings is an additional advantage. The early linguistic environment of the deaf children of deaf parents is in some respects similar to the linguistic environment that we could provide for an experimental subject. This should permit some comparative evaluation of Washoe's eventual level of competence. For example, in discussing Washoe's early performance with deaf parents we have been told that many of her variants of standard signs are similar to the baby-talk variants commonly observed when human children sign.

Washoe

Having decided on a species and a medium of communication, our next concern was to obtain an experimental subject. It is altogether possible that there is some critical early age for the acquisition of this type of behavior. On the other hand, newborn chimpanzees tend to be quite help-less and vegetative. They are also considerably less hardy than older infants. Nevertheless, we reasoned that the dangers of starting too late were much greater than the dangers of starting too early, and we sought the youngest infant we could get. Newborn laboratory chimpanzees are very scarce, and we found that the youngest laboratory infant we could get would be about two years old at the time we planned to start the project. It seemed preferable to obtain a wild-caught infant. Wild-caught infants are usually at least 8 to 10 months old before they are available for research. This is because infants rarely reach the United States before they are five months old, and to this age must be added one or two months before final purchase and two or three months for quarantine and other medical services.

We named our chimpanzee Washoe for Washoe County, the home of the University of Nevada. Her exact age will never be known, but from her weight and dentition we estimated her age to be between 8 and 14 months at the end of June 1966, when she first arrived at our laboratory. (Her dentition has continued to agree with this initial estimate, but her weight has increased rather more than would be expected.) This is very young for a chimpanzee. The best available information indicates that infants are completely dependent until the age of two years and semidependent until the age of four; the first signs of sexual maturity (for example, menstruation, sexual swelling) begin to appear at about eight years, and full adult growth is reached between the ages of 12 and 16 (Goodall, 1965, p. 425; Riopelle and Rogers, 1965, p. 449). As for the complete lifespan, captive specimens have survived for well over 40 years. Washoe was indeed very young when she arrived; she did not have her first canines or molars, her hand-eye coordination was rudimentary, she had only begun to crawl about, and she slept a great deal. Apart from making friends with her and adapting her to the daily routine, we could accomplish little during the first few months.

Laboratory Conditions

At the outset we were quite sure that Washoe could learn to make various signs in order to obtain food, drink, and other things. For the project to be a success, we felt that something more must be developed. We wanted Washoe not only to ask for objects but to answer questions about them and also to ask us questions. We wanted to develop behavior that could be described as conversation. With this in mind, we attempted to provide Washoe with an environment that might be conducive to this sort of behavior. Confinement was to be minimal, about the same as that of human infants. Her human companions were to be friends and playmates as well as providers and protectors, and they were to introduce a great many games and activities that would be likely to result in maximum interaction with Washoe.

In practice, such an environment is readily achieved with a chimpanzee; bonds of warm affection have always been established between

Washoe and her several human companions. We have enjoyed the interaction almost as much as Washoe has, within the limits of human endurance. A number of human companions have been enlisted to participate in the project and relieve each other at intervals, so that at least one person would be with Washoe during all her waking hours. At first we feared that such frequent changes would be disturbing, but Washoe seemed to adapt very well to this procedure. Apparently it is possible to provide an infant chimpanzee with affection on a shift basis.

All of Washoe's human companions have been required to master ASL and to use it extensively in her presence, in association with interesting activities and events and also in a general way, as one chatters at a human infant in the course of the day. The ASL has been used almost exclusively, although occasional fingerspelling has been permitted. From time to time, of course, there are lapses into spoken English, as when medical personnel must examine Washoe. At one time, we considered an alternative procedure in which we would sign and speak English to Washoe simultaneously, thus giving her an additional source of informative cues. We rejected this procedure, reasoning that, if she should come to understand speech sooner or more easily than ASL, then she might not pay sufficient attention to our gestures. Another alternative, that of speaking English among ourselves and signing to Washoe, was also rejected. We reasoned that this would make it seem that big chimps talk and only little chimps sign, which might give signing an undesirable social status.

The environment we are describing is not a silent one. The human beings can vocalize in many ways, laughing and making sounds of pleasure and displeasure. Whistles and drums are sounded in a variety of imitation games, and hands are clapped for attention. The rule is that all meaningful sounds, whether vocalized or not, must be sounds that a chimpanzee can imitate.

TRAINING METHODS

Imitation

The imitativeness of apes is proverbial, and rightly so. Those who have worked closely with chimpanzees have frequently remarked on their readiness to engage in visually guided imitation. Consider the following typical comment of Yerkes and Learned (1925):

> Chim and Panzee would imitate many of my acts, but never have I heard them imitate a sound and rarely make a sound peculiarly their own in response to mine. As previously stated, their imitative tendency is as remarkable for its specialization and limitations as for its strength. It seems

to be controlled chiefly by visual stimuli. Things which are seen tend to be imitated or reproduced. What is heard is not reproduced. Obviously an animal which lacks the tendency to reinstate auditory stimuli—in other words to imitate sounds—cannot reasonably be expected to talk. The human infant exhibits this tendency to a remarkable degree. So also does the parrot. If the imitative tendency of the parrot could be coupled with the quality of intelligence of the chimpanzee, the latter undoubtedly could speak (p. 53).

In the course of their work with Viki, the Hayeses devised a game in which Viki would imitate various actions on hearing the command "Do this" (Hayes and Hayes, 1952). Once established, this was an effective means of training Viki to perform actions that could be visually guided. The same method should be admirably suited to training a chimpanzee to use sign language; accordingly we have directed much effort toward establishing a version of the "Do this" game with Washoe. Getting Washoe to imitate us was not difficult, for she did so quite spontaneously, but getting her to imitate on command has been another matter altogether. It was not until the 16th month of the project that we achieved any degree of control over Washoe's imitation of gestures. Eventually we got to a point where she would imitate a simple gesture, such as pulling at her ears, or a series of such gestures—first we make a gesture, then she imitates, then we make a second gesture, she imitates the second gesture, and so on—for the reward of being tickled. Up to this writing, however, imitation of this sort has not been an important method for introducing new signs into Washoe's vocabulary.

As a method of prompting, we have been able to use imitation extensively to increase the frequency and refine the form of signs. Washoe sometimes fails to use a new sign in an appropriate situation, or uses another, incorrect sign. At such times we can make the correct sign to Washoe, repeating the performance until she makes the sign herself. (With more stable signs, more indirect forms of prompting can be used—for example, pointing at, or touching, Washoe's hand or a part of her body that should be involved in the sign; making the sign for "sign," which is equivalent to saying "Speak up"; or asking a question in signs, such as WHAT DO YOU WANT? or WHAT IS IT?) Again, with new signs, and often with old signs as well, Washoe can lapse into what we refer to as poor "diction." Of course, a great deal of slurring and a wide range of variants are permitted in ASL as in any spoken language. In any event, Washoe's diction has frequently been improved by the simple device of repeating, in exaggeratedly correct form, the sign she has just made, until she repeats it herself in more correct form. On the whole, she has responded quite well to prompting, but there are strict limits to its use with a wild animal—one that is probably quite spoiled, besides.

Pressed too hard, Washoe can become completely diverted from her original object; she may ask for something entirely different, run away, go into a tantrum, or even bite her tutor.

Chimpanzees also imitate, after some delay, and this delayed imitation can be quite elaborate (Hayes and Hayes, 1952). The following is a typical example of Washoe's delayed imitation. From the beginning of the project she was bathed regularly and according to a standard routine. Also, from her second month with us, she always had dolls to play with. One day, during the tenth month of the project, she bathed one of her dolls in the way we usually bathed her. She filled her little bathtub with water, dunked the doll in the tub, then took it out and dried it with a towel. She has repeated the entire performance, or parts of it, many times since, sometimes also soaping the doll.

This is a type of imitation that may be very important in the acquisition of language by human children, and many of our procedures with Washoe were devised to capitalize on it. Routine activities—feeding, dressing, bathing, and so on—have been highly ritualized, with appropriate signs figuring prominently in the rituals. Many games have been invented which can be accompanied by appropriate signs. Objects and activities have been named as often as possible, especially when Washoe seemed to be paying particular attention to them. New objects and new examples of familiar objects, including pictures, have been continually brought to her attention, together with the appropriate signs. She likes to ride in automobiles, and a ride in an automobile, including the preparations for a ride, provides a wealth of sights that can be accompanied by signs. A good destination for a ride is a home or the university nursery school, both well stocked with props for language lessons.

The general principle should be clear: Washoe has been exposed to a wide variety of activities and objects, together with their appropriate signs, in the hope that she would come to associate the signs with their referents and later make the signs herself. We have reason to believe that she has come to understand a large vocabulary of signs. This was expected, since a number of chimpanzees have acquired extensive understanding vocabularies of spoken words, and there is evidence that even dogs can acquire a sizable understanding vocabulary of spoken words (Warden and Warner, 1928). The understanding vocabulary that Washoe has acquired, however, consists of signs that a chimpanzee can imitate.

Some of Washoe's signs seem to have been originally acquired by delayed imitation. A good example is the sign for "toothbrush." A part of the daily routine has been to brush her teeth after every meal. When this routine was first introduced Washoe generally resisted it. She gradually came to submit with less and less fuss, and after many months she would even help or sometimes brush her teeth herself. Usually, having finished her meal, Washoe would try to leave her highchair; we would restrain her, signing FIRST, TOOTHBRUSHING, THEN YOU CAN GO. One day, in the tenth month of the project, Washoe was visiting the Gardner home and found her way into the bathroom. She climbed up on the counter, looked at our mug full of toothbrushes, and signed TOOTH-BRUSH. At the time, we believed that Washoe understood this sign but we had not seen her use it. She had no reason to ask for the tooth-brushes, because they were well within her reach, and it is most unlikely that she was asking to have her teeth brushed. This was our first observa-tion, and one of the clearest examples, of behavior in which Washoe seemed to name an object or an event for no obvious motive other than communication.

Following this observation, the toothbrushing routine at mealtime was altered. First, imitative prompting was introduced. Then as the sign became more reliable, her rinsing-mug and toothbrush were displayed prominently until she made the sign. By the 14th month she was making the TOOTHBRUSH sign at the end of meals with little or no prompting; in fact she has called for her toothbrush in a peremptory fashion when its appearance at the end of a meal was delayed. The TOOTHBRUSH sign is not merely a response cued by the end of a meal; Washoe retained her ability to name toothbrushes when they were shown to her at other times.

The sign for "flower" may also have been acquired by delayed imi-tation. From her first summer with us, Washoe showed a great interest in flowers, and we took advantage of this by providing many flowers and pictures of flowers accompanied by the appropriate sign. Then one day in the 15th month she made the sign, spontaneously, while she and a com-panion were walking toward a flower garden. As in the case of TOOTH-BRUSH, we believed that she understood the sign at this time, but we had made no attempt to elicit it from her except by making it ourselves in appropriate situations. Again, after the first observation, we proceeded to elicit this sign as often as possible by a variety of methods, most frequently by showing her a flower and giving it to her if she made the sign for it. Eventually the sign became very reliable and could be elicited by a variety of flowers and pictures of flowers.

It is difficult to decide which signs were acquired by the method of delayed imitation. The first appearance of these signs is likely to be sud-den and unexpected; it is possible that some inadvertent movement of Washoe's has been interpreted as meaningful by one of her devoted com-panions. If the first observer were kept from reporting the observation and from making any direct attempts to elicit the sign again, then it might be possible to obtain independent verification. Quite under-standably, we have been more interested in raising the frequency of new signs than in evaluating any particular method of training.

Babbling

Because the Hayeses were attempting to teach Viki to speak English, they were interested in babbling, and during the first year of their project they were encouraged by the number and variety of spontaneous vocalizations that Viki made. But, in time, Viki's spontaneous vocalizations decreased further and further to the point where the Hayeses felt that there was almost no vocal babbling from which to shape spoken language. In planning this project we expected a great deal of manual "babbling," but during the early months we observed very little behavior of this kind. In the course of the project, however, there has been a great increase in manual babbling. We have been particularly encouraged by the increase in movements that involve touching parts of the head and body, since these are important components of many signs. Also, more and more frequently, when Washoe has been unable to get something that she wants, she has burst into a flurry of random flourishes and arm waving.

We have encouraged Washoe's babbling by our responsiveness; clapping, smiling, and repeating the gesture much as you might repeat "goo goo" to a human infant. If the babbled gesture has resembled a sign in ASL, we have made the correct form of the sign and have attempted to engage in some appropriate activity. The sign for "funny" was probably acquired in this way. It first appeared as a spontaneous babble that lent itself readily to a simple imitation game—first Washoe signed FUNNY, then we did, then she did, and so on. We would laugh and smile during the interchanges that she initiated, and initiate the game ourselves when something funny happened. Eventually Washoe came to use the FUNNY sign spontaneously in roughly appropriate situations.

Closely related to babbling are some gestures that seem to have appeared independently of any deliberate training on our part, and that resemble signs so closely that we could incorporate them into Washoe's repertoire with little or no modification. Almost from the first she had a begging gesture—an extension of her open hand, palm up, toward one of us. She made this gesture in situations in which she wanted aid and in situations in which we were holding some object that she wanted. The ASL signs for "give me" and "come" are very similar to this, except that they involve a prominent beckoning movement. Gradually Washoe came to incorporate a beckoning wrist movement into her use of this sign. In Table 1 we refer to this sign as COME-GIMME. As Washoe has come to use it, the sign is not simply a modification of the original begging gesture. For example, very commonly she reaches forward with one hand (palm up) while she gestures with the other hand (palm down) held near her head. (The result resembles a classic fencing posture.)

Another sign of this type is the sign for "hurry," which, so far, Washoe has always made by shaking her open hand vigorously at the wrist. This first appeared as an impatient flourish following some request that she had made in signs; for example, after making the OPEN sign before a door. The correct ASL for "hurry" is very close, and we began to use it often, ourselves, in appropriate contexts. We believe that Washoe has come to use this sign in a meaningful way, because she has frequently used it when she, herself, is in a hurry—for example, when rushing to her nursery chair.

Instrumental Conditioning

It seems intuitively unreasonable that the acquisition of language by human beings could be strictly a matter of reiterated instrumental conditioning—that a child acquires language after the fashion of a rat that is conditioned, first, to press a lever for food in the presence of one stimulus, then to turn a wheel in the presence of another stimulus, and so on until a large repertoire of discriminated responses is acquired. Nevertheless, the so-called "trick vocabulary" of early childhood is probably acquired in this way, and this may be a critical stage in the acquisition of language by children. In any case, a minimal objective of this project was to teach Washoe as many signs as possible by whatever procedures we could enlist. Thus, we have not hesitated to use conventional procedures of instrumental conditioning.

Anyone who becomes familiar with young chimpanzees soon learns about their passion for being tickled. There is no doubt that tickling is the most effective reward that we have used with Washoe. In the early months, when we would pause in our tickling, Washoe would indicate that she wanted more tickling by taking our hands and placing them against her ribs or around her neck. The meaning of these gestures was unmistakable, but since we were not studying our human ability to interpret her chimpanzee gestures, we decided to shape an arbitrary response that she could use to ask for more tickling. We noted that, when being tickled, she tended to bring her arms together to cover the place being tickled. The result was a very crude approximation of the ASL sign for "more" (see Table 1). Thus, we would stop tickling and then pull Washoe's arms away from her body. When we released her arms, and threatened to resume tickling, she tended to bring her hands together again. If she brought them back together, we would tickle her again. From time to time we would stop tickling and wait for her to put her hands together by herself. At first, any approximation to the MORE sign, however crude, was rewarded. Later, we required closer approximations and introduced imitative prompting. Soon, a very good version of

Table 1.   Signs used reliably by chimpanzee Washoe within 22 months of the beginning of training. The signs are listed in the order of their original appearance in her repertoire (see text for the criterion of reliability and for the method of assigning the date of original appearance).

Signs	Description	Context
COME-GIMME	Beckoning motion, with wrist or knuckles as pivot.	Sign made to persons or animals, also for objects out of reach. Often combined: COME TICKLE, GIMME SWEET, etc.
MORE	Fingertips are brought together, usually overhead. (Correct ASL form: tips of tapered hand touch repeatedly.)	When asking for continuation or repetition of activities such as swinging or tickling, for second helpings of food, etc. Also used to ask for repetition of some performance, such as a somersault.
UP	Arm extends upward, and index finger may also point up.	Wants a lift to reach objects such as grapes on vine, or leaves; or wants to be placed on someone's shoulders; or wants to leave potty-chair.
SWEET	Index or index and second fingers touch tip of wagging tongue. (Correct ASL form: index and second fingers extended side by side.)	For dessert; used spontaneously at end of meal. Also, when asking for candy.
OPEN	Flat hands are placed side by side, palms down, then drawn apart while rotated to palms up.	At door of house, room, car, refrigerator, or cupboard; on containers such as jars; and on faucets.
TICKLE	The index finger of one hand is drawn across the back of the other hand. (Related to ASL TOUCH.)	For tickling or for chasing games.
GO	Opposite of COME-GIMME.	While walking hand-in-hand or riding on someone's shoulders. Washoe usually indicates the direction desired.
OUT	Curved hand grasps tapered hand; then tapered hand is withdrawn upward.	When passing through doorways; until recently, used for both "in" and "out." Also, when asking to be taken outdoors.

Sign	Description	Context
HURRY	Open hand is shaken at the wrist. (Correct ASL form: index and second fingers extended side by side.)	Often follows signs such as COME-GIMME, OUT, OPEN, and GO, particularly if there is a delay before Washoe is obeyed. Also, used while watching her meal being prepared.
HEAR-LISTEN	Index finger touches ear.	For loud or strange sounds: bells, car horns, sonic booms, etc. Also, for asking someone to hold a watch to her ear.
TOOTHBRUSH	Index finger is used as brush, to rub front teeth.	When Washoe has finished her meal, or at other times when shown a toothbrush.
DRINK	Thumb is extended from fisted hand and touches mouth.	For water, formula, soda pop, etc. For soda pop, often combined with SWEET.
HURT	Extended index fingers are jabbed toward each other. Can be used to indicate location of pain.	To indicate cuts and bruises on herself or on others. Can be elicited by red stains on a person's skin or by tears in clothing.
SORRY	Fisted hand clasps and unclasps at shoulder. (Correct ASL form: fisted hand is rubbed over heart with circular motion.)	After biting someone, or when someone has been hurt in another way (not necessarily by Washoe). When told to apologize for mischief.
FUNNY	Tip of index finger presses nose, and Washoe snorts. (Correct ASL form: index and second fingers used; no snort.)	When soliciting interaction play, and during games. Occasionally, when being pursued after mischief.
PLEASE	Open hand is drawn across chest. (Correct ASL form: fingertips used, and circular motion.)	When asking for objects and activities. Frequently combined: PLEASE GO; OUT, PLEASE; PLEASE DRINK.
FOOD-EAT	Several fingers of one hand are placed in mouth. (Correct ASL form: fingertips of tapered hand touch mouth repeatedly.)	During meals and preparation of meals.
FLOWER	Tip of index finger touches one or both nostrils. (Correct ASL form: tips of tapered hand touch first one nostril, then the other.)	For flowers.

(continued)

Table 1. *(continued)*

Signs	Description	Content
COVER-BLANKET	Draws one hand toward self over the back of the other.	At bedtime or naptime, and, on cold days, when Washoe wants to be taken out.
DOG	Repeated slapping on thigh.	For dogs and for barking.
YOU	Index finger points at a person's chest.	Indicates successive turns in games. Also used in response to questions such as WHO TICKLE? WHO BRUSH?
NAPKIN-BIB	Fingertips wipe the mouth region.	For bib, for washcloth, and for Kleenex.
IN	Opposite of OUT.	Wants to go indoors, or wants someone to join her indoors.
BRUSH	The fisted hand rubs the back of the open hand several times. (Adapted from ASL POLISH.)	For hairbrush, and when asking for brushing.
HAT	Palm pats top of head.	For hats and caps.
I-ME	Index finger points at, or touches, chest.	Indicates Washoe's turn, when she and a companion share food, drink, etc. Also used in phrases, such as I DRINK, and in reply to questions such as WHO TICKLE? (Washoe: YOU); WHO I TICKLE? (Washoe: ME.)

Sign	Description	Usage
SHOES	The fisted hands are held side by side and strike down on shoes or floor. (Correct ASL form: the sides of the fisted hands strike against each other).	For shoes and boots.
SMELL	Palm is held before nose and moved slightly upward several times.	For scented objects: tobacco, perfume, sage, etc.
PANTS	Palms of the flat hands are drawn up against the body toward waist.	For diapers, rubber pants, trousers.
CLOTHES	Fingertips brush down the chest.	For Washoe's jacket, nightgown, and shirts; also for our clothing.
CAT	Thumb and index finger grasp cheek hair near side of mouth and are drawn outward (representing cat's whiskers).	For cats.
KEY	Palm of one hand is repeatedly touched with the index finger of the other. (Correct ASL form: crooked index finger is rotated against palm.)	Used for keys and locks and to ask us to unlock a door.
BABY	One forearm is placed in the crook of the other, as if cradling a baby.	For dolls, including animal dolls such as a toy horse and duck.
CLEAN	The open palm of one hand is passed over the open palm of the other.	Used when Washoe is washing, or being washed, or when a companion is washing hands or some other object. Also used for "soap."

the MORE sign could be obtained, but it was quite specific to the tickling situation.

In the sixth month of the project we were able to get MORE signs for a new game that consisted of pushing Washoe across the floor in a laundry basket. In this case we did not use the shaping procedure but, from the start, used imitative prompting to elicit the MORE sign. Soon after the MORE sign became spontaneous and reliable in the laundry-basket game, it began to appear as a request for more swinging (by the arms)—again, after first being elicited with imitative prompting. From this point on, Washoe transferred the MORE sign to all activities, including feeding. The transfer was usually spontaneous, occurring when there was some pause in a desired activity or when some object was removed. Often we ourselves were not sure that Washoe wanted "more" until she signed to us.

The sign for "open" had a similar history. When Washoe wanted to get through a door, she tended to hold up both hands and pound on the door with her palms or her knuckles. This is the beginning position for the OPEN sign (see Table 1). By waiting for her to place her hands on the door and then lift them, and also by imitative prompting, we were able to shape a good approximation of the OPEN sign, and would reward this by opening the door. Originally she was trained to make this sign for three particular doors that she used every day. Washoe transferred this sign to all doors; then to containers such as the refrigerator, cupboards, drawers, briefcases, boxes, and jars; and eventually—an invention of Washoe's—she used it to ask us to turn on water faucets.

In the case of MORE and OPEN we followed the conventional laboratory procedure of waiting for Washoe to make some response that could be shaped into the sign we wished her to acquire. We soon found that this was not necessary; Washoe could acquire signs that were first elicited by our holding her hands, forming them into the desired configuration, and then putting them through the desired movement. Since this procedure of guidance is usually much more practical than waiting for a spontaneous approximation to occur at a favorable moment, we have used it much more frequently.

RESULTS

Vocabulary

In the early stages of the project we were able to keep fairly complete records of Washoe's daily signing behavior. But, as the amount of signing behavior and the number of signs to be monitored increased, our initial attempts to obtain exhaustive records became prohibitively cumbersome. During the 16th month we settled on the following procedure. When a new sign was introduced we waited until it had been reported by three different observers as having occurred in an appropriate context and spontaneously (that is, with no prompting other than a question such as WHAT IS IT? or WHAT DO YOU WANT?). The sign was then added to a checklist in which its occurrence, form context, and the kind of prompting required were recorded. Two such checklists were filled out each day, one for the first half of the day and one for the second half. For a criterion of acquisition we chose a reported frequency of at least one appropriate and spontaneous occurrence each day over a period of 15 consecutive days.

In Table 1 we have listed 30 signs that met this criterion by the end of the 22nd month of the project. In addition, we have listed four signs (DOG, SMELL, ME, and CLEAN) that we judged to be stable, despite the fact that they had not met the stringent criterion before the end of the 22nd month. These additional signs had, nevertheless, been reported to occur appropriately and spontaneously on more than half of the days in a period of 30 consecutive days. An indication of the variety of signs that Washoe used in the course of a day is given by the following data: during the 22nd month of the study, 28 of the 34 signs listed were reported on at least 20 days, and the smallest number of different signs reported for a single day was 23, with a median of 29[2].

The order in which these signs first appeared in Washoe's repertoire is also given in Table 1. We considered the first appearance to be the date on which three different observers reported appropriate and spontaneous occurrences. By this criterion, four new signs first appeared during the first seven months, nine new signs during the next seven months, and 21 new signs during the next seven months. We chose the 21st month rather than the 22nd month as the cutoff for this tabulation so that no signs would be included that do not appear in Table 1. Clearly, if Washoe's rate of acquisition continues to accelerate, we will have to assess her vocabulary on the basis of sampling procedures. We are now in the process of developing procedures that could be used to make periodic tests of Washoe's performance on samples of her repertoire. However, now that there is evidence that a chimpanzee can acquire a vocabulary of more than 30 signs, the exact number of signs in her current vocabulary is less significant than the order of magnitude—50, 100, 200 signs, or more—that might eventually be achieved.

---

[2] The development of Washoe's vocabulary of signs is being recorded on motion-picture film. At the time of this writing, 30 of the 34 signs in Table 1 are on film.

Differentiation

In Table 1, column 1, we list English equivalents for each of Washoe's signs. It must be understood that this equivalence is only approximate, because equivalence between English and ASL, as between any two human languages, is only approximate, and because Washoe's usage does differ from that of standard ASL. To some extent her usage is indicated in the column labeled "Context" in Table 1, but the definition of any given sign must always depend upon her total vocabulary, and this has been continually changing. When she had very few signs for specific things, Washoe used the MORE sign for a wide class of requests. Our only restriction was that we discouraged the use of MORE for first requests. As she acquired signs for specific requests, her use of MORE declined until, at the time of this writing, she was using this sign mainly to ask for repetition of some action that she could not name, such as a somersault. Perhaps the best English equivalent would be *do it again*. Still, it seemed preferable to list the English equivalent for the ASL sign rather than its current referent for Washoe, since further refinements in her usage may be achieved at a later date.

The differentiation of the signs for "flower" and "smell" provides a further illustration of usage depending upon size of vocabulary. As the FLOWER sign became more frequent, we noted that it occurred in several inappropriate contexts that all seemed to include odors; for example, Washoe would make the FLOWER sign when opening a tobacco pouch or when entering a kitchen filled with cooking odors. Taking our cue from this, we introduced the SMELL sign by passive shaping and imitative prompting. Gradually Washoe came to make the appropriate distinction between "flower" contexts and "smell" contexts in her signing, although FLOWER (in the single-nostril form) (see Table 1) has continued to occur as a common error in "smell" contexts.

Transfer

In general, when introducing new signs we have used a very specific referent for the initial training—a particular door for OPEN, a particular hat for HAT. Early in the project we were concerned about the possibility that signs might become inseparable from their first referents. So far, however, there has been no problem of this kind: Washoe has always been able to transfer her signs spontaneously to new members of each class of referents. We have already described the transfer of MORE and OPEN. The sign for "flower" is a particularly good example of transfer, because flowers occur in so many varieties, indoors, outdoors, and in pictures, yet Washoe uses the same sign for all. It is fortunate that she has responded well to pictures of objects. In the case of DOG and CAT this

has proved to be important because live dogs and cats can be too exciting, and we have had to use pictures to elicit most of the DOG and CAT
signs. It is noteworthy that Washoe has transferred the DOG sign to the
sound of barking by an unseen dog.

The acquisition and transfer of the sign for "key" illustrates a
further point. A great many cupboards and doors in Washoe's quarters
have been kept secure by small padlocks that can all be opened by the
same simple key. Because she was immature and awkward, Washoe had
great difficulty in learning to use these keys and locks. Because we
wanted her to improve her manual dexterity, we let her practice with
these keys until she could open the locks quite easily (then we had to hide
the keys). Washoe soon transferred this skill to all manner of locks and
keys, including ignition keys. At about the same time, we taught her the
sign for "key," using the original padlock keys as a referent. Washoe
came to use this sign both to name keys that were presented to her and to
ask for the keys to various locks when no key was in sight. She readily
transferred the sign to all varieties of keys and locks.

Now, if an animal can transfer a skill learned with a certain key and
lock to new types of key and lock, it should not be surprising that the
same animal can learn to use an arbitrary response to name and ask for a
certain key and then transfer that sign to new types of keys. Certainly,
the relationship between the use of a key and the opening of locks is as
arbitrary as the relationship between the sign for "key" and its many
referents. Viewed in this way, the general phenomenon of transfer of
training and the specifically linguistic phenomenon of labeling become
very similar, and the problems that these phenomena pose for modern
learning theory should require similar solutions. We do not mean to
imply that the problem of labeling is less complex than has generally
been supposed; rather, we are suggesting that the problem of transfer of
training requires an equally sophisticated treatment.

Combinations

During the phase of the project covered by this article we made no
deliberate attempts to elicit combinations or phrases, although we may
have responded more readily to strings of two or more signs than to
single signs. As far as we can judge, Washoe's early use of signs in strings
was spontaneous. Almost as soon as she had eight or ten signs in her
repertoire, she began to use them two and three at a time. As her
repertoire increased, her tendency to produce strings of two or more
signs also increased, to the point where this has become a common mode
of signing for her. We, of course, usually signed to her in combinations,
but if Washoe's use of combinations has been imitative, then it must be a
generalized sort of imitation, since she has invented a number of com-

binations, such as GIMME TICKLE (before we had ever asked her to tickle us), and OPEN FOOD DRINK (for the refrigerator—we have always called it the "cold box").

Four signs—PLEASE, COME-GIMME, HURRY, and MORE—used with one or more other signs, account for the largest share of Washoe's early combinations. In general, these four signs have functioned as emphasizers, as in PLEASE OPEN HURRY and GIMME DRINK PLEASE.

Until recently, five additional signs—GO, OUT, IN, OPEN, and HEAR-LISTEN—accounted for most of the remaining combinations. Typical examples of combinations using these four are GO IN or GO OUT (when at some distance from a door), GO SWEET (for being carried to a raspberry bush), OPEN FLOWER (to be let through the gate to a flower garden), OPEN KEY (for a locked door), LISTEN EAT (at the sound of an alarm clock signaling mealtime), and LISTEN DOG (at the sound of barking by an unseen dog). All but the first and last of these six examples were inventions of Washoe's. Combinations of this type tend to amplify the meaning of the single signs used. Sometimes, however, the function of these five signs has been about the same as that of the emphasizers, as in OPEN OUT (when standing in front of a door).

Toward the end of the period covered in this article we were able to introduce the pronouns I-ME and YOU, so that combinations that resemble short sentences have begun to appear.

CONCLUDING OBSERVATIONS

From time to time we have been asked questions such as, "Do you think that Washoe has language?" or "At what point will you be able to say that Washoe has language?" We find it very difficult to respond to these questions because they are altogether foreign to the spirit of our research. They imply a distinction between one class of communicative behavior that can be called language and another class that cannot. This in turn implies a well established theory that could provide the distinction. If our objectives had required such a theory, we would certainly not have been able to begin this project as early as we did.

In the first phase of the project we were able to verify the hypothesis that sign language is an appropriate medium of two-way communication for the chimpanzee. Washoe's intellectual immaturity, the continuing acceleration of her progress, the fact that her signs do not remain specific to their original referents but are transferred spontaneously to new referents, and the emergence of rudimentary combinations all suggest that significantly more can be accomplished by Washoe during the subsequent phases of this project. As we proceed, the problems of these subsequent phases will be chiefly concerned with the technical business of measurement. We are now developing a procedure for testing Washoe's ability to name objects. In this procedure, an object or a picture of an object is placed in a box with a window. An observer, who does not know what is in the box, asks Washoe what she sees through the window. At present, this method is limited to items that fit in the box; a more ingenious method will have to be devised for other items. In particular, the ability to combine and recombine signs must be tested. Here, a great deal depends upon reaching a stage at which Washoe produces an extended series of signs in answer to questions. Our hope is that Washoe can be brought to the point where she describes events and situations to an observer who has no other source of information.

At an earlier time we would have been more cautious about suggesting that a chimpanzee might be able to produce extended utterances to communicate information. We believe now that it is the writers—who would predict just what it is that no chimpanzee will ever do—who must proceed with caution. Washoe's accomplishments will probably be exceeded by another chimpanzee, because it is unlikely that the conditions of training have been optimal in this first attempt. Theories of language that depend upon the identification of aspects of language that are exclusively human must remain tentative until a considerably larger body of intensive research with other species becomes available.

SUMMARY

We set ourselves the task of teaching an animal to use a form of human language. Highly intelligent and highly social, the chimpanzee is an obvious choice for such a study, yet it has not been possible to teach a member of this species more than a few spoken words. We reasoned that a spoken language, such as English, might be an inappropriate medium of communication for a chimpanzee. This led us to choose American Sign Language, the gestural system of communication used by the deaf in North America, for the project.

The youngest infant that we could obtain was a wild-born female, whom we named Washoe, and who was estimated to be between 8 and 14 months old when we began our program of training. The laboratory conditions, while not patterned after those of a human family (as in the studies of Kellogg and Kellogg and of Hayes and Hayes), involved a minimum of confinement and a maximum of social interaction with human companions. For all practical purposes, the only verbal communication was in ASL, and the chimpanzee was maximally exposed to the use of this language by human beings.

It was necessary to develop a rough-and-ready mixture of training methods. There was evidence that some of Washoe's early signs were acquired by delayed imitation of the signing behavior of her human companions, but very few, if any, of her early signs were introduced by immediate imitation. Manual babbling was directly fostered and did increase in the course of the project. A number of signs were introduced by shaping and instrumental conditioning. A particularly effective and convenient method of shaping consisted of holding Washoe's hands, forming them into a configuration, and putting them through the movements of a sign.

We have listed more than 30 signs that Washoe acquired and could use spontaneously and appropriately by the end of the 22nd month of the project. The signs acquired earliest were simple demands. Most of the later signs have been names for objects, which Washoe has used both as demands and as answers to questions. Washoe readily used noun signs to name pictures of objects as well as actual objects and has frequently called the attention of her companions to pictures and objects by naming them. Once acquired, the signs have not remained specific to the original referents but have been transferred spontaneously to a wide class of appropriate referents. At this writing, Washoe's rate of acquisition of new signs is still accelerating.

From the time she had eight or ten signs in her repertoire, Washoe began to use them in strings of two or more. During the period covered by this article we made no deliberate effort to elicit combinations other than by our own habitual use of strings of signs. Some of the combined forms that Washoe has used may have been imitative, but many have been inventions of her own. Only a small proportion of the possible combinations have, in fact, been observed. This is because most of Washoe's combinations include one of a limited group of signs that act as combiners. Among the signs that Washoe has recently acquired are the pronouns I-ME and YOU. When these occur in combinations the result resembles a short sentence. In terms of the eventual level of communication that a chimpanzee might be able to attain, the most promising results have been spontaneous naming, spontaneous transfer to new referents, and spontaneous combinations and recombinations of signs.

ACKNOWLEDGMENTS

We acknowledge a great debt to the personnel of the Aeromedical Research Laboratory, Holloman Air Force Base, whose support and expert assistance effectively absorbed all of the many difficulties attendant upon the acquisition of a wild-caught chimpanzee. We are also grateful to Dr. Frances L. Fitz-Gerald of the Yerkes Regional Primate Research Center for detailed advice on the care of an infant chimpanzee. Drs. Eamanual Berger of Reno, Nevada, and D. B. Olsen of the University of Nevada have served as medical consultants, and we are grateful to them for giving so generously of their time and medical skills. The faculty of the Sarah Hamilton Fleischmann School of Home Economics, University of Nevada, has generously allowed us to use the facilities of their experimental nursery school on weekends and holidays.

REFERENCES

Bryan, A. L. 1963. Curr. Anthropol. 4:297.

Goodall, J. 1965. *In* I. DeVore (ed.), Primate Behavior. Holt, Rinehart & Winston, New York.

Hayes, K. J., and Hayes, C. 1951. Proc. Am. Phil. Soc. 95:105.

Hayes, K. J., and Hayes, C. 1952. J. Comp. Physiol. Psychol. 45:450.

Hayes, K. J., and Hayes, C. 1955. *In* J. A. Gavan (ed.), The Non-Human Primates and Human Evolution. Wayne University Press, Detroit.

Kellogg, W. N. 1968. Science 162:423.

Kellogg, W. N., and Kellogg, L. A. 1967. The Ape and the Child. Hafner, New York. [Originally published 1933, McGraw-Hill Book Co., New York.]

Lenneberg, E. H. 1967. Biological Foundations of Language. John Wiley & Sons, New York.

McCall, E. A. 1965. Thesis, University of Iowa.

Riopelle, A. J., and Rogers, C. M. 1965. *In* A. M. Schrier, H. F. Harlow, and F. Stollnitz (eds.), Behavior of Nonhuman Primates. Academic Press, New York.

Stokoe, W. C., Casterline, D., and Croneberg, C. G. 1965. A Dictionary of American Sign Language. Gallaudet College Press, Washington, D.C.

Warden, C. J., and Warner, L. H. 1928. Q. Rev. Biol. 3:1.

Yerkes, R. M. 1943. Chimpanzees. Yale University Press, New Haven, Conn.

Yerkes, R. M., and Learned, B. W. 1925. Chimpanzee Intelligence and Its Vocal Expression. Williams & Wilkins, Baltimore.

chapter

10

Early Signs of Language in Child and Chimpanzee

R. Allen Gardner*

Beatrice T. Gardner*

Department of Psychology
University of Nevada
Reno, Nevada

In a sequel to Project Washoe, chimpanzees are being taught American Sign Language from birth by humans who are fluent in the language, including persons who are themselves deaf or whose parents were deaf. The first two subjects began to use signs when they were three months old, and these early results indicate that the new conditions are significantly superior to the conditions of Project Washoe. More valid comparisons can now be made between the acquisition of language by children and by chimpanzees.

The exposure of children to their native language begins at birth, and most theories of language acquisition assume that the exposure during the earliest years is particularly significant. What evidence there is on this point is, at best, indirect. Long term negative effects of an impoverished linguistic environment can be demonstrated for children reared in orphanages during the first years of life (Mussen, 1963). Favorable effects of early exposure to language—in this case, sign language—can also be demonstrated by comparing deaf children of deaf parents with deaf children of hearing parents on tests of the ability to speak, read, or write English (Mindel and Vernon, 1971; Schlesinger and Meadow, 1972). Moreover, with the recently developed techniques for recording behavior of neonates, it has been shown that the human infant is responsive to characteristics of adult speech, such as segmentation and the distinction between phonemes, within a month of birth (Eimas et al., 1971; Condon and Sander, 1974). It seems likely that the beneficial effects of early exposure to language can also be demonstrated in attempts to teach language to animals.

Project Washoe was the first attempt to teach sign language to a chimpanzee. Washoe was about 11 months old when her training in American Sign Language (Ameslan) began. Within 51 months, she had acquired 132 signs of Ameslan, as determined by criteria for reliable usage developed during the research (Gardner and Gardner, 1972). As with humans using words, Washoe used her signs for classes of referents rather than for particular objects or events, and used signs in combinations (Gardner and Gardner, 1969, 1971, in press). Brown (1970, 1973), Klima and Bellugi (1970), and other investigators of child language have commented on the many ways in which Washoe's acquisition of sign language parallels the acquisition of spoken language by children, as, for example, in Washoe's generalization of the meaning of signs, in the gradual increase in length of her sign combinations, and in the types of semantic relations expressed by early combinations. Thus, Project Washoe demonstrated that Ameslan is a suitable medium of communication for a chimpanzee, and that, given a suitable medium, a significant

From Gardner, R. A., and Gardner, B. T. 1975. Early signs of language in child and chimpanzee. Science 187:752–753. Reprinted by permission. Copyright 1975 by the American Association for the Advancement of Science.
* Affiliation given reflects the authors' affiliation at time of writing.
Supported by NSF grant GB-35586, by NIMH research development grant MH-34953 (to B. T. G.), and by the Grant Foundation, New York.

level of two-way communication could be achieved. Since then, several chimpanzees in several laboratories have acquired a vocabulary of signs (Fouts, 1973, p. 34), and it is appropriate to pose questions about individual differences, about limits, and about the effectiveness of different methods of teaching sign language. In our current project of teaching sign language to several chimpanzees, we are capitalizing upon our experience in the research with Washoe by improving key features of procedure, and we plan to maintain these more favorable conditions until the subjects reach intellectual maturity. In this way, we can come much closer to describing the highest level of two-way communication that can be achieved by chimpanzees taught a form of human language.

One of the significant improvements in procedure is that several fluent signers, including deaf persons and persons who have deaf parents, are research personnel in the current project. These "native speakers" of Ameslan provide for more adequate models of the language than those we provided for Washoe.

Another improvement is that the exposure of subjects to Ameslan begins one or two days after birth. Chimpanzee Moja was born at the Laboratory of Experimental Medicine and Surgery in Primates, Tuxedo Park, N.Y., on November 18, 1972 and arrived in our laboratory on the next day. Chimpanzee Pili was born at Yerkes Regional Primate Research Center, Atlanta, Ga., on October 30, 1973 and arrived in our laboratory on November 1.

No special difficulties were encountered in maintaining the infants in good health. Their care is similar to that of the human infant: around-the-clock feedings, diapering, inoculations, sanitary precautions such as sterilization of bottles, and so on. In addition, we provided the infants with body contact whenever they were awake. Within a few weeks, the infants appeared responsive to the activities of their human companions, which included a great deal of signing. Even in the earliest months, the infants were attentive and alert. They could grasp toys, imitate actions such as blowing kisses or peekaboo, and differentiate their usual companions from strangers.

Both Moja and Pili started to make recognizable signs when they were about three months old (Figure 1). In Project Washoe, we kept track of new signs by noting spontaneous and appropriate use of the sign. The day that the third of three observers reported appropriate and spontaneous occurrence was taken as the date of the appearance of the new sign in the vocabulary. By this criterion, Moja's first four signs (COME-GIMME, GO, MORE, and DRINK) appeared during her 13th week of life. Similarly, Pili's first sign appeared during his 14th week of life, and he had a four-sign vocabulary (DRINK, COME-GIMME, MORE, and TICKLE) by his 15th week. The first four signs met the three-observer

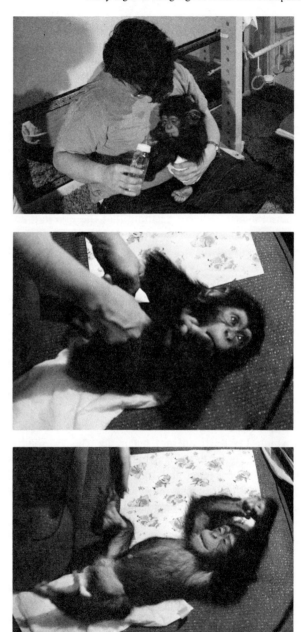

Figure 1.   Chimpanzee Pili, at age four months, using the Ameslan sign DRINK (top) when shown his water bottle, and the sign MORE (bottom) after a bout of tickling. The position of Pili's hands and his orientation toward the human companion when signing MORE are different from those during the preceding bout of tickling (center).

criterion within a few days of each other for both subjects. At the age of six months, Moja's vocabulary consisted of 15 signs, and Pili's of 13 signs. By contrast, Washoe's exposure to sign language did not begin until she was nearly one year old, and the effective start of the exposure was further delayed because the research participants were only beginning to learn Ameslan. After six months of exposure, Washoe's vocabulary consisted of the signs COME-GIMME and MORE.

In the early stages of Project Washoe, we developed a procedure to determine when a new sign had become a reliable item in the chimpanzee's vocabulary. After the third report of a new sign, the sign was added to a checklist. Each day thereafter, the first person to observe Washoe using a sign on the checklist entered a description of its form and context. As the criterion for deciding that the sign had become reliable, we chose a period of 15 consecutive days during which at least one appropriate and spontaneous use of the sign had been recorded (Gardner and Gardner, 1969, 1971, in press).

These 15-day records for the present study show that, even at this early stage, signs were being used, not as mechanical routines, but with variations in form and in appropriate variations of a basic context. For example, in the set of reports on Pili's use of TICKLE during February 14 to 28, 1974, two kinds of context were described. Usually, Pili signed for continuation of tickling when his companion stopped tickling him momentarily or stopped and asked questions such as, WHAT WE PLAY NOW? But in two reports, Pili initiated tickling with his sign. Pili also used another of his early signs, MORE, to request continuation of tickling during this period (Figure 1). But MORE was recorded in several contexts in which TICKLE did not occur, as when we had taken away Pili's water bottle after a bout of drinking or had stopped games other than tickling, such as covering and uncovering Pili's face with a scarf. In forming TICKLE, Pili drew the index finger over the back of his other hand or the back of his companion's hand about equally often. Moja also used both her own body and corresponding parts of the addressee's body as the place for making TICKLE and other early signs; this variation in form has been reported for Washoe and for very young deaf children (Gardner and Gardner, 1972).

Fouts (1973) reported that an infant female, Salome, used the sign FOOD during her fourth month. While the age at which chimpanzees produce their first signs seems early compared to that for first words of humans, it is not very discrepant from the age at which the first signs appear in humans. There are parental reports of first signs between the fifth and sixth months for children exposed to sign language (Mindel and Vernon, 1971; Schlesinger and Meadow, 1972). Possibly, signs are easier to make than words; more likely it is easier for a parent to recognize the infant's poor approximation to a sign than his poor approximation to a spoken word. We consider the early appearance of signs to be an important confirmation of two major procedural improvements in the current project; the exposure of subjects to fluent Ameslan signers and the exposure to language from birth. Of course, it is not the size of early vocabulary per se that is significant but what this promises in terms of further development under the more favorable conditions for the acquisition of sign language.

ACKNOWLEDGMENTS

We thank E. Berger, M.D., for help and advice on the health care of the newborn chimpanzees.

REFERENCES

Brown, R. 1970. Psycholinguistics: Selected Papers by Roger Brown. Free Press, New York.
Brown, R. 1973. A First Language. Harvard University Press, Cambridge, Mass.
Condon, W. S., and Sander, L. W. 1974. Science 183:99.
Eimas, P. D., Siqueland, E. R., Jusczyk, P., and Vigorito, J. 1971. Science 171:303.
Fouts, R. S. 1973. Science Year: World Book Science Annual, 1974. Field, Chicago.
Gardner, B. T., and Gardner, R. A. 1971. In A. M. Schrier and F. Stollnitz (eds.), Behavior of Nonhuman Primates. Academic Press, New York.
Gardner, B. T., and Gardner, R. A. In A. Pick (ed.), Minnesota Symposium on Child Psychology, Vol. 8. University of Minnesota Press, Minneapolis. In press.
Gardner, R. A., and Gardner, B. T. 1969. Science 165:664.
Gardner, R. A., and Gardner, B. T. 1972. In R. Chauvin (ed.), Modeles Animaux du Comportement Humain. Centre National de la Recherche Scientifique, Paris.
Klima, E., and Bellugi, U. 1970. In G. A. Miller (ed.), Forum Series on Psychology and Communication. Voice of America, Washington, D.C.
Mindel, E. D., and Vernon, M. 1971. They Grow in Silence: The Deaf Child and His Family. National Association of the Deaf, Silver Spring, Md.
Mussen, P. H. 1963. The Psychological Development of the Child. Prentice-Hall, Englewood Cliffs, N.J.
Schlesinger, H. S., and Meadow, K. P. 1972. Sound and Sign. University of California Press, Berkeley.

ADDENDUM OF SUGGESTED READINGS

Gardner, B. T., and Gardner, R. A. 1971. Two-way communication with an infant chimpanzee. In A. M. Schrier and F. Stollnitz (eds.), Behavior of Nonhuman Primates, Vol. 4, Academic Press, New York.

Gardner, B. T., and Gardner, R. A. 1974. Comparing the early utterances of child and chimpanzee. *In* A. Pick (ed.), Minnesota Symposium on Child Psychology, Vol. 8. University of Minnesota Press, Minneapolis.

Gardner, B. T., and Gardner, R. A. 1975. Evidence for sentence consitutents in the early utterances of child and chimpanzee. J. Exp. Psychol.: General 104:244–267.

Gardner, R. A. and Gardner, B. T. 1974. Review of R. Brown's *A First Language: The Early Stages*. Am. J. Psychol. 87:729–736.

Gardner, R. A., and Gardner, B. T. 1978. Comparative psychology and language acquisition. *In* K. Salzinger and F. Denmark, (eds.), Psychology the State of the Art. Annals of the New York Academy of Sciences, New York.

chapter 11

Communication and Language in the Home-Raised Chimpanzee

Winthrop N. Kellogg*

Professor Emeritus of Experimental Psychology
Florida State University
Tallahassee, Florida

contents

Oral speech develops in the human infant as an outgrowth of his contact with older humans who are continuously using language. A deaf mute fails to speak because he never hears the acoustic patterns which make up words. He has no sound patterns to follow, no models to imitate. If the ear itself is functioning but the child is mentally retarded, he may be able to hear but not to imitate. Again, he does not learn to speak. A normal ear, a normal brain and speech organs, the continuous hearing of spoken language, and a great deal of imitation are necessary for the completion of the process.

The ear, the speech mechansim, and the capacity to imitate are furnished by the child. The linguistic models come from the human environment in which he lives. Also furnished by the child—perhaps as a result of, or in connection with, his imitation—is a long prespeech period in which he produces both vowels and consonants, but not words. This period of prattling and babbling seems to be a necessary forerunner of the words to come. Children who acquire normal speech habits do so as a kind of outgrowth and expansion of this developmental phase (Smith and Miller, 1966). In the terminology of the experimental psychologist, it may be thought of as a period of "preconditioning" or "pretraining."

If special requirements such as these are necessary for speech to occur in a young human, does any other organism below man possess them? The chimpanzee certainly has a good enough ear, as measurements of auditory sensitivity have demonstrated (Elder, 1934, 1935). So far as the larynx and speech parts are concerned, the general assumption has been that these also are sufficiently well developed to permit the articulation of words—although Kelemen (1948, 1949) takes exception to this position. The chimpanzee is a great imitator of the movements and activities it sees performed, although it is not as good an imitator as the child (Kellogg and Kellogg, 1933a; Hayes and Hayes, 1952). It does not naturally imitate sounds and noises, like the parrot or the myna bird, which can reproduce human word sounds but are less apt at nonvocal imitation. Also, the development of the chimpanzee brain as compared with that of man remains in doubt.

But has a chimpanzee (or any of the other apes, for that matter) ever been given a really adequate opportunity to learn and to imitate human speech signals as they occur in their natural context? Has a chimpanzee been exposed to the environmental sound-models which are necessary—for as long a time and in the same way as human children?

THE APE-REARING EXPERIMENT

The ape-rearing experiment should furnish an answer to such questions. If communication were ever to evolve, it would seem that the environ-

From Kellogg, W. N. 1968. Communication and Language in the Home-Raised Chimpanzee. Science 162:423–427. Reprinted by permission. Copyright 1968 by the American Association for the Advancement of Science.

* Affiliation given reflects the author's affiliation at time of writing.

ment of a human household would offer the most favorable conditions. To be sure, the keeping of infrahuman primates as pets or playthings is by no means a novel practice and can be traced historically as far back as the ancient Greeks and Egyptians (Morris and Morris, 1966). Apes as household pets are not uncommon today and several books by lay authors attest to the problems involved (Kearton, 1925; Hoyt, 1941; Lintz, 1942; Hess, 1954; Harrisson, 1962). Such ventures have never given any indication of the development of human language. But pet behavior is not child behavior, and pet treatment is not child treatment.

It is quite another story, therefore, for trained and qualified psychobiologists to observe and measure the reactions of a home-raised pongid amid controlled experimental home surroundings. Such research is difficult, confining, and time consuming. Too often, unfortunately, its purpose is misunderstood. Since 1932 reports of five such experiments by qualified investigators have been published in the United States and one in Russia. Four of the U.S. studies were sponsored by the Yerkes Laboratories of Primate Biology at Orange Park, Florida[1] The animals used in all instances were chimpanzees.

The Russian research and two of those conducted in America had a human child or children as permanent in-house controls. In the other experiments the chimps were raised in a household with adult humans alone. Table 1 gives some of the characteristics of the different experiments, including the approximate duration of each, the number of child controls, the ages of the chimpanzees, and the names of the investigators. In the present article we deal only with those aspects of these researches having to do with communication and language. The work of Kohts (1935), Kellogg and Kellogg (1932a, 1932b, 1933a, 1933b, 1933c, 1945) C. Hayes (1951), Hayes and Hayes (1950, 1951, 1952, 1953, 1954a, 1954b), and Gardner and Gardner (1967a, 1967b, personal communication) is of special importance in this connection. The observations of Jacobsen, Jacobsen and Yoshioka (1932) do not deal with this topic, and Finch himself never published any of his findings.

THE PRONUNCIATION OF WORDS

The results of such projects show in general that the infant chimp, when properly handled in the home situation, reacts in many ways as a young child does. It adapts rapidly to the physical features of the environment (Hayes and Hayes, 1954b; Kellogg and Kellogg, 1933b, 1933c), shows a strong attachment for its caretaker or experimental mother, passes a

---

[1] Now the Yerkes Regional Primate Research Center of Emory University at Atlanta, Georgia.

Table 1.   Principal chimpanzee-raising experiments

Publi-cation date	Investigator	Approx. duration	Approx. age of chimp at start	Sex and name of chimp	No. of child controls
1932	Jacobsen, Jacobsen, and Yoshioka (1932)	1 year	A few days	F; Alpha	0
1932–1967	Kellogg and Kellogg (1932a, 1932b, 1933a, 1933b, 1933c, 1945)	9 months	7½ months	F; Gua	1
1935	Kohts (1935)	2½ years	1½ years	M; Joni	1
None	Finch	3 years	3 days	M; Fin	2
1951–1954	Hayes and Hayes (1950, 1951, 1952, 1953, 1954a, 1954b)	6½ years	3 days	F; Viki	0
1967	Gardner and Gardner (1967a, 1967b, personal communcation)	In progress	9–15 months	F; Washoe	0

good many of the preschool developmental tests designed for children, and imitates acts performed by adults without special training. Up to the age of perhaps three years, its "mental age" is not far behind that of a child. At the same time, its skeletal and muscular development are much more rapid than those of a child.

With regard to the problem of communication the results at first glance are disappointing. For even in the experimentally controlled environment in which a home-raised chimpanzee is given the same linguistic and social advantages as a human baby, the chimp displays little evidence of vocal imitation. Despite its generally high level of imitative behavior, it never copies or reproduces human word sounds. Yerkes (1943) has written with reference to this matter that in neither the studies of Kellogg nor of Finch "were attempts to imitate speech or other indications of learning to use human language observed" (p. 192). Kohts (1935) noted also that her home-raised chimpanzee displayed not the slightest evidence of trying to reproduce any human vocalizations (p. 576).

Moreover, no ape has ever been known to go through the long period of babbling and prattling which, in the human baby, seems to be the necessary prerequisite to the subsequent articulation of word sounds. Vocalized play of this sort was absent in the Kelloggs' chimp, who made no sounds "without some definite provocation . . . and in most cases this stimulus was obviously of an emotional character" (1933a, p. 281). The Hayeses noted also that their ape was much "less vocal" and was relatively silent as compared to a child (1951, p. 106; 1953).

Despite these observations, the usual chimpanzee noises—such as the foodbark, the "oo oo" cry, and screeching or screaming—were present in all of these experiments and were vigorously employed. The use of these and other sounds as natural communicative signals has been examined by Goodall (1965) for chimpanzees in the wild, and by Yerkes and Learned (1925) for captive animals. It is a question whether such sounds can be modified or shaped to fit the human language pattern.

On the positive side belong the remarkable cases of so-called talking apes. A trained chimpanzee studied by Witmer as far back as 1909 was reported to be able to pronounce the word "mama" but only with great difficulty. The "m" of "mama" was well done, but the "ah" was not voiced (Witmer, 1909).

A few years later, Furness (1916), working diligently with a young orangutan, finally succeeded in getting it to say "papa" and "cup." In training the animal to say "papa," Furness found it necessary to place his fingers on the animal's lips and to open and close them in the proper rhythm.

The best known and most successful of these linguistic efforts is that of the Hayeses (Hayes, 1951), who were able to get their chimpanzee Viki to emit recognizable versions of the words "papa," "mama," and "cup." A beginning was also made toward the sound of "up." Viki thereby exceeded the vocabulary level of either of the other apes, although interestingly enough, she pronounced the same words that they had. She had only one vowel for all of her word sounds, a hoarse and exaggerated stage whisper.

The first step in Viki's speech training was designed to teach her to produce a sound—any sound—on demand. This was done by reinforcing whatever noises she made during the training session, such as the pleasure barks elicited by showing her food, or the "oo oo" which resulted from withdrawing the food. It was five months, however, before the animal could emit a sound promptly on cue, and the noise she made then was a new one: a hoarse "ah," quite unlike the normal chimpanzee vocalizations which had been previously rewarded.

The Hayeses taught Viki to say "mama" by manipulating her lips as she said "ah," then gradually reduced the amount of manipulation as she learned to make the lip movements herself. In this way the animal finally came to say "mama," softly and hoarsely, and without help (although she persisted in putting her own forefinger on her upper lip). Viki's later words were learned more quickly, making use of existing consonant-like mouth sounds which she had often produced in play. Fortunately, her articulation and vocal behavior have been preserved in a sound motion-picture film (Hayes and Hayes, 1950).

These then, "mama," "papa," "cup," and possibly "up," represent the acme of chimpanzee achievement in the production of human speech sounds. But they were learned ony with the greatest difficulty. And, even after she could reproduce them, the animal's words were sometimes confused and were used incorrectly. The most important finding of the Hayeses was perhaps not that their chimp could enunciate a few human sounds. It lay rather in the discovery that these sound patterns were extremely hard for the ape to master, that they never came naturally or easily, and that she had trouble afterward in keeping the patterns straight.

COMPREHENSION OF LANGUAGE

The ability of a home-raised chimpanzee to "understand" or react characteristically to spoken words or phrases is perhaps best illustrated by the Kelloggs' ape Gua. These investigators kept a daily record of the language units which both the chimpanzee and her human control were able to discriminate. In the case of the chimpanzee, the words reacted to varied from such relatively simple commands as "No no" and "Come here" to statements like "Close the door," "Blow the horn" (of a car), "Don't put that in your mouth," and "Go to Daddy," "Go to Mama," "Go to Donald" (as the case might be). In the first four months of the study, the chimp was slightly ahead of the child in the total number of spoken phrases to which she could respond correctly. This was no doubt due to her superior locomotor ability since, in the beginning, the human subject was obviously unable to comply with such commands as "Get up on the chair." During the last five months of the period of comparison, the child surpassed the ape in comprehension. The total score for the entire nine months was 68 specific response patterns for the child and 58 for the chimpanzee (Kellogg and Kellogg, 1933a).

Although the ape was only slightly behind her human control at the end, it is noteworthy that she had earlier scored higher than he. This means that she was overtaken by the child, who accelerated at a more rapid rate. Had the comparison continued for a longer period, all indications are that the human subject would have left the animal far behind in the comprehension of words.

SPONTANEOUS GESTURING

Does an anthropoid ape, maintained in the human household, ever use or develop any system of motions or gestures which carry special significance or meaning? The answer is "yes," the amount and type of gesturing depending upon the particular home environment and the particular animal. Regarding this matter, the Hayeses (1954a) have written about Viki that she "makes relatively little use of gestures of the hand alone"

(p. 299). She would nevertheless take hold of the experimenter's hand and lead him where she wanted to go, an activity earlier observed by Yerkes (1916) in an orangutan with which he worked.

Mrs. Kohts (1935) reports that gestures were commonly employed by her chimpanzee Joni and, surprisingly, that many of the chimp gestures were like those used by her son. "Both infants sometimes show a nearly similar gesture language. Thus 'request' is expressed by extending hand forward, 'rejection of food' by turning face and head aside, 'thirst' by putting hand to mouth, 'desire to draw attention to oneself' by tugging at dress" (p. 544).

The Kelloggs' chimpanzee Gua also employed a kind of language of gesture or of action, but in this instance the gesturing of the ape was generally different from that of the child. Most of Gua's gestures consisted of movement patterns which occurred regularly just before or in advance of some subsequent or final act. In this way they served as preparatory signals for the terminal response to come later. Viewed objectively, these signaling movements can be interpreted as anticipatory reactions which were consistent with and occurred in specific situations. It need not be presumed, therefore, that they necessarily represented conscious or purposeful efforts on the part of the animal to "tell" others what she wanted. Their reliability was confirmed by numerous repetitions. The principal instances of this language of action are given in Table 2.

The most significant of the gestures listed in Table 2 are probably those for "sleep" or "sleepiness," those indicating bladder and bowel needs, and the "help me" signal in drinking a Coke. The latter occurred spontaneously during a minor test problem. The animal was seated upon

Table 2.   Early gesture signals of chimpanzee Gua[a]

Behavior pattern	Human interpretation
Biting or chewing at clothing or fingers of experimenter	"Hungry"
Climbing into high chair	Same
Protruding lips toward cup	"Drink"
Pushing cup away	"Enough"
Removing bib from her neck	"Finished eating"
Taking hand of experimenter and hanging on it	"Swing me"
Throwing self prone on floor	"Sleepy" or "Tired" (goes to sleep at once when put to bed for nap)
Pulling hand of experimenter to Coke bottle	"Help me" or "Lift this for me"
Holding of genitalia	"Need to urinate (or defecate)"

[a] Adapted from Kellogg and Kellogg (1933a, pp. 275–278).

the floor with legs spread apart, and a bottle of Coca Cola with cap removed was placed between her feet. Although she could hold the bottle at the proper angle while drinking, she had not yet learned how to transport it from the floor to her mouth. Unsuccessful attempts consisted of licking or sucking at the opening of the bottle and of overturning it in the crude attempt to pick it up. Finally, after staring at the bottle and looking up at the experimenter, she took his hand in one of her own and drew it gently down to the base of the bottle. This was by no means an isolated instance, since it appeared several times during repetitions of the test. Similar reactions of placing the experimenter's hand on objects to be manipulated were also observed by the Hayeses with their chimpanzee Viki.

TWO-WAY COMMUNICATION BY GESTURE

The spontaneous use of gesture movements by chimpanzees raises the question whether this ability to gesture can be developed into something more. Could an intelligent animal learn a series of regular or standardized signals—as a sort of semaphore system? Even though a chimp may lack the laryngeal structure or neural speech centers of man, it does not necessarily follow that it has deficiencies in general motor activity. Might it therefore be able to communicate back and forth by a series of hand movements, arm signals, and postures? Is two-way communication by gesture possible? This is the question which has recently been asked by the Gardners (1967a, 1967b) and is now under active investigation by them.

It should be understood, however, that the signs and signals employed by the Gardners constitute a systematic and recognized form of voiceless communication. The alphabet language devised for the deaf, in which each word is spelled out by individual hand and finger movements, would obviously be unsuitable. What the Gardners are using is a series of more general or more encompassing hand and arm movements (not involving spelling) which serve as substitutes for entire words, phrases, or sentences. The American Sign Language meets these requirements. This is an accepted form of human language and is in active use today in Canada and the United States, principally by the deaf (Stokoe, Casterline, and Croneberg, 1965).

The chimpanzee subject of the Gardners' study, a young female named Washoe, has been undergoing training in the understanding and transmitting of sign-language signals since June, 1966. The animal lives in a fully furnished house trailer and also has access to children's toys and equipment, as well as to extensive play areas. The human beings who come into contact with Washoe communicate with each other in

Washoe's presence only by means of sign language. She hears no human words except those spoken inadvertently by workmen or others not associated with the project. Conditioning methods have been used to establish many of the signs which are employed.

In support of this new approach is the fact that both chimpanzees and gorillas in the wild state are known to use specific gestures and postures (along with noises) for communicating among themselves (Schaller, 1963; Goodall, 1965). Chimpanzees in laboratory experiments will also adopt characteristic attitudes as a means of communication. An example is the posture of imploring or begging observed by Wolfe (1936). As for the home-raised chimp, the gestures of both Mrs. Kohts' Joni and the Kelloggs' Gua have already been noted (see Table 2). There would seem, therefore, to be considerable promise in the gesture method.

After 16 months of training, Washoe was able to use 19 signs reliably. Five more signs were in the developmental stage. A good many

Table 3.   Some significant gesture-language signs used by chimpanzee Washoe

Sign	Description	Context
COME-GIMME	Beckoning, with wrist or knuckles as pivot.	To persons, dogs, etc.; also for objects out of reach such as food or toys.
UP	Point up with index finger.	Wants a lift to reach object such as grapes on vine, leaves, etc., or wants to be placed on someone's shoulders.
HEAR-LISTEN	Index finger touches ear.	For loud or strange sounds: bells, car horns, sonic booms, footsteps, etc.
TOOTH-BRUSH	Using index finger as brush, rub front teeth.	At end of meals. Once when Washoe noticed toothbrush in strange bathroom.
HURT	The extended index fingers are jabbed toward each other. Can be used to indicate location of pain.	To indicate cuts and bruises on herself or on others. Can be elicited by red stains on a person.
HURRY	Shaking open hand at the wrist. (Correct ASL (American Sign Language) form: use index and second fingers extended side by side.)	Frequently follows signs such as COME-GIMME, OUT, OPEN, GO.
SORRY	Rub bent hand across chest. (Correct ASL form: rub fisted hand, circular motion.)	After biting someone, or when someone has been hurt in some other way (not necessarily by Washoe). When told to apologize for mischief.
PLEASE	Rub open hand on chest, then extend in a begging gesture. (Correct ASL form: use fingertips and circular motion.)	Asking for objects and activities. Frequently combined: PLEASE GO, OUT PLEASE, PLEASE DRINK, etc.

of the movements used by the animal are standard American Sign Language signals. Some are variants of the standard and a few are chimpanzee originals. There is evidence that she understands a great many more signs than she can use herself. Some of the gestures employed by Washoe are given in Table 3.

The most significant thing about these gesture signals is that they are by no means confined to the names of specific persons or things. (They are not all nouns.) Some of them—for example, PLEASE, HURRY, SORRY—are verbs and adjectives which apply in varying social contexts and are used effectively in different situations of the same class. As such they are far in advance of all previous chimpanzee efforts to communicate with human beings.

SUMMARY

Although often misunderstood, the scientific rationale for rearing an anthropoid ape in a human household is to find out just how far the ape can go in absorbing the civilizing influences of the environment. To what degree is it capable of responding like a child and to what degree will genetic factors limit its development? At least six comprehensive studies by qualified investigators have been directed wholly or partly to this problem. All of these studies employed young chimpanzees as subjects and some also had in-house child controls whose day-to-day development could be compared directly with that of the experimental animal. In general, the results of this sort of research show that the home-raised chimp adapts rapidly to the physical features of the household. It does many things as well as a human child and some of them better (for example, those involving strength and climbing).

By far the greatest deficiency shown by the ape in the human environment is its lack of language ability. This eliminates the verbal communication which humans enjoy, and with it the vast amount of social intercourse and learning which are dependent upon language. Even amid human surroundings a chimp never prattles or babbles as a young child does when beginning to talk. Although it imitates the behavior of others readily, it seems to lack the ability for vocal imitation. The neural speech centers of the brain are no doubt deficient in this respect and it is possible also that the larynx and speech organs are incapable of producing the complex sound patterns of human language. One long-time attempt to teach a home-raised chimp to pronounce human words succeeded only in getting the animal to mouth unvoiced whispers of the words "mama," "papa," "cup," and "up."

At the same time, a chimpanzee in the home, as in the wild state, uses gestures or movements as communicating signals. This suggests the possibility of training a home-raised ape to employ a standardized system of gestures as a means of two-way communication. Such an investigation is now under way, using a gesture language devised for the deaf. Considerable progress has already been made in both the receiving and sending of gesture signals by this method. The technique seems to offer a much greater likelihood of success than other methods of intercommunication between chimpanzees and humans.

ACKNOWLEDGMENTS

I am indebted to Dr. Keith J. Hayes who has read most of the material in this article in its preparatory stages and has made a number of helpful suggestions. We are also grateful to Dr. R. A. Gardner and Dr. B. T. Gardner for permission to publish information, from one of their research proposals (see Gardner and Gardner, 1967b), concerning the progress of the chimpanzee, Washoe, for the first part of their experiment: Further development of the chimpanzee in this remarkable research is anticipated. However, the subject matter as presented here is solely my responsibility.

REFERENCES

Elder, J. H. 1934. J. Comp. Psychol. 17:157–183.
Elder, J. H. 1935. Am. J. Physiol. 112:109.
Furness, W. H. 1916. Proc. Am. Phil. Soc. 55:281.
Gardner, R. A., and Gardner, B. T. 1967a. (Parts I and II). Psychonom. Bull. 1:36.
Gardner, R. A., and Gardner, B. T. 1967b. Unpublished proposal and progress report, University of Nevada, Reno.
Goodall, J. 1965. *In* I. Devore (ed.), Primate Behavior, pp. 425–473. Holt, Rinehart & Winston, New York.
Harrisson, B. 1962. Oran-gutan. Collins, London.
Hayes, C. 1951. The Ape in Our House. Harper & Brothers, New York.
Hayes, K. J., and Hayes, C. 1950. Vocalization and speech in chimpanzees (16-mm sound film). Pennsylvania State University, Psychological Cinema Register, University Park.
Hayes, K. J., and Hayes, C. 1951. Proc. Am. Phil. Soc. 95:105.
Hayes, K. J., and Hayes, C. 1952. J. Comp. Physiol. Psychol. 45:450.
Hayes, K. J., and Hayes, C. 1953. J. Comp. Physiol. Psychol. 46:470.
Hayes, K. J., and Hayes, C. 1954a. Hum. Biol. 26:288.
Hayes, K. J., and Hayes, C. 1954b. The mechanical interest and ability of a home-raised chimpanzee (16-mm silent film). Pennsylvania State University, Psychological Cinema Register, University Park.
Hess, L. 1954. Christine the Baby Chimp. Bell, London.
Hoyt, A. M. 1941. Toto and I: A Gorilla in the Family. Lippincott, New York.
Jacobsen, C. F., Jacobsen, M. M., and Yoshioka, J. G. 1932. Comp. Psychol. Monogr. 9:1–94.
Kearton, C. 1925. My Friend Toto: The Adventures of a Chimpanzee and the Story of His Journey from the Congo to London. Arrowsmith, London.
Kelemen, G. 1948. J. Morphol. 82:229–256.
Kelemen, G. 1949. Arch. Otolaryngol. 50:740.

Kellogg, W. N., and Kellogg, L. A. 1932a. Comparative tests on a human and a chimpanzee infant of approximately the same age (16-mm silent film). Pennsylvania State University, Psychological Cinema Register, University Park.

Kellogg, W. N., and Kellogg, L. A. 1932b. Experiments upon a human and a chimpanzee infant after six months in the same environment (16-mm silent film). Pennsylvania State University, Psychological Cinema Register, University Park.

Kellogg, W. N., and Kellogg, L. A. 1933a. The Ape and the Child: A Study of Environmental Influence on Early Behavior. McGraw-Hill Book Co., New York [1967, Hafner, New York].

Kellogg, W. N., and Kellogg, L. A. 1933b. Some behavior characterisitics of a human and a chimpanzee infant in the same environment (16-mm silent film). Pennsylvania State University, Psychological Cinema Register, University Park.

Kellogg, W. N., and Kellogg, L. A. 1933c. Some general reactions of a human and a chimpanzee infant after six months in the same environment (16-mm silent film). Pennsylvania State University, Psychol. Cinema Register, University Park.

Kellogg, W. N., and Kellogg, L. A. 1945. Facial expressions of a human and a chimpanzee infant following taste stimuli (16-mm silent film). Pennsylvania State University, Psychological Cinema Register, University Park.

Kohts, N. 1935. Infant Ape and Human Child. Museum Darwinianum, Moscow.

Lintz, G. D. 1942. Animals Are My Hobby. McBride, New York.

Morris, R., and Morris, D. 1966. Men and Apes. McGraw-Hill Book Co., New York.

Schaller, G. B. 1963. The Mountain Gorilla: Ecology and Behavior. University of Chicago Press, Chicago.

Smith, F. L., and Miller, G. A. (eds.) 1966. The Genesis of Language. The MIT Press, Cambridge, Mass.

Stokoe, W. C., Casterline, D., and Croneberg, C. G. 1965. A Dictionary of American Sign Language on Linguistic Principles. Gallaudet College Press, Washington, D.C.

Witmer, L. 1909. Psychol. Clinic (Philadelphia) 3:179–205.

Wolfe, J. B. 1936. Comp. Psychol. Monogr. 12:1–72.

Yerkes, R. M. 1916. Behav. Monogr. 3:1–145.

Yerkes, R. M. 1943. Chimpanzees. A Laboratory Colony. Yale University Press, New Haven, Conn.

Yerkes, R. M., and Learned, B. W. 1925. Chimpanzee Intelligence and Its Vocal Expressions. Williams & Wilkins, Baltimore.

Section

IV

Strategies for Language and Communication Acquisition

Bruno

Sarah

Editors' Introduction

In studying concept formation or cognitive abilities of infrahuman organisms, the comparative psychologist has been forced to develop techniques for communicating the task or problem to the organism. The trainer of animals for carnivals and circuses is faced with the same problem. The greater the psychologist's or trainer's knowledge of the organism's behavior, anatomy, and physiology, the more likely he is to select a functional technique or communication channel (see Chapter 1, this volume). The important point is that, in developing strategies for language and communication acquisition, it is necessary to take advantage of the behavioral attributes of the species. An example is the repeated failure to teach speech to the chimpanzee (Section III).

Why teach language and communication to an ape? There are many reasons to teach language to infrahuman species, four of which include: 1) to advance knowledge of an infrahuman species, 2) to behaviorally determine the organism's niche on the phylogenetic scale, 3) to use the organism as a model for learning more about the acquisition of language skills, and 4) to develop techniques and methodology to teach language to handicapped persons (e.g., mentally retarded, deaf, and speech impaired). The last reason is the outgrowth of research related to the first three (see Chapters 17 and 19, this volume). No matter the reason for undertaking language research with chimpanzees and gorillas, the important fact is that this work has required the researchers to replace the structural (linguistic) definition of language by a functional one (Premack, 1970 [Chapter 12, this volume]). In other words, what are the important variables in language acquisition? Can strategies be devised for acquisition of language in an infrahuman species?

There will always be philosophical arguments about whether nonhuman primates have or can develop language. In fact, Limber (1977) states, "The ability of apes or even two-year-olds to communicate and use simple names is not sufficient reason to attribute the use of human language to them" (p. 280). However, establishing an association between symbols (names) and environmental referents (objects, etc.) is a step in the right direction (see Hollis and Carrier, 1978). The establishment of the *word* as an essential unit of language (symbolization) becomes a precursor to the *sentence*.

The chapters in this section present the development of different strategies for the acquisition of symbolic and language skills by chimpanzees and gorillas. The strategies differ with respect to linguistic analyses, *receptive modes* (stimulus input), *associative factors* (mediation and cognitive level), and *expressive modes* (symbol selection or symbol production).

FUNCTIONAL ANALYSIS OF LANGUAGE

One limiting factor for language development in the chimpanzee may not be language per se, but the complexity of the response. It has been noted that the speech response mode (expressive language) is inappropriate for the chimpanzee. A second factor involves the operational analysis of language, or a method for analyzing language into its constituent parts, in order to provide a basis for designing training programs.

Within his system Premack (1970 [Chapter 12, this volume]) provides an outline of exemplars, things a chimpanzee (or child) must be able to perform to demonstrate functional language. The initial list of exemplars includes: 1) words, 2) sentences, 3) questions, 4) metalinguistics (using language to teach language), 5) class concepts, 6) the copula, 7) quantifiers, and 8) the logical connective *if-then*. Premack also outlines a training program for teaching these exemplars.

From the standpoint of a communication channel model, Premack's language system uses visual input stimuli (receptive) and plastic symbols for response output stimuli (these required only gross motor movements to demonstrate expressive language). In order to assess the conceptual structure (association, linguistic rules, and so forth), *nonverbal* procedures, such as match-to-sample techniques, are used. Using plastic symbols (chips) makes responses by the chimpanzee selective and semipermanent, thus circumventing the memory problem (see Figure 2, Chapter 1).

In summary, Premack's approach to analyzing and teaching language reduces the cognitive parameters of language to discrete events that can be defined and manipulated. A detailed account of his research on language appears in *Intelligence in Ape and Man* (Premack, 1976).

COMMUNICATION AND COGNITIVE ORGANIZATION

In summing up their discussion of the innateness hypothesis, Stahlke et al. (Chapter 4, this volume) state, "The disparity in linguistic ability between ape and human must then lie in the areas of cognition and intelligence" (p. 104). The view that language is a mapping of already known concepts or existing distinctions has been expressed by Premack (1970 [Chapter 12, this volume]), Bowerman (1978), and others. Although it is inevitable that there be an interaction between the mapping of existing distinctions and language, there must be a cognitive basis for language. The Sapir-Whorf hypothesis holds that cognitive development is dependent on language acquisition (Whorf, 1956). During the 1960s controversy focused upon Skinner's behavioristic approach (Skinner, 1957) versus Chomsky's innate or nativistic approach to language acquisition (Chomsky, 1975). Since then the view that the child undertakes learning language after he has developed basic concepts as a result of nonlinguistic interaction with the environment has been advocated (see Bowerman, 1978, for a detailed discussion).

In discussing communication and cognition, Menzel and Johnson (1976 [Chapter 13, this volume]) suggest that before we can predict how a "word" or "signal" will be responded to by a receiver, we must have considerable knowledge about the psychological organization of the receiver. In this regard Menzel and Johnson state:

> In any event, if successful people-to-people and people-to-animal communication depends on accurate assumptions about the cognitive structure of other beings, it is probably not too farfetched to assume that communication between animals involves similar assumptions about how the world looks to someone else (p. 134 [266]).

This point is also of importance with regard to the development of language acquisition for the mentally retarded and other handicapped children (see Hollis and Carrier, 1978).

Menzel and Johnson (1976 [Chapter 13, this volume]) point out that various sensory channels (see Figure 4, Chapter 1) function together as a coordinated information-getting system. They refer to this process as "triangulation" and suggest that it includes integration of information from verbalizations and gestures, visual and auditory cues, and so forth (see Fouts, Couch, and O'Neil, Chapter 15, this volume; Patterson, 1978 [Chapter 16, this volume]; Wulz and Hollis, Chapter 20, this volume). Wulz and Hollis present a mediated transfer model for receptive, associative, and expressive language components (see Figure 1, Chapter 20). The receptive and associative components provide a paradigm for "triangulation."

Menzel and Johnson view the communication process as a dynamic interaction between participants, objects, intention, and the environment, that is, senders and receivers are not passive but active with respect to assessment of environmental events. Thus, language and communication may require the cognitive ability of the sender and receiver to form "hypotheses" about the behavior of the other.

INITIAL ACQUISITION OF SYMBOLIC SKILLS

In their introduction to acquisition of symbolic skills in the chimpanzee, Savage-Rumbaugh and Rumbaugh (Chapter 14) outline problems frequently encountered in attempting to teach language to the chimpanzee or profoundly alinguistic child. These problems involve: 1) the ability to vocalize, 2) attention span, 3) imitation, 4) cognitive capacity, and 5) individual differences. To overcome some of these problems a computer-based system was developed to provide a general system for structuring linguistic skills (Rumbaugh, 1977). This system provides an environment for the acquisition of language in which there is consistency, feedback, and simplified response output.

In discussing problems encountered during language acquisition training, the issue of whether *requesting* was a more basic skill than *labeling* arose. This question was answered with a qualified yes. It was tentatively concluded that learning to discriminate between relevant and irrelevant lexigrams and learning to discriminate between relevant lexigrams were both important processes in learning symbolization but were not sufficient for language acquisition. Savage-Rumbaugh and Rumbaugh (Chapter 14) describe and discuss several strategies for establishing the relationship between lexigrams (symbols) and their environmental referents. It was only after several failures that a successful strategy evolved.

The reader should note that the mediated transfer model (Wulz and Hollis, Chapter 20, this volume) provides yet another strategy for establishing a relationship between *symbols* and their *environmental referents*. Strategies derived from this model do not require direct training on the association between symbols and their environmental referents.

STRATEGIES FOR PRIMATE LANGUAGE TRAINING

Fouts, Couch, and O'Neil (Chapter 15) provide an overview of the importance of animal research in relation to the study of a behavior such as language. Their work has involved the development of sign language in the chimpanzee. Fouts et al. investigated individual differences among chimpanzees learning sign language (American Sign Language (ASL)); they were also interested in assessing the differences among signs in terms of ease or difficulty of learning. Their findings are reported in Chapter 15.

Prior to the work of Fouts and his colleagues, the Gardners (1969 [Chapter 9, this volume]) had taught the chimpanzee Washoe to use ASL. Critics of their work suggested that Washoe was an intellectual genius. Four chimpanzees in a new study were taught 10 signs. The results showed that Washoe was *not* the only chimpanzee who could learn ASL (see Fouts, Couch, and O'Neil, Chapter 15).

Up to this point primate language studies have used only simple receptive input modes (cf. Hayes and Hayes, 1954 [Chapter 8, this volume]; and Gardner and Gardner, 1969 [Chapter 9, this volume]; Premack, 1970 [Chapter 12, this volume]; Savage-Rumbaugh and Rumbaugh, Chapter 14, this volume). However, the "triangulation" process, as described by Menzel and Johnson (1976 [Chapter 13, this volume]), could include information from verbalizations (speech) and gestures for establishing a relationship between these symbols and environmental referents (cf. Wulz and Hollis [Chapter 20, this volume]). An experiment designed by Fouts and his co-workers involves teaching a chimpanzee to sign in response to vocal English and to select objects in response to vocal English. The results show that a chimpanzee can transfer the sign taught for the vocal English word to the object symbolized by that word without direct training.

The next experiment reported in Chapter 15 concerns the development and assessment of syntactic competence using the manual signing mode. In general, the research supports the notion that a chimpanzee has the capacity for utilizing an active linguistic process. Another experiment has shown that a chimpanzee can learn to sign, to discriminate "same" or "different" between pairs of calls (auditory) produced by a chimpanzee, and also to differentiate between chimpanzees giving the calls (cf. Premack, 1970 [Chapter 12, this volume]).

In subsequent sections of Chapter 15 Fouts et al. discuss application of animal research to child language problems and the use of ASL as a language intervention technique. They give an overview of general strategies for sign language training with chimpanzees and handicapped children, including Total Communication, modeling and imitation, group sessions, and generalization of signs. In general, the purpose of their chapter is to review sign language work with chimpanzees and to illustrate its application to language acquisition in handicapped children.

LINGUISTIC CAPABILITIES OF A GORILLA

On the phylogenetic scale, the gorilla ranks above the chimpanzee but below the human. However, compared to the chimpanzee very little behavioral research has been undertaken with the gorilla (see Schaller, 1963). Some of the animal literature indicates that the gorilla is intractable, negativistic, and intellectually inferior to the chimpanzee.

Patterson (1978 [Chapter 16, this volume]) reports a project concerned with the development of language and communication in the gorilla. Her research explores the parameters of "comparative pedolinguistics." With respect to human language, she states, "It seems to me futile to argue as to whether or not several educated apes 'have' human language—at least until there is a consensus on when a human has language" (p. 162 [327]).

The gorilla project was modeled after Project Washoe (Gardner and Gardner, 1969 [Chapter 9, this volume]), and direct comparisons were made between the gorilla (Koko) and Washoe. Patterson's project differs from Washoe's in several respects: 1) Patterson used native signers, 2) spoken English was used, 3) complete records of utterances were maintained, 4) no attempt was made to control the size and content of Koko's vocabulary, and 5) intellectual functioning was assessed with standard intelligence tests. In training, sign language was used as the primary mode of communication and speech was used as the secondary mode of communication (cf. Fouts, Couch, and O'Neil, Chapter 15, this volume). Patterson was interested in any transfer that might occur between modes. After initial language training, Koko was tested on comprehension of English, sign, and simultaneous communication (both). Results from the test, "The Assessment of Children's Language Comprehension," show that Koko performed significantly better than chance under all three conditions.

In summary, Patterson reports that Koko invented signs and names, talked to herself, and communicated about her feelings. Patterson suggests that a detailed (comparative) investigation of the structure (and functioning) of linguistic communication may be one of the best ways to study primate intelligence (cf. Premack, 1976).

REFERENCES

Bowerman, M. 1978. Semantic and syntactic development. In R. L. Schiefelbusch (ed.), Bases of Language Intervention, pp. 97–189. University Park Press, Baltimore.

Chomsky, N. 1975. Reflections on Language. Pantheon Books, New York.

Gardner, R. A., and Gardner, B. T. 1969. Teaching sign language to a chimpanzee. Science 165:664–672.

Hayes, K. J., and Hayes, C. 1954. The cultural capacity of chimpanzee. Hum. Biol. 26:288–303.

Hollis, J. H. and Carrier, J. K. 1978. Intervention strategies for nonspeech children. In R. L. Schiefelbusch (ed.), Language Intervention Strategies, pp. 57–100. University Park Press, Baltimore.

Limber, J. 1977. Language in child and chimp? Am. Psychol. 32:280–295.

Menzel, E. W., and Johnson, M. K. 1976. Communication and cognitive organization in humans and other animals. In S. R. Harnand, H. D. Steklis, and J. Lancaster (eds.), Origins and Evolution of Language and Speech. The New York Academy of Sciences, New York.

Patterson, F. 1978. Linguistic capabilities of a young lowland gorilla. In F. C. C. Peng (ed.), Sign Language and Language Acquisition—New Dimensions in Comparative Pedolinguistics. Westview Press, Boulder, Col.

Premack, D. 1970. A functional analysis of language. J. Exp. Anal. Behav. 14:107–125.

Premack, D. 1976. Intelligence in Ape and Man. John Wiley & Sons, New York.

Rumbaugh, D. M. (ed.). 1977. Language Learning by a Chimpanzee: The LANA Project. Academic Press, New York.
Schaller, G. B. 1963. The Mountain Gorilla. University of Chicago Press, Chicago.
Skinner, B. F. 1957. Verbal Behavior. Appleton-Century-Crofts, New York.
Whorf, B. L. 1956. Language, Thought, and Reality. The MIT Press, Cambridge, Mass.

chapter

12

A Functional
Analysis of Language

David Premack*

Department of Psychology
University of California at Santa Barbara
Santa Barbara, California

Language has been given a largely structural definition by linguistics, but in order to have a psychological theory of language, the structural emphasis must be replaced by a functional one. What must an organism do in order to give evidence that it has language? More specifically, when is a response a word? A sequence of responses a sentence? What makes one response sequence an assertion or predication, another an imperative, still another a question? In this chapter I try to give these questions the most general answers possible, general in the sense of relieving them of their exclusively human form.

The functions an organism carries out when engaged in language need to be separated from the form these functions take in man. Not only human phonology but quite possibly human syntax may be unique to man; both may encompass mechanisms not found in any other species (Chomsky, 1965; Lenneberg, 1967). But if this is so, it does not commit the mechanisms of logic and semantics to the same status. The latter may be more widely distributed and it may be them, not the human form of syntax and phonology, upon which the basic functions of language depend.

STRICT TRAINING PROCEDURE: A RECIPE FOR TEACHING LANGUAGE FUNCTIONS

This chapter is organized around two interlocking lists. The first is the list of functions, the things an organism must do in order to give evidence of language. The ideal list of this kind will be exhaustive, although presently it is acceptable simply if it avoids glaring lacunae and contains only items that are patently important. The second is a parallel list of strict training procedures. For each function on the first list, the second gives at least one and preferably several alternative ways of producing the function. A strict training procedure is essentially a recipe. Given a decision as to what constitutes, for example, competence in the interrogative—the ability to ask and answer questions—the second list offers a set of instructions showing how to train an organism so as to instill the competence in question. Clearly the difficulties of the first list greatly exceed those of the second. It is far more elusive a task to explicate what interrogation or predication consist of than, given a decision on the former, to prduce a training procedure that will inculcate the competence in question. Indeed, a strict training procedure is no more than an

From Premack, D. 1970. A functional analysis of language. J. Exp. Anal. Behav. 14:107–125. Reprinted by permission. Copyright 1970 by the Society for the Experimental Analysis of Behavior, Inc.

* Affiliation given reflects the author's affiliation at time of writing.

Based upon an invited APA address (Div. I), 1969, Washington, D.C. Mary Morgan, J. Olson, Randy Funk, and Deborah Petersen are the exceptionally patient and ingenious research assistants who made the study possible. The research was supported by NIH grant MH-15616.

ordered series of steps, each one to be accomplished before the next one is begun, and each one so small as to be atomic, i.e., manageable by a docile organism. Although certain species, man notably and even other higher primates, may be capable of taking many steps at a time—so that for them an atomic decomposition of the task was not a necessity to begin with—the strict training procedure is happiest when it reaches the lowliest organism; it knows no other way of doing this than by breaking the task into the smallest steps possible. It should be recognized from the beginning, however, that there is no mechanical procedure for generating recipes. The notion of an atomic step is a primitive. Furthermore, a strict training procedure is not an explanation of how, as a result of carrying out the prescribed steps, the organism accomplished the function in question. A recipe is a method, not a theory, though by merit of its success, often a method in search of a theory.

CHIMPANZEE AS A DRAWING BOARD

The chimpanzee will be our drawing board. I will take only four items from the first list, which elsewhere I am attempting to deal with comprehensively, and show how application of the corresponding training procedures to the chimpanzee results in the functions in question. The functions considered are: word, sentence, question, and metalinguistics. Each one opens out into further topics, some of them classical such as displacement—talking about things that are not present—and predication—asserting a state of affairs (as opposed to requesting it). Displacement and predication have both been cited as uniquely human, as hallmarks of man and language. Certainly they are impossible without language but, as we will see, they are not unique to man. It is unfortunate in a sense to use the chimp as the drawing board, for it is too close to man. It will be more illuminating if later the same functions can be instilled in nonprimates. But teaching an organism language amounts in part to mapping the built-in knowledge of its species; this will be brought out here in a number of examples. And this knowledge is difficult, even perhaps impossible, to disinter in species far removed from man. The greater accessibility of this knowledge in the case of the chimp is the main reason we start with it, more than the fact that it is bright and playful.

PHYSICAL BASIS OF LANGUAGE: PLASTIC WORDS

The physical basis of the language used with the chimp is plastic varying in shape, size, texture, and color. Each word is a metal-backed piece of plastic that adheres to a magnetized slate (see Figure 1). The sentences

Figure 1. The physical basis of the language is plastic, varying in color, size, and shape. Each piece of plastic is a word; the pieces are metal-based and adhere to magnetized slate. Sentences are written on the vertical. A word-by-word translation of the two sentences is: SARAH HONEY BREAD TAKE; NO SARAH JAM CRACKER TAKE. Notice the occurrence of NO or the negative particle as a free morph (independent word) in both Figure 1 and 3, and in the bottom half of Figure 4 as a bound morph appended to NAME OF forming NOT NAME OF.

are written on the vertical, an ancient form of writing once used by certain human groups (Hewes, 1949), but adopted here simply because in the beginning it appeared to be the chimp's preferred style. The two sentences shown in Figure 1 can be paraphrased in English as follows: "Sarah take honey-bread," and "No Sarah take jam-cracker," respectively. Since the language is written rather than spoken or gestured, words are permanent not evanescent, and sentences are displaced in space not time. This has overwhelming advantages for short term memory. Once written on the board, the sentence can remain indefinitely, giving the chimp time to pick its bizarre profile and think the matter through before responding. The permanence of the sentence not only makes it possible to study language without a memory problem, but to study memory in the context of language by regulating the duration for which the sentence remains on the board.

In addition, because the experimenter makes the words—the chimp merely uses them—he can control their supply. The words available to the chimp at any moment in time can be varied in number, kind, type/token ratio, etc. as the experimenter chooses. The adult animal, or one proficient in the language, can be given an unlimited supply of words along with the opportunity to produce sentences at will. Then the physical organization of its vocabulary can be observed; whether, and if so how, it lays the words out in piles to enhance their availability for sentence construction, or the degree to which it can be trained to adopt favorable organizations. But the main advantages are to the training of the naive animal; since the number of alternatives can be controlled, so can the difficulty of the problem.

There are no phonemes in the language, the most elementary unit being quite deliberately the word. Elsewhere we have described a phonemic system suitable for the chimp (Premack and Schwartz, 1966), and can also describe a system intermediate between the present one and the earlier phonemic one, a system of words with an implicit phonemic structure that can be made explicit at any time the experimenter considers propitious. But the implications of these different systems are merely practical. Although the systems vary in their assets and liabilities, no one of them is in any sense a necessary condition for the general functions of language.

Human phonology is an adaptation to specific needs that are intrinsic to the human condition but not to language. These needs can be eliminated, obviating the need for mechanisms to resolve them, and the system that remains is still language. For example, the principal traits of human phonology, the phoneme and the auditory channel, are both parts of a solution to a common problem. Limitations on man's memory on the one hand, and ability to generate discriminably different responses on the other, make it impossible or highly inefficient for him to attempt to map a large world by devising an irreducibly different response for each word. Rather than attempt to generate and store 40,000 or even 5,000 different words, he produces instead only about 50 or so different phonemes. By combining these manageably few responses, he produces the large number of words needed to map his complex world.

The auditory channel also makes its contribution to the same problem; indeed, in an important sense it makes the combinatorial approach possible. Not the auditory channel per se, but the fact that the modality of man's language is different from the primary modality in which he perceives his world. Man is predominantly visual, while his language is auditory. It might be thought that an auditory language is merely a profound convenience—conferring the possibility of whispering while copulating or speaking while writing on the board—but the contribution is of a far deeper nature. To begin with, if the modalities were not different, it would be impossible to distinguish at a glance a member of the language system from a member of the system referred to by the language. This simple distinction—telling a word from that which the word refers to—would require an inquiry of a kind that is nearly impossible to appreciate if your experience with language is confined to the human case. You must work in an artificial system to appreciate this problem; in Figure 3 I have deliberately included a case where a member of the language system and a member of the world referred to by the language not only both belong to the same modality, but overlap so markedly in dimensional values that one can barely be told from the other. There is no sense in dwelling on this point, however, since its impact, I fear, is very dependent upon experience with artificial systems that do not provide for those critical separations so much taken for granted in the human system.

But the minor confusions that can result when words and designata are not immediately distinguishable is the least of the damage that could be done the combinatorial approach. If the language modality and that of the primary perception of the world did not differ, the language would very probably end up iconic not phonemic. The tendency to match items on the basis of similarity is as strong as the tendency to associate them on the basis of contiguity, probably stronger. But if language elements were to match the salient characteristics of the objects which they name, there would be as many irreducible language elements as there are objects named in the world. Such a development would be in complete opposition to the need for a small set of meaningless elements—meaningless in the sense that they match nothing in the world—whose combinations are used to produce words. But the only arrangement that could fully guard against this iconic possibility is a disparity in modality, a difference in the channels in which the language is expressed and the world is perceived. Nothing could more effectively preclude matching and thus allow for the emergence of language elements fewer in number than the number of elements named by the language. Thus, a primarily visual organism like man would require an auditory or at least a nonvisual language, even as an auditory organism if there were one might end up with a visual language.

But this whole set of problems reflects limitations on human information processing; it has little to do with the logically necessary properties of language. Neither the need to map a "large" world nor a limitation in operating characteristics leading to the desirability of a combinatorial approach to lexicon, are pressures which a system must accommodate in order to qualify as language. An artificial subject (computer) or prosthetics added to an experimental subject might extend memory or make for a superior response generator; or we might simply accept a thoroughly iconic language: no general language function would appear to be precluded by an iconic lexicon. Alternatively, we might operate upon the world instead, reducing its elements. The latter is an attractive alternative, since carrying out the basic language functions does not appear to require a world of human complexity. All the essential functions of language apparently can be carried through in small spaces—arbitrary "corners" of a real world, or a diminished artificial world. For example, the chimp to be described here has about 40 words at present. In all likelihood, this could be 400, if the focus were vocabulary. But I have no interest in vocabulary per se, not a large one in any case. Indeed, the more intriguing question is: what is the smallest lexicon in which it is possible to carry through all the basic functions of language?

GENERAL FUNCTIONS: WORD

Unlike the phoneme, which is an adjustment to a nonessential problem, the word is an essential unit of language. It reflects some of the most basic features of experience, among them the consensus that perceptual experience can be divided into stable elements, and the agreement that all such elements can be represented or referred to by responses of the organism.

The introduction of language to a totally naive organism is substantially different from introducing new words to an organism already equipped with a bit of language. "X is the name of Y" is a powerful device that can be used to teach words to the advanced subject, as is shown in the section on metalinguistics. But here we are talking of first words and a totally naive subject. With this subject, a vital first step is to establish a simple social transaction between the subject and the trainer. We establish this transaction well, assuring ourselves that it holds no concepts of which the subject is incapable, for it is this transaction we will map with language. Mapping, as the many examples to follow will show, amounts to dividing a routine into its component classes, displaying the range of values that each class can take, and assigning a name to each of the values.

A feeding routine makes an effective transaction with a young chimp. The trainer places an edible item on the table between him and the subject and looks by benevolently while the chimp takes it and eats it. Once or twice, after giving the fruit to the chimp, the trainer may "request" that the fruit be given back to him; he extends a cupped hand and extrudes his lip to the best of his ability, mimicking the supplication chimps direct at one another, but the imitation is unsuccessful. The chimp looks puzzled, even hesitant, but never gives back the fruit, so the trainer goes on with that part of the routine that is successful, laying fruit out and watching the chimp eat it.

Then one day, after the transaction is well established, the trainer places an element from the language system, a piece of colored plastic, alongside a piece of fruit, say, a banana. The banana is now farther back than usual, out of reach, while the plastic chip is forward, easily within reach. The animal is induced to make a prescribed response with the language element, in this case, place it on the language board, after which she is given the fruit. The chimp is almost immediately proficient in this act. Causing objects to adhere to a vertical surface is something it does readily, in contrast, for example, to producing human sound. (Notice that in this system, unlike the human one, production need not lag behind comprehension. The subject does not make but merely uses the words, and can do so from the beginning without having to undergo elaborate motor learning. Thus, the earliest training can occur in the production, as well as in the comprehension, mode. This can be an advantage in training young subjects, since the control of attention is more certain when the subject is required to respond rather than merely observe.)

What does the piece of plastic mean to the chimp? The question is hopelessly premature at this stage for, in a sense, all of the training that lies ahead is an attempt to inculcate a system that will make it possible to answer questions of that kind. The question is one to which the subject's own answers can contribute importantly, provided we can make the subject susceptible to questions. How to confer question-answering ability upon a chimp is illustrated in the section on the interrogative.

The rest of the training consists of making simultaneous changes in some aspect of the transaction and in some aspect of the language system, so as to establish a correspondence between the two systems. For example, we may start with the fruits that are offered. The set of possible objects is defined by offering different fruits on different trials and each time with a corresponding change in the language element. When the fruit is banana the plastic chip is of one kind, when apple of a different kind, and when orange still a third kind. On each trial the chimp's task is the same: place the piece of plastic that is alongside the fruit on the board before receiving the fruit.

Two kinds of tests will show whether or not the subject has formed an association between members of the object class and of the corresponding language class. Trials on which the chimp is given two would-be words but only one piece of fruit will determine whether it can match the word with the fruit. But the subject may know more than such choice trials reveal. If the subject is less interested in the fruit that is offered on a particular trial than the fruit that is not offered, it may use the "wrong" word essentially as a request for the fruit that it prefers. This possibility can be detected by obtaining independent preference orderings on the fruits and on the words. For example, allow the subject to choose between all possible pairs of fruits and on another occasion all possible pairs of words. If its preferences among the words agree with its preferences among the fruits, then the subject must know what word goes with what fruit, whatever its choice behavior may suggest to the contrary.

The next perceptual class is mapped in the same fashion. Each change in fruit was accompanied by a change in the language element; now, in similar fashion, each change in donor—the person giving the fruit—is accompanied by a change in the second language element. For example, when Mary is present and the fruit is apple, the chimp (Sarah) must write, MARY APPLE, to receive the apple; with Randy present, RANDY APPLE, etc. Associations for members of the donor class can be tested in the same way as for members of the object class. With one trainer present but two or more donor words, the subject must match the word to the trainer. Similarly, if necessary, a preference ordering can be determined for donors' and would-be donors' names, and the concordance between the two orderings taken as evidence of an association.

In addition to being required to place two pieces of plastic on the board, the chimp is required to observe a proper order. MARY APPLE is accepted but APPLE MARY is not. In the sentence toward which she is progressing, words will occur in the one order but not in the other. Thus, in the target sentence, MARY GIVE APPLE SARAH we find MARY APPLE but not the reverse. The correct order is required from the beginning so that incorrect orders will not have to be unlearned later. In addition to the order requirement, we observe an anti-regression rule. Once she reaches a two-word state, we reject one-word fragments, even as we reject two-word fragments when she reaches a three-word stage, etc. (This rule is rigidly enforced only at this tender stage, when there is uncertainty not only in her use of language but, more important, in our estimate of how much language she actually knows. At a later stage, fragments are welcomed, it being of interest to see what the proportionality may be between her use of fragments and the redundancy in the situation.)

The fruit and the donor are easily mapped; the other two classes in this example present difficulty, though of a practical kind. For example, the attempt to map the recipient by varying who it is that receives the fruit runs into difficulty of a predictable kind; the chimp is reluctant to produce response sequences calling for a recipient other than herself. Similarly, the attempt to map the operator, by varying the action upon the fruit—sometimes giving it as before but other times cutting it or inserting it in a pail—encounters the same problem; some of the outcomes are so nonpreferred that, once she has associated the language element with the undesired action, she will not form the sentence. These are strictly practical problems, however; they can be dealt with for the most part by arranging appropriate contingencies; e.g., when Sarah writes MARY GIVE APPLE JIM, thereby effectively denying herself the apple, she can be given a tidbit more preferred than apple. If reinforced, altruism can become quite reliable.

The order in which the transaction is mapped—fruit, donor, operator; or donor, recipient, etc.—is not something we have tested yet. Also, it may make a difference how many members of one class are established before a new class is introduced; this too remains to be tested. Notice, however, that while we may puzzle over these minor parameters, we have no comparable hesitation in deciding a far more basic matter, viz., how to partition the transaction in the first place. Why is this so?

The effect of the order of the mapping can readily be converted into an experimental question, as can the number of entries that should be established in one class before proceeding to another, for we have no difficulty in proposing alternative orders or numbers. But the effect of alternative partitionings, of dividing the transaction one way rather than another, does not go over into an experimental question, for we are incapable of proposing significantly different partitionings. We see the situation one way and one way only. There is a recipient, a donor, the object that is exchanged, and the act of giving. All alternative partitionings that we may propose will turn out to be trivial variations on this one, proposals either to omit a class or to slice an existing class more finely. Our freedom in this matter consists in our choice of situations to map; thus, rather than start with feeding, we might begin with body care and lead into the operator WASH and names for parts of the body. We are not free in how to divide this situation. We are free to choose the situation but not free in our choice of how to divide it.

These perceptual constraints must have a great practical advantage, however. The organism being trained in language could not be less circumscribed perceptually than we are. If both organisms see the situation the same way this must greatly facilitate the training, in ways that we have not yet fully worked out.

In summary, while many variations remain to be explored, the basic procedure for teaching words to a naive organism is extremely simple. A transaction is established between the subject and the trainer and a decision is made as to the salient perceptual classes into which the transaction should be divided, a decision that will prove to be remarkably easy. Then each class is rotated through a series of values, in the present case, apple, banana, etc.; Mary, Randy, etc.; give, insert, etc.; Sarah, Jim, etc., the other classes being held constant. As the value of the perceptual class is changed, a corresponding change is made in the language element. And as each new class is mapped, the language requirement is increased. In the beginning, the chimp merely took the fruit, looked over benevolently by the trainer. Then one word was required, two, three, until finally target sentences were realized such as MARY GIVE APPLE SARAH.

GENERAL FUNCTIONS: SENTENCE

The subject may produce properly ordered strings of words and yet give no essential evidence that the string is a sentence. A sentence differs from a string of words in that it has an internal organization, a knowledge of which is a necessary condition for correctly responding to it. The knowledge can be represented by a tree diagram of the sentence or the application of parentheses, both of which will show the dependencies between any one word in the sentence and all the others (e.g. Chomsky, 1965). I will deal with this topic under two headings—two-term relations and hierarchical organization—in the course of which we will see some examples of the dependencies that distinguish a sentence from a string of words.

SYMMETRICAL RELATIONS

The conditions leading to the necessity for syntax are general, involving information that is commonplace rather than exotic. Perhaps the simplest condition is the symmetrical two-term relation such as can be found in geometrical propositions, for example, and in some of the verbs of social behavior. These semantically disparate topics have in common relations whose terms can be interchanged. For example, A on C but also C on A; X talks to Y but also Y talks to X. This interchangeability makes it impossible to distinguish physically the class of items that can take one position in the relation from the class that can take the other position. In the limiting case the membership of the two classes can be completely interchanged, so that, for example, anything that can be on top can also be on the bottom, and anything that can talk can also be talked to. In cases of this kind there is no other way to identify the position of the item in the relation than by the order of the corresponding word in the sentence. This state of affairs contrasts with what we may call a *closed* relation, where there is a well-marked difference between items that take one position in the relation and those that take the other position, and for which a semantic covariation rule is a sufficient kind of organization.

For example, the verb *insert* as we have used it with Sarah involved a closed relation and could be dealt with by a semantic rule. In Sarah's experience as in ours, she (and Mary and Randy and Jim) insert(s) pieces of fruit in dishes and pails, but pieces of fruit do not insert her (or Mary or Randy or Jim). Inserters are one kind of thing, insertables a different kind. INSERT could therefore be treated as a relation between two classes defined on the basis of physical or functional properties of the membership, which is what a semantic covariation rule amounts to. On this treatment SARAH INSERT BANANA, BANANA INSERT SARAH, INSERT BANANA SARAH, etc. should not differ from one another; if the subject's training included experience with variable word order, so as to safeguard emotional reactions to novel forms, its response should be the same to all possible forms of the string. (Notice that one limitation of semantic covariation rules is already evident. The world need not change, and oranges begin to insert Marys, in order that we may want to talk about such possibilities. But such talk would not be possible with semantic covariation rules; semantic rules set limits on speculative discourse that syntactic formulations do not.)

The prepositions *on, under,* and *to the side of* involve physical relations which we do not doubt that the chimp can discriminate and which can be trained in a manner that will assure a complete interchange of the items that take the two positions in the relation. To evaluate the chimp's capacity for syntax we must make certain that the prepositions are in fact learned on a syntactic basis. This is possible only if the application of the preposition is restricted to so-to-speak semantically neutral domains—cases where one form of a relation is as sensible as the other. For example, objects that differ only in their color will fulfill this condition, for red on green has no semantic edge over green on red, unlike, for example, fly on horse, which is notably more probable than the reverse. This restriction is necessary because, although prepositions are in principle symmetrical, they may be used asymmetrically in the beginning and defined improperly as a result. For instance, the regularity with which children go on bikes, cups on saucers, plates on tables, lamps on floors, etc., may lead the child to define *on* as a semantic rule in which the larger of two items goes on top and the smaller on the bottom. Only accidents in which, for example, bike ends up on child or plate ends up on food, not to mention later sexual experience, may induce the child to abandon the initial semantic formulation and redefine the word on purely syntactic grounds. Since, however, our control of the training sample is better than that of the average parent, we need not rely on accidents to assure that our subject uses syntactic definitions from the beginning.

Four color words—RED, GREEN, BLUE, and YELLOW—had been taught the subject earlier, and we used them in training the prepositions. Two by four cards, painted one of the four colors, but indistinguishable otherwise, were used as the objects. The cards were placed on top of each other with the top one offset a bit so that the bottom one could be seen. The four color words make possible 12 different cases, e.g., RED ON GREEN, GREEN ON RED, BLUE ON RED, etc. ON, UNDER, and TO THE SIDE OF have special interest in a language written on the vertical. The order of the elements in the sentence and the order of the elements referred to by the sentence are the same in the case of ON, opposite in the case of UNDER, and unrelated in the case of TO THE SIDE OF. We are interested in determining whether the isomorphism between the two orders or the lack of it will affect the rate of learning; unfortunately, at the moment, ON is the only one for which the training has been completed.

Using the colored cards as described, we trained her in the comprehension mode, where she was required to respond to our sentences and then subsequently tested her ability to produce the same sentences herself. The training proceeded in three steps, the first restricted to one pair of colors, the second dealing with her ability to generalize to new colors, and the last examining her transfer from comprehension to production.

In the first step of the training, the red card was placed on the table before the subject, the trainer wrote on the board GREEN ON RED, handed Sarah the green card, and then induced her to place it on the one that was already there. I describe this procedure, which is in no way unusual, simply to illustrate the general strategy of a strict training procedure: to bring about the desired behavior by limiting the possibility for other kinds of behavior. The step used is hardly the only possible one, and had it failed we would have tried others, which illustrates a second characteristic of strict training procedures: they are based on judgment not algorithms.

Next, the opposite sentence RED ON GREEN was presented, now with the green card down and the red card handed to the subject as the one to be placed on top. Subsequently, the subject was given both cards and presented first with one form of the sentence and then with the other. Once she was proficient at producing the card arrangement called for by the sentence, she was given sentences using all four color words, e.g., YELLOW ON BLUE, RED ON YELLOW, etc. She performed as well on the 10 new cases as on the two training cases (red, green), demonstrating that she had not simply memorized the training cases but could apply the preposition to new cases. (These tests do not demonstrate that she could use ON in any domain other than color—or indeed even with colored blocks rather than cards—but that question, though intriguing, is not germane to the present discussion of syntax.)

The last step concerned her ability to produce sentences appropriate to the trainer's behavior, rather than, as in the initial training, to behave in ways appropriate to the trainer's sentences. On each trial she was given three words, two color words and ON, and required to place them on the board in a way that corresponded to, or described, the trainer's placement of the cards. Thus, if the trainer put the blue card on the green one, Sarah, who held the words GREEN, BLUE, and ON in her substantial hand, was required to write BLUE ON GREEN and not vice versa. Her proficiency at this was 80% in the first set of 10 trials, which is indicative of a high order of transfer, since about 80% correct is her usual asymptotic performance level for essentially all problems.

HIERARCHICAL ORGANIZATION

Consider the sentence, in chimp language, SARAH INSERT BANANA PAIL APPLE DISH. Translated into English this is the instruction to separate the banana and apple, to put the former in the pail and the latter in the dish. But to carry out that quite simple instruction, or instructions of that general kind, requires a knowledge of the internal organization of the sentence. That organization can be shown by using parentheses to indicate the dependencies among the words. For example, {Sarah insert [(banana pail) (apple dish)]} shows that BANANA and PAIL go together, likewise APPLE and DISH; that INSERT applies not only to BANANA-PAIL but to both cases, and finally that it is Sarah who is to carry out the action.

This example carries us beyond word order to a second contribution of syntax—hierarchical organization of the sentence. How essential is that factor? What would be lost if, for example, the strings of words in the language were sensitive to order but were not organized hierarchically? We can answer that question by comparing the subject's behavior to the above sentence under conditions in which an understanding of it was based on either of three levels of organization: 1) word knowledge or gross semantic rule, 2) refined semantic rule, or 3) hierarchical.

Several years ago in working with psychotic children, R. Metz and I devised some tests of language comprehension to determine whether the severely impaired speech production, which characterized these children, was owed to performance factors or to something deeper. Having earlier confirmed Lenneberg's (1967) surprising claim that the feeble-minded child is grammatical, I was distinctly surprised when some of the psychotic children failed all of the comprehension tests (while at the same time performing adequately on nonlanguage tests). They had what we ended up calling "word knowledge" but, so far as our tests could determine, little else. Response to the sentence in question at the level of word knowledge would amount to the following.

Understanding of the word SARAH would result in Sarah's carrying out whatever action was carried out rather than waiting for, say, Mary to act, as she would on the occasion of sentences that began with MARY. Secondly, an understanding of the word INSERT would assure action of one kind—putting one thing into another—as opposed to cutting, taking, giving, some of the other verbs or operators that she knows. Third, the objects acted upon would be confined to those named. But with no more than word knowledge, there would be great latitude in what was inserted into what. Every object could be inserted into every other; thus, the dish could go into the pail as readily as the banana go into the dish, etc. Clearly, the specific pairing of banana with pail and apple with dish that would alone constitute evidence of an understanding of the (hierarchically organized) sentence would not be guaranteed by a knowledge limited to individual words.

A higher level of organization could be provided by semantic covariation rules; they could limit the possible outcomes, bringing them closer to the desired one, but would still fall short. Actually, what we have called word knowledge could be formulated as a coarse semantic covariation rule; the second level of organization would then amount to the addition of a second semantic rule which would have the effect of refining the first rule. Thus, the first case could be analyzed in a manner already suggested above, as a rule in which the verb was the predicate and the agents and objects were the arguments taken by the predicate. This could be diagrammed as:

INSERT

agents   objects

emphasizing the focal role of the verb or operator and the secondary role of that which instanced the verb, inserters on the one hand, and objects of insertion on the other.

The addition of a second semantic rule could differentiate the object class, separating the containers (dish, pail) from that which gets contained (apple, banana, etc.). This better defined situation could be diagrammed as:

INSERT

agents   objects

fruits   containers

The additional definition of the semantic space would further delimit the subject's behavior, e.g., it would keep the dish out of the pail, but it would no more assure the exact outcome indicative of an understanding of the hierarchically organized sentence than the first organization. Indeed, no combination of semantic rules could assure that outcome since, so to speak, pails and dishes will accept one kind of fruit as readily as the other.

TRAINING PROCEDURE
FOR THE COMPOUND SENTENCE

I will now describe the procedure we used to teach the chimp to respond correctly to the sentence in question, though without claiming that she is therefore unquestionably proficient in syntax. Proving competence in syntax is ticklish, not impossible, but difficult or at least arduous. Testing any highly inferential matter is, of course, more troublesome than when the hypotheses lie closer to the surface of the data. The problem is aggravated by a factor which the reader might guess simply by recalling his own childhood. Grammar is not the chimp's favorite subject. There is a limit to the number of tests she will accept on a grammatical topic, and that limit is not always sufficient to include all the control sentences one might desire.

The training proceeded by three steps, all in the comprehension mode. First, she was trained individually on each of the four simple sentences of which the compound sentence in question could be composed. These included:

SARAH INSERT BANANA PAIL.
SARAH INSERT APPLE PAIL.
SARAH INSERT BANANA DISH.
SARAH INSERT APPLE DISH.

The trainer wrote each sentence on the board, at the same time offering a choice of fruits and containers, and requiring the subject to place the designated fruit in the designated container. Next, she was given all possible pairs of the sentences, side by side, in the manner of a paragraph. For example,

SARAH	SARAH
INSERT	INSERT
BANANA	APPLE
DISH	PAIL

Since no change was made in the composition of the individual sentences, this step was intended merely to accustom her to carrying out two acts of insertion, as is required by the compound sentence.

In the final step, all possible pairs of sentences were again combined, this time one immediately above the other, and this conjunction of two simple sentences was gradually converted into one compound sentence. The procedure generated sentences of this kind:

(1)	(2)	(3)
SARAH	SARAH	SARAH
INSERT	INSERT	INSERT
BANANA	BANANA	BANANA
PAIL	PAIL	PAIL
SARAH	INSERT	APPLE
INSERT	APPLE	DISH
APPLE	DISH	
DISH		

Neither the deletion of the second use of SARAH nor the subsequent deletion of the second use of INSERT disrupted her performance. She was performing at between 75% and 80% correct, her customary level, and continued to do so when the changes were made. Nor was the subject disrupted by the subsequent generalization tests we have carried out. These tests are incomplete in that while we have substituted fruit names (e.g., grape, apricot, orange) for those used in training, we have not yet changed the verbs, and these may present more difficulty. Also, there are some ad hoc rules that she might be using in processing the compound sentences, not all of which have been explicitly eliminated by test. I will describe just one as an example of the several that could apply.

For example, she might use a rule that said, in effect, apply the container word to the object word above it. This would work for the individual sentences but would run into trouble when one sentence was written above the other; then the bottom-most container word would apply to two object words, one directly and one indirectly above it. In the compound sentence in question, the rule would lead her to apply dish correctly, but pail incorrectly, for pail would apply to both apple and banana, both of which are above it. There was no evidence for an error of this kind.

This error could be overcome, however, if the rule were expanded to read apply the container word to the fruit word *immediately* above it. But this modification would fail in the case of sentences of this kind:

SARAH
INSERT
APPLE
DISH
APPLE
BANANA
PAIL

for apple would go into dish but would fail to make it into pail. That is, the effect of "immediately" would be to confine pail to banana. This is one of the control cases we have not yet tested.

Notice that these ad hoc rules, though not yet explicitly eliminated by test, are *not* necessarily more parsimonious than the kind of rules that could generate the hierarchical organization which could equally well account for her present performance. Nevertheless, the question of her syntactic competence must remain undecided for the time being, until we have examined a larger portion of the sentences that she is capable of making.

**INTERROGATIVE AND THE
CONCEPT OF SAMENESS OR IDENTITY**

Except for formulations like RED ON GREEN, etc., which the chimp produced in conformity to the trainer's placement of the cards, and which can be interpreted as declaratives, the other sentences—both those of the trainer and the subject—were in the imperative mood; e.g., MARY GIVE BANANA SARAH, SARAH TAKE BANANA PAIL ORANGE DISH, etc. There have been no questions and no metalinguistic propositions. By the latter I have in mind the use of language to teach language, as in the case of "X is the name of Y," where a so-far unnamed object is given a name, or "X is a synonym for Y," where an object with one name is given another one.

We will treat the interrogative first. It can be introduced in several ways, of course, though we found highly effective a procedure that exploited the concept of sameness or identity. Thus, some of the very first questions we asked the chimp were, in English paraphrase, "What is the relation between those objects, identity or non-identity?" Identity or sameness is a concept for which the chimp can readily distinguish between positive and negative instances. It is therefore an ideal subject matter for questions, since in the beginning at least there is no point in asking the chimp questions she cannot answer. Also, the procedure leads naturally from the Wh- form of the question to the yes/no form. Hence, the advantage of the procedure is that the chimp is asked questions she can answer and the several forms of the question develop in a natural succession from a common situation.

What are the concepts that the chimp knows? Fortunately, we need not guess but can answer that question directly through matching-to-sample procedures. For example, if given a cup and a spoon, and another cup set somewhat apart from the other two objects, the subject will indicate by whatever gesture we choose, that the cups go together or participate in a relation which the cup and spoon do not. This procedure, which does not depend upon language and which can be applied broadly, is a boon to the teaching of language. With it we can determine what it is that the subject already knows and thus can avoid wasting time attempting to teach the subject names for concepts it does not know. Only with rare exceptions—of a kind I will deal with in the section on metalinguistics—does language teach the subject new concepts. Mostly it merely teaches names for concepts the subject already knows.

The matching procedure is not restricted to object identity but can be used to inventory the overall conceptual knowledge of the subject. For example, the subject can be given objects that match on no other basis than that of color, or shape, or size; or sets of objects that match on no other basis than that of area, volume, or number. Similarly, it can be used to assess the capacities for perceptual transformations. The subject can be required to match (three-dimensional) objects to their (two-dimensional) pictures, or vice versa—something that Sarah does nicely—as well as match one orientation of an object or picture to another orientation. Whenever it is shown that the subject can distinguish between positive and negative instances of the concept in question, it is reasonable to attempt to introduce a name for the concept. For the procedure by which a name is taught for the most abstract concept is no different from the one by which a name is taught for the most mundane object.

Having established that the subject is capable of matching like objects, a name is established for the fact of sameness or identity—as well as a name for nonidentity—in the same way names were previously established for objects, actions, and agents. We establish a consistent relation between positive instances of the concept and one language element and negative instances and a second language element. In the actual training, two objects, say two cups, were placed before her at a small distance from one another. She was given a piece of plastic, intended to mean same or identical, and required to place it between the two like objects. On other trials she was given objects that were not the same and required to place a different language element between them, one intended to mean nonidentical or different. (Notice how an exactly analogous procedure can be used to map the concept of equality and inequality. For example, three marbles are set slightly apart from three sticks, and the subject is required to place an equality sign between them. On other trials, two marbles are set apart from five sticks, and the subject is required to place an inequality sign between them. Both the schema for identity and for equality are so far hybrid, i.e., contain elements from the world and from the system mapping the world. For example, XXX = YYY, or stick, stick, stick = marble, marble, marble, rather than 3 = 3. To convert the hybrid sentence into a pure form requires naming the objects so that the relation can be stated between names of objects rather than objects themselves. Likewise, converting the hybrid equation into a pure form requires naming the number of the objects so that the relation can be stated between numbers rather than number of objects. The traditional question about the arithmetic ability of infrahuman primates has been misformulated. Can chimps be taught to count or to do arithmetic? That is a misleading way to put the question. A better way is: do chimps recognize numerosity? That is, can they match sets of objects that have nothing in common except the fact of their equal number? That question can be answered, in a matter of hours, with matching-to-sample procedures. If the answer is positive, there would be little doubt but that they could be taught to count. But if the answer is negative and the chimp cannot recognize numerosity, though some might remain sanguine I would not wish to be the instructor. Teaching a concept and mapping one that already exists are different enterprises.)

Were the proper associations formed between the language elements on the one hand and cases of identity and nonidentity on the other? That was established in the usual manner. She was given both the words for same and different in the presence of a case of, say, identity on one trial and nonidentity on the next, and required to match the word to the case. She was also given generalization tests to determine whether she had merely memorized the training cases. We tried her on a variety of new cases, including new combinations of old items, entirely new items, and new items for which names had and had not been previously taught. But these experimental niceties proved to be in vain, for she made so few overall errors that one condition could not be differentiated from another. Also, she made no more errors on nonidentity than on identity. Thus, in principle, the subject could go about the cage, picking up pairs of objects, and labeling them identical or nonidentical. Any instance of this kind, which she could previously recognize, she could now label as such. That is what the language training contributed. The matching-to-sample procedure established that she could distinguish between positive and negative instances of identity; the language training simply provided her with a name for a concept that already existed.

INTERROGATIVE

In the identity exercise above the chimp is already being asked a question. If you were to instruct an English-speaking subject in the same task as the chimp's, you would say something along these lines: "What is the relation between the two objects, are they the same or different?" The chimp is asked the same question but without benefit of an explicit interrogative marker. The only marker she has so far is the implicit one of the space between the objects—into which she is to insert her answer—along with the fact that the trial does not end until she completes the schema by adding the third item.

The question can be made explicit by any one of the three standard linguistic devices: inflection, word order, or an interrogative particle. We chose the latter as the simplest both in the sense of involving the least change for the subject and of being most compatible with the present physical system. So we simply added a question marker to the schema she was already receiving. For example, where we previously wrote:

A   A
IDENTICAL   NONIDENTICAL

we henceforth wrote

A   ?   A
IDENTICAL   NONIDENTICAL

We are now in a position to look at examples of all three types of questions which the identity exercise generates. The first two are Wh-types—what or which—while the last one is of the yes/no form. Examples of two versions of a Wh-type question are shown in the lower panel of Figure 2; they can be paraphrased as "A is what to A?" and "A is what to B?" The alternatives for both versions are IDENTICAL or NONIDENTICAL and the subject's task in both cases is to replace the interrogative marker with the word appropriate to the case.

Two versions of a second type of Wh-question are shown in the upper panel of Figure 2; they can be paraphrased as "A is the same as what?" and "A is not the same as what?" The alternatives are no longer the words IDENTICAL or NONIDENTICAL but the objects themselves. The subject's task remains essentially the same, however: to replace the interrogative particle with the appropriate object.

The yes/no question, which is shown in Figure 3, has four forms rather than two as in the Wh-questions, and these can be paraphrased as 1) "Is A the same as A?", 2) "Is A not the same as A?", 3) "Is A not the same as B?", and 4) "Is A the same as B?" Her alternatives now are neither the words IDENTICAL or NONIDENTICAL nor the object A and B, but the words YES and NO. Her task remains the same: to replace the question mark with either YES or NO.

The chimp is capable of answering correctly all the question types shown, for an essentially unlimited variety of items, words as well as objects. In this case, too, the generalization tests, requiring that she recognize the concept when applied to items not used in training, proved that she had not merely memorized the training cases but could apply the concept broadly. Indeed, the subject has never failed a generalization test. Though often trained on no more than two positive and two negative

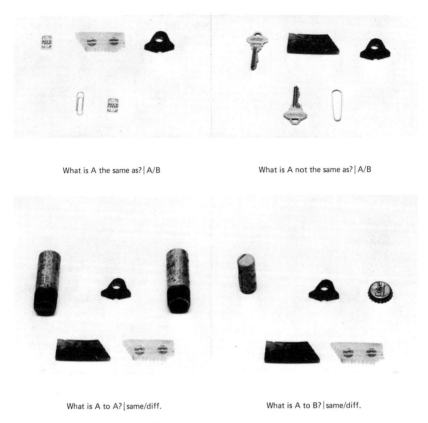

What is A the same as? | A/B   What is A not the same as? | A/B

What is A to A? | same/diff.   What is A to B? | same/diff.

Figure 2.   Four Wh-type questions, with English paraphrases.

instances of the concept, she has always been able to apply the words to cases not used in training. How shall we explain this? If we adopt the position that in teaching a new word we are at the same time teaching a new concept, generalization emerges as a mystery. But if we recognize that concepts antedate the language training, there is then little mystery in the subject's ability to apply words beyond the training cases. Only failures in generalization would speak against the existence of concepts that antedated the language training.

Consider three objections to calling the above expressions questions. First, each case has the form of a one-to-one substitution: The interrogative particle is removed and replaced by a single item. Human interrogation does not suffer from this limitation since answers may be of any length.[1] But in fact, the present system is not restricted to one-word

---

[1] I am indebted to E. Klima for this interesting observation.

Is A the same as A? | yes/no   Is A the same as B? | yes/no

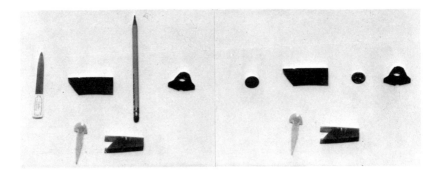

Is A not the same as B? | yes/no   Is A not the same as A? | yes/no

Figure 3. Four yes/no-type questions, with English paraphrases. Notice how one of the objects shares dimensional values with the language elements and, though not a word, is easily confused with the words.

answers either. The answers considered have been short because the language is simple; in addition, there are already counter-examples in which answers consist of more than one word. For example, if we give her as alternatives, NO and IDENTICAL—rather than IDENTICAL and NONIDENTICAL—when the question asked of her is A?B, i.e., "What is the relation between A and B?", she will answer NO IDENTICAL, which though laconic is nonetheless a two-word answer and is thus no longer a case of one-to-one substitution. (Her ability to use the negative particle in this fashion is of considerable interest in its own right, though not to the present discussion.)

Second, she has answered but never asked any questions. This would be a serious objection if she failed to ask questions when given an opportunity to do so. But so far the omission is in the training program, not the subject. Our failure to have tested her ability to produce questions is a failure to have found a simple condition in which to make the test. (On one occasion the chimp offered her own solution to this problem. She stole the test materials for the lesson, as she does from time to time, and went on both first to produce and then to answer many of the questions we had taught her.)

Third, a quite different kind of objection might be made on the grounds that the questions are not themselves genuine. In human affairs, a question is often taken as evidence of 1) the speaker's ignorance and 2) his assumption that the listener is less ignorant. Thus, a person may ask, "What time is it?" because 1) he does not know and 2) he believes his listener does know. It is clear that the questions asked the chimp do not belong to this paradigm.

But it is equally clear what paradigm they do fit and also that the paradigm above is only one of several that figure in human interrogative behavior. Another strong paradigm is based on exactly the opposite assumption about the distribution of knowledge; it is the mainstay of the teacher's business and is the paradigm that is applicable here. The teacher knows the answer to the question and therefore asks it of the student to find out whether he too knows the answer. Thus, a father may ask his son, "What time is it?" thereby determining whether or not the boy can tell time. Although the distribution of knowledge is now the opposite of that in the first case, the utterance is no less a question.

METALINGUISTICS

The relation that now concerns us can be paraphrased as "X is the name of Y." In the relation just dealt with, viz., "X is identical with X," the items instancing the relation were both objects. But the items instancing the present relation are a word and an object, a word which in positive instances of the concept is the name of the object, and a word which in negative instances is not the name of the object. The training procedure for establishing a name for this concept is nonetheless the same as for all the cases already described. In brief, positive instances of the concept are associated with one language element, negative instances with another.

The well-established words for apple and banana along with the corresponding objects were the training materials used. Thus, positive instances consisted of the pairs, APPLE-apple and BANANA-banana, and negative instances of the pairs, APPLE-banana and BANANA-apple. That is, positive instances consisted of a word and the object named by the word, negative instances of a word and an object not named by the word.

The subject was given a word-object pair set slightly apart and required to place between them the language element intended to mean "is the name of." Parallel trials were given on negative instances, i.e., a pair such as BANANA-apple was set before her and she was required to place between them the language element intended to mean "is not the name of." Should we proliferate the vocabulary by introducing an independent word for the negative case, or should we economize and require her to form the name for the negative ("is not name of") by applying the negative particles to the name for the positive case? We compromised by introducing an independent name for the negative case which consisted, however, of the negative particle attached as a single unit to the name for the positive case (see Figure 4).

Following the training in which the words NAME OF and NOT-NAME OF were associated with the negative and positive cases respectively, her associations were tested in a manner that took advantage of her competence in the interrogative. First, she was asked a Wh-type question, in effect, "What is the relation between APPLE and apple?" Her alternatives were NAME OF and NOT-NAME OF and her task was to replace the interrogative marker with the word of her choosing. Next, her associations were tested with yes/no questions. For example, she was

APPLE is the name of apple

BANANA is not the name of apple

Figure 4. Examples of the relation "X is the name of Y" and "X is not the name of Y." Note that the name for the negative relation amounts to the negative particle built onto the name for the positive relation.

asked in effect, "BANANA is the name of apple?" and required to choose between the alternatives YES and NO. She was tested on both versions of the Wh-question as shown in Figure 2, and all four versions of the yes/no question as shown in Figure 3. The questions were confined at first to the four word-object pairs on which she had been trained, but once it was clear that she had mastered the training cases, this restriction was lifted and the same kinds of questions were asked of a number of word-object pairs that had not been used in training, some of them the names of fruits like those used in training and some of them not, e.g., DISH and PAIL. Once again her performance on the generalization test did not differ materially from her performance on the training materials, indicating that she was able to apply the names beyond those few cases on which she had been trained.

PRODUCTIVE VERSUS RECOGNITIONAL USE OF A CONCEPT

I have emphasized all along that language training is primarily a mapping of existing knowledge; it gives the subject names for distinctions that he or she could draw in advance of the language training. In the concept "name of" we have an important exception. This concept was inculcated by the language training and would not have existed otherwise. An interesting and powerful consequence of this fact is that this kind of concept can be used to generate new instances of itself.

In the standard generalization test, the subject may recognize instances of the concept that were not used in training, but this is not the same thing as using a concept to generate new instances of itself. In the generalization test, the cases called "new" are so only in the limited sense that they were not used in the training of the word in question. They are otherwise old, established cases. For example, when we found that the chimp could apply NAME OF to APRICOT-apricot (and NOT-NAME OF to APRICOT-raisin), we proved that she could apply the words to cases other than those used in training. But the pair APRICOT-apricot was not a new pair. It was an old pair with a history of use in sentences that the chimp had both produced and comprehended, some part of which history—exactly which part we do not yet know—enabled the chimp to identify the pair as an instance of "name of." This is quite different from introducing new words by telling the subject that this piece of plastic is the name of this object; and then finding that the piece of plastic is henceforth used appropriately in sentences dealing with the object in question. We will call the application of a word to new cases in a generalization test *recognitional*, to distinguish it from this second and more powerful use which we will call *productive*.

Figs and Crackerjacks were objects that interested the subject but which had never been given names. We used them as the first objects to name with the use of the concept "name of" rather than the more laborious procedure of rotating a class through a range of values while at the same time changing the corresponding language elements (which, however, is the only procedure that can be used to teach a naive subject its first words. See above for a description of this more laborious procedure). A three-step procedure was used to introduce the new words, as well as test the effectiveness of the introduction by subsequently requiring her to use the word in a sentence.

First, a piece of plastic (potential word) and a fig were placed slightly apart and the word NAME OF set between them; next a second piece of plastic was placed slightly apart from a fig and the word NOT-NAME OF was placed between them. Had the subject paid attention to the lesson or had her attention wandered like that of students in classrooms everywhere? In order to answer this question we resorted to the interrogative, as teachers do everywhere, giving the subject both the Wh-and yes/no forms of the question. In effect, she was asked, "What is the relation between the piece of plastic and fig?" for which the alternatives were NAME OF or NOT-NAME OF and "Is this piece of plastic the name of fig?" where the alternatives were YES and NO. Her generally correct answers permitted us to move to the last step, which required that she use the appropriate word in a sentence.

The materials set before the subject were a fig and a number of words; FIG, the piece of plastic she had been told was not the name of fig, the names of two other fruits, GIVE, SARAH, and MARY. The subject was given the fig when she produced the sentence MARY GIVE FIG SARAH, which she did correctly on eight of the first 10 trials, never using the incorrect form for fig but twice using other established fruit names, perhaps as a request for these fruits (a methodological problem noted earlier). She was equally proficient when later exactly the same training procedure was applied to Crackerjacks. Notice that the negative trials—on which she is told that X is not the name of Y—serve to rule out the possibility that the name is conferred simply by the geometry, by the physical contiguity between the language element and the object. Both when it is asserted that X is the name of Y, and when it is denied, the spatio-temporal relation between the language element and the object are identical. Yet only in the case of assertion does the subject go on to use the language element as the name of the designated referent.

INTERNAL REPRESENTATION: WHEN IS A PIECE OF PLASTIC A WORD?

When does a piece of plastic cease to be a piece of plastic and become a word? We might answer by saying, when it is used as a word: when it occurs along with other words of appropriate grammatical class in sentences, and when it occurs as the answer or part of the answer to questions. For example, we consider a small piece of blue plastic to be the name for apple because 1) it is the word used when, for example, the subject requests apple, and 2) it is the answer given when the subject is asked, "What is the name of apple?" This is a standard treatment, and we cannot improve upon it, though we may be able to add to it. We might say in addition that the piece of plastic is a word when the properties ascribed to it are not those of the plastic but are those of the object designated by the piece of plastic. By what means can we determine whether this condition obtains?

This can be done quite directly by using match-to-sample procedures to obtain independent-features analyses of both the word and its referent. For example, to obtain a features analysis of apple the subject was given a series of trials on which an actual apple was presented along with two alternatives. Her task was to indicate which of the two alternatives was more like the apple than the other. The most explicit version of this test would make use of such words as "similar" or "more like than" but these words were not a part of her vocabulary at the time, and we did not find it necessary to instill them before doing the present tests. The subject's disposition to match-to-sample was strong enough so that the three items had only to be set before her in the established geometrical arrangement; this was sufficient to assure that she would select one of the alternatives. The alternatives used in the present tests were: a red plaque versus a green one; a square plaque versus a round one; a square plaque with a stem-like protruberance versus a plain square one; and a square plaque with a protruberance versus a plain round one. The alternatives could be words, rather than objects instancing the properties named by the words. That is, the subject could be required to decide whether the apple was more like words "red" and "green" rather than the red and green plaques. We did not use words because of limitations in Sarah's vocabulary.

After obtaining a features analysis of apple, we repeated the test exactly except for replacing the object apple with the name for apple. Once again the subject was required to indicate whether the sample—now a piece of blue plastic—was, for example, red or green, round or square, etc. Although the sample was no longer a shiny red apple but a piece of blue plastic, the subject assigned to the plastic the same properties she earlier assigned to the apple (see Figure 5). Surely if we did not know that the plastic stood for apple, we would be confused by her analysis of it; we might reasonably conclude that she did not understand matching-to-sample. But this is ruled out by her analysis of the object apple, which accords nicely with the human analysis. The

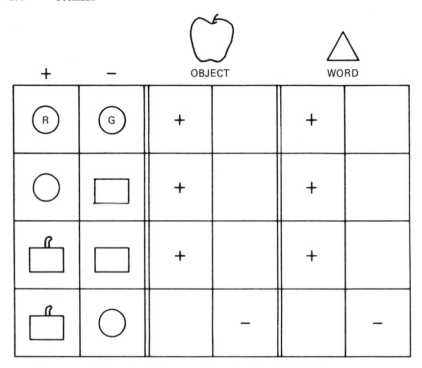

Figure 5.   Features analyses of apple and APPLE.

properties she assigns to the word are immediately sensible if we consider that her analysis of the word is not of its physical form but of that which the form represents.

Bertrand Russell in an early work (1940) noted that uttering a word is like jumping in that both the word and the jump are responses, but that the word differs from the jump in that it has meaning. Skinner (1957) commended the first part of Russell's observation, but rejected the second part on the grounds that a behavioral analysis of language should eschew or at least does not need the concept of meaning. Since I can think of no philosopher more admirable than Russell, nor any psychologist whose reputation is more enviable than Skinner's, I am pleased to suggest that they are both wrong: Skinner in holding that we do not need meaning, and Russell in suggesting that the distinction between responses with and without meaning is a radical one. On the other hand, there is a sense in which both men are right, and their correct judgments lead more surely to the points that need attention now than their more fallible judgments.

Russell is correct in arguing that a response may represent some-thing other than itself. The identical-features analysis which the chimp ascribes to apple on the one hand and to the name of apple on the other supports that conclusion directly. But Skinner is correct in urging that the process by which a response becomes a word is not a unique one, not a process different in principle from the one by which a pigeon learns to peck a key when it is lighted. Words do not require special training methods. The procedures that train animals will also produce words.

REFERENCES

Chomsky, N. 1965. Aspects of the Theory of Syntax. The MIT Press, Cambridge, Mass.

Hewes, G. W. 1949. Lateral dominance, culture, and writing systems. Hum. Biol. 21:233–245.

Lenneberg, E. 1967. Biological Foundations of Language. Wiley, New York.

Premack, D., and Schwartz, A. 1966. Preparations for discussing behaviorism with chimpanzee. In F. Smith and G. A. Miller (eds.), Genesis of Language, pp. 295–335. The MIT Press, Cambridge, Mass.

Russell, B. 1940. An Inquiry into Meaning and Truth. George Allen, London.

Skinner, B. F. 1957. Verbal Behavior. Appleton-Century-Crofts, New York.

chapter 13

Communication and Cognitive Organization in Humans and Other Animals

Emil W. Menzel*

Marcia K. Johnson*

Department of Psychology
State University of New York at Stony Brook
Stony Brook, New York

Chomsky (1967) once remarked that if animal communication has any fundamental properties in common with human language, the place to look for these properties is not at the level of ethological displays (i.e., the motor aspects of performance) or linguistic analysis, but rather at the level of perceptual and cognitive organization (see also Osgood, 1971; Count, 1973; Eisenberg, 1973). In this chapter we consider those aspects of human and nonhuman communication which seem most interesting from a functionally oriented, cognitive, and comparative point of view.

A FUNCTIONAL POINT OF VIEW

First of all, all communication systems may be viewed as means to an end. They are mechanisms whereby humans or nonhumans solve the basic problems of coordinating and regulating their societies; discriminating each other's specieshood, sex, age, social background, group membership, emotional and motivational states, and the state of other objects and events in the environment; transmitting the capacity for similar accomplishments to subsequent generations; and thus ultimately securing all of the requisites for the survival and reproduction of the phenotype. Inasmuch as all living species are, almost by definition, capable of achieving their basic goals under natural conditions, it seems chauvinistic to ask whose communication systems are the "best," or to attempt to train animals in our languages before learning theirs.

Communication is Part of the General
Information-Processing Activities of an Organism

Communication is embedded in the general perceptual and cognitive activities of the organism, and these activities have the primary characteristic of being adaptive and purposeful. To separate communication from the overall information pickup and transmission capabilities of the individual would be a tour de force on the part of the human observer. Obtaining information from language or other specialized signal systems must share common features with obtaining information from any source.

Meanings Have Multiple Signs and
There Are Multiple Meanings for Signs

Communication is symbolic, but the symbols do not correspond to meanings in any simple one-to-one fashion. An animal moving through the woods might hear a single vocalization or the sound of several footsteps, or see a footprint in the sand, or smell the slight trace of urine or body

---

From Menzel, E. W., and Johnson, M. K. 1976. Communication and cognitive organization in humans and other animals. Ann. N. Y. Acad. Sci. 280:131–142. Reprinted by permission.

* Affiliation given reflects the authors' affiliation at time of writing.

odor in the air. Any number of these "sign stimuli" might stop him in his tracks, cause him to hypothesize or conclude that "something is out there," and that "it is probably over there rather than elsewhere," and "it is an X animal rather than a Y," and so forth. It is not the stimulus as such, but what that stimulus might *represent* which makes the stimulus biologically or cognitively significant. There is probably no one "innate releasing stimulus" for any particular hypothesis, and the same general conclusion can be reached in a host of different ways. Conversely, the "same" nominal stimulus can often represent a number of objects or events. What is a snake? It depends on whether you are talking to a student of biology, a fundamentalist preacher who is about to baptize you, a two-year-old child who is about to set foot in a Louisiana swamp, your psychoanalyst, a dance leader, a crapshooter. Neither the calls of monkeys nor the words of people *directly* stand for things. As Olson (1970) and others have suggested, words serve to provide information relative to a given set of alternatives. This reduces the likelihood that a dictionary approach—assigning signs to meanings in a direct one-to-one fashion—will be adequate for characterizing any communication system.

The Importance of "Triangulation"

In the everyday world information comes from multiple sources, and except perhaps for organisms with split brains (Gazzaniga, 1967) or those in highly specialized laboratory experiments (Held, 1965), various channels function together as a coordinated, if not in some sense a unified, information-getting system. As Hornbostel (quoted by Gibson, 1966) put it, "it matters little through which sense I realize that . . . I have fallen into a pigsty" (p. 54). Many different forms of stimulus energy can all carry the same information; and information about the world can be obtained with any cue system alone or with many combinations of cues working together. D. T. Campbell (1966) gives the latter process a very apt name: "triangulation." The most obvious form of triangulation is intramodal binocular vision or the ability to integrate the information received by each eye separately into a single percept. Other forms of triangulation would include the integration of information from verbalizations and gestures, visual and auditory cues, and so on.

The Importance of Cognitive Structures

A fundamental characteristic of information processing in general, as well as of language, is that two or more individuals do not reach the same understanding without similar cognitive structures. This is, of course, because the meaning of a message depends on the cognitive structure or schema to which it is referred (e.g., Bransford and Johnson, 1973). *Move out of the way* means one thing if someone is trying to run a vacuum cleaner around you and another if a large truck is coming toward you. Similarly, the sound of leaves rustling probably means one thing if you know a friend is near the source of the noise and another if you have reason to believe that a predator might be near. Thus, not only is there "triangulation" of information from various sources, but also there is considerable "filling in" or redintegration on the basis of the cognitive structures which are active at any given moment. Probable inferences based on past experience and reasonable hypotheses in any given situation are an integral part of information utilization (e.g., Kintsch, 1972; Johnson, Bransford, and, Solomon, 1973; Johnson, 1975).

Taking into Account the Cognitive Structure of Someone Else

In ordinary human discourse, the appropriate cognitive organization may be given by the immediate environment, as in the *Move out of the way* example. Or it may be given by experience and conventions; to use John Searle's example, *Could you pass the salt?* does not ordinarily mean *Are you able to pass the salt?* but rather *Please pass the salt.* However, environmental cues and the habits of conventions are often only partial cues to meaning. Frequently, much of the appropriate cognitive structure must be established during the interaction of speaker and listener.

One of the most interesting aspects of practical communication situations is that people continually assess and take into account the cognitive competencies and cognitive structures of others and tailor their communications accordingly. If you were looking for the TWA gate at Kennedy Airport, you would be more likely to ask a person in an airport uniform than a randomly selected passerby. If you wanted to buy marbles, you would be more likely to ask a child where to go than to ask an adult. Similarly, if the airport guard or child were giving you directions, he or she would very likely start by determining something about your current state of knowledge about the environment. "Well, do you know where the airport restaurant is? Good. Turn left there and it's about three gates down."

An ongoing series of studies by David Goldstein and some of his colleagues indicates that children communicate more effectively the more familiar they are with the environment they are communicating about (Goldstein and Kose, personal communication). More importantly, children are more likely to use gestures in interactions with younger children than in interactions with adults (Goldstein et al., personal communication); and the length of children's verbalizations is affected by the age of the listener (Shatz and Gelman, 1973). Apparently, by the age of four or five, if not sooner, children are beginning to tailor their communication to fit the presumed cognitive outlook of their listeners. As adults, many specific features of our communications (e.g., word choice, gestures, length of sentences, tone of voice, our rate of speech) are determined partially by the presumed capacities and actions of someone else.

Successful Communication
Is Based on the Above Characteristics of the Process

In general, successful communication depends on accurate assumptions about the cognitive organization of others and creative ways of using the entire communication process—making gestures, facial and body expressions, drawing pictures, making analogies, in addition to "straight" verbalization. This point is important not only in people-to-people exchanges, but also in people-to-animal exchanges. Most behavioral work with animals (like that with human infants) is largely a communication problem. Since we cannot verbally question an octopus about whether he can tell the difference between black and white, we have had to find some other ways to ask such questions. The most successful behavioral researchers are probably those who have particularly good intuitions about the way the world might look from someone else's point of view. As Konrad Lorenz put it, the first requirement of good research is that you be thoroughly familiar with your animal.

Since successful communication depends on accurately assessing the available cognitive structures of other beings, and animals integrate information from various sources, it is misleading to think of communication as one individual transmitting information to another who knows absolutely nothing about the intended message. The more two individuals share common structures, assumptions, knowledge, and values, the more efficient their communication. This is one reason why it is easier to teach a human language to a chimpanzee than to a rhesus monkey. Perhaps this is partly why animal communication systems appear less elaborate than our own. In their societies, more information is shared information. Thus there is less variability in psychological organization to overcome.

In any event, if successful people-to-people and people-to-animal communication depends on accurate assumptions about the cognitive structure of other beings, it is probably not too farfetched to assume that communication between animals involves similar assumptions about how the world looks to someone else.

LOOKING AT ANIMALS
COLLECTING AND TRANSMITTING INFORMATION

With this background of assumptions, consider a "simple" interaction between an animal and an unknown object or being. Suppose that a normal, free-ranging monkey is strolling through the woods and suddenly comes into sensory contact with an object. How would he go about sizing up the situation? How would he know whether he was dealing with another living being, and if so, how would he determine its intent? If it were a conspecific, how would he determine whether it knows better than he does the lay of the land, the whereabouts of food, predators, and the rest of the social group?

Intentional Triangulation and Testing Hypotheses

Even if our monkey could conceivably be viewed as a "passive receiver" at the instant he perceives the first signal or cue (a glimpse, an odor, etc.), he does not remain passive for long. In nature, few situations can be sized up with certainty on the basis of a single distal cue; and in most cases the monkey will accordingly not "automatically" race toward or away from the source of the signal, but rather he will seek out additional information, or indulge in what Pavlov called the "what is it?" reflex. He might turn his head this way and that, send out an answering call, sniff the air further, possibly climb a tree to scan the area visually. In this way, whatever "hypothesis" or "question" was posed initially can be further probed or checked out. We doubt very much that monkeys, like theorists (e.g., Marler, 1965), sort various signals or cues into different categories according to what sensory modality is involved. They are, in other words, probably even less aware of and interested in their raw sensations as such than are human beings.

The Problem of Context

The extent to which our monkey will continue to indulge his curiosity depends upon many factors in addition to his initial hypothesis about the object. It depends, for example, upon his general familiarity with this particular portion of woods, whether or not the area includes large vertical structures that might provide cover or escape, how far away he is from his companions, how hungry he is, and so on. Those scientists who relegate such considerations to a garbage-pail category of "contextual factors" and focus their attention on "signals as such" should ask themselves: How do we, as observers, know which stimuli are "context," *psychologically speaking*, and how do we know which stimuli are the "core" of the animal's attention, at any given instant? As Floyd Allport (1955) has shown, the "core vs. context" distinction might be useful in informal discussion, but it is based on inadequate theories of cognitive structure and meaning (see also Menzel, 1969).

To give an illustration, consider why it is so difficult to do good auditory "playback" experiments on primates, if not on many other higher mammals. If you record the "alarm call" of some bird species and play it back on a high-fidelity tape recorder, birds of that species will often respond very much as they would to the live event. Try the same experiment on a rhesus monkey or a chimpanzee, however, and he will probably glance at the recorder, then at you, and soon go on about his business. There are at least two ways in which the experiment could be changed to increase the chances of getting a "better" outcome: either add further cues that would tend to support the same hypothesis, or eliminate those cues (starting with the visible presence of a human being and a strange looking gadget) which might give rise to alternative hypotheses. Thus, for example, if the call came from behind some bushes that might easily conceal both a monkey and something about which a monkey might well become alarmed, and if the call were the voice of a known individual who was not in sight but whom the subject had seen walking over toward those bushes a few minutes earlier, and if, moreover, the subject himself had heard a leopard growling within the last several hours, we would predict without hesitation that his response would be less sanguine. It is not merely what animals know but what they don't know (and are capable of hypothesizing) that gives the signal its specific meaning. The call constitutes an "alarm cry"—i.e., it has the customary "dictionary" meaning which the Darwinian student of animal behavior has tried to assign it—only under certain sets of circumstances. With animals, as with people, we have to take into account what Orne (1973) calls "communication by the total experimental situation."

Novelty: Assimilating Something New

Back to our monkey in the woods. In the interest of brevity, we will henceforth concentrate our attention on visual cues. Certainly the monkey would take into account whether the object looks like other objects with which he is already familiar, particularly in this part of the forest. There is a fairly high positive correlation between the phyletic status of the animal and the length of time he will spend in exploring a strange object (Glickman and Sroges, 1966) and with most (but by no means all) classes of objects, the young will continue to respond longer than will adults. From our point of view, this cannot be attributed simply to motivational differences. Confronted with something new or unusual, animals attempt to make some sense of it, to organize it within a known framework, to discover what it is and what it does and what it might be good for. The more complicated the object and the more complicated the perceiver, the more possibilities there are to be explored. Adults of a given species might explore simple objects less than a youngster would, because they can evaluate such objects more quickly.

Assessing Someone Else

Apparent Size Generally speaking, objects that look large are approached much more tentatively than are objects that look smaller. For example, the same object usually produces quite different reactions according to whether it is standing upright or lying on its side, and the upright position usually produces greater caution. It is striking that so many of the visually mediated "aggressive displays" of so many different species are based on the simple principle of "making oneself look bigger" (via sitting up versus lying down, standing bipedally versus standing quadrupedally, showing piloerection, and so on). Conversely, one way to get a timid animal or child to approach is to stoop down or otherwise make yourself look smaller. A puzzling problem is why even presumably intelligent animals such as monkeys and men, who show excellent size constancy in other situations, often do not see through such tricks.

Visual Capacity Of all the static visual cues that lead a monkey to respond to an object as if it were a living being, one of the most important is anything that looks like eyes. Two buttons attached to a rectangular piece of fur, for example, will produce a much more pronounced reaction than the fur alone. To be really effective the buttons should be located together on one end of the rectangle. A monkey will characteristically circle the object and then make his first close approach from the "tail end" of the object—that is, the end opposite from the eyes. Using a doll as the test object, one can in fact often cause the direction of the monkey's approach to vary simply by having the doll's eyes either opened or closed. A radio-controlled doll which would open its eyes and rotate its head toward the monkey as he was sneaking in cautiously from the rear would probably produce a striking effect. It should go without saying that similar behaviors occur if the test objects are other living beings, particularly other monkeys; the phenomenon of "gaze aversion" is by now very well known. One of us (Menzel) kept a record for about two months of all the times that he was approached and threatened by free-ranging rhesus monkeys as he was sitting passively in the woods. The data of principal interest were the direction of approach and the monkey's location when he sounded his first threat vocalization. A large majority of the monkeys (especially the smaller ones) made their approach from the rear, and in addition, many of these came in from overhead. They approached much closer, too, than those who did not come in from outside the test person's field of vision.

We could add many more examples of such behaviors, but perhaps their major point is already clear. Not only does the monkey seem to know the layout of the environment and his own behavioral and information-processing potentials, but also, he seems to be making hypotheses or somehow taking into account what behavioral and perceptual capacities *the other being* might possess. Was this indeed not true almost from the start, when our imaginary monkey received its first cue about the presence of the object? From a phenomenological point of view we might be stretching the data in putting forth such a claim; but from an evolutionary and functional point of view the claim is most plausible. In other words, we would argue that *most* species-specific behaviors, if not most morphological characteristics of living things (such as the eye-spots of a moth which frighten off predatory birds, and the bright colors of flowers which attract bees) in some way "take into account" the perceptual and cognitive organization of other living beings. Just where in the foregoing description of the monkey's behavior one is actually warranted in positing phenomenological knowledge or understanding on the monkey's part is a matter that future research will have to settle, but we are convinced that the question is not a trivial one (Bastian and Bermant, 1973).

Behavior Potentials   Up to now we have said nothing about motion, and this is undoubtedly the most important single visual feature that gets and holds an animal's attention and assists him in distinguishing between a living being, a dead animal, and an inanimate object. Indeed, the general attention-getting value of movement most likely evolved in the first place because moving things are so apt to be either living beings or objects that are being acting upon by living beings; that is, certain types of movement are a fairly reliable sign of life, and hence of food, danger, or something else that might be of biological significance. A pile of leaves or a series of bushes that rustle and stir in a regular progression (as if they were being moved by a live animal burrowing or walking through them) will frequently be investigated, and the monkey does not investigate all points along this line of movement, but only the *last* point.

Even more pertinent to our present discussion, monkeys are capable of learning very quickly to discriminate between two static objects, one of which will move in one way (suddenly and rapidly toward you) when it is approached and another of which will move in a different way (slowly and away from you). In other words, the animals seem to learn a particular object's *potential ability* to move in a particular way; the object does not have to be moving at any given instant to produce its differential effect. It would be very surprising to us if normally raised monkeys could not, like people, take into account the following sorts of facts when they confront "new" animals: if the beast has wings and feathers, it is probably capable of traveling through the air; if it has no appendages at all, it probably cannot travel through the air; if it has big teeth, it can probably bite; and, in general, the more it looks like me, the more likely it can do whatever I can do.

While the general nonrandomness of an object's movement and the suddenness and directionality of this movement are highly effective determinants of a monkey's response, these animals seem also to be highly sensitive to whether or not the object's movement (and, of course, its other behaviors) are nonrandom *specifically with respect to their own behavior.* For example, a radio-controlled doll that moves its head up and down on a randomly determined schedule would probably be much less apt to inhibit a monkey from taking food that lay at the doll's feet than another doll that performs precisely the same movements but "looks down" only when the monkey is about to put his hand on the food.

Many aspects of the stalking behavior and play of mammals have some of the characteristics we have discussed so far. Consider, for example, how a monkey tries to sneak up on another animal for a "surprise attack." Not only will he move slowly, silently, and low to the ground, circle in from the rear if possible, and keep trees, rocks, bushes, or any available visual barrier between himself and the victim, but, also, he will continually keep a watch on what the victim is doing. If he steps on a dry leaf he will freeze and watch the victim, and if the victim pricks up its ears, he will probably take greater care not to make any noise. If the victim starts visually to scan the area in the monkey's direction, the monkey might move quickly and duck behind a tree. If the victim plops down on the ground and closes its eyes, the monkey moves in faster than before, and so on.

Certainly it is not farfetched to say that the monkey perceives the correlation or the lack of correlation between his own behavior and that of the other animal (*and vice versa*) and varies his behavior appropriately. Is it possible that he also tries to guess what the other animal is hypothesizing, or even, conceivably, to control the other animal into hypothesizing one thing rather than another? Such a question might at first glance seem absurdly anthropomorphic. However, as Norbert Wiener suggested many years ago in his classical description of a fight between a mongoose and a snake, a principal advantage that the "higher" animal has is that he can use higher orders of information and feedback than the "lower" animal. In a fight he can correct his own moves in mid-course according to cues received from the other animal, rather than responding on an all-or-none basis; he can feint in one way to draw the other animal out, and then utilize this "opening"; he can keep himself in a favored location and gradually maneuver the other animal into a corner; he can learn what the other animal's potentials for certain types of movement will be as it gets more and more tired, and so proceed on the principle of first wearing the other animal down before the killing move is made. By the objective criteria that authors such as Tolman (1951), Sommerhoff (1950), and Rosenblueth, Wiener, and Bigelow (1943) have proposed, not only monkeys and mongooses but possibly even the snake could be said to know something about other animals' behavior potentials, hypotheses, and intentions.

Communicating about Others, Objects, Intentions, and the Environment

A still more complicated form of interaction is that which involves a third party in addition to the sender and the receiver. Can animal A perceive the fact that animal B's behavior is nonrandom with respect to animal C or with respect to an object? Since such behavior may be said to involve communication about the environment, and since it has been an accepted dogma for many years that animals other than man do little if any communicating about the environment, there are many authors who would be understandably skeptical about the ability of monkeys on this score. Consider, however, the following examples, which we are sure almost every field observer of primates has seen:

1. A human observer stares hard at an infant, then leans down to pick up a rock. The infant's mother, who is 20 yards off, starts to threaten the observer.
2. Monkey A, monkey B, and a big ripe banana are all located 20 feet from each other, like three points of an equilateral triangle. Monkey A happens to see the banana first and starts for it. Monkey B, who is dominant to A, looks up at A, then immediately spots the banana too, and gives a gruff vocalization and gets up and starts for the same goal. A stops short at B's vocalization, glances once or twice between B and the banana, and sits down and grimaces at B.
3. Monkey A and monkey B are sitting a few yards apart. Monkey A spots something behind a bush and cocks his head and stares toward the bush. Monkey B immediately stares in the same direction, then gets up and walks over and looks behind the bush.

We could, of course, extend this sort of analysis to four-party, five-party, or N-party interactions, and ask how many independent factors a monkey is capable of taking into account simultaneously before responding, but unfortunately there is very little empirical data available on such "higher order" situations. A majority of the available studies of primate behavior focus attention on simple dyadic relations (see Kummer, Götz, and Angst, 1974, for a cogent critique). It is, however, safe to predict that although probably all species of primates are capable of taking into account two or three independent factors, various species of primates would differ greatly in the sheer number of independent factors they could handle simultaneously (Nissen, 1958).

Perhaps the major point that we are trying to make here is that any statement to the effect that "animals other than man are capable only of communicating their internal emotional states and cannot convey information about objects" is predicated upon a false dichotomy and a very narrow view, even of emotional and expressive behavior. As Michotte (1950) pointed out some years ago, human beings, if not other animals also, characteristically perceive "emotion" as a modification of a signaler's behavior *in regard to* oneself or *in regard to* some object or event. That is, we judge the character and meaning of another being's internal state not merely from his motor patterns and vocalizations and other molecular reactions, but also from the relation of these reactions to the rest of the environment.

When we see an individual acting excited or even just walking rapidly in a straight line, we tend to assume that the individual is not performing some isolated activity, but rather that his behavior has some external referent or cause, if not some goal or purpose. A whole group of monkeys startles and leaps for the trees when one member does so, not because of what the leader's behavior portends about his internal state, but because of what such behavior might portend (or has in the past portended) about the environment and the receiver's odds of survival. A chimpanzee heads over in the direction of another chimpanzee who is giving loud "food calls" not because the calls indicate how happy the signaler is (and happiness is contagious), but because of what the calls suggest about the receiver's odds of getting something for himself.

Chimpanzees that have seen a member of their group orient toward an object which they themselves cannot see will often search the field in the indicated direction. It is not necessary that the signaler accompany them or even that he be in the situation at the time of group response. Moreover, there can be a considerable temporal delay between the leader's signal and the followers' response. Further, the followers react quite differently if the hidden object is a snake than if it is a pile of food, and they can similarly discriminate the difference between a large versus a small pile of food or a preferred versus a less preferred type of food (Menzel, 1974).

To give one more example, consider a group of semidesert-dwelling hamadryas baboons that sleep every night on one of several cliffs but that forage up to several miles from these cliffs during the day (Kummer, 1968). Assume that on a given day the group is at a position from which each cliff lies in a different direction, and that the leader of the group starts to glance alternately toward the setting sun, the cliffs, and the other animals, and then strides off in the direction of one of the cliffs. Would it really be so remarkable if the other adult group members could predict the leader's (and the group's) destination an hour or so and a few miles in advance? Does the leader actually need a vocal or gestural language to get across to the human observer or to his followers that it is late in the day and time to move out, and that he intends to spend the night at the same place the group put up a few nights ago?

It seems to us that one function of communication is to reduce the others' uncertainty in situations that are not already clear, and that the more information the sender and receiver already have in common and the better they can evaluate each other's knowledge and momentary predispositions, and the greater the number of alternative ways they have for filling in the few remaining blanks of information, the less necessary is any particular "signal."

According to Suzanne Langer (1942), two of the clearest suggestions of symbolization in nonhuman species, and hence two of the clearest precursors of language-like processes are 1) the "mere sense of significance" that animals attach to strange-looking objects and new situations and 2) expressive movements and "dances." Maybe she did not go far enough. Almost any motor behavior, even simple locomotion, is "symbolic" in the sense that it usually has some external referent or "refers to" objects and events that the animal has either encountered in the past or expects to encounter in the future. Actions may also be said to possess most of the formal design features by means of which other investigators have tried to characterize language. The ability of nonverbal animals to "tell" each other the nature and location of objects and events is limited only by the richness of a signaler's behavioral organization and a receiver's knowledge of the signaler and the common environment in which they are operating.

SUMMARY AND CONCLUSIONS

Our major goal has been to indicate some primary features of a cognitively oriented, functional account of communication. In summary, we have argued that communication is part of the general perceptual and cognitive activities of an organsim. Before we can predict how a "word" or a "signal" will be comprehended in a particular situation by a particular receiver, we must presuppose a good bit about the psychological organization of the receiver. Specialized signals supplement and complement the information that is available from other sources, including internal schemata and hypotheses. Some of the most interesting of these hypotheses involve assumptions about the perceptual and cognitive capacities of someone else. Sometimes these assumptions may be wrong, but many animals, and especially primates (including us) seem to be able to correct them even in the mid-course of an action on the basis of feedback from another individual. Where language leaves off and nonlanguage begins, or where "cues" leave off and "context" begins, is an open question, and in our opinion it is not a very central one.

These considerations suggest that it is time to question, if not lay to rest, many of the assumptions that still linger on in the area of animal communication, especially the assumptions that there are one-to-one correspondences between particular signals and particular meanings (the principle of the dictionary and the ethogram), that the relative communicative ability of species can be measured in terms of how many different signals they make (vocabulary size), that nearly all nonhuman communication patterns are involuntary and nonintentional, that the hallmark of human language is the ability to indicate objects rather than purely internal states, that without language animals can convey nothing about the past or the future or about objects that are not present to the senses. In particular, we would argue that any theory of communication that ignores the ability of animals to use many different interchangeable means for getting across the same general message (which ability has been called "paraphrasing" and "translation" in linguistics, "means-ends-readiness" in the area of problem solving, and "equifinality" in biology) is of little value for understanding primate communication or its biological roots or its cognitive base.

Some investigators have argued that sentences or propositions rather than words or phonemes are the appropriate units for a structural analysis of verbal language. For a functional analysis of language and communication in general, the more appropriate units are the larger events in which sentences *and* nonverbal cues occur. The amount of information conveyed by a signaler to a receiver cannot be specified from any more molecular form of analysis.

The more we think about the fact that communication is part of the general information-processing activities of an organism, the more obvious it becomes that beneath the "deep structure" of human language and human thought there are indeed "deep-deep" structures that we share with other species, and that it is on these structures that our linguistic abilities are predicated.

REFERENCES

Allport, F. H. 1955. Theories of Perception and the Concept of Structure. John Wiley & Sons, New York.

Bastian, J., and Bermant, G. 1973. Animal communication: An overview and conceptual analysis. *In* G. Bermant (ed.), Perspectives on Animal Behavior. Scott, Foresman & Co., Glenview, Ill.

Bransford, J. D., and Johnson, M. K. 1973. Consideration of some problems of comprehension. *In* W. Chase (ed.), Visual Information Processing. Academic Press, New York.

Campbell, D. T. 1966. Pattern matching as an essential in distal knowing. *In* K. R. Hammond (ed.), The Psychology of Egon Brunswik. Holt, Rinehart & Winston, New York.

Chomsky, N. 1967. The general properties of language. *In* F. L. Darley (ed.), Brain Mechanisms Underlying Speech and Language. Grune & Stratton, New York.

Count, E. W. 1973. Being and Becoming Human. Van Nostrand-Reinhold Co., New York.

Eisenberg, J. 1973. Mammalian social systems. Are primate social systems unique? *In* Symposia Fourth Inter. Cong. Primatology, Vol. 1: Precultural Primate Behavior. S. Karger, Basel, Switzerland.

Gazzaniga, M. 1967. The split brain in man. Sci. Am. 217:24–29.

Gibson, J. J. 1966. The Senses Considered as Perceptual Systems. Houghton Mifflin Co., New York.

Glickman, S. E., and Sroges, R. W. 1966. Curiosity in zoo animals. Behaviour 26:151–188.

Held, R. 1965. Plasticity in sensory-motor systems. Sci. Am. 213:84–94.

Johnson, M. K., Bransford, J. D., and Solomon, S. K. 1973. Memory for tacit implications of sentences. J. Exp. Psychol. 98:203–205.

Johnson, M. K. 1975. Constructive aspects of memory: Historical antecedents. Presented at 83rd Annual Convention of the American Psychological Association, September, Chicago, Ill.

Kintsch, W. 1972. Notes on the structure of semantic memory. In E. Tulving and W. Donaldson (eds.), Organization and Memory. Academic Press, New York.

Kummer, H. 1968. Social Organization of Hamadryas Baboons. S. Karger, Basel, Switzerland.

Kummer, H., Götz, W., and Angst, W. 1974. Triadic differentiation: An inhibitory process protecting pair bonds in baboons. Behaviour 59:62–87.

Langer, S. K. 1942. Philosophy in a New Key. Harvard University Press, Cambridge, Mass.

Marler, P. 1965. Communication in monkeys and apes. In I. DeVore (ed.), Primate Behavior. Holt, Rinehart & Winston, New York.

Menzel, E. W. 1969. Naturalistic and experimental approaches to primate behavior. In E. Williams and H. Rausch (eds.), Naturalistic Viewpoints in Psychological Research. Holt, Rinehart & Winston, New York.

Menzel, E. W. 1974. A group of young chimpanzees in a one-acre field. In A. M. Schrier and F. Stollnitz (eds.), Behavior of Nonhuman Primates, Vol. 5. Academic Press, New York.

Menzel, E. W. Communication of object-locations in a group of young chimpanzees. In D. Hamburg and J. Goodall (eds.), Behavior of the Great Apes. Holt, Rinehart & Winston, New York. In press.

Michotte, A. 1950. The emotions regarded as functional connections. In Feelings and Emotions: The Moosehart Symposium. McGraw-Hill Book Co., New York.

Nissen, H. W. 1958. Axes of behavioral comparison. In A. Roe and G. G. Simpson (eds.), Behavior and Evolution. Yale University Press, New Haven, Conn.

Olson, D. R. 1970. Language and thought: Aspects of a cognitive theory of semantics. Psych. Rev. 77:257–273.

Orne, M. T. 1973. Communication by the total experimental situation: Why it is important, how it is evaluated, and its significance for the ecological validity of findings. In P. Pliner, L. Krames, and T. Alloway (eds.), Communication and Affect. Academic Press, New York.

Osgood, C. E. 1971. Where do sentences come from? In D. D. Steinberg and L. A. Jacobvitz (eds.), Semantics: An Interdisciplinary Reader in Philosophy, Linguistics, and Psycholgoy. Cambridge University Press, Cambridge, Mass.

Rosenblueth, A., Wiener, N., and Bigelow, J. 1943. Behavior, purpose and teleology. Phil. Sci. 10:18–24.

Shatz, M., and Gelman, R. 1973. The development of communication skills: Modifications in the speech of young children as a function of listener. Monogr. Soc. Res. Child Dev. No. 152.

Sommerhoff, G. 1950. Analytical Biology. Oxford University Press, Oxford, England.

Tolman, E. C. 1951. Behavior and Psychological Man. University of California Press, Berkeley.

chapter

14

Initial Acquisition of Symbolic Skills Via the Yerkes Computerized Language Analog System

E. Sue Savage-Rumbaugh

Duane M. Rumbaugh

Georgia State University
Atlanta, Georgia
and
Yerkes Regional Primate Research Center
of Emory University
Atlanta, Georgia

THE ANIMAL MODEL PROJECT:
COMMON PROBLEMS IN TEACHING LANGUAGE TO
CHIMPANZEES AND ALINGUISTIC HUMANS

The animal model research project at the Yerkes Regional Primate Research Center was initiated following the success of the Language Analog (LANA) Project and the use of a computer-based system as an aid in language instruction with an alinguistic organism (Savage and Rumbaugh, 1977). The basic goals of the program are to determine whether or not the chimpanzee is a feasible animal model for the study of factors important to the development of language processes in children who, for a variety of reasons, do not acquire language in a spontaneous fashion. If the chimpanzee proves to be a viable animal model, then many types of language-based studies can be conducted with apes that would not be feasible to conduct with human children because of lack of control over their environment and, in some instances, because of ethical constraints. The determination of whether or not the chimpanzee can be used as a workable model depends upon demonstrating:

1. That similar training techniques are feasible for both chimpanzee and human subjects.
2. That problems encountered during training tend to be of a similar nature as revealed by error analysis.
3. That solutions to training problems are basically the same for both species.
4. That the developmental progress and hierarchical structuring of both linguistic and cognitive world views are of a common nature for chimp and human being although perhaps different in their specifics.

The chimpanzee, as an experimental model for the study of language acquisition skills, provides the researcher with numerous ready-made problems. Contrary to common expectations, these problems do not generally stem from the fact that the chimpanzee is a different, albeit closely related, species. Instead, they stem from a variety of environmental and cognitive factors which the alinguistic chimpanzee and retarded child share in common. It is these common factors, quite apart from any innate, linguistic, and/or biological similarities, that render the chimpanzee language animal model concept a possible alternative to the human child in the study of language acquisition processes.

Problems that must be faced in an attempt to teach chimpanzees language are surely familiar to all who have worked with profoundly retarded alinguistic children. They include the following:

1. There is frequently little, if any, voluntary control over the vocal apparatus; thus, some form of nonvocal instruction must be employed.

Supported by National Institutes of Health grants HD-06016 and RR-00155.

2. The attention span, initially, is relatively brief, especially when faced with a problem that cannot be readily solved. Lack of understanding often (but not always) results in a preservation of errors rather than a searching for alternative solutions.

3. Although imitation occurs on occasion, chimpanzees are not highly imitative without training, and thus imitation as an initial training strategy is not particularly useful.

4. They often do not understand that the skills which they are asked to acquire are part of any form of communicative system, i.e., lexigrams, signs, etc., are not initially recognized as words or even as stimuli of specific import.

5. They possess little or no linguistic receptive skills.

6. Practically nothing is known about their cognitive capacities, what their limits are, or how they develop.

7. Creative symbolic play is absent and tool-use skills are minimal.

8. In captivity, they often suffer from the general institutionalized problems of lack of motivation as a result of:
   a. expecting to have the necessities of life provided for them.
   b. depression and stereotypic behaviors caused by separation from mothers and social groups.

9. They display extreme individual variability in both intellectual skills and personality.

10. Linguistic instruction requires a high degree of subject-instructor rapport and understanding in a one-to-one setting.

Without a considerable understanding of the personality and problems of each individual animal, language-training efforts are futile. Premack's (1976) success with Sarah, and his difficulty with other apes, illustrates this problem. Work at the Georgia Retardation Center has revealed that the same sort of rapport is equally necessary with human subjects. This places a great demand on the trainer and requires constant interpretation of, and sensitivity to, the nature of the subject's difficulties. It is far too easy to presume that the reason a particular subject is not learning is because of his stupidity and not the trainer's lack of insight. The most difficult aspects of training language skills revolve around determining what it is that the subject does not understand, and determining how to arrange environmental contingencies so the subject will attend to the significant aspects of the task.

ADVANTAGES OF USING A COMPUTER-BASED SYSTEM

A computer-based keyboard system provides unique ways of dealing with many of the problems outlined above. In general, a graphic computer-based system allows the structuring of linguistic skills to occur in an environment that emphasizes consistency and interpretable feedback, orients attentional factors appropriately, and simplifies response output. Advantages of this system as contrasted with other nonvocal, noncomputer-based approaches include:

1. The extreme simplicity of the motoric response.
2. The orienting of attentional responses via the brightening of a key as it is depressed, followed by its appearance on the projectors. Both serve to indicate to the subject that a word has just been produced, and the maintenance of that word on the projectors (until it is erased) allows for the continuance of sequential cognitive processes which otherwise might be disrupted because of difficulties with short term memory storage.
3. The response initiators (PLEASE) and terminators (PERIOD) erase the entire phrase if depressed out of sequence. Their distinctive color, form, and erase function allow the subject to separate the *act* of communication from the message which is to be communicated. They require attention to message type (question, statement, etc.) before its formulation, and they force attention to a message's completion or termination.
4. The linking of the keyboard to the computer allows repeatable, identical, environmental occurrences to be programmed following a chosen series of properly arranged key depressions. It is after the first vague realization that there is a reliable connection between pressing keys, which are embossed with particular geometric figures, and environmental happenings, that the chimpanzee comes to discriminate between lexigrams and to treat them as a significant element of his visual surrounding.
5. A computer-based system with a programmable grammar analyzer permits the subject repetitious practice using syntactically ordered word strings. The subject can work at his own pace, can stop midsentence if distracted, and is provided with constant feedback about the syntactic elements that have already been executed.
6. Interpretation of the animal's response and, consequently, the feedback given for that response, is always consistent since there are no problems in accurately decoding the response (as there might be with poorly executed signs or vocalizations). Proper interpretation of, and consistent feedback for, each type of response are extremely critical parameters of initial language acquisition, because at that point the subject has no understanding of the general nature of the task, nor of the significance of the symbols. Irrelevant or extralinguistic factors are invariably attended to by alinguistic subjects, and, without a fully consistent mapping between language-based responses and environmental events, these extralinguistic factors tend to interfere continually with performance. Fully consistent mapping is possible only if both the computer and the human experimenter reliably interpret each

response. With less structured approaches, such as American Sign Language for the Deaf, this sort of reliability and consistent response interpretation is not possible.

7. The fact that the computer itself can be used as a communicative partner often prevents the kind of frustrating response that occurs when a teacher or experimenter requires a subject to produce or practice a sequence of correct responses. Frequently the chimp (or child) is aware that the experimenter knows what he (the child) desires, but is nevertheless requiring that the request for that item be executed in a particular manner. This situation can be particularly frustrating if the request task needs to be practiced or executed repeatedly, because it then becomes very obvious that the task is not one of communication but one of pleasing the instructor, doing a "trick" for a reward, so to speak. While both chimpanzee and child will "perform" in such a situation, the attendant's frustrations de-emphasize the communicative function of the response.

8. The use of computer-controlled devices, set in a Plexiglas training module, allows the instructor to control the subject's world in a manner that focuses the subject's attention on the relevant aspects of the task—or at least on those aspects that the instructor delimits as relevant.

The keyboard-controlled computer system is often mistakenly viewed as mechanistic and impersonal. In actual operation, however, quite the contrary proves to be true. The keyboard and the computer are merely vehicles of communicative processes. The real communication is between the subjects and their trainers. The "machine" can provide repetitive practice, but none of the subjects behaves as though he is communicating, in any social sense, with the "machine." The communication between animates, which is mediated via the keyboard, is as rich in non-verbal overtones and complex social exchanges as is communication via any other system, be it verbal, gestural, or whatever. Indeed, were this not the case, it is doubtful if language skills could be acquired and used in any real communicative sense. They would instead be limited problem-solving skills.

PERSPECTIVES ON LANGUAGE TRAINING
DERIVED FROM THE ANIMAL MODEL PROJECT

Initially, the Language Analog (LANA) Project began with an open-ended question (Rumbaugh, Gill, and von Glasersfeld, 1973): Could a young chimpanzee acquire language via a computer-based system? Because a positive answer was in doubt from the start, everything that could conceivably be thought of to ensure that Lana attended to the proper cues of the task was incorporated into the initial system design and training strategy. Additionally many things that were not initially perceived as possibly crucial, but were convenient from a mechanical or engineering standpoint (Plexiglas room, PERIOD and PLEASE, location of dispensers, etc.), were also included in the system and task design. Much to the surprise of both the designers and the trainers, Lana came easily to attend to the lexigrams, to their projected display, and to the critical fact that they were meaningful representational symbols. That she did so facilely and (in addition) came to differentiate among her stock sentences and even among elements within those sentences, on the basis of what appeared to be merely opportunity to practice, led to the initial conclusion that given the opportunity to work at such a keyboard the chimpanzee comes to acquire the most crucial skills of its own accord, namely to discriminate between lexigrams, to use the lexigram as a symbol, to combine lexigrams in order to employ them as a mode of functional two-way communication. The critical elements facilitating the acquisition of these skills appeared to be: 1) simplicity of response (button press), 2) attention-orienting factors (illuminated keys, which increased in brilliance when depressed, were projected above the keyboard), 3) practice or repeated pairing of lexigrams and that for which they stand, and 4) requirement of proper syntax. (Even if some units in the sentence were redundant or otherwise meaningless, syntactically ordered sentences were viewed as a prerequisite skill for the development of later meaningful syntactically correct sentence constructions.) Thus, in brief, the display and feedback features of the system, coupled with the innate cognitive capabilities of the chimpanzee, were sufficient to bring about language acquisition (Rumbaugh and Gill, 1976). The main function of the human in this situation was to decide which lexigram represented what and pair the two (lexigram and that for which it stood) in strict accordance so that the chimpanzee could come to learn the proper meaning.

It was from such a viewpoint that the design of the animal model project and the initial experiments to be conducted therein were derived. Because Lana appeared to acquire her initial language skills with relative ease, and because we knew well the kinds of things Lana could do but did not really understand the conceptual processes she employed during the execution of these language processes, the important questions to be asked of other animals appeared to revolve around laying bare the fundamental operations involved in these cognitive linguistic processes. In so doing, it was hoped that information useful to the programming of training strategies with mentally retarded humans could be more insightfully devised. Premack (1976) has taken a similar approach in his attempt to set forth and teach the basic functions of language. Although such functions (*same-different, if-then*) are important language processes, it is the use of words in combination to increase the specificity and preciseness of meaning, and the further use of such combinations in a communicative ordered exchange, that a child (or any alinguistic organism) must have if his communications are to be functional ones. Language must be developed in a hierarchical fashion, with each new element fitting into a meaningful framework; otherwise the subject exhibits a set of impressive problem-solving skills but nothing more.

The parameters important in producing initial language acquisition with Lana were thought to lie in the computerized feedback and the innate capabilities of the animal. Although chimpanzees were not reported to use any form of artificial symbolic communication in the wild, or in captivity without training, the questions of why Lana had done so and what were the critical parameters that brought about this ability were not raised. In retrospect, this shortcoming might be difficult to understand, but the parameters involved in initial acquisition of symbolic skills have also been ill defined by other chimpanzee language projects and by many of the programs that attempt to teach language to retarded children.

The initial language task presented to the four young animals chosen for the extended LANA Project involved the presentation and naming of single items. While the procedural details of the first design are not critical here, it is important to note that the task was basically a labeling or naming one (i.e., the experimenter held up one of several objects and the chimpanzee was to depress a single key which stood for that object). A food reward was given for proper key depression. Daily training was begun in May, 1976, and four months later none of the animals had shown signs of learning names for the training objects. By contrast, after four months of training Lana had learned three stock sentences of four to five words in length and could make meaningful substitutions at the appropriate point in the sentence in accordance with the given state of affairs. (For example, if the stock sentence PLEASE MACHINE GIVE M&M PERIOD was not appropriate because there were no M&Ms in the M&M vendor, but there was a ball in the object vendor, Lana would say, PLEASE MACHINE GIVE BALL PERIOD.) Clearly one of two things was implied. Either Lana was a very exceptional chimpanzee or one or more critical and essential aspects of Lana's initial training situation had been overlooked. Lana had come easily to treat lexigrams as labels, but the new animals, in spite of four months of training to do so, had not. What was wrong? If Lana and the other animals had been retarded human children and not chimpanzees, the conclusion might have been that Lana was a high level child and the others were too profoundly retarded to make them viable candidates for a language-learning program. However, all were chimpanzees. Hence, that conclusion was unacceptable. It could not be the chimpanzees; it had to be the training program. The coupling of the innate cognitive capabilities and the technology of the Yerkish system was not enough in and of itself to produce language acquisition.

Not only had the new animals not learned names of objects, they also had not learned some other very important prerequisites regarding the system *per se*. When given free access to the keyboard, they pressed dimly lighted, brightly lighted, and unlighted keys indiscriminately, making no use of the feedback information about key state (unlighted keys are inoperative, dimly lighted keys are functional, brightly lighted keys have already been depressed). If, after four months of training, they had not learned to discriminiate between functional and nonfunctional keys on the basis of back lighting, how could they possibly discriminate between the small geometric figures themselves or consequently ever come to understand that these figures served as symbols? The young chimpanzees were not alone in their difficulty. Two of the subjects at the Georgia Retardation Center were having similar problems—one was even given extensive tests to determine whether or not he possessed a degree of visual acuity sufficient to permit him to see the lexigrams. He did.

Discrepancies between the original training which the young animals had been given and that which Lana had received were reviewed. The differences, which had seemed less important at the outset of the project, now appeared numerous and profound. They included the following:

1. Lana had undergone match-to-sample training with hand-drawn representations of the lexigrams before any access to the keyboard.
2. Lana had intially learned a "sentence" or more correctly a "stock phrase": PLEASE MACHINE GIVE M&M PERIOD. Thus from the beginning she was required to depress a series of keys in proper sequence to receive a food reward. The young animals had been required to press only one key per trial.
3. Lana was not initially asked by the experimenter to depress a particular key for a given object. Instead she was vended whatever she requested. Thus she did not have to press M&M if Tim held up an M&M, or BALL if the trainer held up a ball. Instead she received whichever item she requested via her stock sentences. Whether or not she intentionally requested the item she received was, at first, a moot issue.
4. Lana lived in constant 24-hour contact with her keyboard. By contrast, the young animals lived as a social group in a large colony room and had access to the keyboard only a few hours each day.

5. Lana turned on her own keyboard by depressing a bar directly overhead. If she released this bar the entire keyboard was turned off. The experimenter turned the keyboard on and off for the young animals.

6. All liquid food, solid food, and object computer-controlled vending devices were clearly in view of Lana and she received the majority of her food from them. By contrast, the vending devices were not used with the young animals because they were not learning "stock sentences." The Yerkish parser only operated the vending device upon receipt of a grammatically correct sentence. Correct single-key depressions of the young animals were food reinforced by the experimenter.

There were other differences, but these seemed sufficient to begin a search for the important factors that had been involved in Lana's initial mastery of symbolic skills.

The ability to discriminate functional from nonfunctional or previously depressed keys resulted from giving the animals free access to the keyboard and allowing them to depress any and all keys at will instead of allowing them one response per trial on a discrete trial basis. This permitted the animals to press any and all keys as frequently as they wished: however, they were reinforced only upon correct key depression. Discrimination of a key's functional capacity occurred by the second day, but there was no indication that they had begun to attend to the colors or geometric figures on the surface of the keys, merely to their state of illumination. Consequently, irrelevant or meaningless keys were added to the display and the position of each lighted key was changed on every trial. This meant that the only way an animal could be correct more often than chance (which would have been 20%) was to ignore position and attend to the lexigrams. This attentional orientation occurred quickly. Within two to three days, lexigrams that stood for food were distinguished from the irrelevant lexigrams. However, although the initial dichotomy between relevant and irrelevant keys was easily acquired, reliable discriminiations between relevant keys linked to the objects for which those keys stood proved to be much more difficult.

In brief, we found that, through procedural alterations that were specifically designed to manipulate attentional factors, it was possible to quickly focus the animal's attention on key brightness, color, and geometric design. Once the animal comes to attend to these factors, certain types of learning occur very rapidly, namely, any type of all-or-none processes associated with that feature (i.e., unlighted keys work, lighted keys do not work; keys with lexigrams of set A work, keys with lexigrams of set B do not). The essential skill, that of recognizing that there is a one-to-one symbolic correspondence between a lexigram and a particular object in the environment, was a much more elusive phenomenon.

Prior to *name-of* training, Lana had not been required by the experimenter to demonstrate that she actually knew items or actions by name. Rather, she simply used her stock sentences to request items whenever those items were available. Pressing the proper lexigram as a "name" for an object, when that object was held up by the experimenter, was not instituted until six months of training had elapsed, during which time Lana had learned to use several stock sentences to request items. This suggested that perhaps learning to request an item was a more basic skill than labeling that item. Request tasks differ from labeling tasks in two fundamental ways:

1. The subject is always reinforced because he gets what he requests, even if he makes an error and requests an item he does not desire. This means that the information value in each trial is always equivalent in that it permits the subject to link together the lexigram and the object for which it stands, without having to draw the inference that it was a lexigram which he did not choose that was correct.
2. In labeling tasks, the subject is reinforced only if he is correct. He does not decide which symbol is to be employed and then register the consequences. Instead, the experimenter decides which object is to be named at any given time and the subject must try to determine the answer. Thus the labeling task removes from the alinguistic subject the only modicum of control that he has, that of determining what he will receive, even if wrong.

Is requesting a more basic skill than labeling, and, if so, does it foster the kinds of processes necessary for labeling at a later date? When these questions were asked with the four young chimpanzees in the LANA Project, the answer, at least to the first part of the question, definitely was yes. The two animals allowed to request any one of four foods that they wanted readily learned to discriminate between the four lexigrams that stood for those foods, while the two animals asked to label the same foods (when they were held up one at a time) took several weeks to discriminiate reliably between two foods and never came to discriminate with accuracy between three or four foods. The number of trials required to reach a discrimination of 90% or better, across two consecutive sessions, for two foods, was 2,616 for the label group (one animal never got above 80%) and 304 for the event group.

Thus, requesting and labeling seem to involve somewhat different capabilities, with labeling being a higher level or at least a more difficult task than simply requesting (Savage-Rumbaugh and Rumbaugh, 1977).

It should be emphasized at this point that, although the animals who were allowed to request any of four foods came to distinguish reliably between the lexigrams that represented those foods, this did not mean that they employed those lexigrams as symbols for the food. They seemed instead to have learned that pressing a particular lexigram, if it was illuminated, resulted in the attainment of a particular food item. It would perhaps be more accurate to state that the lexigrams came to serve, when lighted, as differentially rewarded S^Ds for key depression. This finding led us, and we feel should lead others, to a more critical assessment of the parameters involved in stating that a chimpanzee, or any alinguistic organism, has x number of words in its vocabulary simply because it can make a set of differential responses. The ways these differential responses are linked to environmental occurrences is critical. Until it is demonstrated that the animal's set of differential responses (be they button presses, signs, etc.) is correlated in a one-to-one fashion with environmental changes, it is not sound methodological practice to accept words which the animal produces as attempts to describe or explain its desires, wishes, and thoughts. With a modicum of practice and a keyboard, signs, or chips, animals come to combine their responses in interesting ways. But to place a "rich interpretation" (Fouts, 1974; Gardner and Gardner, 1975) upon these responses is misleading, and the animals appear to say complex things for which there is no contextual validation. Thus, we must not be satisfied with lists of skills and poetic metaphors but must understand how those skills came to be, how they are used, and how they are altered in reliable ways with changes in the environment. The LANA Project to this point had demonstrated that, while 1) learning to discriminate relevant from irrelevant lexigrams and 2) learning to discriminate between relevant lexigrams were important processes leading to the attainment of true symbolic functioning, these processes alone were not sufficient to produce symbolic capabilities.

What was? Again Lana's original training situation was considered, and it was decided to introduce a chaining together of words. Perhaps some intrinsic attentional factors, required by an ordered sequencing of responses, would facilitate a true symbolic linking between lexigram and object. A two-word chain was chosen in the interest of asking this question in the most conservative manner possible. The animals learned, one at a time, eight short two-word sentences. When asked to discriminate in a reliable manner between sentences or between elements within a sentence, or to execute one sentence when elements of another were also lighted on the keyboard, they could not do so. Apparently there was no magic in chaining, at least as far as fostering the initial emergence of symbolic capacity was concerned.

Again there remained the question, how could we make manifest the relationship between lexigrams and their environmental referents? In teaching the two-word sentences one at a time we had purposely removed the element of choice with the intent of assessing whether or not, given a variety of short stock sentences, the animals could learn to discriminate reliably between them without the element of choice. The fact that the animals treated all lexigrams associated with food as equivalent and all lexigrams not associated with food as equivalently irrelevant, became apparent when we simultaneously illuminated the sentences GIVE ORANGE and POUR COKE. The animals responded with GIVE POUR ORANGE COKE, POUR COKE GIVE ORANGE, POUR GIVE COKE ORANGE, etc. Keys not previously associated with food presentation (CELERY, CARROT, and BREAD) were not depressed. These results strengthened the finding that we had attained with the initial one-word request versus labeling task, namely, if not allowed to make a self-instigated choice, the animals did not come to learn which keys stood for which food. While the implications of this finding were clear for those language-training programs that attempt to teach words by repeatedly pairing them with referents, we still had not provided a reasonable method of bringing symbolic processes into fruition.

Coupled with choice, which was now obviously a critical parameter, we next attempted to provide the animals with a greater degree of control over their own responses and with more obvious control over their environmental surrounding. To this end, two additional changes were instigated. The food dispensers, which had been located approximately six inches above the animals' heads as they sat in front of the keyboard (to maximize work space outside the experimental chamber) were lowered and placed in full view of the animals as they sat at the keyboard. Thus they could, at all times, without moving, assess the state of the dispensers (i.e., whether or not a given dispenser was loaded with food, how much food, and what type of food). The PLEASE and PERIOD keys were also added to the already established two-word chains. The addition of these keys permitted the animals to initiate, terminate, and erase messages of their own accord and to work at their own speed. Furthermore, the addition of these keys permitted the Yerkish parser to handle each sentence and to automatically activate the dispenser when a sentence was correctly executed.

With the dispensers in full view, the animals initially asked for food, regardless of whether or not the dispenser was loaded, revealing that they interpreted key depression as something which mysteriously produced food. Previously, the experimenter had always kept the dispenser filled when working on a given problem; also, the location of the dispenser had rendered it somewhat difficult to see. Thus this result was not a surprising one, although it had not been foreseen. Within a few days, the test behaviors of the animals changed dramatically. They attended keenly, not only to the state of the dispenser, but also to the preparation and loading of the food. Responses occurred only if the dispenser was filled with food, and, as the last piece dropped out, the animal moved away from the keyboard. When the dispenser was reloaded, responding began again immediately. Choice was provided by loading two dispensers simultaneously and lighting the elements of two possible sentences: PLEASE GIVE BANANA PERIOD and PLEASE GIVE ORANGE PERIOD. The animal was then allowed to choose the fruit he wanted. If he executed the sentence PLEASE GIVE ORANGE PERIOD until that dispenser was empty, he then had to switch to PLEASE GIVE BANANA PERIOD to empty the remaining dispenser. Thus, two factors were now involved simultaneously: 1) making a choice between two foods, and 2) correlating that choice with the state of the dispensers. Therefore, if the animal chose BANANA when the banana dispenser was empty and the orange dispenser was filled, his choice was inappropriate. Moreover, if he chose BANANA under those conditions, the banana dispenser still functioned, i.e., the tray revolved, a buzzer sounded, and the brush turned as though to push out a piece of banana, but no food was vended. This allowed the animal to see that the sentence, as executed, was a correct sentence, but that he had not made the proper choice based on the state of affairs that existed in his world, namely, orange was there but banana was not.

This maneuver turned out to be a critical one. Very quickly, elements of the sentences came to be distinguished from one another. Double-ending errors, such as PLEASE GIVE BANANA ORANGE PERIOD, disappeared rapidly. Not only did such endings not produce food, but they also did not operate either dispenser. The inference that if one ending was incorrect, the other one had to be correct, was drawn almost immediately by all animals. The state of affairs to be dealt with by the animals at this point could be described as follows:

1. There were two possible sentences.
2. There were two possible dispensers.
3. There were two possible fruits.

Their goal was to make the proper dispenser (proper being either the one that was not empty or the one that was filled with the more desirable food) operate. To prevent the animals from always associating a particular food with a particular dispenser, both fruits were placed occasionally in the dispenser to the left and occasionally in the dispenser to the right.

With some hesitancy, the animals began to request each fruit according to preference or presence or absence in the dispenser; with this, the first essence of true symbolic performance appeared to occur. However, tests revealed that the animals had not learned to associate one sentence (or more precisely one sentence ending) with banana and the other with orange. Instead, they had learned that one sentence operated one dispenser and that the other sentence operated the other. Apparently the revolving and brushing actions of the dispenser were more salient and distinguishable aspects of the tasks than type of food. Additionally, with only two dispensers, regardless of which fruit was placed in which dispenser initially, only one trial was needed to see which sentence operated which dispenser. Had five or six dispensers been employed simultaneously, perhaps this strategy would not have been viable; but, with only two, it allowed the subject to be 100% correct after one information trial. Could this be interpreted as symbolic functioning? If the foods had been reliably placed in only one dispenser or the other, then the BANANA lexigram would stand for one dispenser and the ORANGE lexigram for the other. However, the shifting of the foods forced the animals to employ the strategy, "If PLEASE GIVE BANANA does not operate the dispenser on the left, then it operates the one on the right." Therefore, symbolic functioning can be said to have occurred, though not in the manner we had anticipated. That it occurred at all appeared to be a function of the animals' capability to see and understand the relationship between depressing lexigrams and the ensuing control of significant environmental aspects which they gained thereby.

It thus became obvious that the initial use of the lexigrams as a symbol for objects was a difficult process. The animals were inclined at every point to attend to actions, as opposed to objects, and to try to solve each new task on the basis of position rather than lexigram whenever the task was a difficult one.

The return to reliance on positional cues when components of the task changed or increased in difficulty, and the preponderance of attention to actions, as contrasted with objects, have, through the course of the work to date, become identified as problems that must be dealt with repeatedly during the initial acquisition of language skills. Only by eliminating these factors through carefully controlled procedures that focus the animal's attention appropriately can the desired symbolic skills be attained.

The first unquestioned example of naming skills arose only after the animals had: 1) the ability to initiate and terminate their own responses, 2) shown sensitivity to the state of the dispensers and to their own ability to operate a dispenser whether it was full or empty, 3) shown the ability to discriminate between elements of sentences and eliminate double-naming errors, 4) and indicated that they could track a given food, by appropriate request, from one dispenser to another, even as the locations of keys on the keyboard were changed.

Once these skills were developed, the lexigram for "banana" was located nearest the banana dispenser and the lexigram for "beancake" nearest the beancake dispenser. After this relationship was learned, the positions of the keys were changed, then the foods were placed in the opposite dispensers, and finally both foods were sequentially vended from the same dispenser. The initial attention to the spatial location of the dispensers, following a clarification of spatial location and food, with attention then centering on food, came to be an essential series of steps for each animal. Trying to force attention to the food by initially placing both foods in the same dispenser did not work and caused numerous frustration-related behaviors to appear and to interfere with learning. By the time both foods were vended sequentially from the same dispenser, the preceding skills and discriminative abilities enabled the animals to avoid many errors of incorrect task interpretation and thereby to begin responding on a symbolic basis, i.e., attaching the proper symbol to the proper referent. Once this skill was acquired, it transferred readily to other symbols with which the animals were familiar, but had not previously reliably associated with the presence or absence of given food referents. Furthermore, once the animals reached this level of performance, they transferred this capacity back to food names they had learned in their original single-word teaching under the event and label conditions. All animals, including those that had never come to distinguish reliably between two or three food lexigrams, now integrated those old lexigrams in a few trials into their new conceptual framework. They reliably discriminated between these lexigrams and placed them appropriately in a sentence, asking that the items be GIVEN or POURED, depending or whether the ingestible was a solid or a liquid. This reintegration of previously learned inadequate skills into a new conceptual framework without training supports the Piagetian (1963) view of cognitive development and indicates that the language skills learned by the animals are not merely task-specific, but are instead powerful cognitive tools that can reorganize their conceptual world.

Perspectives derived thus far from attempts to apply a computer-based-system—in an experimental manner—to the investigation of the parameters of language acquisition in chimpanzees have, in summary, revealed the following:

1. There are many important similarities with reference to language acquistion difficulties between chimpanzee and retarded child.
2. The initial acquisition of symbolic capacity, via the chosen symbolic mode (geometric figures), cannot be achieved by rote pairing of symbol and referent.

3. Before symbolic functioning occurs, the subject must come to attend to lexigrams as significant aspects of his environment.
4. The subject must also perceive the use of the lexigrams as providing him with control over his environment in a real and tangible manner. (Following the depression of a lexigram with the presentation of the food for which it stands is not sufficient. The food presentation is perceived as associated with the key depression, but not produced by it. Rather, it is the experimenter who is seen as causing the food to appear in response to the animal picking the key the experimenter wants.)
5. The subject must be able to ignore the positional cues which are only reliably associated with the proper lexigrams in a temporary manner.
6. The subject must learn the concept (and not numerous rote associations) that a lexigram can be used to identify its referent. This should be exemplified by the ability to transfer this idea to other lexigrams and other referents.

In contrast to earlier work with single animals, the LANA Project is concerned not with demonstrating what a chimpanzee can do but with developing training procedures that specify the important parameters of how the animals come to emit linguistic behaviors, and to document these in detail for translation to work with retarded humans. Animals not particularly adept or behaviorally pleasant to work with are nevertheless kept in the project. Such animals help us sort out procedural difficulties that would otherwise be overlooked. By working with more animals we have come to acquire a far better sense of the important elements of initial training. Presently, procedures developed through work with these animals are being implemented with six new human subjects at the Georgia Retardation Center. It is through such direct implementation that the true test of the chimpanzee as an animal model will be made.

REFERENCES

Fouts, R. S. 1974. Language: Origins, definition and chimpanzees. J. Hum. Evolu. 3:475–482.
Gardner, B. T., and Gardner, R. A. 1975. Evidence for sentence constituents in the early utterances of child and chimpanzee. J. Exp. Psychol. General 104:244–267.
Piaget, J. 1963. Le language et les operations intellectuals. In Problems de Psycholinguistique: Symposium de L'association de Psychologic Scientifique. Presse Universitaires de France, Paris.
Premack, D. 1976. Intelligence in Ape and Man. John Wiley & Sons, New York.
Rumbaugh, D. M., and Gill, T. V. 1976. Lana's mastery of language skills. In H. Steklis, S. Harnad, and J. Lancaster (eds.), Origins and Evolution of Language and Speech, Vol. 280. Annals of the New York Academy of Sciences, New York.

Rumbaugh, D. M., Gill, T. V., and von Glasersfeld, E. C. 1973. Reading and sentence completion by a chimpanzee (*Pan*). Science 182:731-733.

Savage, E. S., and Rumbaugh, D. M. 1977. Communication, language and Lana: A perspective. *In* D. M. Rumbaugh (ed.), Language Learning by a Chimpanzee: The LANA Project, pp. 287-309. Academic Press, New York.

Savage-Rumbaugh, E. S., and Rumbaugh, D. M. 1977. Initial acquisition of graphic symbolic skills by chimpanzees. Paper presented at the First American Primatological Society Conference, March, Seattle.

chapter

15

Strategies for
Primate Language Training

Roger S. Fouts

Joseph B. Couch

Department of Psychology
University of Oklahoma
Norman, Oklahoma

Charity R. O'Neil

Parsons Research Center
Parsons State Hospital and Training Center
Parsons, Kansas

contents

IMPORTANCE OF COMPARATIVE RESEARCH

Behavioral studies of the great apes enable us to examine a nonhuman being that is both very similar to, and quite different from, a human being. Such research can provide scientists with a wealth of information about the mental and behavioral capacities of the nonhuman primates. In addition, this information can provide comparative data that assist in the understanding of human behavior, including communicative behavior. There are differences, important differences, that reflect the respective individuality of the various primates: realizing the many millions of years of separate primate evolution it would be naive not to expect differences. It would be just as naive, however, to assume that these species do not have similarities, including the basis for a behavior such as language. The assumption that language developed solely in the human species pushes the mechanisms we know of genetics and evolution to an extreme (and probably incorrect) conclusion. In fact, the striking physiological similarities between humans and chimpanzees with regard to blood protein and type, chromosomal characteristics, and structural similarities in the two brains would lead one to the opposite conclusion. King and Wilson (1975) compared the blood protein, amino acids, and immunologies in the blood of chimpanzees, humans, and other great apes and found that the chimpanzee's blood differed from human blood by only 0.2%, while gorilla blood showed about an 0.8% difference. These similarities were so striking to King and Wilson that they referred to the chimpanzee as a "sibling species" of *Homo sapiens*.

Although behavioral characteristics and their functions provide further evidence of the similarity of the two species, the use of sheer function of behavior to support this notion must be viewed with caution. As Schnierla (1972) points out, ant caste systems bear remarkable similarity to human caste systems but have an entirely different basis. He warns that when comparing phenomena one should look for the *bases* for the similarities and differences and emphasize these according to their respective importance. If Schnierla's position is correct, then assuming a different basis for two behaviors that show such striking similarity of behavioral and functional characteristics, as does language in humans and chimpanzees, would involve the inverse of the error against which Schnierla warns. In other words, given the extreme similarity of the chimpanzee and the human on behavioral, physiological, neurological, and other such measures, it would seem simplistic to assume anything other than a common basis for behaviors in the two species. Chomsky (1967), however, seems to ignore the similarities of the two species by stating that language is a result of a mutation in human evolution and is therefore unique to that species. Hewes (1973) commented on Chomsky's mutation hypothesis by stating that it ". . . seems wholly simplistic, and hardly more plausible than the idea of language as a gift of the gods" (cf. Ploog, 1968). To this point Sarles (1972) states, "Biologically speaking, we expect continuity and relationship, not emergence and saltation and we are rightfully suspicious when told that man is more than a bit outside of nature" (p. 4).

In a similar vein Lashley (1951) states:

> I am coming more and more to the conviction that the rudiments of every human behavioral mechanism will be found far down in the evolutionary scale and also represented even in primitive activities of the nervous system. If there exist, in human cerebral action, processes which seem fundamentally different or inexplicable in terms of our present construct of elementary physiology of integration, then it is probable that the construct is incomplete or mistaken, even for the levels of behavior to which it is applied (pp. 135–136).

Lashley's statement would support the conclusion that the differences found between human and chimpanzee language acquisition are differences of degree rather than of kind. In order to determine to what degree these two species are similar and different, the process of establishing the mental capacities of the chimpanzee must continue. Several studies which we hope will assist in this process have been conducted over the past several years at the Institute for Primate Studies in Norman, Oklahoma.

THE RESEARCH WITH CHIMPANZEES

Soon after the publication of Project Washoe (Gardner and Gardner, 1969 [Chapter 9, this volume]) the question arose in the scientific community as to whether this chimpanzee's sign language acquisition was not simply attributable to an abnormally high intellectual capacity. Washoe was called a mutant intellectual genius, and these critics posited that other chimpanzees might never be able to acquire American Sign Language (ASL). Therefore, after the arrival of Washoe and Dr. Fouts at the Institute for Primate Studies, an experiment (Fouts, 1973) was conducted to demonstrate that other chimpanzees also had the ability to acquire sign language. This study also investigated individual differences among chimpanzees with regard to sign language acquisition and provided a comparison among signs in terms of ease or difficulty of acquisition.

Four chimpanzees, Booee, Bruno, Cindy, and Thelma, served as the subjects for the study. The experiment consisted of teaching each chimpanzee 10 signs using molding (Fouts, 1972) as the training method. (Molding is a type of guidance in which the teacher forms the subject's hands into the desired response, thus forcing the subject into a passive response.) The acquisition time for each sign was recorded in minutes, with an acquisition criterion of five consecutive unprompted responses by the subject. No ceiling was established on the amount of training, which continued until the acquisition criterion was met. To ensure that the chimpanzees were not simply making one sign for every exemplar, each newly acquired sign was integrated into the training session. Once the subject acquired all 10 signs, they were given a double-blind box test similar to the double-blind slide test used in Project Washoe (Gardner and Gardner, 1969 [Chapter 9, this volume]).

The results showed a significant variation in acquisition across signs (9.7 min to 316 min to acquisition), and an expected significant difference in acquisition across chimpanzees (54 min to 159 min mean acquisition times).

All the subjects scored above the chance level of responding during testing. Cindy, who needed large amounts of love and reassurance, understandably fell to 26 percent correct responses during the testing situation in which no such love and affection could be administered. Thelma and Booee scored 58 percent and 59 percent, respectively, while Bruno topped the group with an impressive 90 percent correct responses. Indeed, Washoe was *not* the only chimpanzee who could acquire signs in ASL.

Lucy, a chimpanzee reared in a human home since the age of two days, served as the subject for the next experiment (Mellgren, Fouts, and Lemmon, 1973). She was seven years old at the time the research was conducted. She had been trained in ASL for two years and possessed a vocabulary of 75 signs. This study was designed to investigate the relationship between generic and specific signs, while also testing the conceptual ability of a chimpanzee with regard to the categories of items in its vocabulary.

Lucy had in her vocabulary five signs that related to food. Three of these (FOOD, FRUIT, and DRINK) she used in a generic manner, while two (CANDY and BANANA) she used in a specific manner. Lucy was taught a new sign, BERRY (a cherry served as the exemplar), and then records were kept to see if the sign became generic or specific in relation to a category of items. Twenty-four fruits and vegetables made up the category of items, with the exemplars ranging from a piece of watermelon and a grapefruit to cherry tomatoes, blueberries, and radishes.

The 24 items were presented in a random order every day to Lucy (interspersed between at least two items that were in her vocabulary but not on the list), and she was asked WHAT'S THAT? in ASL. She could pick the item up, play with it, chew on it, or do whatever she wanted to do with it, and her responses were recorded.

To establish Lucy's usual response to the items, four days of baseline data were recorded before the BERRY sign was introduced. Four days after the introduction of the new sign, BERRY remained specific to cherries. After the eighth day Lucy was again taught the

BERRY sign, but with a blueberry as the exemplar. After the next two days, in which she called blueberries BERRY, Lucy returned to her original sign for "blueberry." Interestingly, she returned to using the BERRY sign for cherries, obviously preferring to use this sign in a specific manner.

The investigation of Lucy's conceptualizations of fruits and vegetables also proved to be quite interesting. The results showed that Lucy dichotomized the two categories when signing. To label fruit items she used the FRUIT sign 85 percent of the time while using the FOOD sign only 15 percent of the time. When signing to the vegetable exemplars the reverse was true, with the FOOD sign preferred 65 percent of the time as opposed to only 35 percent for the FRUIT sign. The odiferous qualities of the four citrus fruits used apparently did not go unnoticed by Lucy. She referred to them as SMELL FRUIT 65 percent of the time.

Lucy's novel combinations of signs were also of interest. For the first three days she signed FRUIT FOOD or DRINK when presented with the radish. However, on the fourth day she bit into the radish, spit it out immediately and signed CRY HURT FOOD. After that she signed either CRY or HURT to the radish exemplar. Lucy also used the signs CANDY DRINK or DRINK FRUIT to describe the piece of watermelon, although the experimenter continued to use the signs WATER and MELON. Lucy had demonstrated the ability of a chimpanzee not only to form new combinations of signs from an existing sign language vocabulary but also to express concepts of items in the environment.

Home-reared chimpanzees receive a great deal of exposure to vocal English. In fact, the human parents of these chimpanzees have often expressed the belief that their chimpanzee child could understand a great deal of spoken English. This supposition was intriguing, and a study was conducted to investigate the relationship between these chimpanzees' understanding of vocal English and their ASL vocabularies.

This experiment (Fouts, Chown, and Goodin, 1976) was carried out with a young male home-reared chimpanzee named Ally. First, Ally was given vocal commands: "Give me the spoon," "Pick up the spoon," "Find the spoon," etc. He then had to obey these commands by picking out the requested object from a group of objects. Ally met the criterion for understanding when he had obeyed a given command five consecutive times. In this way Ally's understanding of 10 vocal English words was established.

For testing, these English words were divided into two groups of equal number. Using only the vocal English word as the exemplar, one experimenter attempted to teach Ally the signs for the five words in one group. Ally was then tested by a second experimenter on all five objects corresponding to those vocal English words. The second experimenter was not told which, if any, of the words had been taught or acquired. A reversal of this procedure was used on the other five-word group. The results revealed that Ally could, in fact, transfer the sign taught for the vocal English word to the object which represented that word. A process similar to second-language acquisition in humans, with cross-modal implications, had thus been shown to occur in a chimpanzee.

Chimpanzees had demonstrated the ability to create novel combinations of signs, as mentioned earlier, from signs already in their vocabulary. The next study (Fouts, Chown, Kimball and Couch, 1976) consisted of two experiments that tested the ability of a chimpanzee to comprehend novel commands and to use a grammatical system. Ally, the young male chimpanzee mentioned earlier, again served as the subject for both experiments in this study.

In the first experiment Ally was first taught to pick, on command, one of five objects out of a box and to put it in one of three locations (i.e., PUT THE BABY IN THE PURSE). After Ally had learned the procedure, new items were placed in the box, and in addition, a new location was added in which to place the items.

During testing, the experimenter placed the five new items into a box into which Ally could not see. To further prevent the possibility of cueing, a screen was placed between the experimenter and the three possible locations in which the item was to be placed. The experimenter then gave Ally the commands, and his responses were recorded. Chance level of responding was determined to be approximately 7 percent, with five items from which to choose and three possible locations in which to place the item.

The results showed that Ally scored 40 percent correct for total commands. Ally is a hyperactive chimpanzee and often grabbed the correct item and rushed to the different possible locations before the experimenter had completely finished signing the command. A breakdown of the data revealed that there was as much as a 60 percent difference between percentage correct for the object and percentage correct for the location. Therefore, although the 40 percent correct figure is far above chance level, it is probably conservative in assessing Ally's ability to comprehend novel commands.

Previous studies (Premack, 1971a, 1971b; Premack and Premack, 1972; Rumbaugh, Gill, and von Glasersfeld, 1973) had provided evidence of syntactic competence in the chimpanzee. Therefore, the second experiment in this study was designed to demonstrate the active application of a syntactic system by a chimpanzee. The syntactic system expressed spatial relationships between objects in the environment, which were easily specified by short sequences of signs; however, syntax was essential for the expression of proper meaning. The order of the signs (subject, preposition, location) expressed the relationship, while the rules of grammar generated all permissible sequences and no ungrammatical sequences. Although the system was not formally complex, it did contain all of the essential aspects of language in rudimentary form.

The experiment began by first teaching Ally the relations *on*, *in*, and *under*. This was accomplished by placing physical objects (noun exemplars) in the appropriate arrangements, and then teaching Ally to describe the situation accurately in ASL.

Once training was over, tests of acquisition were conducted. The testing consisted of placing the objects in a given arrangement and asking Ally to describe them. For example, a ball would be placed on a chair and the experimenter would sign to Ally WHERE BALL? To make a correct response Ally had to make the appropriate signs in the proper order. Testing situations were varied from the familiar (arrangements used in training) to the completely novel. Again, the possibility of cueing by the experimenter was controlled by the use of a double-blind testing procedure.

Results showed that Ally expressed the prepositions correctly in 84.9 percent of the familiar situations (F) and in 76.9 percent of the novel situations (N). Locations were expressed correctly 77.9 percent (F) and 64.3 percent (N). Ally expressed the total relationship correctly 67.4 percent (F) and 50.0 percent (N). Ally often did not sign the subject of the relationship, but this was not counted as an incorrect response. However, if Ally did sign the subject it had to be correct, or else the entire relationship expressed was counted as incorrect. During the 240 trials, he signed the entire relationship (subject, preposition, location) 44 times. Ally made the correct sign for the subject 42 times, for 95.5 percent accuracy.

Even though these figures were far above a chance level of responding, they were greatly affected by several interesting errors in Ally's responding. For example, a "purse" was used as a novel location and proved to be the source of a great many of Ally's errors. This may have been because of the physical attributes of the exemplar, an old red laundry bag. When placed on the floor, it was impossible for Ally to determine if the subject (noun exemplar) was *in* or *under* the purse since both conditions resulted in a lump in the red bag. Ally also often made a conceptual error in responding by confusing the "purse" exemplar with the "blanket" exemplar. When laid on the floor, the two exemplars were strikingly similar. Another error Ally committed involved the relationship *ball under box*, which he frequently signed as BALL UNDER IN BOX. This response was counted as incorrect because two prepositions were used. Interestingly, later when asked WHAT THIS? (pointing to the box), Ally often signed IN BOX. Therefore, this error could easily have been a functional one, since the box was in fact used to transport the exemplars from the storage area to the training area: the box was an object that things were placed *in*—an IN BOX. When the errors involving the purse and box were deleted, the results showed that Ally had signed the total relationship correctly 68.6 percent of the time. Of special interest is the fact that, although Ally had to construct the relationship entirely on his own, not once did he make a grammatical error.

These two experiments provided support for the notion that a chimpanzee has the capacity for using an active linguistic process.

The last experiment to be discussed (Beatty, Fouts, and McDivit, in preparation) was in many ways the most fascinating. John Beatty, an anthropologist from Brooklyn College, wanted to investigate the capacity of a chimpanzee to differentiate between various chimpanzee calls. In order to do this, he brought with him to the Institute recordings of chimpanzee calls made by Peter Marler at the Gombe Stream Reserve. Although Washoe was originally to be the subject for this study, she proved to be more interested in Beatty than in the recordings. Bruno (an eight-year-old male at the time of the study) was therefore pressed into service as the new subject.

Bruno was first taught the signs for "same" and "different" by simultaneously presenting him with objects which were the same and objects which were different. After Bruno was responding reliably to the objects, he was presented with tape recordings of both high- and low-pitched sounds. Once again he was taught the SAME and DIFFERENT signs, this time to the appropriate pairings of sounds. Reliability of responding was established to these auditory stimuli and then testing began.

In testing Bruno was presented with the following pairs of calls: chimpanzee A bark, chimpanzee B scream; A bark, A scream; A bark, B bark; A bark #1, A bark #2; A bark #1, re-recording of A bark #1. The results showed that on trial 1 of the first day Bruno responded by signing DIFFERENT to each pair of calls. However, on trials 2–5 his responses were exactly the same: DIFFERENT; SAME, DIFFERENT; SAME, DIFFERENT; SAME; SAME. It appeared that a pattern had developed in Bruno's responding, and so the test was repeated the next day. Except for the response to the fourth pair on trial 3, Bruno's responses were identical to those of trials 2–5 on the first day. At first it seemed as though Bruno had failed the discrimination test by responding SAME, DIFFERENT to two pairs of calls. However, a closer analysis of the data showed that Bruno was not only differentiating between calls but also between the chimpanzees giving the calls. Certainly it is important for a chimpanzee to know not only what call is being given but who is giving it. His responding, then, was quite appropriate. That is, A bark, B

scream was different both in chimpanzee and type of call (DIF-
FERENT). A bark, A scream was the same chimpanzee, different call
(SAME, DIFFERENT). A bark, B bark also constituted a SAME, DIF-
FERENT situation for the type of call was the same but the chimpanzee
was different. Bruno interpreted the last two pairs of calls as same chimpanzee, same type of call (SAME). Bruno had indeed provided the
experimenters with much more information than was first imagined.

Investigations into the cognitive capacities of chimpanzees continue
at the Institute for Primate Studies. Research dealing with verbal discrimination processes in signing chimpanzees is in progress as are studies
involving chimpanzee-to-chimpanzee ASL communication.

APPLICATIONS OF ANIMAL RESEARCH
TO CHILD LANGUAGE PROBLEMS

Studies with chimpanzees, such as those mentioned above, are compelling for several reasons. Experimental controls are more easily maintained when chimpanzees rather than children serve as subjects, thus
allowing the experimenters more confidence in the data obtained.
Furthermore, the natural language acquisition process in human children
is a lengthy one when compared to adult chimpanzee language acquisition, which can be induced in as little as one year. Consequently, much
more data concerning language acquisition can be collected from such
nonhuman subjects in a given segment of time. More important, though,
is the advantage that sign language acquisition and grammar studies with
chimpanzees have in providing a suitable comparison to deaf human
signing behavior. Gorcyca, Garner, and Fouts (1975) commented on this
advantage:

> Examination of the results of chimpanzees and deaf human signing behavior
> yields many similarities. Previous comparisons for the chimps and deaf
> signers have been drawn from oral English speaking humans. Yet, ASL is a
> language in its own right (Klima and Bellugi, 1972; Stokoe, Casterline, and
> Croneberg, 1965), making the oral English comparison somewhat faulty,
> especially in the area of syntax and other aspects of grammar. Comparing
> the chimps with deaf signers allows for generalizations based on a common
> language (p. 3).

One must be careful not to view the chimpanzee as some sort of defective
human child, however. The chimpanzees in our language studies are completely intact organisms that function very adequately before they
acquire human language skills. Experience with chimpanzees may be
particularly valuable in the training of nonverbal children, because in
both situations one is forced to suspend the assumptions of vocal-verbal
competence under which one normally interacts with other humans.

Basic animal research can also serve to suggest language intervention techniques with exceptional children. The research of Overmier and Seligman (1967) and Seligman and Maier (1967) provides an example. Their findings indicated that presenting uncontrollable events to animals or humans resulted in an interference with later learning. This phenomenon was termed "learned helplessness" (Maier, Seligman, and Solomon, 1969). Typically, a learned helplessness experiment consists of first presenting the organism with inescapable shock under Pavlovian conditioning procedures. Next, the organism is placed in a shuttle box, a two-sided chamber that allows the organism to jump a barrier in order to escape the shock. Organisms that have not received the inescapable shock conditioning rapidly learn to escape. However, those organisms that have received inescapable shock training become quite passive and are unable to make the appropriate response for the situation. It should be noted that this phenomenon has also been shown to occur in experiments involving uncontrollable reward procedures (Hiroto and Seligman, 1975). Seligman (1974) addresses the issue of an organism's inability to control events in the environment by hypothesizing that when "an animal or a person is faced with an outcome that is independent of his response, he learns that the outcome is independent of his response." Seligman also discussed three types of disruptions caused by this uncontrollability: "The motivation to respond is sapped, the ability to perceive success is undermined, and emotionality is heightened." Of further importance, Hiroto and Seligman (1975) demonstrated that the phenomenon of learned helplessness produced in one situation will generalize to other, different situations. This suggests that much of an organism's adaptive behavioral repertoire may be weakened by uncontrollable events in its environment.

The extent to which this experimental phenomenon can be used to understand and explain the behavior associated with nonspeaking children is significant. The inability to speak creates a tremendous loss of control over one's environment, producing a situation analogous to that of learned helplessness. Consequently, these children should be passive and indifferent with regard to communication behaviors, and this passivity should generalize to situations not involving communication. Furthermore, these children should demonstrate lower overall motivation and greater emotionality when compared to normal children. The observations of nonspeaking cerebral palsied children (Crickmay, 1966; Cruickshank, 1966) do, in fact, show that these behavioral characteristics commonly occur.

The theory of learned helplessness also suggests the possibility of reversing this phenomenon. If, in fact, the lack of response initiation is caused by the expectation of the organism that responding will *not* work, a reversal in expectation should eliminate, or at least reduce, this inappropriate passivity (Seligman, 1974). This hypothesis may be directly applied to the problem of establishing communication with nonspeaking children. By teaching these children communicative behaviors that can be transmitted to, and interpreted by, others (thus providing the children with more control over their environment), their expectations about the use of communication can be changed. These communicative behaviors could be produced be either helping them to establish and develop vocal speech or by introducing a means of communication not requiring the use of the possibly impaired vocal apparatus. Pointing to symbols or using a manual communication, such as ASL, are excellent ways of establishing a nonvocal communication system.

THE USE OF ASL AS A LANGUAGE INTERVENTION TECHNIQUE

We have found several unique advantages to the use of ASL as a language intervention mode, as opposed to the traditional oral strategies. Although oral language is the ultimate goal of our child language programs (except where vocal-auditory deficits prohibit), ASL is often appropriate as an *initial* strategy. As will become apparent, we do not ignore oral communication, we simply elect a more potent method when oral intervention has proved unsuccessful.

Gestural language has a history presumably as old as *Homo sapiens*, and its basis can be traced far back into evolution. Nonverbal communication, be it vocal, gestural, postural, or pheromonal, is an integral part of the behavioral repertoire of most vertebrates and some invertebrates. The instances of complex, nonverbal communication in the animal world are too numerous to be mentioned here. Peter Marler (1965) states:

> In most situations it is not a single signal that passes from one animal to another, but a whole complex of them, visual, auditory, tactile, and sometimes olfactory. There can be little doubt that the structure of individual signals is very much affected by this incorporation in a whole matrix of other signals (p. 583).

The primates seem particularly expressive, at least to their fellow primate *Homo sapiens*, although this apparent wealth of expressiveness may merely be an artifact of the commonality of our communicative acts; to humans, other primates are easy to "read." Chimpanzees use specific gestures, postures, and vocalizations in specific instances, with specific results. Some of these behaviors are largely involuntary or emotive (notably vocalizations), while others seem quite deliberate, possibly even denotative or propositional. Presumably, preverbal human beings relied upon much the same communicative acts as do other primates.

Indeed, Lieberman, Crelin, and Klatt (1972) assert that Neanderthal man possessed a vocal tract similar to that of today's chimpanzee (*Pan troglodytes*). Van Hooff (1972) has actually traced the evolution of the smile and laughter from primitive mammals to contemporary man, and within the human race of primates certain gestures and facial expressions, such as the eyebrow flash, seem to be universal (Eibl-Eibesfeldt, 1972).

Gordon Hewes (1973) states, "Propositional communication by means of gestures is a capacity not only innate to man, but, in a rudimentary form at least, may go back to the undivided common stock from which modern pongids and hominids have descended." Hewes has summarized and extended the evidence that man's first language consisted of arm and hand signals, as opposed to vocal signals. Acceptance of the language abilities in chimps like Washoe, Sarah, and Lana, he states, implies that the cross-modal associative capacities required for the integration of vocal-auditory and visual-tactile inputs must have evolved later than the basic language capacity. Hewes speculates that early hominids would have found it much more natural to acquire a propositional language system based on the visual perception of patterned hand, finger, and arm movements than to suddenly leap to the controlled vocal articulations necessary for human speech. The fact that counting is universally accomplished with reference to digital enumeration adds to the potency of the gestural glottogenesis theory of language. Nonverbal accompaniments to contemporary speech are pervasive, and contemporary man is surprisingly skillful at relaying information purely nonverbally, as is evidenced by the performance of visitors in a foreign country who manage to convey their needs without benefit of the appropriate local language skills. Kimura (1976) notes that, not only do certain specific manual motions accompany the speech of the hearing, but vocalizations accompany the signing of the deaf, suggesting an intimate relationship between speech and gesture.

Formal gestural languages have been used by various populations in the course of history. Some American Indians, for instance, used a sign language that was also occasionally employed by explorers to communicate with newly discovered peoples. And, of course, the deaf and the mute the world over have used signed languages for centuries. Today, ASL comprises the natural language of a small but significant population within this country: the deaf and the nonspeaking. ASL was the first manual language widely used here and is still the most common one, although other languages such as SEE-1, signed English, and fingerspelling are coming into use among the younger set. Since the deaf form an increasingly cohesive population, a growing number of public events cater to this audience. Certain television shows, for instance, are simultaneously translated into ASL in an effort to bring the deaf into the mainstream of American life. Cultural events, such as the performances of the American Theatre for the Deaf augment the diversions available to an ASL user. It is likely that the scope and number of educational activities and entertainments designed for this population will widen in the near future. Programs at traditionally hearing colleges have also been started for the deaf in order to facilitate their integration into hearing communities, and, of course, the long established Gallaudet College in Washington, D.C., was founded specifically for the deaf. Thus, ASL users are by no means limited to communication with their own teachers and families.

ASL has its own morphology, syntax, and semantics. Other criteria of language, such as productivity, rapid fading, interchangeability, complete feedback, speculization, arbitrariness, discreteness, displacement, openness, prevarication, tradition, and learnability, are met by ASL, but of course it does not meet the requirement of a vocal-auditory channel (Hockett, 1960; Thorpe, 1972). One of the great beauties of a gestural language is its flexibility, and by this measure ASL is markedly superior to artificial language methods such as language boards or computers. To begin with, the only equipment required to speak ASL is two reasonably agile hands, a requirement easily met by most of the children we encounter. Furthermore, the equipment is completely portable, contrasting sharply with the very specialized and rather bulky devices required by artificial languages. Use of ASL, then, need not be limited to preplanned sessions. The user may sign at will—at any place, at any time—whether or not a receiver is present. Normal children go through a stage in language acquisition when they babble to themselves, and eventually they talk to themselves; they seem to practice their language when they are alone. Washoe, too, used to sign to herself when she was alone, as do deaf children. ASL affords the total spontaneity that is necessary for private babbling and which is a quality essential to truly useful language.

Beyond the convenience afforded by ASL, this method meets another requisite of language—creativity. Artificial methods severely circumscribe the possible scope of their language, because the teacher or experimenter limits the available language elements to a certain number of plastic blocks or computer keys. Although keys and blocks may be added, they are added at the will of the teacher, not of the language learner. With a manual language, the child may make up idiosyncratic signs himself for needed vocabulary if the teacher has not demonstrated the appropriate ones. Children are naturally expressive in a gestural mode and are adept at signifying their needs without benefit of formal language or signs. Washoe made up signs of her own; one of her more descriptive ones was an outline of a bib on her chest to replace the

WIPER sign used for bibs as well as for other wiping items. Individually created signs are generally easily understood by the teacher because they are usually iconic in nature. This brings up another advantage of ASL use: many of the ASL signs, particularly those likely to comprise a beginner's or child's vocabulary, bear an obvious visual resemblance to their referents.

A further benefit of ASL instruction is that the individual signs are easily molded by the teacher. The teacher may actively manipulate the child's hands to form the desired sign, thus entering it directly into the child's gestural repertoire. When oral responses are being taught, the teacher must rely upon the fortuitous utterance of certain sounds or on the child's ability to imitate the required sounds. The lips may be externally molded, but neither the vocal tract nor the tongue may be molded without great difficulty. Some evidence (Fouts, 1972), mentioned in detail later, indicates that molding of signs is a more efficient training technique than imitation. At any rate, in order for a response to be imitated, it must first be in the subject's repertoire (Hayes and Hayes, 1952), and, since signs may be molded, they are easily inserted into the repertoire. Regardless of which specific technique may be best in which situation, the fact remains that the availability of *both* molding and imitating as instructive techniques must be advantageous.

An objection occasionally raised to the prospect of teaching a manual language to a child whose vocal and auditory systems are intact is that the acquisition of an alternative mode of communication will actually inhibit the eventual acquisition of vocal language. The fear exists that, if one language is acquired, the child will have no need to learn another language and, therefore, would not. Numerous studies have disproved this notion.

Fulwiler and Fouts (1976) elected to teach sign language to a five-year-old noncommunicating autistic child. After 20 hours of training, the boy used approximately 25 signs appropriately and combined them into two- and three-word phrases. The most exciting outcome of this project, however, was the spontaneous generation of vocal words and phrases by the subject. Although the Total Communication technique was used, the experimenters had not intentionally tried to elicit vocal responses. Another by-product of these sessions was a marked improvement in the child's behavior. Attentiveness and initiations of social contact increased, as did manageability in general.

Hunsicker and Fouts (1976, personal communication) had similar success with a nonspeaking eight-year-old cerebral palsied child who had control over gross motor activity of his arms and hands. After 13 30-minute sessions, the child had acquired about 73 signs and had produced approximately 150 different sign combinations, including sequences up to six signs in length. Toward the end of the training series, the child showed an increase in vocalizations, although no comprehensible words were recorded.

Miller and Miller (1973) report the results of sign training of 19 autistic children. All 19 children acquired some signs, one of them progressed to vocal language, and all of them learned to respond to spoken words that had been paired with signs. Barnes (1973) taught signs to six autistic children in a six-month program. All the children learned signs, with vocabularies ranging from 12 to 50 words. Four children began to vocalize, and one signed in phrases and learned some abstract signs. The children signed spontaneously and in situations other than the training sessions. All subjects also became more interactive with the people in their environment.

Schlesinger and Meadow (1972) concur that the acquisition of sign language, if anything, facilitates speech in deaf children, as well. Berger (1970), in a language program for atypical deaf children (those with accompanying mental, emotional, or physical handicaps), has recognized the importance of a multimodal, rather than a strictly oral, approach to language intervention. In her program, a manual language is taught *first*, and it serves as a foundation upon which more complex language can be built.

The literature clearly indicates that sign language acquisition may facilitate vocal language acquisition. Given this fact, it would seem a grave mistake to deny the noncommunicating child the opportunity to learn at least a manual language. Certainly all children will not miraculously progress from signs to speech, but communication in any mode is better than none at all, and behavior problems are the inevitable result of the inability to communicate in a child.

Kimura (1976) discusses the thesis that certain language deficits should be viewed not as impairments in symbolic functioning but as impairments in motor sequences that lend themselves naturally to communication. In an analysis of the functional systems associated with speech, she observed that certain hand movements are more frequently associated with speaking than with silence or nonverbal vocalizing (humming) in the hearing, and that vocalizations are associated with signing in the deaf. Furthermore, she found an association between hand preference and speech lateralization. She postulates an overlap between the neural control of speech and that of certain motor activities, particularly serially organized manual movements. A close neural relationship between speech and manual gestures might explain the spontaneous appearance of speech skills in autistic children that coincides with the acquisition of a manual language.

The above studies reveal two additional points. First, almost all the studies report that a side benefit to the sign language acquisition was a rather dramatic improvement in overall behavior. The learned helplessness theory mentioned above may explain this side effect. The child who suddenly overcomes the communicative barrier may realize that he exercises control over other aspects of the immediate environment. Second, the reader has no doubt noted that autistic children were the subjects of several of these studies. We have reason to believe that sign language is a particularly appropriate communication mode for autistic children for the reasons described below.

Speech training of autistic children using operant techniques has proved discouragingly time consuming and unproductive (Hingtgen and Churchill, 1969). Recent evidence (Gillies, 1965; Lovaas et al., 1966; Bryson, 1970, 1972) indicates that the vocal-auditory mode may be inappropriate for language in these subjects, because cross-modal visual-auditory associations may be impaired. Autistic children seem to be more adept at tasks requiring primarily visual integration than at tasks requiring primarily auditory integration (Davis, 1970). Bettelheim (1967) reports that once autistic children *do* acquire speech they often have quite well developed syntax and vocabularies. These observations would be compatible with the notion (Fulwiler, 1976) that the sensory systems of the autistic child are essentially separate. Thus, the senses may develop at quite different rates: one sense (say, vision) may be normally developed but another (say, audition) may not be. If the normal communicative sense (verbal-auditory) is deficient, or if cross-modal associations are impossible, then the information in the perfectly adequate sensory system will not be tapped via normal communication. Fulwiler suggests that autistic children, because of deficient verbal abilities, are forced to rely upon representational forms of memory. Representational memory utilizes iconic, or visual, information, as opposed to verbal-auditory information (which is more efficiently stored by normal children). Representational processing is not only an inefficient memory process, but it is also very difficult to transmit representationally stored and processed information from person to person.

Autistic children do, however, seem to use gestures in a meaningful way (Jakab, 1972). Several researchers (Pronovost, Wakstein, and Wakstein, 1966; Ruttenberg and Gordon, 1967) note that autistic children respond to the gestures and facial expressions of others, and that communication is impossible without such nonverbal signals. Lovaas (1966) and Senn and Solnit (1968) reported that autistic children are particularly responsive to tactile stimulation. A manual language seems singularly appropriate for these children for the following reasons: it capitalizes on the senses (visual and tactile) to which the autistic child is most responsive, it avoids problems with cross-modal (visual-auditory) associations, it is an appropriate method of transmission for representationally stored information, and it utilizes the child's naturally communicative gestures and expressions.

Other studies involving sign language training of autistic children that do *not* mention concomitant vocal development include Webster et al., (1973) and Bonvillian and Nelson (1976). In the first study, the subject learned to obey signed commands and spontaneously issued signed commands to others; this successful program was instituted after the failure of an operant oral language program. In the second study, some sign language was acquired, but it apparently had no influence on vocalizations.

GENERAL STRATEGIES FOR SIGN LANGUAGE TRAINING

Biological Considerations

Robert Hinde (1974) has stated that if we are to gain control over our own behavior we must understand our own biology. This would hold true for any organism. In order to affect, change, or control an organism's behavior one must understand its biology, a fact that experimental psychologists have had to relearn. Psychologists, for example, have frequently used mazes to study learning in rats. Mazes were used because the particular rat used (*Rattus norwegicus*) runs in burrows in the wild; in Europe it was known as the "cellar" rat. When it is frightened it runs downward, and it is an excellent performer in a maze. An open plains animal, such as the antelope, would seem an idiot in a maze as compared to another burrowing animal, such as the pocket gopher. This crucial sort of information was forgotten by some behaviorists of the 1930s, who assumed that all behavior was learned, and who ignored the biological characteristics that each organism brought to the experimental situation. Breland and Breland (1961) have noted several amusing occasions when animals learned a behavior but later reverted to biological or instinctive behaviors which destroyed the experiment. Rats may be taught to press a bar because they manipulate objects in the environment with their paws; pigeons, however, are studied using keys because they naturally peck. These examples suggest a moral which can be illustrated with a more obvious example: you cannot teach a dog to fly. No matter how you reward it, and no matter how high you teach it to jump, the dog will not learn to fly. It is imperative, then, before engaging in research or therapy, to understand the subject's biology and to adjust the methodology to fit the subject rather than vice versa.

This notion is especially important in the case of exceptional children, because they often have physiological or neurological dysfunctions. One must take into account not only their biology as a member of their species, but also their physiological differences from the species norm. For example, since autistic children seem to have a dysfunction in their ability to make auditory-visual associations, it would be better to adjust the therapy to avoid tasks requiring this ability (Fulwiler and Fouts, 1976). Along with this general approach the individual nature of each child should also be considered.

Establishment of the Relationship

Language or communication requires at least two individuals—a sender and a receiver—and, where there are two individuals, these persons must exist in some sort of relationship. If there is no relationship, communication is severely limited. The establishment of a good working relationship between teacher and child is essential to learning. Behaviorism has tended to ignore the all-important social aspects of communication. Most animals must form a relationship with another animal at some point in their existence, at least in order to breed. The relationship between two animals is perhaps their most important behavioral pattern, with respect to the survival of the species. With more complex species, intraspecific relationships become even more important. The long childhood and adolescence of the chimpanzee is an excellent example. It is within the mother-infant bond that most of the chimpanzee's social learning takes place (van Lawick-Goodall, 1975). Robert Yerkes (1943) once stated that one chimpanzee is no chimpanzee, reflecting the importance of the social relationship in this gregarious species. Of course, this also holds true for *Homo sapiens*. Given experimental psychologists' traditional methodologies, it is easy to forget this point and to be more concerned with the input-output of an organism than with the role that relationships play in its behavior.

Individual Differences

Comprehension of an organism's biology helps one to recognize the environmental stimuli that comprise that organism's salient cues. Thereafter, the establishment of a relationship with the organism becomes relatively easy. This is a fine start, but one must also take into account the individual differences of the particular subject. Individual differences are an especially important consideration when dealing with exceptional children, and one method of assessing these individual qualities is to treat the exceptional child as a member of a different species. Simply observe the child, paying particular attention to the unique manner in which he deals with the world. Does the child seek visual, auditory, tactile stimuli?

In what modalities does the child produce stimulation? Once these observations are catalogued, act upon them. In essence, then, listen to the child's music and adjust your approach to the child, based on this information.

Implicit in this approach is the assumption that the child is an active, information-seeking organism (although the exceptional child may not seek information in a manner typical of normal members of the species). This assumption is extremely important in light of early behavioristic approaches, which seemed to assume instead that the child is a passive organism, waiting for some stimulus to goad it into a response. Historically, behavior modification approaches placed more emphasis on the methodology than on the organism. These approaches ignore the give-and-take of a relationship in favor of popping M&Ms into the child's mouth as a reinforcer, the assertion being that with the proper number of M&Ms the child will come under the experimenter's control. The pitfalls of this philosophy become quite apparent when working with chimpanzees. Some react well to food rewards, and others do not. For example, if one were to use candy as a reward for a chimpanzee named Lucy, one would become very fat. Lucy takes the reward, puts it in the experimenter's mouth, and watches the process of consumption. So, too, a given child may be fascinated by telephone books, pipes, or music, but be untouched by the allure of a more standard reward. Rather than operating on preconceived notions of what constitutes a reward, let the child demonstrate the positive and negative reinforcers in his own existence.

The Child's Behavior and Its Effect on the Environment

It is most important that noncommunicating children be shown that they can affect their environment in a reliable manner. A common feature of noncommunicating children is that their activities tend to relate to themselves alone rather than to their environment. By demonstrating to children that their responses result in reliable and corresponding responses from their environment, children learn that their behavior has consequences. This is easily accomplished in the context of establishing a communicative relationship. For example, by molding the child's hands into the DRINK sign and then offering a drink, the child begins to discern that his activities can control the behavior of another person. Once the child realizes this power, the motivation to interact with the teacher and the environment is dramatically increased.

Perils of the Overstructured Situation

Many experiments that deal with communication problems are conceived on the basis of the experimenter's a priori assumptions as to what constitutes the behavior of language. Such approaches have been categorized as synthetic by Turney (1977), who compared this strategy to the analytic strategy in chimpanzee language studies. He points out that the synthetic approach deduces features of human languages and then attempts to synthesize them in the chimpanzee experiments by using traditional animal learning paradigms. Turney contrasts this approach to analytic approaches which expose the chimpanzee subject to an existing human language and then attempt to verify certain aspects of the subsequent acquisition of the human language. He notes that the analytic approach as used by Gardner and Gardner (1971) makes no a priori assumptions concerning the necessary or descriptive features of language. The Premacks' (1972) research is an example of the synthetic model, in that it deduces the constituents of language and then examines the chimpanzees' ability to employ these features. Similarly, Fouts, Chown, Kimball, and Couch (1976) examined the elements of productivity and openness in a chimpanzee's production of novel prepositional phrases. These experiments tend to tell us more about the experimenters' preconceived notions than about the subject's preferences or natural behaviors that might accomplish the same ends. Such studies, although valuable in certain ways, demonstrate capacities or potentials for human behaviors rather than letting the organism demonstrate linguistic tendencies spontaneously. Pertinent to this discussion, Wolfgang Kohler (1971) made the following points in 1921:

> Lack of ambiguity in the experimental setup in the sense of an either-or has, to be sure, unfavorable as well as favorable consequences. The decisive explanations for the understanding of apes frequently arise from unforeseen kinds of behavior, for example, the use of tools by the animals in ways very different from human beings. If we arrange all conditions in such a way that, so far as possible, the ape can only show the kinds of behavior in which we are interested in advance, or else nothing essential at all, then it will be less likely that the animal does the unexpected and thus teaches the observer something (p. 215).

In short, the methodology used may unnecessarily restrict the subject to the preconceived notions of the experimenter. A very structured approach is often necessary in the pilot or demonstration stage of a study, but it may be deleterious when carried further into experimentation. For example, if a highly structured program is developed out of pilot experiments, it may have drastically different effects when applied by someone other than the original experimenter. The inexperienced individual tends to rely more upon the program itself than on the program's interaction with the peculiarities of a particular subject. It is common knowledge that promising new therapy programs often cease to be effective once the person who initiated them leaves the program. These therapeutic methodologies should be viewed as tools, but it should be emphasized that other necessary skills, such as developing interpersonal relationships, should be considered an integral part of the program. One is reminded of the salesperson at a state fair who makes vegetable chopping and cutting look so very simple. Unfortunately, the buyers usually find when they get their shiny new tools home that they do not have the years of experience and finesse necessary to do the job, and they end up breaking the new machines and multilating both the vegetables and their fingers.

Another problem with a highly structured program is that it not only teaches the subjects what to do, but it also tacitly teaches them what *not* to do. As a result, such programs run the risk of reducing the amount of generalization from the experimental situation to other settings. Formal conditioning procedures seem particularly susceptible to these problems. Hewett (1965) and Lovaas (1966) reported the establishment of verbal behavior in the repertoire of autistic children through the use of operant conditioning procedures. Although these and other studies since (e.g., Schell, Stark and Giddan, 1967) have reported some success, an evident problem is the lack of response generalization outside the therapy situation. Lovaas (1966) reported generalization, but Schell et al. (1967) reported that the increase in speech occurred only in therapy sessions. Sulzbacher and Costello (1970) and Hartung (1970) reported that the generalization of speech outside the therapy situation had to be specifically taught—it was not spontaneous. Formal techniques apparently have not been the panacea that some had hoped. The problems encountered by such procedures seem to stem from an emphasis on methodology rather than on relationships, and from a lack of concern for the biological characteristics of the subjects, along with their individual differences.

SPECIFIC TECHNIQUES OF SIGN LANGUAGE TRAINING

Total Communication

Among the specific techniques we recommend for sign training is Total Communication. Total Communication refers to the simultaneous use of gestural and vocal communication. Brady (1975) compared Total Communication methods to sign training alone and to reinforcement for vocalization alone in an autistic boy, and found the Total Communication strategy to be most effective. Konstantareas et al. (1974) claim success with a Total Communication approach with five autistic children. Four of them acquired some gestures (the program lasted only five weeks), and their interactive behavior increased. The contiguity of redundant stimuli, one of the most basic prerequisites of learning, is the key to such successes. With Total Communication we provide contiguous vocal and auditory stimuli, thus increasing the probability that the stimuli will be associated by the subject. The child's response may spontaneously shift from control by gestural stimuli to control by vocal stimuli, because of their consistent contiguity in time and space. Bonvillian (1976, personal communication), however, cautions that for some children communication through two modalities may have a deleterious effect on learning. Auditory stimuli *may* have a disruptive effect with autistic children, although obviously this is not always the case (cf. Fulwiler and Fouts, 1976).

Molding and Imitation

A technique we have cited earlier, which has proved efficient in sign language tuition, is the use of *molding*. Molding is a form of guidance in which the teacher forms the child's hands into the desired manual response, thus forcing the child into a passive response. As the child begins to approximate the correct motions himself, the molding is systematically faded until no prompting whatsoever is necessary. Imitation, on the other hand, does not involve direct contact with the subjects, although active collaboration on the subject's part is required. Molding has been successfully used with autistic children (Lovaas et al. 1966) and mentally retarded children (Baer, Peterson, and Sherman, 1967). Fouts (1972) discovered that molding was more effective than imitation when he taught signs to the young (three-year-old) Washoe. Baer et al. (1967) found that mentally retarded children did not imitate a model (e.g., raising an arm) when given the command "Do this." It was necessary to first mold the subject into the correct position and then to fade the molding so that the subject could match the model's movements. Apparently, certain children, such as the mentally retarded and also the very young, do not possess imitative abilities at all. Imitation is a developmental milestone, which may be reached late or never at all in some exceptional children. Fouts, who had found in 1972 that the then three-year-old Washoe did not learn well using imitation, repeated the study with the now nine-year-old Washoe and another signing chimp, eight-year-old Lucy (Fouts and Goodin 1974). He found that both of these older chimps responded equally well to molding and imitation as training techniques. Imitation, of course, is easier on the teacher—and, if the subject is a reliable imitator, it is probably the preferred technique. If, though, the teacher is faced with a nonimitating subject, molding would be the more efficient technique. The teacher should, however, be alert to the cognitive development of the child and be ready to try imitation should it become appropriate. It might be sensible during the transition phase from molding to imitation for the teacher to face in the same direction as the child when demonstrating a sign, so that mirror-image reversal is not a problem.

It is certainly important to wean the child from a passive response (molding) to an active response (imitating). Konorski (1967) found it extremely difficult to change a passive movement into an instrumental response. We believe that this problem can be avoided if the passive response is not allowed to persist for an inordinate length of time; therefore, fading of the molding prompts should begin as soon as possible. This procedure is consistent with the finding that passively moving the subject through its paces is beneficial to response acquisition during early trials, but is deleterious if carried too far (Koch, 1923; Ludgate, 1923; Carr, 1930).

Group Sessions

Two other specific training techniques deserve brief mention. It has been the experience of at least one of the authors that certain children may respond better in training sessions involving another child. To some children, of course, the presence of another pupil is inhibiting or distracting. To other children, however, another child may stimulate friendly rivalry, and signing games involving some competition may be created by the teacher. Still other children may benefit from the emotional support afforded by the presence of a peer. Another benefit of a group session is that communication among children may be actively encouraged so that it will more rapidly generalize to situations when the children are together outside of training sessions.

Generalization of Signs

The last point to be made also involves generalization of signed responses. Most signs will initially refer to very concrete objects, because the teacher will pair a given sign with a given exemplar, such as a toy, that is available in the training room. It is of paramount importance that the demonstration of a particular sign be extended beyond one particular exemplar. The sign for "car," for instance, will probably be applied first to a toy car, but after initial acquisition the sign should be demonstrated with other toy cars, larger and smaller than the original exemplar. Then, of course, it should be extended to actual cars on the streets. After successful generalization of a response in this manner, the teacher may proceed from physical referents to pictorial representations of the exemplars (Barnes, 1973). Transfer of a signed response from the physical object to its two-dimensional representation demonstrates a rather abstract level of linguistic and conceptual development.

SUMMARY

It has been the purpose of this chapter to review some of the animal research, particularly our own work with chimpanzees, and to illustrate its applications to child language acquisition. The review is by no means exhaustive, and details of additional studies with our "sibling species" may be obtained from various review articles (see Fouts and Rigby, 1975). Research into both the linguistic abilities and the purely conceptual abilities of the animals at the Institute for Primate Studies continues. Work with nonspeaking children also continues at the Cerebral Palsy Center in Norman, Oklahoma, and at the Child Studies Center in Oklahoma City, where children with a wide range of physiological, mental, and emotional dysfunctions are treated. It is hoped that new insights into language intervention strategies will result from these studies.

REFERENCES

Baer, D. M., Peterson, R. F., and Sherman, J. A. 1967. The development of imitation by reinforcing behavioral similarity to a model. J. Exp. Anal. Behav. 10:405–416.
Barnes, S. 1973. The use of sign language as a technique for language acquisition in autistic children; an applied model bridging verbal and nonverbal theoretical systems. Unpublished doctoral dissertation, California School of Professional Psychology, Los Angeles.
Beatty, J., Fouts, R. S., and McDivit, A. Same-different discrimination of chimpanzee vocalization by an ASL responding chimpanzee. In preparation.
Berger, S. 1970. A clinical program for developing multimodal language responses with atypical deaf children. In J. McLean, D. Yoder and R. L. Schiefelbusch (eds.), Language Intervention with the Retarded, pp. 212–235. University Park Press, Baltimore.
Bettelheim, B. 1967. The Empty Fortress: Infantile Autism and the Birth of Self. Collier, London.
Bonvillian, J., and Nelson, K. 1976. Sign language acquisition in a mute autistic boy. J. Speech Hear. Disord. 41:339–346.
Brady, D. 1975. The effects of simultaneous treatments for language acquisition in an autistic child. Unpublished master's thesis, University of Oklahoma, Norman.
Breland, K., and Breland, M. 1961. The misbehavior of organisms. Am. Psychol. 16:681–684.
Bryson, C. Q. 1970. Systematic identification of perceptual disabilities in autistic children. Percept. Mot. Skills 31:239–246.
Bryson, C. Q. 1972. Short-term memory and crossmodal information processing in autistic children. J. Learn. Disabil. 5:81–91.
Carr, H. A. 1930. Teaching and learning. J. Genet. Psychol. 37:189–218.
Chomsky, N. 1967. The formal nature of language. In E. Lenneberg (ed.), Biological Foundations of Language, pp. 397–342. John Wiley & Sons, New York.

Crickmay, M. C. 1966. Speech Therapy and Bobath Approach to Cerebral Palsy. Charles C Thomas, Springfield, Ill.

Cruickshank, W. M. (ed.). 1966. Cerebral Palsy: Its Individual and Community Problems. Syracuse University Press, Syracuse, N.Y.

Davis, B. J. 1970. A clinical approach to the development of communication in young schizophrenic children. J. Commun. Disord. 3:211–222.

Eibl-Eibesfeldt, I. 1972. Similarities and differences between cultures in expressive movements. In R. Hinde (ed.), Non-Verbal Communication, pp. 297–312. Cambridge University Press, Cambridge, England.

Fouts, R. S. 1972. The use of guidance in teaching sign language to a chim-
· panzee. J. Comp. Physiolog. Psychol. 80:515–522.

Fouts, R. S. 1973. Acquisition and testing of gestural signs in four young chim-panzees. Science 180:978–980.

Fouts, R. S., Chown, W. B., and Goodin, L. 1976. Transfer of signed responses in American Sign Language from vocal English stimui to physical object by a chimpanzee (Pan). Learn. Motivation 7:458–475.

Fouts, R. S., Chown, W. M., Kimball, G., and Couch, J. 1976. Comprehension and production of American Sign Language by a chimpanzee (Pan). Paper presented at the XXI International Congress of Psychology, July, Paris.

Fouts, R. S., and Goodin, L. 1974. Acquisition of signs in chimpanzees: A comparison of training methods. Paper presented at the Psychonomic Society Meeting, November, Boston.

Fouts, R. S., and Rigby, R. L. 1975. Man-chimpanzee communication. In T. A. Sebeok (ed.), How Animals Communicate, pp. 1034–1054. Indiana University Press, Bloomington.

Fulwiler, R. L. 1976. Autism reconstituted: An ontogenic hypothesis. Unpublished manuscript, Langely-Porter Institute, University of California at Berkeley, Berkeley.

Fulwiler, R., and Fouts, R. 1976. Acquisition of American Sign Language by a noncommunicating autistic child. J. Aut. Child. Schizo. 6:43–51.

Gardner, B. T., and Gardner, R. A. 1971. Two-way communication with an infant chimpanzee. In A. M. Schrier and F. Stollnitz (eds.), Behavior of Non-human Primates, pp. 117–184. Academic Press, New York.

Gardner, R. A., and Gardner, B. T. 1969. Teaching sign language to a chim-panzee. Science 165:664–672.

Gillies, S. M. 1965. Some abilities of psychotic children and subnormal controls. J. Ment. Defic. Res. 9:89–101.

Gorcyca, D. A., Garner, P., and Fouts, R. S. 1975. Deaf children and chim-panzees: A comparative sociolinguistic investigation. Paper presented at the Speech Communication Association Convention, December, Houston.

Hartung, J. R. 1970. A review of procedures to increase verbal imitation skills and functional speech in autistic children. J. Speech Hear. Disord. 35:203–217.

Hayes, K., and Hayes, C. 1952. Imitation in a home-raised chimpanzee. J. Comp. Physiolog. Psychol. 45:450–459.

Hewes, G. W. 1973. Primate communication and the gestural origin of language. Curr. Anthropol. 14:5–24.

Hewett, F. 1965. Teaching speech to an autistic child through operant condition-ing. Am. J. Orthopsychiatry 35:927–936.

Hinde, R. A. 1974. Biological Bases of Human Behavior. McGraw-Hill Book Co., New York.

Hingtgen, J. N., and Churchill, D. W. 1969. Identification of perceptual limitations in mute autistic children: Identification by the use of behavior modification. Arch. Gen. Psychiatry 21:68–71.

Hiroto, D. S., and Seligman, M. E. P. 1975. Generality of learned helplessness in man. J. Personal. Soc. Psychol. 10:48–57.

Hockett, C. 1960. The origin of speech. Sci. Am. 203:88–96.

Jakab, I. 1972. The patient, the mother and the therapist: An interactional triangle in the treatment of the autistic child. J. Commun. Disord. 5:154–182.

King, M. C., and Wilson, A. C. 1975. Evolution at two levels in humans and chimpanzees. Science 188:107–116.

Kimura, D. 1976. The neural basis of language qua gesture. In H. Avian-Whitaker and H. A. Whitaker (eds.), Studies in Neurologuistics. Academic Press, New York.

Klima, E., and Bellugi, U. 1972. The signs of language in child and chimpanzee. In T. Alloway, L. Krames, and P. Pliner (eds.), Communication and Affect: A Comparative Approach, pp. 67–96. Academic Press, New York.

Koch, H. L. 1923. The influence of mechanical guidance upon maze learning. Psycholog. Monogr. 32(5).

Kohler, W. 1971. Methods of psychological research with apes. In M. Henle (ed.), The Selected Papers of Wolfgang Kohler, pp. 197–223. Liveright, New York.

Konorski, J. 1967. Integrative activity of the brain. University of Chicago Press, Chicago.

Konstantareas, M. M., Opman, J., Webster, C. D., Fisher, H., and Miller, K. 1974. A five week simultaneous communication programme for severely dysfunctional children: Outcome and implications for future research. Paper presented at the Annual Meeting of the Psychonomic Society, November, Boston.

Lashley, K. S. 1951. The problem of serial order in behavior. In L. A. Jeffross (ed.), Cerebral Mechanisms in Behavior, pp. 112–136. John Wiley & Sons, New York.

Lieberman, P., Crelin, E., and Klatt, D. 1972. Phonetic ability and related anatomy of the newborn and adult human, Neanderthal man, and the chimpanzee. Am. Anthropol. 74:287–307.

Lovaas, O. I. 1966. A program for the establishment of speech in psychotic children. In J. K. Wing (ed.), Early Childhood Autism: Clinical, Educational and Social Aspects, pp. 115–144. London: Pergamon Press, 1966.

Lovaas, O. I., Berberich, J. P., Perloff, B. F., and Schaeffer, B. 1966. Acquisition of imitative speech by schizophrenic children. Science 155:705–707.

Ludgate, K. E. 1923. The effect of manual guidance upon maze learning. Psycholog. Monogr. 33(1, Whole No. 148)

Maier, S. F., Seligman, M. E. P., and Solomon, R. L. 1969. Pavlovian fear conditioning and learned helplessness. In B. A. Campbell and R. M. Church (eds.), Punishment and Aversive Behavior, pp. 299–342. Appleton-Century-Crofts, New York.

Marler, P. 1965. Communication in monkeys and apes. In I. DeVore (ed.), Primate Behavior: Field Studies of Monkeys and Apes, pp. 544–584. Holt, Rinehart & Winston, New York.

Mellgren, R. L., Fouts, R. S., and Lemmon, W. B. 1973. American Sign Language in the chimpanzee: Semantic and conceptual functions of signs. Paper presented at the Midwestern Psychological Association Meeting, May, Chicago.

Miller, A., and Miller, E. E. 1973. Cognitive developmental training with elevated boards and sign language. J. Aut. Child. Schizo. 3:65–85.

Mounin, G. 1976. Language communication in chimpanzees. Curr. Anthropol. 3:65–85.

Overmier, J. B., and Seligman, M. E. P. 1967. Effects of inescapable shock upon subsequent escape and avoidance responding. J. Comp. Physiolog. Psychol. 63:28–33.

Ploog, D. 1968. Kommunikationsprozesse bei Affen. Homo 19:151–165.

Premack, D. 1971a. Language in chimpanzees? Science 172:808–822.

Premack, D. 1971b. On the assessment of language competence and the chimpanzee. In A. M. Schrier and F. Stollnitz (eds.), Behavior of Nonhuman Primates, pp. 186–228. Academic Press, New York.

Premack, J., and Premack, D. 1972. Teaching language to an ape. Sci. Am. 227:92–99.

Pronovost, W., Wakstein, P., and Wakstein, P. 1966. A longitudinal study of the speech behavior of fourteen children diagnosed as atypical or autistic. Except. Child. 33:19–26.

Rumbaugh, D., Gill, T. V., and von Glasersfeld, E. C. 1973. Reading and sentence completion by a chimpanzee (Pan). Science 182:731–733.

Ruttenberg, B. A., and Gordon, E. G. 1967. Evaluating the communication of the autistic child. J. Speech Hear. Disord. 32:314–324.

Sarles, H. B. 1972. The search for comparative variables in human speech. A symposium paper presented at the Animal Behavior Society Meetings, June, Reno, Nev.

Schell, R. E., Stark, J., and Giddan, J. J. 1967. Development of language behavior in an autistic child. J. Speech Hear. Disord. 32:51–64.

Schlesinger, H. S., and Meadow, K. P. 1972. Sound and Sign. University of California Press, Berkeley.

Schnierla, T. 1972. Problems in the biopsychology of social organization. In L. R. Aronson, E. Tobach, J. Rosenblatt, and D. Lehrman (eds.), Selected Writings of T. C. Schnierla, pp. 417–439. W. H. Freeman and Co., San Francisco.

Seligman, M. E. P. 1974. Helplessness. W. H. Freeman and Co., San Francisco.

Seligman, M. E. P., and Maier, S. F. 1967. Failure to escape traumatic shock. J. Exp. Psychol. 74:1–9.

Senn, M. J. E., and Solnit, A. S. 1968. Problems in Child Behavior and Development. Lea and Febiger, Philadelphia.

Stokoe, W. C., Casterline, D. C., and Croneberg, C. G. 1965. A Dictionary of American Sign Language on Linguistic Priniciples. Gallaudet College Press, Washington, D.C.

Sulzbacher, S. I., and Costello, J. M. 1970. A behavioral strategy for language training of a child with autistic behaviors. J. Speech Hear. Disord. 35:255–276.

Thorpe, W. H. 1972. Comparison of vocal communication in animals and man. In R. A. Hinde (ed.), Nonverbal Communication, pp. 27–47. Cambridge University Press, Cambridge, England.

Turney, T. H. 1977. Synthetic and analytic approaches to the study of language in chimpanzees. In preparation.

Van Hooff, J. A. R. A. M. 1972. A comparative approach to the phylogeny of laughter and smiling. In R. Hinde (ed.), Nonverbal Communication, pp. 209–238. Cambridge University Press, Cambridge, England.

van Lawick-Goodall, J. 1975. The chimpanzee. In V. Goodall (ed.), The Quest for Man, pp. 130–159. Phailen, London.

Webster, C. D., McPherson, H., Sloman, L., Evans, M. A., and Kuchar, E. 1973. Communicating with an autistic boy by gestures. J. Aut. Child. Schizo. 3:337–346.

Yerkes, R. 1943. Chimpanzees: A Laboratory Colony. Yale University Press, New Haven, Conn.

chapter 16

Linguistic Capabilities of a Lowland Gorilla

Francine Patterson

Department of Psychology
Stanford University
Stanford, California

The forma mentera of psycholinguistics has in recent years shifted from a reverence for Chomskian grammars innately imprinted and genetically unfolded to an appreciation of language as a cognitive process fundamentally similar to other intelligent behaviors. One way to reach an understanding of the basic cognitive processes involved in language is to examine its characteristics in a mode other than vocal. The approach being taken in this symposium ["An Account of the Visual Mode: Man versus Ape," February, 1977, Denver, Colorado] is precisely this. Another method is to study its form and function in a species other than *Homo sapiens*, a method that underlies the second theme of this symposium. By switching modes or species we can sort out the characteristics essential to language from those that are merely consequences of its association with a particular mode or its use by a particular species.

This statement reveals one of my basic assumptions: human language is not a redundant phrase—language is an ill defined phenomenon in communication which may have many manifestations, including the possibility of nonhuman forms. A recent critic of the ape language experiments, Georges Mounin (1976) states that ". . . the criteria for human language . . . cannot be obtained through mere generalization of its present features, but must be sought through a comparative . . . study of all systems of communication, including animal communication" (p. 2).

What I am exploring in my work with the gorilla Koko are the parameters of—dare I say it—comparative pedolinguistics. It seems to me futile to argue as to whether or not several educated apes "have" human language—at least until there is a consensus on when a human has language. A more productive approach might be to chart the similarities and differences in its form and function in child, chimp, and gorilla, thus discovering more about the various paths the evolution of intelligence can take.

Project Koko began as the result of a fortunate series of coincidences. In 1972, the Gardners lectured at Stanford on the acquisition of American Sign Language by the chimpanzee Washoe, an event which fired me with the ambition to become involved in the examination of the language abilities of the great apes. Shortly thereafter, a visit to the San Francisco Zoo gave me my first glimpse of Koko, then three months old. I immediately singled her out as a likely subject for a language experiment, but the zoo intended to keep her with her mother. Disappointed but undaunted, I enrolled in a course in sign language, in the event that

From Patterson, F. 1978. Linguistic capabilities of a lowland gorilla. *In* F. C. C. Peng (ed.), Sign Language and Language Acquisition—New Dimensions in Comparative Pedolinguistics, pp. 161–201. Westview Press, Boulder, Col. Association for Advancement of Science. Reprinted by permission.

This research was made possible by grants from the Spencer Foundation and the National Geographic Society and support from the recently established Gorilla Foundation of Menlo Park, California.

the opportunity to work with an ape should present itself. Nine months later, I discovered that Koko, a victim of malnutrition and shigellosis, had been separated from her mother but had since recovered in the zoo's nursery and was a thriving 20-pound infant. When I again asked for permission to initiate the sign language study, the director immediately granted my request. The next day, July 12, 1972, I began work.

Modeling my study after Project Washoe, I held the expectation that Koko would prove the peer of Washoe in language acquisition, despite a literature which depicted the gorilla as intractable, negativistic, and intellectually disadvantaged in comparison with the chimpanzee. Robert Yerkes (1925) described gorillas as aloof, independent, and at times obstinate and negativistic: "In degree of docility and good nature the gorilla is so far inferior to the chimpanzee that it is not likely to usurp the latter's place . . . in scientific laboratories" (p. 74). He noted that in direct contrast to chimpanzees, gorillas showed a low level of motivation and a positive resistance to imitation. Similar conclusions have been drawn from more recent investigations of gorilla intelligence (Knoblock and Pasamanick, 1959):

> There is little question that the chimpanzee is capable of conceptualization and abstraction that is beyond the abilities of the gorilla. It is precisely because of these limitations, which are apparently genetically determined, . . . that it is more difficult to work with them (p. 703).

My experience was quite different from what might have been expected following a reading of this literature. Koko was highly sociable (at times to a fault—her exuberant show-off behavior in the presence of visitors often proved disruptive to training which was initially carried out in the children's zoo nursery in front of the public). She was also responsive to social reinforcers such as praise and tickling.

Although the gorilla learned signs most rapidly through the technique of molding (a process she initially resisted), Koko showed a substantial amount of imitation; in fact, her first recorded sign, DRINK, was a result of this process and not of molding. Before long, she was imitating domestic tasks, such as cleaning with a sponge, and at times I have had the experience of having my every activity and posture mimicked much to my amusement and sometimes to my embarrassment. Some days, Koko follows me like a shadow—writing, scrubbing the floor, using the phone, filing her nails, thoughtfully tapping her chin (cf. Figure 1).

Negativism has reared its ugly head on occasion but it is by no means a dominant characteristic of Koko's behavior. Incidence of negativistic behavior seemed higher when she was in the "terrible twos" and "fearsome fours"—but it has always been more a situation-specific response than a generalized trait. One routine I devised to test Koko's

Figure 1.   Koko's imitative behavior. Koko frequently imitates the behavior of her human companions. This and all photographs in this chapter are by Ronald H. Cohn, Ph.D.

comprehension of signs and relations involved asking her to perform a certain task as a condition of being allowed to come out of her room. For example, I would ask her to find the yellow ball, or the small shoe, or to put the baby under the blanket. Sometimes, the request was completely ignored, but more frequently she would bring me everything in the room except the requested item. Alternatively, she would put various objects, in, on, or under other objects, but, again, executing every permutation and combination except the correct one. It was an exasperating experience and I had the sneaking suspicion that she was more reinforced by our signs of frustration than by the end reward of her freedom. One way to gain her cooperation was to threaten to leave her completely alone—suddenly, albeit reluctantly, she made the correct response.

At times, Koko's contrary behavior is more amusing than frustrating. For instance, she has signed FROWN or SAD, when asked to smile for a photograph. Occurrences such as this are informative in that they demonstrate her grasp of the concept of opposites.

Koko failed to match the gorilla stereotype in more ways than she fit it, however. Her acquisition of a large American Sign Language vocabulary and her performance in test situations, including standardized intelligence tests, call into question the widespread belief that the chimpanzee is the most intelligent of all nonhuman primates.

This brings us to the data on Koko that I would like to discuss in this chapter, some of which are strictly comparative in nature. Initially, Project Koko was structured in form and intention quite similarly to Project Washoe in that I sought to investigate many of the same parameters: vocabulary development, generalization, semantic relations, comprehension, and productivity. My aim was to create a body of data from which direct comparisons could be made between Koko and Washoe and Koko and human children. Consequently, certain aspects of my methodology were similar: daily inventories of signs, double-blind tests of vocabulary and comprehension, naturalistic observations on the use of sign, and studies of behavioral development.

Vocabulary is a valuable index of cognitive and linguistic development. In fact, tests of vocabulary are considered to be the best single index of human intelligence. Koko's vocabulary is closely comparable in content and size to those of children and chimpanzees.

To be considered a reliable part of Koko's vocabulary, a sign must meet a criterion of spontaneous and appropriate use on at least one-half the days of a given month. This is somewhat different from the Gardners' (1969, 1972) criterion (spontaneous and appropriate use for a period of 14 consecutive days) but it has seemed desirable to avoid daily drill sessions which might be imposed just for the sake of meeting such a criterion. Koko's sign vocabulary grew at the rate of approximately one sign per month during the first year and a half; by the end of January, 1974, 22 signs had met my criterion. This compares favorably with the progress of Washoe, who acquired 21 signs during the first 18 months of her training. Since neither ape was exposed to a sign language environment until she was about one year of age, it is difficult to compare their vocabulary development with that of human children who are exposed to their native language from birth. However, despite her disadvantage, Koko built a vocabulary of approximately 100 signs by the time she was three and a half (30 months of training), a figure in the normal range for human children who build vocabularies ranging in size from 30 to 400 words between their second and third years. For example, one report of a deaf child inventoried 132 signs at age three (Olson, 1972). During the next year, Koko's vocabulary doubled in size; at age four and a half, she had approximately 225 signs at her command (cf. Figure 2).

In order to directly compare Koko's vocabulary development with that of Washoe, I applied the Gardners' 14-consecutive-day criterion to Koko's data. The Gardners report that after 36 months of training, 85 of Washoe's signs had met their strict criterion. At an identical point in her training, 112 of Koko's signs had met the Gardners' criterion. Table 1 presents the vocabularies of Koko and Washoe in a manner that shows

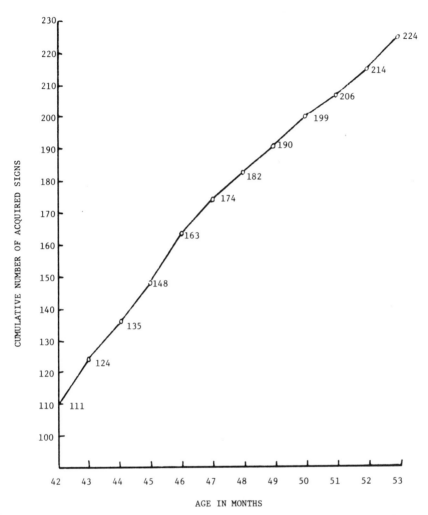

Figure 2.   Cumulative number of signs in Koko's vocabulary from age 42 to 53 months.

the considerable overlap between the two. Forty-seven of the 112 signs acquired by Koko within 36 months of training were also acquired by Washoe in the same period of time.

Another figure available for comparison from the published data on Washoe is the amount of signing at dinnertime. The Gardners started sampling Washoe's signing in the 29th month of their project. At this time, she used 50 signs during a 15- to 20-minute session taken at the evening meal. During a one-hour dinnertime sample (5:00 p.m. to 6:00 p.m.) in month 29 of this project, Koko used 251 signs. (This would be approximately 63 every 15 minutes.) While more direct quantitative com-

Table 1.   Signs in Koko's vocabulary meeting the strict Gardner and Gardner criterion as of July 1, 1975 (approximately three years of training)

Signs acquired by Koko within three years of training not in Washoe's vocabulary at the same point in her training

ALLIGATOR	EARRING	PINCH-SKIN
APPLE	EGG	POTATO
ARM	FEATHER	POUR
AROUND	FISH	RUBBER
ASK	FORK	SANDWICH
BAG-PURSE	GRAPE	SCRATCH
BEAN	HAIR	SMALL
BIG	KOKO	SMILE
BITE	LIPSTICK	SOAP
BLANKET	MATCH	SOCK
BOTTLE	MILK	SPICE
BRACELET	MONEY	STAMP
BUTTER	MOUTH	STRAW
CABBAGE	NECKLACE	TAPE
CAKE	NOSE	TASTE
CANDY	NUT	TEETH
CEREAL	ON	THIRSTY
CHASE	ONION	TIGER
COLD	ORANGE	TIME
COOKIE	PEACH	WATER
CRACKER	PICK-GROOM	
DRY	PILLOW	

Signs in common with Washoe at same point in training

BABY	GO	QUIET
BANANA	GOOD	RED
BERRY	HAT	RIDE
BIRD	HURRY	SLEEP-BED
BOOK	KEY	SORRY
BRUSH	LIGHT	STRING
BUG	LISTEN	SWEET
CAT	LOOK	THERE-THAT
CATCH	ME	TICKLE
CHEESE	MEAT	TOOTHBRUSH
CLEAN	MINE	TREE
COME-GIMME	MORE	UP
DRINK	OPEN	WHITE
EAT-FOOD	OUT	WIPER (BIB)
FLOWER	PEN-WRITE	YOU
FRUIT	PLEASE	

Signs acquired by Washoe within three years of training not in Koko's vocabulary at the same point in her training

BLACK	FUNNY	OIL
CAR	GRASS	PANTS
CHAIR	GREEN	ROGER

Table 1.   (continued)

CLIMB	GREG	SHOES
CLOTHES	HAMMER	SMELL
COMB	HELP	SMOKE
COVER	HUG	SPIN
COW	HURT	SPOON
DIRTY	IN	SUSAN
DOG	KISS	WASHOE
DOWN	LEAF	WENDE
DR. G.	MRS. G.	WINDOW
ENOUGH	NAOMI	YOURS

parisons will have to await the release of additional data on Washoe, these figures indicate that at similar points in their training in sign language, the performances of Koko and Washoe were closely comparable.

Words represented in the early vocabularies of children (Nelson, 1973) are very similar in semantic content and proportion to those of Koko. For both, the most prominent category is food and drink, followed by animals, then clothing and personal items. The only category present in children's vocabularies but absent in both Koko's and Washoe's was that of places (e.g., pool, school). This category was the least frequently represented in the child lexicons and is understandably missing from those of the apes because of their more restricted environment.

Koko's vocabulary has expanded in every conceptual domain, with the greatest increase occurring in the object name category (cf. Table 2). This parallels the development of human children (Nelson 1973). Koko has acquired some words relating to the concept of time (e.g., *now, time, finished*) but she has not yet consistently used question words such as *who, what,* or *why*, although she can appropriately answer questions employing these words.[1] Many children in the earliest stages of language acquisition do not use Wh- words to express questions (Bowerman, 1973). However, since the third month, Koko has used gestural intonation (retaining the hands in the sign position at the end of an utterance and seeking direct eye contact) to express questions.[2] For example, one

---

[1] Responses to Why questions have not yet been reported for chimpanzees learning language. Koko now regularly answers such inquiries. For example, one day, a deaf companion pursued her most cherished ball under the trailer in a game of Keepaway, and gained possession of it in violation of Koko's special rules (which I had failed to adequately explain to her opponent). Koko's response was to give her companion a play bite on the posterior. About 20 minutes later, when asked why she bit her friend, she replied, HIM BALL BAD.

[2] In the following example, taken from the diary records, Koko's companion described the interrogative intonation in a way very similar to Fischer's description of it for the deaf: "Yes-no questions are marked by a raising of the eyebrows and an expectant look on the face."

Table 2.   243 distinct[a] signs acquired[b] by Koko within 50 months of training

Type	Number	Tokens
Proper nouns	4	KOKO, KATE, PENNY, RON
Pronouns	3	ME, MYSELF, YOU
Animate nouns	22	ALLIGATOR, BABY, BEAR, BIRD, BUG, CAT, CLOWN, COW, DOG, ELEPHANT, FISH, FROG, GIRAFFE, GORILLA, MAN, MONKEY, MOUSE, PIG, RABBIT, SKUNK[a], TIGER, MOOSE
Edible nouns	46	APPLE, BANANA, BERRY, BEAN, BONE, BREAD, BUTTER, CABBAGE, CAKE, CANDY, CARROT, CEREAL, CHEESE, COOKIE, CORN, CRACKER, CUCUMBER, DRINK[a], EGG, FOOD[a], FRUIT, GRAPE, GRASS, GUM, JELL-O, LEAF, LEMON, LOLLIPOP–ICE CREAM, MEAT, MEDICINE, MILK, NUT, ONION, ORANGE, PEACH, PEPPER, POTATO, PUDDING, RAISIN, SALAD, SALT, SANDWICH, SPICE, TREE, WATER
Other nominals	85	AIRPLANE, ARM, BALL, BAG-PURSE, BED[a], BELT, BELLYBUTTON, BLANKET, BRUSH, BOAT, BOOK, BOTTLE, BOTTOM, BOX, BRACELET, COMB, CIGARETTE[a], CHIN, CLAY, CLOTHES, DRAPES, EAR, EARRING, EYE, EYE MAKEUP, FINGER, FEATHER, FLOWER, FOOT, FORK, HAT, HAIR, HEAD, HURT[a], INJECTION, KEY, KISS[a], KNIFE[a], LEG, LIGHT, LIGHTER, LIP, LIPSTICK, MASK, MATCH, MIRROR, MOUTH, NAIL, NAIL CLIPPER, NECK, NECKLACE, NOSE, OIL-LOTION, PANTS, PAPER, PEN-WRITE[a], SHOULDER, SKIN-PINCH[a], PILLOW, PIMPLE, RING, RUBBER, SHELL, SOAP, SOCK, SPONGE, SPOON, STAMP, STETHOSCOPE, STOMACH, STRAW, STRING, SWING[a], SWEATER, TAPE, TASTE[a], TEETH-GLASS, TELEPHONE, TIME, TOILET, TONGUE, TOOTHBRUSH, TRAIN, WHISTLE, WIPER
Modifiers	34	ALL, BAD, BIG, BLACK, CLEAN[a], COLD, DIFFERENT, DIRTY, DRY[a], GOOD, GREEN, HOT, HUNGRY, HURRY, MAD, MINE, MORE, NOW, OLD, PINK, QUIET, ROTTEN, RED, SAD, SAME, SMALL, SMOKE[a], SORRY, STINK[a], SWEET, THIRSTY, THAT-THERE, WHITE, YELLOW
Negatives	5	CAN'T, DON'T-NOT, DON'T KNOW, NO, NOTHING

Table 1.   (continued)

Type	Number	Tokens
Verbals	50	ASK, BITE, BLOW, BREAK, CATCH, CHASE, CLEAN[a], COME-GIMME, CUT[a], DO, DRAW, DRINK[a], DRY[a], EAT[a], FINISHED, FROWN, GO, HAVE, HELP, HELPMYSELF, HIDE, HUG-LOVE, HURT[a], KISS[a], KNOW, LIKE, LISTEN, LOOK, MAKE-FIX, OPEN, PLAY, PICK-GROOM, PINCH-SKIN[a], PLEASE, POUND, POUR, RIDE, SIP, SCRATCH, SIT, SLEEP, SMELL, SMILE, SWING[a], TASTE[a], THINK, TICKLE, TURN-AROUND, WANT, WRITE-PEN[a]
Prepositional	6	DOWN, IN, OFF, ON, OUT, UP
Interjections	2	DARN, HI-BYE
Total:	5	

[a] Indicates signs occurring in more than one category because of overlap in usage. For example, DRINK can be both a noun and a verb, and the sign for KNIFE (noun) is the same as the sign for CUT (verb).

[b] Acquired indicates signs used spontaneously and appropriately half the number of days or more in a given month.

day in response to a woodpecker's tapping outside, one of Koko's companions, Barbara, signed, KOKO, LISTEN BIRD. Koko responded, BIRD? As she signed, she turned her head toward Barbara, cocked it, and opened her eyes wide—almost raised her eyebrows. Barbara said, "Yes, that is a bird tapping outside. Listen" . . . Then, Barbara tapped on the counter and pointed outside when the woodpecker made the noise again. This time, Koko signed, LISTEN BIRD, with a definite declarative intonation.

As in the case of children and chimpanzees learning language, certain words are more difficult for Koko to articulate than others. Signs which require a great deal of manual dexterity are often simplified by the gorilla. For example, WATER and RUBBER are simplified from the "w" and "x" hand configuration to a forefinger extended from a loose hand or compact fist. Manual dexterity is not the only problem; some signs are physically impossible for Koko to articulate correctly (e.g., SAND and PURPLE) because of the small size of her thumb.

I have noticed a developmental change in the case of articulation of a certain group of signs in which the hands do not contact the body (noncontact signs) which parallels that reported for Washoe (Fouts, 1973). Both Koko and Washoe acquired noncontact signs more slowly than contact signs before the age of four. Prior to the time when Koko could properly articulate noncontact signs, such as FINISHED (cf. Figure 3) and MILK, she tried to convert these signs into contact signs

Figure 3. Koko's MILK. Koko signs MILK, a nontouch sign which is performed as if milking a cow with one hand. [Cohn]

by changing the place of articulation from a point away from the body to one on the body.

Koko, like Washoe (Gardner and Gardner, 1971) and human children (Clark, 1973), has spontaneously generalized and overgeneralized her signs to novel objects and situations. For example, the sign for STRAW, learned initially with reference to drinking straws, was spontaneously used to label plastic tubing, a clear plastic hose (¾ inch in diameter), cigarettes, and a car radio antenna; OPEN, used initially with reference to locked doors, was generalized to boxes, covered cans, drawers, and cupboards; NUT, learned as a name for packaged nuts, was later used to refer to pictures of nuts in magazines, peanut butter sandwiches, roasted soybeans, and sunflower seeds (but in this case only after tasting some—she had first labeled them CANDY FOOD); TREE, learned with reference to acacia branches and celery, was overgeneralized to asparagus, green onions, and other tall thin objects presented vertically.

Not only has the gorilla demonstrated a capacity for acquiring a sizable vocabulary, she has also spontaneously combined these words into meaningful and sometimes novel strings of two or more signs. The first juxtaposition of gestures that might be interpreted as a sign combination, GIMME FOOD, was recorded on film during the second month of the project when Koko was about 14 months old. The signing was elicited by a drink held out of reach, so an alternative interpretation might be that this sequence was a combination of a natural reaching gesture plus a sign. This second interpretation is supported by the finding that children pass through a stage prior to the first joining of words in which words and actions are combined to express a statement (Greenfield and Smith, 1976). The sequence FOOD DRINK, elicited by a bottle of formula, was also recorded during the second month, but notes taken at the time state that Koko may have been correcting herself, for we always referred to the formula (cereal plus milk) as DRINK.

During the third month of training, when Koko was 15 months old, she acquired the sign for MORE and soon began to use it spontaneously in conjuction with the signs for FOOD and DRINK. The first recorded combination using this sign was FOOD MORE for an additional serving of fruit. Washoe's first recorded combination of signs was GIMME SWEET at approximately 21 months of age. That this happens to be close to the age when human children begin to combine words may, however, be more of a coincidence than a parallel in development, because the Gardners' second chimpanzee subject, Moja, combined signs (GIMME MORE) at the tender age of six months (Gardner and Gardner, 1975a). It might be noted that GIMME, which is one of the chimps' early combiners, is a gesture present in the repertoire of chimpanzees in the wild (van Lawick-Goodall, 1968).

In the months following their first conjoining of words, human children exhibit only a few kinds of semantic relations in their utterances. Brown (1973) lists ten structural meanings that account for 75% of the first two-word sentences in child speech. Four of these are operations of reference (nomination, notice, recurrence, and nonexistence) in which a constant term is joined with a variety of other words. The remaining six are relations (attribution, possession, location, agent-action, agent-object, and action-object) in which forms, such as verbs or nouns, are combined in several grammatical relationships. Table 3 lists all of these terms but one, NOTICE (to be discussed later), plus two other relations that occur somewhat less frequently in early child speech (person-affected dative, and dative of indirect object) along with utterances by Koko, Washoe, and deaf children which exemplify each relation.

It is evident that close parallels exist between Koko and the other subjects for each category. The correspondences extend to finer aspects of the data as well. For example, in both Stage I children and Koko, the possessive construction is limited to the expression of property-territory

Table 3. Early semantic relations expressed by gorilla Koko, chimpanzee Washoe, and deaf children

Relation	Koko	Washoe[a]	Deaf children[b]
Nomination	THAT CAT, THAT BIRD	THAT FOOD, THAT DRINK	COOKIES MORE, PLEASE MORE
Recurrence	MORE CEREAL, MORE POUR	MORE FRUIT, MORE GO	GOOD FINISHED
Nonexistence	ME CAN'T	ME CAN'T	(ME) ANGRY, WANT OPEN
Affected person, state	SORRY ME, ME GOOD	WASHOE SORRY	
Attributive	HOT POTATO, RED BERRY	DRINK RED, COMB BLACK	THAT PINK, RED SHOES
Genitive	KOKO PURSE, HAT MINE	BABY MINE, YOU HAT	BARRY TRAIN
Locative	GO BED, YOU OUT	GO FLOWER, LOOK OUT	DADDY WORK, (ME) GO HOME
Dative	GIVE-ME DRINK	GIVE-ME FLOWER	GIVE-ME ORANGE
Agent-action	YOU EAT, ME LISTEN	YOU DRINK, ROGER TICKLE	ME EAT, MAN WORK
Action-object	OPEN BOTTLE, CATCH ME	TICKLE WASHOE, OPEN BLANKET	EAT CRACKER, GRAB BOY
Agent-object	ALLIGATOR ME (CHASE)		DADDY SHOE (TAKE OFF)

[a] Examples drawn from Gardner and Gardner (1971, 1973).
[b] Examples drawn from Klima and Bellugi (1972) and Schlesinger and Meadow (1971).

338

and part-whole relationships. While examples of the former relation, such as those given in Table 3, are frequent, the expression of part-whole relations is much less common in children and in Koko. BABY-HEAD, signed simultaneously for the head of a doll, is one of the few examples found in our samples.

Koko has also made a number of the same mistakes in word usage as some children; for instance, she signed MORE CHEESE to request a first helping, and MORE SWING for another push on her trapeze. Her early use of MORE as a simple request form and her use of MORE in conjunction with verbs and even adjectives are patterns of overgeneralization reported in child language literature (Bloom, 1970; Brown, 1973).

Brown's (1973) finding that "about 75% of all utterances from all Stage I children studied . . . are classifiable as expressions of this small set of semantic roles or relations" (p. 40) is one that may hold true for young apes learning language as well. Gardner and Gardner (1971) analyzed the 294 different two-sign sequences produced by Washoe during a 26-month period when she was reported to be between two and four years old, and found that a similar set of semantic relations accounted for 78% of the total. Using the categories listed in Table 3 plus an appeal category (e.g., UP PLEASE and HURRY GO), analogous to that in the Gardner and Gardner (1971) scheme, the two-sign combinations produced by Koko during 40 hours of samples in 1974 (eight hours each in the months of January, February, June, November, and December) were analyzed. These 12 semantic relations accounted for 75% of the 719 two-sign combinations (or 451 distinct utterance types). Thus, Koko resembles closely both Washoe and human children with respect to the early expression of relational meanings.

Although Koko has produced uninterpretable strings (as do some children) most of her utterances are well suited to the situation. Koko's linguistic interchanges with her companions indicate her comprehension of their utterances and illustrate her appropriate use of signs in a given context, as seen in the following example:

K: YOU CHASE ME.
B: MY NAME IS BARBARA.
K: BARBARA CHASE.
K: YOU TICKLE ME.
B: WHERE?
K: TICKLE ARM.

Because sign language is used by Koko primarily in social situations in which she and her companions are cognizant of the context surrounding linguistic exchanges and have direct access to events and objects that serve as topics of conversation, it might be argued that her use of signs and our interpretation of them are dependent upon these extrinsic factors. That is, it is possible that Koko's use of sign language is not truly spontaneous, but elicited by cues and prompts that she receives from her companions. Double-blind tests were administered to evaluate Koko's performance under conditions in which she had to respond linguistically to a stimulus that she alone could see. Lacking funds for a more sophisticated method, I employed the box test devised by the Gardners. A plywood box, 12 inches high by 14 inches wide by 14 inches deep, one side of which was a removable Plexiglas window, was used. One experimenter baited the box with a random selection from a pool of objects representing 30 of the nouns in her vocabulary, and then covered the box with a piece of opaque material. A second experimenter, who did not know the contents of the box, stood behind it and when Koko started the trial by uncovering the box, asked her what she saw (Figure 4). This test situation required a fair amount of discipline, and curiously enough we found that, like Washoe, Koko's interest and cooperation could be secured for no more than five trials a day and two sessions per week. Her methods of avoiding the task were varied—she would either respond to all objects

Figure 4.   Correct response. TIGER is a correct response given by Koko on a trial of the "box test." [Cohn]

with the same sign, refuse to respond at all, or regress to an earlier pattern of asking to have the box opened.

Despite the difficulties, Koko's responses on these tests were correct about 60% of the time. On a series of tests administered when Koko was four years old (September, 1975), she gave the correct response on 31 of 50 trials (62%). This compares favorably with the level of performance reported for Washoe (54%).

Koko's errors on the box test were of four basic types (in order of frequency).

1. Requests to have the box opened (e.g., KEY BOX and KEY OPEN)
2. Conceptually related errors in which the response was for another item in the same class of objects (e.g., CANDY or CRACKER)
3. Perseverative errors (e.g., CLOWN on two trials succeeding one on which it was the correct response).
4. Formally related errors in which the sign given was similar in articulation to the sign for the correct response (e.g., CLOWN for FLOWER).

On one interesting trial, Koko frowned, then signed CAT RED when the box contained a red stereoscopic viewer. Upon examination, I found that the slide in the viewer depicted a lion. Possibly, this was an unrelated error; alternatively, she may have been recalling what she had last seen in the viewer. (Incidentally, this response was scored as an error.) Gardner and Gardner (1971) comment that many of Washoe's errors in the double-blind tests of her nouns were errors of the second type, that is, conceptually related.

In addition to the information such tests yield on categorization and performance errors, they also show that Koko's appropriate use of signs is not dependent upon cueing from her teachers and companions, but is the result of an ability to retrieve and produce linguistic symbols spontaneously.

The usefulness of the form of double-blind test is limited, however. Only object names can be tested and the procedure is expensive in terms of time and personnel required, and often fails to elicit the gorilla's cooperation.

Other techniques, including the use of videotaped session in which experimenters with no knowledge of sign language are employed and the presentation of animate relational stimuli on film, are being devised and implemented.

It is also true that when the response required in a test situation is verbal (as opposed to forced choice) the probabilities of the subject emitting the correct response by chance or as a result of cueing of some kind by the experimenter are quite small. For example, the probability of the gorilla uttering the appropriate sign by chance, spontaneously, or in response to a question, is about one in 245, given a vocabulary of 245 signs. The chances of her uttering a correct string of signs by accident are even more remote. Therefore, I believe that there is even better evidence of Koko's ability to retrieve, manipulate, and combine linguistic symbols appropriately in our records of her day to day signing under completely naturalistic conditions.

These records take the form of repeated samples of Koko's signed utterances which have been routinely recorded since week 15 of the project. Initially, all linguistic exchanges between Koko and her companions, along with notes on the nonlinguistic contest, were recorded during a 4- to 5-hour period several times a week. As the gorilla began to produce increasing numbers of utterances, a decision was made to limit sampling to 8 to 10 hours per month. Each hour of the day between 9 o'clock and 5 o'clock was sampled once each month, so that Koko's signing in the spectrum of her activities during the day would be represented. Assignment of sampling hours to days of the month was done on a random basis. After the 40th week, these samples were recorded on audio tape cassettes.

In order that a more accurate picture of the pace and volume of Koko's signing during the course of a day would be obtained, one 8-hour long sample was taken once each month in addition to the eight 1-hour samples from month 12 of the project to the present. Videotaped samples (30 to 90 minutes per month) have been taken since the 16th month (November, 1973). These will be invaluable in the analysis of certain subtle characteristics of her signed utterances, such as form, intonation, and segmentation, that only a visual record can fully capture.

The following is an excerpt from an eight-hour sample taken at the end of last month (January, 31, 1977, 9:00 a.m.):

(It is time for Koko's breakfast which normally consists of a square of rice bread and a glass of milk.)

P: WHAT DO YOU WANT?
K: APPLE DRINK.
P: HOW ABOUT . . . (Penny is about to suggest her usual rice bread but Koko interrupts, signing)
K: APPLE.
P: WHAT TIME IS IT? WHAT TIME? (Penny wants to elicit a new sign in her vocabulary, BREAKFAST. Koko is persistently requesting some apple juice—her favorite beverage which is not a usual breakfast item.)
K: DRINK.
P: BREAKFAST.
K: BREAKFAST.

P: O.K., YOU WANT BREAKFAST?

K: GOOD HAPPY.

P: WHAT DO YOU WANT FOR BREAKFAST? (A rhetorical question—Penny is not really going to give her a choice, and gets out rice bread, saying [vocally] as she does so:)

P: I've got something good for gorillas . . . right here's breakfast. (Penny offers rice bread to Koko.)

K: BOTTLE THERE APPLE. (Koko indicates a bottle of apple juice in the refrigerator.)

P: KOKO? (Penny, who does not intend to alter the breakfast menu, firmly closes the refrigerator door, gets the rice bread out of the bag.)

K: MEAN . . . (Koko had never before used this sign and Penny did not comprehend her utterance at the time, but recorded its configuration. Koko seemed to be trying to clarify her own intentions.)

P: WHAT'S THIS?

K: BOTTLE APPLE . . . NICE THERE (points to her palm).

P: KOKO, YOU ARE SIGNING WRONG THINGS. (Penny wants Koko to sign for the rice bread but Koko rephrases her request.)

K: PLEASE MILK, PLEASE ME LIKE DRINK APPLE . . . BOTTLE.

P: HOW ABOUT FIRST BREAKFAST?

K: BREAKFAST EAT SOME COOKIE EAT. (Now Koko has either made an error or another unacceptable request—gorillas, like children, do not get sweets for breakfast.)

P: NO, NO, BREAD. (Penny molds BREAD and gives it to Koko. A glass of milk will complete Koko's breakfast. Penny has a glass of water out for powdered milk; Koko touches it and, then, the container of milk powder.)

K: HURRY DRINK MILK.

P: YES, PENNY MAKE?

K: GLASS ALL MILK. (Perhaps Koko is suggesting that Penny put all the milk powder in her glass. Penny molds MAKE and makes it.)

P: O.K., NOW WHAT?

K: TIME MILK. (Koko is allowed to drink the glass of milk. Koko, across the counter, hands Penny the empty glass and looks at a new doll a few feet away.)

K: HURRY GIMME.

P: WHAT? (Koko reaches for the new doll, but Penny stops her from getting it.)

K: BABY COME-ON HAPPY. (Penny picks up the doll.)

P: THIS IS BABY ALIVE.

K: LIKE BABY NEW.
P: YES! (Penny gives the doll to Koko.)
K: GOOD HAPPY. (Koko lies down on floor, the doll in her arms signing:)
K: SLEEP. (Koko seems to have forgotten all about the apple juice . . .)

In addition to these comprehensive samples, I have also been gathering data on Koko's responses to questions. This aspect of the study is particularly important, because it can provide information on Koko's understanding of abstract concepts, such as causality and time (abilities so far not well documented in apes) as well as evidence for a grasp of major sentence constituents, an ability demonstrated by Washoe (Gardner and Gardner, 1975). Again, desiring to obtain data from which direct comparisons between Koko and Washoe could be made, I employed a methodology similar to that of the Gardners'. In order to examine the full spectrum of Koko's abilities, however, I included a wider variety of question frames including Why and How, and two additional modes, spoken English and simultaneous communication, or the use of sign accompanied by speech.

This study is still in progress and will be the subject of a future paper, but it introduces the second major point I wish to make: although similarities in approach and methodology were important for comparative purposes, from its inception, Project Koko diverged from Project Washoe in a number of significant respects.

1.   Deaf personnel have been employed as teachers and companions for the gorilla from the beginning of the project.
2.   The use of spoken English in the presence of Koko has been allowed and the methodology has provided for samples and tests of the gorilla's production and comprehension under conditions in which the two modes (sign and English) are separated.
3.   Complete records of the gorilla's signed utterances along with a description of the context in which they occurred have been kept so that analyses of sign order can be performed.
4.   No attempt has been made to limit the size or control the content of Koko's vocabulary.
5.   Secondary examinations of the gorilla's intelligence featuring the use of standard infant and preschool intelligence tests and Piagetian techniques have been carried out on a regular basis, thus providing data on her cognitive abilities directly comparable in a quantitative way to those available on human children and apes.

I made no attempt to eliminate spoken language from the gorilla's environment, in part because the conditions of the facility housing of the project for the first year, San Francisco Children's Zoo nursery, precluded the possibility of such control. Instead, I decided to turn this situation to advantage by adopting a method known as simultaneous communication, or the use of American Sign Language accompanied by spoken English. I provided Koko with native signers as teachers and companions on a day-to-day basis and used sign language as the primary mode of communication because it would yield data most directly comparable to that available on the language acquisition of both child and chimpanzee. Speech was used as a secondary mode of communication. Early research had shown that, although apes could learn to produce fewer than a half dozen spoken words, even after years of training, the animals' comprehension skills were in all cases far superior to their production skills. Koko had lived for a time in the home of the Director of the Children's Zoo, and, when I began to work with her, she was already responsive to several spoken words. We hoped that Koko would comprehend a considerable amount of English, even though she probably would not come to produce speech to a significant extent. Furthermore, it seemed possible that the redundancy of information conveyed by the two modes might facilitate learning (Ferster, 1964). In short, the use of simultaneous communication would allow for the study of any receptive and productive skills the gorilla might develop in the vocal as well as the manual mode and for the possibility of the transfer of information between modes. In addition, this method of teaching might allow an evaluation of the validity of claims such as the following: "apparently it is the child's innate capacity for auditory analysis that distinguishes him from the chimpanzee" (Hebb, Lambert, and Tucker, 1974, p. 153).

The gorilla's responsiveness to spoken requests in our daily interaction with her suggested that she did possess a considerable capacity for complex auditory analysis. She would often surprise us by translating English words and phrases into signs during the course of the day. For instance, once a visitor asked Koko's companion what the sign for GOOD was. Before an answer was given, Koko demonstrated the sign for GOOD to the visitor. On another occasion, Koko's companion was making her a sandwich and asked if she wanted a taste of butter (in English only, since her hands were occupied) and Koko responded TASTE BUTTER. She will also frequently respond to spoken suggestions to put refuse into the garbage, kiss a companion, find a towel, etc.

The problem with evidence of this type is that most speech to the gorilla (as to children) occurs in situations in which a good guess on her part will yield the correct interpretation of a sentence and/or an appropriate linguistic response.

To circumvent this difficulty, I administered a standardized test to assess the extent of Koko's comprehension of English, sign, and simultaneous communication early in 1976, when Koko was four and a half years old. The test, "The Assessment of Children's Language Comprehension" (Foster, Gidden, and Stark 1973), consisted of 40 large cards, 6 inches by 14 inches on which were printed four to five black-and-white line or silhouette drawings representing objects, attributes, or relationships between objects (cf. Figure 5). The first 10 cards, used to test single vocabulary items, depicted five objects each for a total of 50 vocabulary items. The remaining 30 cards tested comprehension of phrases, consisting of from two to four critical elements (e.g., little clown; little clown jumping; happy little clown jumping). Ten items at each of these three levels of difficulty were administered under three conditions (sign only, English only, and sign and English simultaneously) for a total of 90 trials. All trials were recorded on videotape and the sign-only and voice-only trials were alternated (so that these two conditions were tested simultaneously) and administered blind. That is, a second experimenter independently preselected the target picture for each trial, and compiled a list of items corresponding to the numbered cards (which were arranged in order of level of difficulty). The person administering the test followed the list without looking at the cards (which were kept face down until trial time) and presented them in such a way that only the video camera and the gorilla could see the stimulus pictures. After Koko had responded by pointing to one of the pictures, the experimenter looked at the card to determine whether or not her response was correct and rewarded her accordingly.

Koko performed significantly better than chance under all three conditions and at all levels of difficulty (cf. Tables 4 and 5). I had

Figure 5.   Assessment of Children's Language Comprehension test. Examples of four (top) and five (bottom) critical element items from The Assessment of Children's Language Comprehension test. (From Rochana Foster, Jane Gidden, and Joel Stark, 1973. Courtesy of Consulting Psychologists Press, Inc., Palo Alto, California.)

Table 4.   Koko's performance on the Assessment of Children's Language
Comprehension test

Number of critical elements	Chance	Sign + Voice (%)	Sign (%)	Voice (%)	Total (%)
Vocabulary—one (50 items)	20	72			
Two (e.g., happy lady)	25	70	50	50	56.7
Three (e.g., happy lady sleeping)	25	50	30	50	43.3
Four (e.g., happy little girl jumping)	20	50	50	30	43.3
Totals (two, three and four elements)		56.7	43.3	43.3	47.7

anticipated that comprehension might be enhanced under the
simultaneous communication condition. Although there was a trend in
this direction, it was not statistically significant. The data do clearly indicate that Koko comprehends novel statements in sign language and
spoken English with equal facility. An unexpected finding was that
Koko's performance at all levels of difficulty was quite similar. She
responded correctly to 43% of the 30 most difficult items (four critical
elements), a level of performance that matches the norm for educa-
tionally handicapped children four to five years old. Her performance on
the two critical element items was slightly better than her performance

Table 5.   Results of Chi-square tests on Koko's level of
performance on the Assessment of Children's Language
Comprehension Test

Variable	χ^2 (1)	Significance level
Sign + Voice (2, 3, and 4 critical elements)	18.6	0.001
Sign only (2, 3, and 4 elements)	6.7	0.01
Voice only (2, 3, and 4 elements)	6.7	0.01
Two critical elements (all conditions)	16.0	0.001
Three critical elements (all conditions)	5.4	0.025
Four critical elements (all conditions)	10.2	0.005
Sign + Voice versus sign only (all levels)	2.1	ns
Two versus three critical elements (all conditions)	2.1	ns

on items at the next two levels of difficulty, but not significantly so. This seems to indicate that some factor other than complexity of the phrase was operating to limit her performance. Evidence from her behavior during testing sessions indicated that motivation may have been the limiting factor. From session to session and even from trial to trial, Koko showed wide variations in her level of motivation to do the task. Her best performance was obtained on the first phase of the test (simultaneous communication, two critical elements). The gorilla's level of motivation was also highest at this stage—the test was novel and she quickly completed all 10 problems in one session. In the subsequent phases of the experiment, her performance frequently fell below chance in sessions consisting of more than five trials. After responding correctly on the first few trials of a session, Koko would lapse into a series of consecutive errors. She seemed to use incorrect responses and/or responses without considering each of the alternatives as ways of signalling that she had had enough testing.[3]

I have encountered this difficulty when repeating other standardized tests—once Koko is familiar with the materials and the novelty is gone, she may either refuse to do the task or her performance may deteriorate. The standard laboratory phenomena of learning to learn and practice effects would lead one to expect improvement under these conditions. Paradoxically, it may be that an exposition of the gorilla's intellectual capacities will prove to be a test of our ingenuity in devising stimulating new tasks.

A number of innovations have marked Koko's progress over the past four and a half years: She has invented signs and names for novel objects; she talks to herself; she engages in imaginative play using sign; and she has used language to lie, to express her emotions, and to refer to things displaced in time and space.

The first evidence of her innovative ability occurred very early in the study. Koko produced gestures which closely resembled the signs for COME or GIVE-ME, GO, HURRY, and UP. These were distinctive, because they appeared without direct training at a time when the great majority of Koko's signs were being acquired by molding. Because these same gestures have been noted in observations of other young gorillas in captive conditions, who have not been exposed to sign language, they

---

[3] One other interesting source of errors, not due simply to inability to respond correctly, and perhaps due to her boredom with the task, was the following. In some instances, Koko would attend to the instructed phrase, and even after correctly translating or imitating the signs in the instruction, sign about another object pictured on the card, and then point to the item containing that object. For example, when given the instruction, find BALL UNDER TABLE, Koko signed CAT and pointed to the cat under the table. Making up her own rules?

may be part of the gorilla's natural repertoire of gestures.[4] Other gestures which resemble signs, but which have not been observed in untrained gorillas, have been spontaneously produced and used productively by Koko. These signs seem to qualify as true "inventions," for they are not standard forms in Ameslan. Examples are: BITE, TICKLE, STETHO-SCOPE, and DARN.

The sign for BITE is done by clamping one clawed hand onto the side of the other hand held flat, palm down. Koko's sign for BITE (open mouth contacting the side of the hand held palm down) originated quite dramatically one afternoon: Koko had play-bitten Ron, one of her companions, just a little too hard and once too often and he bit her back on the knuckles. Taken by surprise, and perhaps even a little shocked, she came to me for comfort. When I asked, WHAT HAPPENED? Koko cast a woeful glance at the offender and placed her mouth on her hand—the meaning was unmistakable. She has continued to use this form of the sign appropriately (even in imitation of our correctly formed version of the sign) ever since.

Since there is no Ameslan sign for TICKLE, I adopted the sign used by the Gardners, which is executed by drawing the index finger across the back of the hand. Though her companions have repeatedly modeled and molded this sign, Koko has consistently used a more iconic gesture of drawing her index finger across her underarm which I have come to accept as a variant of the TICKLE sign with a perhaps more logical place of articulation.

I learned the sign for STETHOSCOPE (index finger of one hand to the ear; the other hand in a fist on the chest) only after Koko invented her own (in which she placed an index finger to each ear).

One interesting invention of Koko's is a sign done by hitting the back of a tight fist onto a surface or object (cf. Figure 6). This gesture closely resembles a natural killing motion observed in chimpanzees but which has not been reported in gorillas in the wild (as far as I know). Koko uses the sign to express herself in situations in which her goals have been frustrated in some way or in which she seems annoyed by something, and I have translated it as DARN. For instance, she signed DARN BIRD BIRD, while a bird outside was giving a cry resembling a distress call for several minutes (it seemed like hours—I had tried and failed to locate the bird).

Two other gestures invented by Koko are less clearly iconic. One can only be defined as meaning "walk-up-my-back-with-your-fingers" (both hands are placed palm up on the floor, behind the back). This ges-

---

[4] However, Dian Fossey (personal communication) has not observed the "hurry" gesture in free-living mountain gorillas.

Figure 6. The sign of DARN. DARN is Koko's invented expletive. It is performed by hitting the back of a hand in a clenched fist onto a surface or object. Note the facial gesture accompanying the sign—lips drawn in, mouth compressed—which is a natural sign of annoyance in both gorillas and humans. [Cohn]

ture is not often used in conjuction with other signs and has not been included in Koko's vocabulary. The other gesture had me completely mystified for some time. It is executed by quickly stroking the index finger across the lips and is preceded or followed by a noun or the pointing gesture, THAT. It is not directed to companions but occurs when

Koko is looking through magazines, playing by herself with toys, nesting, or noticing an object in passing. When forced to give it an English equivalent, I called it NOTE, and later realized its resemblance to the construction "hi" and noun, found by Bloom (1970), which is used by children not as a greeting but in taking notice of the presence of an object.

Another creative aspect of Koko's use of sign language is her practice of varying the place of articulation of several action signs, such as TICKLE, PINCH, or PICK, to convey slight differences in meaning. (See the characteristic of directionality mentioned by Peng, 1978.) At times, she will sign TICKLE on her inner thigh instead of her underarm or on both underarms (as a kind of emphasis). The location of the PINCH sign is highly variable: It may be done on her leg, stomach, arm, neck, etc., rather than on the back of the hand, indicating exactly where she wants to be pinched. The sign, PICK, is properly done on the index finger, but Koko signs it on her teeth when she needs help dislodging food stuck between her teeth, or as a request for dental floss. In addition, Koko has signed SCRATCH on her back (to request a back scratching) and on her finger (when confronted with a recently inflicted scratch wound on her companion's finger), as well as on the back of the hand, which is the correct form.

These variations are used consistently, are readily interpretable, and seem to be deliberate and efficient alterations made by Koko to express her desires. I have observed another use of sign with this simultaneous aspect (cf. the characteristic of simultaneity in Peng's article) not only in Koko's, but also in my own signing, which seems fortuitous.

Two distinct signs are merged into one by combining the place of articulation of one with the hand configuration of the other. An example produced by Koko was CHUCK-TOILET—a C done on the nose. The hand configuration was that of the proper name but the location was that of the toilet sign. This occurred after Chuck had emptied her potty. I have done similar gestures unintentionally, usually when I am signing rapidly (e.g., APPLE-DRINK with the drink sign done on the side of the face instead of at the mouth). This phenomenon resembles Hockett's (1959) description of blending, a process exemplified by the word "slithy," a combination of "lithe" and "slimy."[5] Hockett stated that such words can be created by this process without conscious planning, and hypothesized that the roots of productivity lie in such forms; ". . . in

---

[5] Note that there is a significant difference between Patterson's description of the combination of two signs, such as CHUCK-TOILET and APPLE-DRINK, and Hockett's description of the combination of "lithe" and "slimy" for "slithy." The former is a simultaneous combination, in the sense described by Peng (1978), whereas the latter is a linear combination—[AAAS Editor].

[our] prehuman . . . ancestors . . . [when] a few blends were communicatively successful . . . the closed circle was broken and productivity was on its way" (1959, p. 37). Signs such as PREFER may have originated in this way—the place of articulation is that of the sign for LIKE and the hand configuration is that of the sign for BETTER.

In addition to creating new signs, Koko invents names for new objects in her environment, some of which are strikingly apt. For example, she called a ring a FINGER BRACELET, a zebra a WHITE TIGER, a mask an EYE HAT, and a Pinocchio doll an ELEPHANT BABY. Koko also spontaneously comments to her human companions about occurrences in her surroundings. For example, she signed LISTEN QUIET when an alarm clock stopped ringing in the next room, and SEE BIRD when she saw a picture of a crane in a stereo viewer.

Not all of Koko's utterances are directed to her human companions, however. She has been observed talking to herself, her dolls, various animals, and to another gorilla. Her habit of talking to herself, that is, using signs meaningfully but directing them to no one but herself, has increased in frequency over time and the utterances have gradually increased in length as well. Often, while nesting in clothes or blankets and toys, she will stop arranging the nest momentarily and sign THAT RED (indicating a piece of red cloth), or ME SLEEP and lie down in the nest. Frequently, while looking through magazines, she will comment to herself about what she sees; for example, THAT TOOTHBRUSH and THAT NUT. Recently, I noticed Koko signing THAT KOKO to a picture of King Kong depicted on a bowl I bought for her at the supermarket. At times, Koko seems embarrassed when her companions notice that she is signing to herself, especially when it involves her dolls and animal toys. The other day, while Koko was signing KISS, after kissing her alligator puppet, I caught her eye. She abruptly stopped signing and turned away. At times, when her companions have been otherwise occupied, Koko has taken her toy gorillas into the room furthest from them and engaged in sign by herself while playing. One day, she seemed to structure an imaginary social situation between two gorilla dolls. She placed the gorillas before her and signed BAD, BAD, while looking at the pink gorilla, then, KISS to the blue gorilla. Next, she signed CHASE TICKLE and hit the two of them together (making them play?), then joined in and wrestled them both at once. When the play bout ended, she signed GOOD GORILLA, GOOD, GOOD. At this point, Koko noticed that Cathy, her teacher, was watching and left the dolls.

This observation and others like it have strengthened my expectation that, given the opportunity, Koko would sign to other gorillas and perhaps even teach them. In his recent review, Mounin (1976) asserted that Washoe did not have language, because she did not use it to lie or to convey what she had learned to her conspecifics. There is preliminary evidence that Koko does both of these things.

For the past several months, Koko has had contact with Michael, a three-and-a-half-year-old male gorilla with whom she now shares the project trailer. Almost as soon as they met, the gorillas were signing COME to each other through the fencing that separates their rooms. During their play sessions together, Koko frequently signs to Michael. CHASE is a common request and Michael, who has just acquired this sign, will often respond by pursuing Koko. She has also asked him to do such things as COME TICKLE-FOOT. One day, she signed ME HIT YOU, then, followed up her threat by initiating a play-fighting bout with a few blows. Michael has used his small but growing vocabulary of signs to communicate with Koko as well.

Although it is difficult to empirically demonstrate intent, Koko has made statements in response to questions about her misbehavior which appear to be lies. For instance, once she was caught in the act of trying to break a window screen with a chopstick she had stolen from the silverware drawer. When asked what she was doing, Koko replied SMOKE MOUTH and proceeded to place the stick in her mouth as though she was smoking it (this is a game we engage in frequently with sticks and other cigarette-shaped objects). On another occasion, Koko, who had just tipped the scales at 90 pounds, sat on the kitchen sink and it sank about 2 inches. Not knowing how it had happened, I asked Koko, DID YOU DO THAT? and Koko signed KATE THERE BAD, pointing to the sink. Kate, my deaf assistant who had witnessed the incident, defended herself by explaining the situation.

Koko's apparent prevarications usually take place under interrogation at the scene of the crime, immediately following the misbehavior. However, Koko will often respond to questions about such incidents long after their occurrence, indicating that she is capable of using language to refer to events and objects removed in time and space. This ability, known as displacement, is considered to be a fundamental characteristic of human language (Hockett, 1960; Bronowski and Bellugi, 1970). For example, the day after Koko bit a companion, I asked her WHAT DID YOU DO YESTERDAY? She replied, WRONG, WRONG. WHAT WRONG? I queried. BITE. Data being collected in the question-answer study give further evidence of this ability:

Q: WHAT DID I SAY YOU COULD HAVE AFTER BREAKFAST?

A: COOKIE (An accurate response; the promise was made about an hour earlier.)

Q: DO YOU REMEMBER WHAT HAPPENED THIS MORNING?

A: PENNY CLEAN (Not the answer I expected, but again accurate. Koko had been upset by something prior to my arrival that morning and had made a mess of her room. It took me the better part of an hour to clean it.)

The following conversation took place three days after the event discussed:

P: WHAT DID YOU DO TO P?
K: BITE.
P: YOU ADMIT IT? (Previously, Koko had referred to the bite as a scratch.)
K: SORRY BITE SCRATCH (P shows Koko the mark on her hand—it really does resemble a scratch.)
K: WRONG BITE.
P: WHY BITE?
K: BECAUSE MAD. (A few moments later, it occurred to P to ask Koko:)
P: WHY MAD?
K: DON'T-KNOW.

The preceding example is noteworthy, because Koko makes reference to a past emotional state, her anger, without actually experiencing it at the moment. This is a clear indication that she is able to separate affect from the context of her utterances, another important feature of displacement.

There is other evidence that Koko can reflect upon and report about her feelings. She has spontaneously informed her companions that she is happy or sad or tired and regularly answers questions, such as HOW ARE YOU? and HOW DO YOU FEEL? The gorilla has even reported about her fears: Koko has always been repulsed by lizard-like creatures and toys. One day, several hours after a play session in which she avoided direct contact with the gorilla, Michael, I asked her if she was afraid of him. She made no response, so I rephrased the question.

P: WHAT ARE YOU AFRAID OF?
K: AFRAID ALLIGATOR.

What can be concluded from this brief and partial overview of Project Koko? As an early and partial answer to this question, I would like to reformulate a statement made by Noam Chomsky in 1968, by substituting the word *primate* for "human" and the phrase *linguistic communication* for "unique human possession":

> ... There is no better or more promising way to explore the essential and distinctive properties of primate intelligence than through the detailed (com-

parative) investigation of the structure (and functioning) of . . . linguistic communication.

ACKNOWLEDGMENTS

I would like to acknowledge the San Francisco Zoo for making the gorilla Koko available and Professors Richard C. Atkinson and Karl H. Pribram for their invaluable support. I am especially grateful to Ronald H. Cohn and Barbara F. Hiller for their continued assistance with the project.

REFERENCES

Bloom, L. 1970. Language Development: Form and Function in Emerging Grammars. The MIT Press, Cambridge, Mass.
Bowerman, M. 1973. Early Syntactic Development: A Cross-linguistic Study with Special Reference to Finnish. Cambridge University Press, Cambridge, England.
Brown, R. 1973. A First Language. Harvard University Press, Cambridge, Mass.
Bronowski, J. S., and Bellugi, U. 1970. Language, name, and concept. Science 168:699–773.
Clark, E. V. 1973. What's in a word? On the child's acquisition of semantics in his first language. In T. E. Moore (ed.), Cognitive Development and the Acquisition of Language. Academic Press, New York.
Ferster, C. G. 1964. Arithmetic behavior in chimpanzees. Sci. Am. 210:98–104.
Foster, R., Gidden, J. T., and Stark, J. 1973. Assessment of children's language comprehension. Consulting Psychologists Press, Inc., California.
Fouts, R. S. 1973. Acquisition and testing of gestural signs in four young chimpanzees. Science 180:978–980.
Gardner, R. A., and Gardner, B. T. 1969. Teaching sign language to a chimpanzee. Science 165:644–672.
Gardner, R. A., and Gardner, B. T. 1971. Two-way communication with an infant chimpanzee. In A. M. Shrier and F. Stollnitz (eds.), Behavior of Nonhuman Primates, Vol. 4. Academic Press, New York.
Gardner, R. A., and Gardner, B. T. 1972. Communication with a young chimpanzee: Washoe's vocabulary. In R. Chauvin (ed.), Modeles Animaux du Comportement Humaine, 198:241–264. C.N.R.S., Paris.
Gardner, R. A., and Gardner, B. T. 1975a. Early signs of language in child and chimpanzee. Science 187:752–753.
Gardner, R. A., and Gardner, B. T. 1975b. Evidence for sentence constituents in the early utterances of child and chimpanzee. J. Exp. Psychol. 104:244–267.
Greenfield, P. M., and Smith, J. H. 1976. The Structure of Communication in Early Language Development. Academic Press, New York.
Hebb, D. O., Lambert, W. E., and Tucker, G. R. 1974. A DMZ in the language war. In J. B. Maas (ed.), Readings in Psychology Today, pp. 152–157. Ziff Davis, California.
Hockett, C. F. 1959. Animal "language" and human language. In J. N. Spuhler (ed.), The Evolution of Man's Capacity for Culture, pp. 32–38. Wayne State University Press, Detroit.
Hockett, C. J. 1960. Origin of speech. Sci. Am. 203:88–96.
Klima, E. S., and Bellugi, U. 1972. The signs of language in child and chimp. In

T. Alloway, L. Krames, and P. Pliner (eds.), Communication and Affects. Academic Press, New York.

Knoblock, H., and Pasamanick, B. 1959. The development of adaptive behavior in an infant gorilla. J. Comp. Physiolog. Psychol. 52:699–704.

Mounin, G. 1976. Language, communication, chimpanzees. Curr. Anthropol. 17:1–21.

Nelson, K. 1973. Some evidence for the cognitive primacy of categorization and its functional basis. Merrill-Palmer Q. 19:21–40.

Olson, J. R. 1972. A case for the use of sign language to stimulate language development during the critical period for learning in a congenitally deaf child. Am. Ann. Deaf 117:397–400.

Peng, F. C. C. 1978. Sign Language and Language Acquisition—New Dimensions in Comparative Pedolinguistics. Westview Press, Boulder, Col.

Schlesinger, H. S., and Meadow, K. 1971. Deafness and Mental Health: A Developmental Approach. Langley Porter Neuropsychiatric Institute, University of California at San Francisco.

van Lawick-Goodall, J. 1968. A preliminary report on expressive movements and communication in the Gombe Stream chimpanzee. In P. C. Jay (ed.), Primates: Studies in Adaptation and Variability, pp. 313–374. Holt, Rinehart & Winston, New York.

Yerkes, R. M. 1925. Almost Human. Century, New York.

Section

V

Application of
Primate Language
Strategies
to Children

Editors' Introduction

Two chapters in this section are based on the work of David Premack. The authors, Carrier (1974 [Chapter 17]) and Hodges and Deich (Chapter 18) are acquainted with Premack and have discussed their work with him. Nevertheless, prior to the personal exchanges, they had already worked out most of their extrapolations from his published work. This fact is mentioned to point out that they were able to make their plans (including the alterations that make the program suitable for retarded children) from Premack's published explanations.

Premack's information (1970 [Chapter 12, this volume]) makes it clear that his language functions involve cognitive parameters reduced to discrete symbolic events that can be defined and manipulated. The discrete events are exemplars, i.e., words, sentences, questions, metalinguistics (using language to teach language), class concepts, the copula, quantifiers, and the logical connective, *if-then*.

SYMBOL PROGRAMS

Such functions cover a range of semantic classes and represent a fascinating accomplishment in primate research. Nevertheless, the list of exemplars does not constitute a full language program for children. Neither of the application programs are literal replications of Premack's program. For instance, Carrier elected to construct and teach a seven-unit horizontal sentence made from plastic forms similar to those used by Premack. His plan differs markedly from Premack's. Although it specifies the symbol functions with the same visual-motor response mode, it involves a selective rather than a productive response. The most complete version of Carrier's work is now available as Non-SLIP (Nonspeech Language Initiation Program) (Carrier and Peak, 1975).

Hodges and Deich (Chapter 18) also use Premack's modes of symbol designation. They, too, validated the procedures with low functioning retarded children. Although the two instructional programs (Carrier and Hodges and Deich) are structured and sequenced differently, the effects are remarkably similar. Many retarded children are able to learn these symbol programs, to initiate spontaneous vocalization, and to imitate the trainer's speech patterns and intonations (also see Kuntz, Carrier, and Hollis, 1978).

Fortunately, each study provides extensive explanations about the design of the programs and how the authors overcame the problems encountered in creating them. These explanations can serve as helpful suggestions for clinicians and applied researchers who are making their own extrapolations and designs.

The applications from the Language Analog (LANA) Project reported by Parkel and Smith (Chapter 19) have interesting implications for planning feasible symbol tasks for low functioning, nonverbal children. The Parkel and Smith applications have apparatus, lexicon, computer circuits, and communication board format similar to those used in the experimental project, but the instructional mode does differ markedly from the instruction with Lana. The teacher sits with the retarded child and uses verbal instructions (as well as the visual symbol board) in communicating with the child. The child responds by indicating appropriate visual symbols (lexigrams) on the board. It is apparent that the Language Analog (LANA) Project is literally applied to retarded children, except for modifications necessary to function with the child in a one-on-one instructional arrangement.

Apes and children, although apparently similar in their ability to process visual-motor tasks and to handle strings of visually presented symbols, are different in the range of concepts they have available for creating symbol repertoires. They do not share the same environments and do not acquire the same knowledge. Although each may learn the same referential symbol behavior as indicated by a task series, the ecology and the experience ranges are not similar. Children and chimpanzees are not destined for similar life roles. For this reason the lexicons that the two species need for functional communication vary greatly. In addition to the semantic variance, there is also a great difference in the grammar a child needs for polite discourse as compared to the correlational grammar Lana used in communicating in her environment. This point highlights the pragmatic differences between the two species. The social context that a child encounters, and in which he is asked to communicate, is not predicted by the chimp language models of Premack and Rumbaugh. What then do their language models offer for human programming?

First, the models are based upon a functional analysis of language and upon an operational system for instructing the primate to acquire the functions. The analyses involve the nonspeech language mode, the form of the symbol system, the referent functions to be symbolized, and the task difficulties in the instructional program relative to the dispositions of the organism. It is apparent that a nonvocal child must be approached functionally and the resulting analyses must answer similar questions. The applications from ape programs consider the what and the how of language instruction. Extrapolations should produce a fit with the human conditions under which these categories of instruction will be performed.

However, considerations of practical alterations might also address the questions of *why* and *when*. The Premack and the Rumbaugh models can be used as speech activation systems. There is evidence that the task sequences in their models do indeed evoke conventional speech as well as capabilities for performing nonspeech symbol functions. Very probably, too, they assist the child, as well as the chimp, to make symbolic relationships between the physical, object-event world and the visual symbol forms. However, even if one accepts these possibilities, one still does not have a full answer to the *why* and the *when* of language.

SIGNING MODELS

There is evidence that primates, in the wild, use signs, both vocal and gestural, to communicate with each other. The evidence of gestural signs led the Gardners to plan a manual sign program (using Ameslan) for Washoe. The same insight led Fouts to continue the signing program in his work at the University of Oklahoma. Fouts is the first to consider a common signing model for both apes and children. His analysis suggests that signing enables the nonspeaking organism to control the environment and thus to escape a condition of helplessness. The implication of this approach is that ASL is a functional communication system that either an ape or child can use in expressing, requesting, or controlling. If so, this system suggests an answer to the question of *why* or *what for*. The primary reason for a handicapped child to use language is to communicate. Fouts provides several explanations relative to the functional utility of ASL as a communication system. The system is flexible, it is available for use in various contexts, and it is easy to learn and use. It also meets the critical tests of a functional, syntactic language.

Wulz and Hollis (Chapter 20) provide supporting evidence for the functional nature of manual signs by building such a system into a reading program. The gestures are presented simultaneously with the auditory labels. Their plan is to evoke gestural signs or equivalent communication board responses with established equivalences among sets of symbols, production labels, and referents. They find that equivalences between two linguistic media can be established with no direct training, and that the equivalences between auditory and visual media can be established by contiguous presentation.

The work of Wulz and Hollis, with the work of Fouts, Couch, and O'Neil (Chapter 15, this volume), and Patterson (1978 [Chapter 16, this volume]), suggests that the intervention specialist can vary the input and the response modes without disrupting the symbolization learning of the child.

SUMMARY

The analysis of the functional advantages of different nonspeech modes of language is presented in more detail in the next volume of this series, *Nonspeech Language and Communication: Analysis and Intervention.* An analysis of the contributions of work with the apes, however, is limited primarily to this volume.

A tentative summary of the contributions of language research with apes to language interventions with children may now be presented.

1. The analysis, planning, designing, and implementation steps in primate research (technologically and experimentally) can be employed in developing language programs for handicapped children.
2. Functional language, including linguistic structures and functions, can be taught with various nonspeech symbol forms.
3. Both apes and children are able to produce generative forms and functions with nonspeech symbol repertoires.
4. Both apes and children demonstrate concept equivalence across stimulus modes.
5. The research with apes is strongly data oriented and provides explicit instructions for designing the operational maintenance.
6. The research with apes highlights both the similarities and the differences encountered in designing programs for the human child. Perhaps the similarities are greatest in symbol mapping and in referential language exchanges. They differ greatly in regard to the semantic range of, and pragmatic designs required for, a fully functional language.

REFERENCES

Carrier, J. K. 1974. Application of functional analysis and a nonspeech response mode to teaching language. ASHA Monogr. No. 18.

Carrier, J. K., and Peak, T. 1975. Non-speech language initiation program. H & H Enterprises, Lawrence, Kan.

Kuntz, J. V., Carrier, J. K. and Hollis J. H. 1978. A nonvocal system for teaching retarded children to read and write. *In* C. E. Meyers (ed.), Quality of life in severely and profoundly mentally retarded people: Research foundations for improvement. AAMD Monogr. 3.

Patterson, F. 1978. Linguistic capabilities of a young lowland gorilla. *In* F. C. C. Peng (ed.), Sign Language and Language Acquisition—New Dimensions in Comparative Pedolinguistics. Westview Press, Boulder, Col.

Premack, D. 1970. A functional analysis of language. J. Exp. Anal. Behav. 14:107–125.

chapter
17

Application of Functional Analysis and a Nonspeech Response Mode to Teaching Language

Joseph K. Carrier, Jr.*

Bureau of Child Research
University of Kansas
Lawrence, Kansas
and
Parsons Research Center
Parsons State Hospital and Training Center
Parsons, Kansas

See Section VII, pages 517–520, for recent research related to this chapter.

The work presented here is research in the development of tactics for language training with children with severe communication handicaps. These tactics are characterized by 1) evoking symbolic language in response modes other than oral speech, 2) establishing complex overt rote responses (with certain linguistic properties) before teaching meaning, and 3) programming sequences derived from functional analysis and logic systems rather than from developmental data.

This work began as a simple attempt to replicate, with severely retarded children, the language-training procedures Premack (1970 [Chapter 12, this volume]) used to teach language functions to a chimpanzee. Later, when data became available from a similar application of Premack's procedures (Schmidt, Carrier, and Parsons, 1971), revisions were made in this programming to make the procedures more directly applicable to teaching language to humans. The disciplines of linguistics, programming, and logic have all made significant contributions to this endeavor.

The critical need for the development of language-training tactics for severely impaired children is obvious to individuals familiar with institutions for retarded children. Although there are some excellent teachers and well constructed programs, the fact remains that many institutionalized children do not acquire speech and language. For them, something more than a simple language-training program is needed.

As a child learns language, he begins to conceptualize his environment in a manner that relates to the way other persons conceptualize theirs. He learns the critical parameters for making discriminations among environmental events, and he learns to respond differentially to symbolic stimuli and with symbolic responses. As he learns the nonlanguage skills that are appropriate to adaptation into society, he is often required to make discriminations between environmental events, to respond to symbolic stimuli (verbal instruction), and to make use of other sorts of linguistic skills. The interaction between language and nonlanguage learning is so strong that it is doubtful that a child can make much progress in learning one without acquiring skills in the other.

RESPONSE MODE IN LANGUAGE TRAINING

One way of training severely impaired children in language was suggested by Premack (1970 [Chapter 12, this volume]). His use of a nonspeech symbol system and his treatment of language from the perspective of its

From Carrier, J. K. 1974. Application of functional analysis and a nonspeech response mode to teaching language. *In* L. V. McReynolds (ed.), Developing systematic procedures for training children's language, ASHA Monogr. 18:47–96. Reprinted by permission.

* Affiliation given reflects the author's affiliation at time of writing.

Some of the work reported and discussed herein should be credited to the following federally funded projects: NICHHD 00870, NICHHD 05088, and OEG-0-71-0449(607).

function rather than its structure greatly simplify the language-training process.

If language is defined as a set of rules and principles by which meanings and symbolic representations are correlated, it becomes immediately apparent that language is not overt behavior per se, but that language skills can be demonstrated only by overt responses—symbolic representations in which symbols are selected and arranged in linguistically determined fashions. The response mode most commonly associated with language is oral speech, which can be defined as various phonemic responses arranged to create morphemes, which, in turn, may be arranged to create grammatical utterances. The symbols to be selected and arranged are various combinations of phonemic responses (morphemes), and the response topography is quite complex. Similar conclusions can be made about the complexity of written language and manual communication systems used by the deaf. All these communication systems require a response topography in which the user must, in addition to selecting and arranging symbols, actually produce each individual symbol. This is a complex behavior in any response mode.

Premack's response mode eliminated the need for a complex response topography and, therefore, suggested a fresh approach to teaching language. He used plastic shapes as symbols and required nothing more than the simple placement of the shapes on a response board for responses. In such a system the student is not required to go through the complex response sequences involved in actually producing symbols (articulating, writing, or signing). However, in order to respond appropriately he must still recognize the rules and principles for correlating meanings and symbolic representations; he must still know semantic and syntactic aspects of language. It seems reasonable that a response mode similar to that used by Premack would have the effect of greatly simplifying the language-learning process by eliminating the requirement of symbol production and thus facilitating language acquisition in children who could not succeed if speech were required.

Premack's work led to a functional analysis of language—a perspective that eliminates the need to explain the cognitive parameters of language. His work suggested that to learn language a child has only to learn discriminations among different symbols, environmental events, and different sequential arrangements of symbols. When the child appropriately matches specific arrangements of symbols to environmental events, he is in fact demonstrating language.

Finally, it is worth noting that such a symbol system eliminates the transient qualities of speech responses. The shapes remaining in front of the child make it easier for him to monitor himself and correct his sequences.

DEFINING WHAT TO TEACH

It is important for a programmer to define operationally what is to be taught. Program goals such as teaching language or teaching linguistic rules and principles are too vague. It is necessary to specify rules and principles as well as the behaviors that will demonstrate their mastery.

Premack (1970 [Chapter 12, this volume]) specified functions of linguistic behavior (that is, identification and interrogation) and then designed response classes to demonstrate these functions. He was interested in demonstrating linguistic functions in a chimpanzee rather than in teaching communication skills to a child and thus had considerable latitude in his selection of specific semantic and syntactic elements to be taught. He chose semantic elements and designed syntactic structures that would permit maximum efficiency in training strategies, but that were not necessarily identical to those used by communicating humans.

The task of teaching children to communicate, of course, does not permit such latitude. The language system of a child's environment is a fact of life, and, however inefficient it may be, is the one the child must learn. Thus, the process of determining program goals for children requires not only a consideration of language functions, but also a consideration of semantics and syntax as they actually exist. In other words, the programmer must select linguistic responses that will serve the communication needs of the child. In the work reported here, it was assumed that it was not necessary to teach language functions separate from environmental language systems, and that the simultaneous teaching of the two would prove more efficient. To this end, an attempt was made to define those operations that an individual might go through to generate grammatical strings that would adhere to the rules and principles and serve the functions of language.

The model generated by this work was in no way intended to simulate any actual processes in which humans engage. For example, no attempt was made to accommodate data describing the normal acquisition of language; the normal development process does not appear to be efficient logically, and, indeed, some language-deficient children may fail to learn language because of the inefficiency of that process. The model used in this work is intended only as a definition of operations that can efficiently generate responses that incorporate linguistic principles—processes that can function in helping to determine sequences, specific steps, and behavior goals for programs.

A MODEL FOR LANGUAGE

Our current language model is quite large and complex, and no attempt will be made to present it in its entirety. Rather, representative portions of the model will be isolated to help the reader understand some of the program rationale.

The first step in the development of this model was an attempt to define operationally two sets of rules and principles, each of which is an integral part of language. Semantic rules consist of those used for the selection of symbols to represent meanings. In writing, the symbol *boy* may be used to represent a young male human. Syntactic rules determine the sequential arrangement of symbols in a standard grammatical response. For example, in an active declarative sentence, the subject noun precedes the verb, and articles precede nouns. In the current analysis, semantic and syntactic systems are treated separately, although each is certainly dependent on the other for ultimate linguistic performance. It should be further noted that this means of operationally defining syntactic and semantic systems was strictly for the purpose of generating a workable model and was not intended, in any way, as an argument relating to their treatment in linguistic literature.

Syntactic Model

The purpose of the syntax parameter of the model was to define operations that would result in correctly arranged sequences of symbols. This is a complex task if one attempts to consider all the transformations suggested in linguistic literature. But, if the problem is approached from a functional perspective, it is somewhat simpler.

Skinner (1957) provided a reasonable and simple means of defining function when he presented the basis for distinguishing between tacts and mands. For the purpose of this analysis these terms were interpreted as meaning that a response might be directed more strongly toward either an antecedent or a consequent event. Operationally, those responses designed to bring about specific consequences are directed toward consequent events and are called *mands*. All others, more strongly directed toward antecedent events, are called *tacts*. The grammatical class called declarative sentences consists of tacts, and the classes called interrogative and imperative sentences are mands. Interrogative and imperative sentences are interchangeable at this level; they can serve the same function. Thus, development of a functional syntax model becomes a matter of describing operations necessary to generate two types of syntactic strings—declarative and either interrogative or imperative sentences. Of the latter two, interrogative forms were chosen because these appeared to have more general applicability.

Interrogative and declarative sentence types have certain properties in common. Both consist of one or more noun phrases and one or more verb phrases with similar constituents. However, the interrogative sentence type is usually marked by a question indicator (*do* and Wh-words) or a change in the sequential arrangement of constituents; the

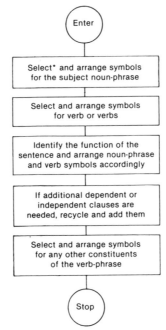

Figure 1. Schematic of major modules of syntax. The asterisk indicates the point at which symbols must be selected. The operations for selection are defined in the semantic charts (for example, Figure 2).

declarative *The boy is going* has the same constituents as the interrogative *Is the boy going?* but an obvious word-order difference. The model can, in many respects, treat these sentence types similarly, but is also equipped to handle their differences.

The current model consists of several components defining a series of operations to generate grammatical strings (Figure 1). The first component is designed to construct subject-noun phrases. The second component directs the construction of the verb, and the third component consists of those operations necessary to sequence the constituents of the noun phrase and the verb. Additional operations, such as the inclusion of Wh- words for interrogatives, prepositional phrases, direct objects, and adverbs, are then included in the model, and operations are delineated for forming compound or complex sentences. Figure 1 is only an outline of the actual model and does not detail the numerous discrete operations within each component. The actual model, at this stage, does not permit many of the transformations referred to in psycholinguistic literature, but it does appear to be adequate for grammatically arranging symbols to represent any meaning.

Semantic Model

As mentioned earlier, the function of the semantic model is to delineate operations necessary to select symbols. The semantic model, because there are many functionally determined classes of symbols, consists of several different parts. Each part defines the operations necessary for selecting a specific member from that class. The operations are nothing more than a series of binary discriminations, performed in specific sequences. The critical discriminations and their sequences were logically derived using decision logic tables (McDaniel, 1968) and schematized in

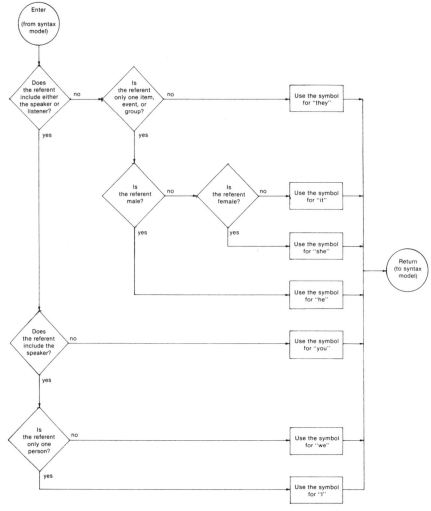

Figure 2.   Flow chart of subject pronoun selection operations.

flow chart form. An example for such an analysis appears in Figure 2, where the operations necessary for proper selection of subject pronouns are presented. The user, with a specific referent in mind, enters the model and must answer the question "Is the referent either the speaker or listener?" If the answer is no, the user exits that box from the right side. If the answer is yes, the user continues vertically to the next box. He continues to make similar decisions until he has eliminated all but one option and is instructed to use a particular symbol. This schematic permits the user to perform one semantic operation called for in the syntax schematic. The child who learns those operations will be able to make such selections.

Obviously, similar schematics are required for the other classes within the semantic system. Flow charts have been designed for the selection of members of easily quantifiable classes such as articles and conjunctions. Other classes with more members, such as prepositions, nouns, and verbs, are currently being treated in part. That is, systems are being designed to handle only a limited number of entries—vocabulary items chosen as those to be taught earliest in the program sequences.

Application of a Language Model to Programming

With such a model, the matter of determining tactics for language training becomes no more complex that the process of programming any other carefully defined behavior. The model defines those binary discriminations, semantic and syntactic, and a set of operations that will result in appropriate linguistic responses. The program sequences can thus begin with responses already in the child's repertoire and then establish behaviors that indicate mastery of each of the operations specified in the model.

For example, if we set out to teach sentences of the form article + noun + verb, we might begin by teaching the child to sequence properly any set of three items cued in a particular way. We might color cue symbols: all article symbols cued red, all noun symbols yellow, and all verb symbols blue. The child's task, when presented with any combination of three of these symbols, would simply be to arrange them, left to right, in the proper sequence—red, yellow, blue. When he had learned this discrimination, he would be emitting behavior with certain properties of syntactically determined sequences. The sequence would be by color cue rather than symbol function. Nevertheless, it would be identical to the correct syntactic arrangement. A schematic for this behavior (Figure 3A) shows that the behavior represents only a very small portion of the total model, but that it is an approximation of what is desired.

A next step would be to teach the child, through the semantic model, to select appropriate nouns. Successful acquisition of such behavior would add another box to the child's performance schematic (Figure 3B)

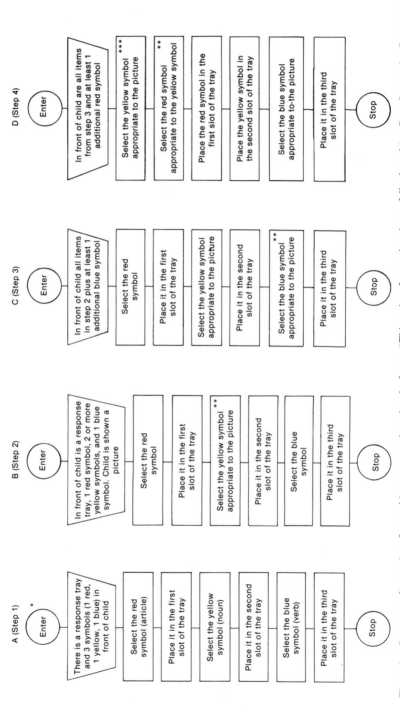

Figure 3. Sequence of operations for teaching sentences by using the forms. *This series of operations is carefully shaped (see Rote Sequencing Program for details). **These operations represent gradual approximations of terminal performance. ***The noun must be selected before the article, since article selection depends on noun properties. This phase in the sequence of operations might require an additional step between Steps 3 and 4.

372

and make it more closely approximate the final model. Figures 3C and D show the inclusion of additional steps in which the child is taught to select verbs and articles. In each step of the program, the index of language acquisition would increase, and the schematic of the child's performance would expand to more closely approximate ultimate goals. The model, therefore, in addition to suggesting programming sequences, permits continual comparison of the child's performance, via his performance schematic, to the terminal goals of the programs.

There is another very reasonable application of the language model. The child is exposed to a communication environment outside of any therapy room, and he usually has opportunities to learn linguistic rules and principles there. This generalization of the language acquisition process is probably critical to successful language training, and its measurement could, therefore, provide useful information to the programmer. With a master model and the child's performance model, the programmer can observe samples of the child's linguistic performance and precisely identify those operations acquired outside of therapy. Such information might then be used to develop program sequences further and to provide a rationale for deleting steps designed to teach behaviors most children can learn outside therapy.

LANGUAGE PROGRAMS

Although the programs to be presented here do appear to have certain implications for the clinical requirements of language training, they are not intended for direct clinical application in their present form. Rather, they represent ongoing research. Their purposes, to date, have been to test the feasibility of the language model and to begin to develop a program model that might later be applied to the actual process of teaching functional language to severely impaired children. Consequently, it has been necessary to impose certain restrictions that would not be necessary, or even efficient, in actual clinical application. The purpose of presenting information here is not to delineate clinical procedures but to report preliminary research and suggest directions for additional research and eventual clinical application.

The nature of the children for whom such programs are being designed is an important consideration. All children for whom data are available have been residents of institutions for retarded children. All were at least eight years of age when the data were collected, and none had been observed using speech for communication. Similarly, none had been able to imitate speech responses of more than one intelligible word. Some were enrolled previously in language therapy in which they were asked to use a speech response mode and failed to make progress.

In addition, many of these children, when initially seen for therapy, would not follow simple directions or show changes in frequency of responses that the clinician provided consequences for in traditional ways.

The language programs to be presented here all have the following features in common:

1. The symbols for various morphemes to be taught are geometric forms cut from 3-inch squares of masonite. Each form is marked on its face with colored tape to indicate the grammatical class of the linguistic constituent it is to represent (noun, verb, article, plural marker, and so on) along with the written representation (the latter primarily for the clinician's use) of the actual constituent.
2. The response board is a simple plywood tray similar to the tray of a chalkboard. It is 24 inches long and divided into eight 3-inch sections by lines drawn on its face. Figure 4 shows the tray and a sample set of forms to represent the sentence *The boy is sitting on the floor*.
3. The child's response topography is essentially the same as that used by Premack (1970 [Chapter 12, this volume]) except that ordering of

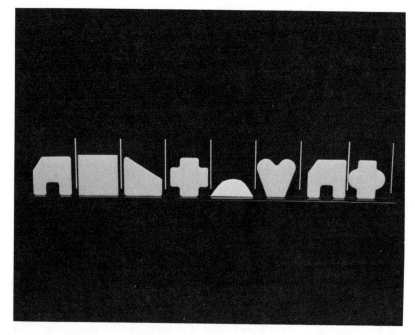

Figure 4.   Symbolic representation of *The boy is sit ing on the floor* (written with geometric forms).

the forms is done horizontally rather than vertically. It was felt that this might facilitate eventual transfer to conventional reading and writing tasks if such a transfer was later indicated.

4. In all program steps, the child is seated at a table with the response directly in front of him. Before the child responds, the clinician places, between the child and the tray, those geometric forms designated by the appropriate step of the program.

5. In all programs, the children are on a continuous schedule of reinforcement for correct responses. Reinforcers are selected on the basis of child preference before each session. The most common reinforcers have been pieces of candy, cereal, or a few drops of soda pop or water. No attempt is made to provide consequences for incorrect responses.

6. The data recorded include pretest and posttest responses (correct and incorrect), records of every correct and incorrect response in each step of the program, and, where appropriate, probe-test performance indicating stimulus or response generalization. Records also include precise identifying information about stimuli (geometric forms and, where appropriate, pictures) and reinforcers. These data are kept with a cumulative recorder. The cumulative record introduces two new parameters to the data: the child's rate of responding (responses/unit of time) and a measure of the time required for the clinician to perform various operations.

The reliability of the records of correct and incorrect responses, stimuli presented, and reinforcers used has been predictably high. All discriminations required of the record keeper are simple and clear, and the occasional scoring of sessions by an independent observer has indicated 100% agreement. The reliability of the temporal measures provided by the cumulative recorder may, however, be another matter. With the clinician activating the time markers on the recorder when stimuli are presented and when the child responds, the validity of these measures may be in question. Until validity is established, the matter of reliability is a moot question.

Labeling Program

The first program in the series was designed to teach a child to use 10 symbols to represent 10 environmental events that might, ordinarily, evoke noun responses. This program uses procedures similar to those often used to teach single nouns to children. Picture stimuli represent each of the 10 objects, and 10 different geometric forms are used as the symbols. The pretests and posttests and procedures for administering this program are presented in Appendix A.

After the child has been pretested and program sequences to meet his individual needs have been planned (completion of the stimulus key), he is taught that, when one form is between him and the tray and he is shown a picture, he is to place the form in the tray. In the next step, he is presented a choice of two forms, for example, a square for *boy* and a circle for *girl*, and, from one trial to the next, he is shown a randomly selected picture of either a boy or a girl. When he has responded correctly 10 consecutive times, another form is added, for example, a square for *boy*, a circle for *girl*, and a triangle for *man*, and pictures of the three nouns are presented randomly until 10 consecutive correct responses have been emitted. The randomization procedure, at this and all future steps, is designed to ensure that about 50% of all pictures presented will be of the noun being learned at this step (for example, *man*) and that the other 50% will be randomly selected from the nouns already learned in previous steps. This progression is continued until the child has met criterion (10 consecutive correct responses) at a step on which all 10 forms are in front of him and all 10 pictures have equal probability of being presented. He is then posttested. If he scores 100% correct, he is moved to the next program. If he scores less than 100%, he is continued in this program, learning the items failed in the posttest. The program is reviewed, the teaching of appropriate items continued, and the posttest repeated until criterion is met.

This program has been quite successful with children for whom clinician control and attending behavior were not serious problems. Such children have progressed very rapidly (see Table 1 for a summary of the data), usually completing the program in about two hours of training time. Error rates have usually been below 10%, and most children have shown total retention when retested one to two weeks after completing the program.

Unfortunately, the program has not been so successful with some children who do not attend or who do not show responsiveness to clinician control when first entered in the program. They show no apparent progress even after several sessions in which they are required to do nothing more than place a form on the tray. Such children have been removed from the program, run through procedures for establishing clinician control, and then placed back in the program. Under these circumstances some progress has been observed, but it has been extremely slow compared to that of the other children.

It seems unlikely that the children who fail simply cannot learn the appropriate discriminations, although such a possibility may exist for some. The response topography (placing a form on the tray) is not a problem in itself, although, just as speech responding may interfere with language acquisition, this response class may be interfering with discrimi-

Table 1. Summary of data for 60 subjects completing the Labeling Program

	Total responses	Total errors	Training times (minutes)
Mean	695.86	86.98	125.38
Standard deviation	671.32	124.04	111.86
Range	58–3469	0–728	8.18–512.2

nation learning. For some children, it may be necessary to program more carefully the stimuli that are to be presented, as Sidman and Stoddard (1966) did, or begin with responses of even less complex topography similar to procedures suggested by Carrow (1971) for testing. In addition to being a successful means of establishing some basic language behavior in some children, the labeling program seems to be a means for probe testing to determine which children may require even more basic types of programs before acquiring labeling behavior.

Rote Sequencing Program

The second program of this series is designed to teach a child to arrange sequentially from left to right, by color and number cues, eight geometric forms in the response tray. The forms that are to be placed in the slot at the left of the tray are always marked with one red stripe, which, in subsequent programs, will indicate that that form is the symbol for an article. The form for the second slot of the tray has one red marker to designate a noun. The form for the third slot has a green marker to designate a verbal auxiliary. For the fourth slot a dark blue marker is used to designate a verb. The fifth slot has a light blue marker to designate a verb ending (-*ing* or *ed*), and the sixth slot has a black marker indicating a preposition. The form for the seventh slot has two red markers, and the form for the eighth slot has two orange markers, indicating by color that they are articles and nouns, but by number of markers that they do not go in the subject portion of the sentence sequence. If the child were to know the meaning of the sequences being constructed in this program, all sequences would take the form article + noun + verbal auxiliary + verb + verb ending + preposition + article + noun. This response sequence, when established, is intended to serve as a rote-response skeleton that will function as the vehicle for teaching the child the operations suggested by the semantic and the syntactic models. At this level it does not function communicatively, and, in that sense, is not syntactic performance. However, it is precisely the same behavior that, emitted in a communicative context, will serve as evidence of syntax acquisition. Figure 5, in which this behavior is schematically represented, shows the child's first actual approximation of the syntax model.

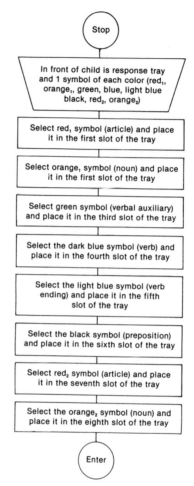

Figure 5. Operations performed by child completing the Rote Sequencing Program. Red₁ and orange₁ are symbols for articles and nouns that go in the subject noun phrase (they have one color marker). Red₂ and orange₂ are symbols for articles and nouns that go in the prepositional phrase (they have two color markers).

Procedures in this program include pretests and posttests in addition to program steps in which the terminal response topography is gradually shaped. The child is pretested and, if he makes no correct responses, is first taught to place a form with two orange markers in the last slot of the tray. This task is learned easily because a wooden covering is placed across the tray, concealing all but the last slot, and only one form is presented to the child. In the next step, however, the last two slots are uncovered and the child is presented two forms, one with two orange markers (noun) and one with two red markers (article). His task is to place the red-marked form in the first open slot of the tray, then to place the orange-marked form in the last slot. When he performs this task successfully without assistance, new geometric forms with the same color markers are presented to him. To complete this step of the program he must demonstrate generalization to the new forms, that is, demonstrate that he is responding to the color markers. The teaching is continued until such generalization is observed, and then a black marked form is added and the next slot in the tray is made available. This process of adding forms, training and probing for generalization, is continued until the child can take any set of eight appropriately colored and numbered forms and place them, from left to right, in the tray in their correct slots. He is then posttested to ensure his generalization of color cues and the acquisition of the behavior.

The data for 60 subjects who have completed this program are presented in Table 2. Most children show a pattern in which criterion is reached quickly in the first lesson, attained more slowly in Lesson 2, and reached more slowly still in Lesson 3. Most children seem to acquire the concepts of sequencing and placing the new form in the slot farthest to the left, and the remaining tasks are learned very quickly. Some do, however, have unusual difficulty with the last two steps. The children who have been given this program have learned the rote sequencing performance in a mean time of about 3½ hours and maintained the behavior in subsequent programs.

Subject Selection Program

When a child enters this program, he has learned to select symbols (subject nouns) out of context, and he has learned to sequence, by rote, the eight constituents of one sentence type. The program was designed to combine these two behaviors, that is, to teach the child to select and sequence in one series of operations. The flow chart for these operations (Figure 6) is a step closer to that of the master language model discussed earlier in this writing.

Before entering the Subject Selection Program, the child is again posttested on the 10 nouns learned earlier in the Labeling Program, since the retention of that behavior is necessary for performance on this

Table 2.   Summary of data for 60 subjects completing the Rote Sequencing Program

	Total responses	Total errors	Training times (minutes)
Mean	1761.28	136.86	199.35
Standard deviation	1886.60	177.52	217.20
Range	179–9125	5–1119	16.68–908.7

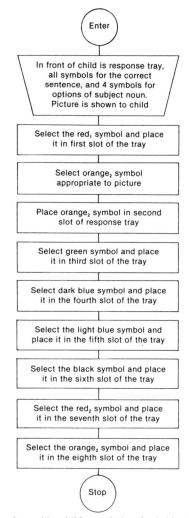

Figure 6.   Operations performed by child completing the Subject Selection Program.

program. If he makes errors in that test, the Labeling Program is repeated until posttest criterion is met.

The child is then pretested for behavior in the Subject Selection Program. In this pretest, only five of the nouns taught in the labeling Program are used. The child has in front of him the geometric form symbols to produce a complete sentence appropriate to a picture to be presented, just as he did in the Rote Sequencing Program. But, mixed in with these are four additional symbols representing inappropriate subject nouns. When the child is shown a picture, he is to select the correct article and place it in the first slot of the tray, select the correct subject noun and place it in the second slot, and then place properly, by color and number cues, the other constituents of the sentence. This procedure is used for five different sentences, each with a different subject noun.

If the child does not successfully complete the pretest scoring 100% correct, he begins the program in which only the other five nouns from the Labeling Program are used. Since he has already learned the behaviors required in the program, but has learned them in response to different types of environmental events, the responses required throughout this program have the same basic topography (described in the preceding paragraph); but the events used to evoke the responses are varied to approximate gradually the final desired conditions. Two parameters of these evoking events are varied systematically. The child begins with only two subject-noun options. Then, as he progresses, he is presented three, then four, and finally five possibilities. Similarly, at any level where the numer of options is being held constant (two, three, four, or five), the sequence and manner in which the geometric forms are presented are changed gradually (Figure 7). That is, in the first step the child is presented only one form, the article from the first slot of the tray, and then, after correctly placing that form, he is presented the forms for the appropriate number of noun options. Finally, after selecting and placing the noun, he is presented the forms for the rest of the sentence. In the second step the article and noun forms are first presented simultaneously, the responses with these forms completed, and the forms for the rest of the sentence presented. In the third step, forms for the sentence are presented at the same time but placed in two separate groups on the table—article and subject noun options in one group and the rest of the sentence in the other group. In the fourth step, the article and noun groups are placed together and the other forms are placed randomly around that group. In the final step all forms are mixed on the table in front of the child.

Criterion for completing this program is successful generalization from the behavior specific in the pretest. Probes for testing this behavior are made periodically throughout the program and continued until criterion is met, demonstrating that the child has learned the operation of noun selection in conjunction with the sequencing behavior.

The program for teaching this behavior, presented in Appendix C, is lengthy, primarily because of its experimental nature. The gradual changing of the evoking events adds many steps to the program, and the frequent probe tests and procedures for going back to the Labeling Program to teach new nouns make the program, when visually inspected, appear to be extremely long. Although this kind of care is necessary to answer research questions, the data indicate that, for many children,

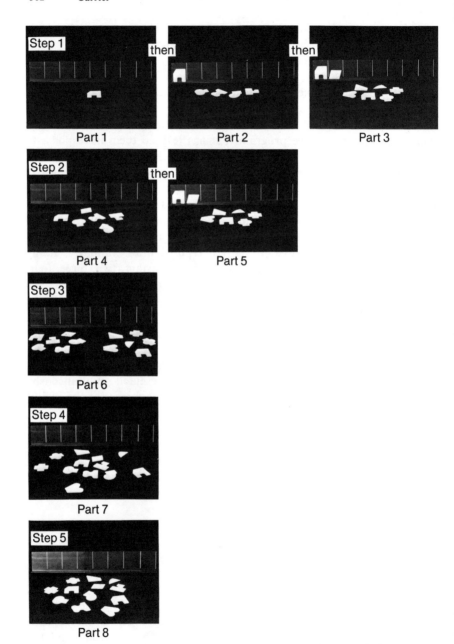

Figure 7.   Manner of presenting forms for Subject Selection Program (in five steps).

several of the steps that add to the program's length probably will be unnecessary for clinical application.

The children for whom data are available in this program (see Table 3) typically show some of the target performance during the pretest. Some (as in the Labeling Program) select the proper subject nouns and place them in the tray, but ignore the rest of the forms. Others, as in the Rote Sequencing Program, place forms with the correct color and number markers in the appropriate slots, but do not properly select correct subject nouns. Many children actually begin combining the two behaviors and respond correctly in several of the pretest items.

Typically, program time for these children has been very short. In fact, most children have met target criterion in the probe test following the first step of the program in which only two choices for subject nouns were available. The mean training time for the program has been about 1.25 hours.

Verb Selection Program

This program is similar in structure to the Subject Selection Program, but there may be a subtle difference in the nature of the learning process required of the child. Before beginning the Noun Program, the selection process had already been taught in the Labeling Program. In the Verb Selection Program, the selection process is taught at the same time all previously learned behaviors are being required, that is, in context. The schematic of the terminal behavior, again a step closer to that of the master language model, is presented in Figure 8. This program is not presented in the appendices because of its similarity to the Subject Selection Program.

The Verb Selection Program is very similar in basic structure to the Subject Selection Program in that the general response topography is held constant throughout and only the evoking events are varied. In Step 1 the child is presented forms for the appropriate article, for all nouns previously taught, and for the appropriate verbal auxiliary. He is shown a picture, and, after completing this first part of the sentence, the verb option forms are presented. Finally, the forms for the rest of the sentence are presented. In the next step, the forms (including noun and verb

Table 3. Summary of data for 50 subjects completing the Subject Selection Program

	Total responses	Total errors	Training times (minutes)
Mean	75.52	11.16	75.83
Standard deviation	75.51	30.66	74.24
Range	8–388	0–214	9.7–328.63

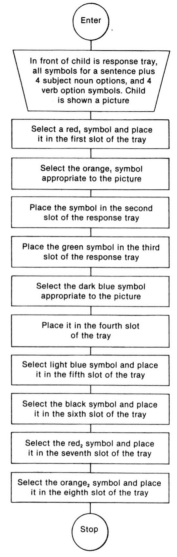

Figure 8. Operations performed by child completing the Verb Selection Program.

options) through the sentence verb are presented, that part of the response completed, and the rest of the forms presented. The same basic five steps used in the Subject Selection Program are used. Then another verb is added and the procedures for Steps 1 through 5 repeated. In this work only five verbs have been taught to each child, but it is reasonable to conclude from the children's performance that the procedures could be used to teach a greater number of verbs if this were desired.

The data for this program (Table 4) show rapid acquisition of verb selection, with a mean training time of under 2 hours. However, it should be noted that some children have unusual difficulty with the first two verbs and thus require much longer training times.

DEVELOPMENT OF ADDITIONAL PROGRAMS

The Verb Selection Program essentially completes the program model required for teaching a sentence of a specific structure, in this case, article + noun + verbal auxiliary + verb + verb ending + preposition + article + noun. In other words, children should learn to use the additional constituents to pluralize and select verb tense following the same basic procedures employed in the Verb Selection Program. Rather than verbs being varied, as in the Verb Selection Program, options for other constituents, such as articles or prepositions, might be presented. Some data are available regarding such an application of the program model to nouns in prepositional phrases. These data show patterns and rates of acquisition that are very similar to those observed in Verb Selection Program data. Figure 9 illustrates the general nature of the child's task after completing this program.

When children have learned to select various symbols and arrange them appropriately for this type of declarative sentence, a reasonable progression in the programming might be to begin to teach the child, using symbols already learned, to produce other declarative sentences with different syntactic structures. For example, the child might be taught that certain situations do not call for responses with prepositional phrases, but, rather, call for responses with direct objects or adverbs following the verb. Such training has not yet been undertaken, but it is hypothesized that the program model for such training will include steps similar to those of the Rote Sequencing Program, except that the child will be permitted options in sequences. The choice of options will be determined by characteristics of the evoking events. For example, a pic-

Table 4. Summary of data for 30 subjects completing the Verb Selection Program

	Total responses	Total errors	Training times (minutes)
Mean	412.13	108.63	363.42
Standard deviation	421.93	137.70	453.12
Range	57–1660	3–552	59.15–2240

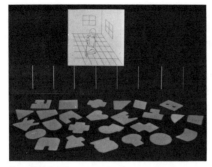

1. Stimuli presented.

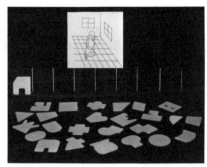

2. Places first article forms.

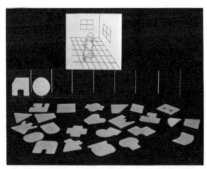

3. Selects and places subject noun.

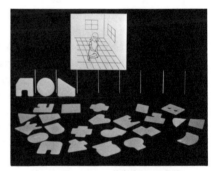

4. Places verbal auxiliary form.

5. Selects and places verb.

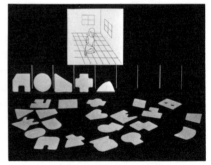

6. Places verb ending form.

Figure 9.   Sequential performance completing the Object of Preposition Program.

ture of a boy sitting on the floor might call for production of the prepositional phrase sequence, while a picture of a boy eating candy might call for a direct object construction. It seems reasonable that a child could learn such discriminations if he could learn some of the others in previously completed programs.

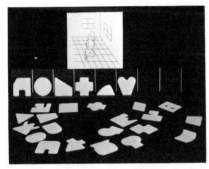

7. Places preposition form.

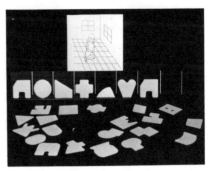

8. Places second article.

9. Selects and places object of preposition.

Figure 9. (*continued*)

It is anticipated that procedures similar to those used to teach declarative sentence discriminations will also be used to teach interrogative and perhaps imperative sentences. During this process, vocabulary could also be easily expanded.

APPLICATION OF PROGRAMS

As previously mentioned, these programs currently are being used on an experimental basis, and they are far from ready for effective clinical application. However, there are certain implications of this preliminary work that may have direct application to clinical procedures.

Effectiveness of Nonspeech Symbols in Language Training

First, as suggested by Premack (1970 [Chapter 12, this volume]), it seems clear that the process of language acquisition can be separated from complex response topographies such as speech, writing, and manual signing. Further, this work suggests that many children who typically learn very slowly when speech responses are required can learn language (rules and principles) when the symbols are provided for them. This does not mean that all language-handicapped children should learn language in a nonspeech response mode, but it does indicate that such an approach might be effective and efficient for many who have particular difficulty with more traditional approaches.

Indications are, however, that even this type of approach to language training may be too complex for some children. The programs using the nonspeech symbols, reported in this work, appear to be effective with some of the children for whom they are intended. Still more basic programming is indicated for others.

Transfer to a More Functional Response Mode

A major problem with a response mode such as the one being used here is the obvious fact that the specific communication system being taught to the child is not likely to be functional in an environment where other symbol sets such as speech are used. There seem to be several ways of approaching the problem of making language functional outside the therapy setting. One such approach was used in some of the earlier pilot work with these procedures. As children "wrote" responses with the forms, the clinician spoke the words being represented. Many children began imitating these words and soon the clinician's utterance was faded and the child continued emitting the speech responses. Reports on one such child, after less than a year of therapy, indicate that he is beginning to speak in other environments and is using some of the complex grammar taught in therapy. This approach is not yet built into the program and cannot be carefully evaluated at this time, but clinical experience does suggest it may be very effective for some children. Eventually, variations of the nonspeech program, designed specifically for clinical application, will probably include such procedures.

A second obvious approach has not been investigated at this time but will quite probably be necessary for some children. This approach would involve carefully programmed transfer of the application of linguistic rules and principles to another, more functional response topography (that is, speech, writing, or manual signing). The nature of such programming would likely be shaping functional responses and gradually substituting them for the geometric forms.

Finally, it might be reasonable in certain very structured activities, to use the geometric forms for actual communication. The children who are candidates for nonspeech programs presented here are typically children who are also engaged in learning certain basic nonlanguage skills, such as putting on clothes. In those cases where communication between teacher and child might facilitate learning, it would be possible to teach the child language responses appropriate to a specific nonlanguage behavior and introduce a set of forms and a response tray into the other learning situation. The teacher using the written words on the forms as cues would arrange the forms to represent instructions, and the child could ask questions and provide other types of appropriate feedback. Such procedures could be initiated easily where sequences for teaching nonlanguage behaviors were specified carefully and when teachers of those skills were willing to cooperate. This type of functional usage of the geometric forms is certainly not the ideal, but it might be extremely useful for making all of the child's learning experiences more efficient and for demonstrating the power of communication to him.

Initiating Training in Another Response Mode

It should be mentioned that neither the language model nor the program model discussed in this work need be restricted in application to training procedures using the geometric form symbols. Although there is no evidence in this work to validate the application of the models to language training using other response modes, it does seem logical to make such a generalization. The application of such models to language therapy to teach speech or manual signing might greatly simplify the programming task of the clinician and result in very specific program strategies that might enable some clinicians to be very precise in describing their therapy and its relation to the total process of language training. Such a switch in the response mode would involve no program changes except slight variations in specific evoking events and criteria for calling responses correct.

Nonessential Parameters of the Program Model

Although lack of substantive data makes positive conclusions impossible at this time the data from performance on the Verb Selection Program strongly suggest that the Labeling Program is probably not essential to the language intervention process for many children. If children learn verbs in context, as they do in the Verb Selection Program, it would seem reasonable that they might learn various other constituents in context. If such is the case, the Labeling Program is not necessary for teaching nouns per se. It might, however, as suggested earlier, serve either as a convenient means of beginning discrimination training at a simple level or as a source for certain kinds of prognostic or diagnostic information.

Use of More Functional Evoking Events

All the work presented here has used pictures as events to evoke responses; however, although pictures were the most convenient stimuli for this kind of experimental work, their use in clinical application is certainly questionable. A child in his out-of-therapy environment is seldom asked to respond to pictures. Rather, he is faced with environmental events, such as questions, bladder pains, sensations of hunger, and the like. It would seem much more functional to teach responses to such situations to a child so that responses learned in therapy could be easily used to generate consequences in his everyday environment. Descriptive information about the environment and activities of children could be inspected to deduce specific linguistic responses that might have high probabilities of being used. These responses could be taught using the same language and program models.

CONCLUSIONS

The purpose of the work reported here has been to begin to develop two models—one for operationally defining goals for language intervention and the other for specifying actual program sequences. This research appears to have clinical implications but has not yet advanced to the point where the programs presented should be recommended for actual clinical application.

In operationally defining language program goals, the unmanageable number of correct linguistic responses was viewed in terms of two of its components—an operationally defined semantic system and an operationally defined syntactic system. Each of these, excluding dialectical variance and temporal change, can be treated as a finite set and, if defined separately, should permit a quantifiable, all-inclusive description of language. Tactics for developing a language model were derived from functional analysis as suggested by Premack (1970 [Chapter 12, this volume]), linguistic literature, and logic systems. The results of such analysis have been used as rationale for programming tactics.

The language programs presented in this chapter are unlike traditional language programs in a number of ways. It was assumed that the complex nature of the speech response system often interferes with language acquisition when speech-response-system responses are required in language remediation. Therefore, a nonspeech response mode, similar to that used by Premack (1970 [Chapter 12, this volume]), was substituted for speech. In this mode, geometric forms function as linguistic constituents and the child has only to select and correctly arrange forms appropriate to the meaning to be conveyed.

A second feature of these programs is derived from the results of the linguistic analysis. The child is taught, very early in the programming sequence, to produce grammatically correct sentences by rote. These sentences are not necessarily meaningful to the child but are grammatical responses to the stimuli presented. The effect is that the child always uses complete responses and is never reinforced for a partial response as he is in the response-shaping strategies more commonly used in language therapy. Complete responses are established by rote and, as they are repeatedly evoked, the child is taught the differential functions (meaning) of each of the constituents of his response.

A third feature of these programs is that they follow logical rather than developmental sequences. In most instances the two models suggest similar sequences but, where they do differ, the directions indicated by the logic model appear to have higher probability of improving overall language functions.

The specific programs presented in this chapter include: 1) a program to teach a child to label, 2) a program to teach a child to arrange geometric forms of varying grammatical classes into their correct syntactic order, 3) a program to teach a child to select correct subject nouns and use them in sentences, and 4) a program to teach a child to select correct verbs and use them in sentences.

These programs are still in need of at least two kinds of refinement. First, there remains a need for effective procedures for children who do not progress significantly in these programs. Second, there is a need for considerable work in preparing the programs for clinical application. If these needs can be met, this approach to language intervention may become useful in the process of teaching severely impaired individuals.

REFERENCES

Carrow, E. 1971. Assessment of speech and language in children. *In* J. E. McLean, D. E. Yoder, and R. L. Schiefelbusch (eds.), Language Intervention with the Retarded: Developing Strategies. University Park Press, Baltimore.

McDaniel, H. 1968. An Introduction to Decision Logic Tables. John Wiley & Sons, New York.

Premack, D. 1970. A functional analysis of language. J. Exp. Anal. Behav. 14:107–125

Schmidt, M. J., Carrier, J., and Parsons, S. 1971. Use of a non-speech mode for teaching language. Paper presented at the Annual Convention of the American Speech and Hearing Association, Chicago.

Sidman, M., and Stoddard L. 1966. Programming perception and learning for retarded children. *In* N. Ellis (ed.), International Review of Research in Mental Retardation. Academic Press, New York.

Skinner, B. F. 1957. Verbal Behavior. Appleton-Century-Crofts, New York.

APPENDIX A: LABELING PROGRAM

This program is designed to teach a child to label, that is, to use symbols to represent stimuli from the environment.

In this program the stimuli to be used are pictures (of a man or a dog, for example) and the symbol for each picture is a different geometric form cut from masonite (triangle = man, circle = dog). To label, the child must select (from a group of forms in front of him) the one representing the stimulus presented and place that form on a response tray similar to the tray on a chalkboard.

Entry Behavior. Before entering the program, the child should be attentive (look at pictures shown by the teacher) and responsive to some external control (interact with the teacher in a play situation and show consistent increase(s) in frequency of responses that are responded to contingently by teacher-administered events).

Terminal Behavior. Upon completion of the program, the child will be able to label, in the described fashion, 10 objects represented in pictures.

Contingencies. Specific reinforcers are not designated in the program because of the tremendous variance from child to child. A reinforcer is anything presented after the response that results in an increased frequency of the response. For most children pieces of candy, cereal, a few drops of soda pop, or a similar edible item will be effective. For others, verbal praise or a pat on the arm may be adequate. The teacher should begin by hypothesizing a reinforcer and viewing its effect (on a record sheet). If the child is not learning and has met entry criteria, a new reinforcer should be tried.

Administrative Sequences. The program should be preceded by a pretest (Labeling Program Test). After completion of this test, a guide to program sequences, tailored to the needs of the individual child, should be prepared (Stimulus Key Construction). All lessons of the program are then administered (Labeling Program), and upon their completion the Labeling Program Test is repeated as a posttest. If the child does not complete this test with 100% accuracy, a new stimulus key is constructed and he repeats those parts of the program with which he is having difficulty. He continues to recycle through the entire sequence until he scores 100% correct on the posttest. He then goes on to the next program.

Labeling Program Test Record Sheet

Name _____   √ = correct
Date _____   X = incorrect
Pretest   Posttest 1

Form no.	Response	Form no.	Response	Form no.	Response	Form no.	Response
1	___	5	___	1	___	5	___
2	___	4	___	2	___	4	___
3	___	3	___	3	___	3	___
4	___	2	___	4	___	2	___
5	___	1	___	5	___	1	___
6	___	10	___	6	___	10	___
7	___	9	___	7	___	9	___
8	___	8	___	8	___	8	___
9	___	7	___	9	___	7	___
10	___	6	___	10	___	6	___

Labeling Program Test

Teacher in chair
Reinforcers
Record sheet
10 pictures
Table
Response tray
10 forms (random arrangement)
Child in chair

Materials
1. Labeling Program Test Record Sheet and pencil
2. Reinforcers
3. 10 forms
4. 10 pictures

$$\begin{bmatrix} boy & dog \\ girl & cat \\ man & bird \\ lady & horse \\ baby & cow \end{bmatrix}$$ Arrangement of materials

5. Response tray

Before Administering Program
1. Record identifying information (name, date, and so on) on record sheet.
2. Arrange materials as indicated above.
3. Shuffle pictures.

(*continued*)

Labeling Program Test (continued)

Administering Labeling Program Test

Step	Evoke the response	Evaluate the response	Provide consequences	Record the response	Select the next step
1	Show top picture to child.	*Correct:* Child places matching form on tray. *Incorrect:* Child does not place matching form on tray or places more than one form on tray.	*If correct:* Reinforce. *If incorrect:* Do nothing.	*If correct:* Record ✓ and form number on first unused blank on record sheet. *If incorrect:* Record X and form number on first unused blank on record sheet.	After each stimulus presentation, place the picture just used in another pile. AND Repeat Step 1 showing one picture at a time until all pictures are used. THEN

If child did not have 10 correct, go to Stimulus Key Construction.

If child had 10 correct, shuffle pictures and repeat Step 1 for 10 more responses.

THEN

If child did not have 10 more correct, go to Stimulus Key Construction.

OR

If child had 10 more correct, go to the Rote Sequencing Program Test.

Stimulus Key Construction

Materials
1. Stimulus Key blank and pencil
2. Labeling Program Test Record Sheet

Procedures
1. Identify the numbers of all items missed on the Labeling Program Test.
2. Enter each of these numbers, one item per row, in the blanks in Column A of the Stimulus Key. Stop when each error number has been entered once.
3. Identify the numbers of all items with correct responses on the Labeling Program Test.
4. Enter all these numbers on the Lesson 1 row of Column B of the Stimulus Key. If there were no correct responses, enter 0.
5. In the next row of Column B, enter all items from Columns A and B of the preceding row.
6. Continue Step 5 until Column B has an entry in every row for which there is an entry in Column A.
7. Go to the Labeling Program.

Stimulus Key

Lesson no.	Box A	Box B	Completed
1	_____	_____	_____
2	_____	_____	_____
3	_____	_____	_____
•	_____	_____	_____
•	_____	_____	_____
•	_____	_____	_____
20	_____	_____	_____

Labeling Program

Materials

1. Stimulus Key (completed)
2. Reinforcers
3. Labeling Program Record Sheet and pencil
4. Tray
5. Random selection list[a]
6. 10 pictures
7. 10 masonite forms

Arrangement of materials

boy, girl, man, lady, baby
dog, cat, bird, horse, cow

Stimulus Key
10 pictures
Place on table for Pile B
Place on table for Pile A
10 forms
Table
Response tray
Child in chair

Teacher in chair
Record sheet
Random Selection List
Reinforcers

Before Administering Program

1. Record identifying information (name, date, and so on) on record sheet and number the first trial *1*.
2. Arrange materials as indicated above.
3. Select the first uncompleted lesson from the Stimulus Key.
4. Place picture in Column A of Stimulus Key in Pile A on table.
5. Place picture(s) (if any) in Column B of Stimulus Key in Pile B on table.
6. Place one form for each of the pictures in Piles A and B on table between child and tray.

(continued)

397

Administering the Program

Labeling Program *(continued)*

Step	Evoke the Response	Evaluate the response	Provide consequences	Record the response	Select the next step
1	Show child the picture from Pile A.	*Correct:* Child places matching form on tray. *Incorrect:* Child does not place matching form on tray or places more than one form on tray.	*If correct:* Reinforce. *If incorrect:* Do nothing.	*If correct:* Record a √ and the picture number on the first unused blank of the record sheet for this trial. *If incorrect:* Record an X and the picture number on the first unused blank of the record sheet for this trial.	*If correct:* Go to Step 2. *If incorrect:* Go to Step 3.
2	Arrange all materials as they were before administering program. Select the first unused letter from the Random Selection List. Draw a line through that letter to indicate you have used it. Show child a picture from that pile (A or B).	Same as Step 1.	Same as Step 1.	Same as Step 1.	*If correct:* Continue Step 2 until child makes an error or completes 10 consecutive correct responses. Mark that lesson "completed" on Stimulus Key. If this was the last lesson on the Stimulus Key go to the Labeling Program Test. If not, repeat procedures from "*Before Administering*

				Program" (above) and begin the next lesson at Step 1 ("Administering the Program").
3	Arrange all materials as they were before administering the program. Show child the same picture used for the last response. Point to the correct form.	Same as Step 1.	If *correct:* Record a √ beside the mark for the last response. If *incorrect:* Record an X beside the mark for the last response.	If *incorrect:* Go to Step 3. If *correct:* Begin a new trial on the record sheet, number it, go back to Step 1, and use, for the first response, the same picture just used. If *incorrect:* Go to Step 4.
4	Arrange all materials as they were before administering the program. Show child the picture on which he was just incorrect. Point to the correct form and then to the tray.	Same as Step 1.	If *correct:* Record a √ beside the mark for the last response. If *incorrect:* Record an X beside the mark for the last response.	If *correct:* Go back to Step 3. If *incorrect:* Go to the Hand-Shaping Program.[b]

[a] The Random Selection List (not presented here) is simply a series of columns containing randomly selected *A*s and *B*s.
[b] The Hand-Shaping Program is not presented here. It is a carefully sequenced branch program in which the child is first physically "put through" the correct response and then the assistance involved in "putting-through" is gradually faded.

399

Labeling Program Record Sheet

Name _____

Date _____

	Lesson No. _____				Lesson No. _____	
	Trial No. _____				Trial No. _____	
	Form no.	*Response*			*Form no.*	*Response*
1	_____	_____		1	_____	_____
2	_____	_____		2	_____	_____
3	_____	_____		3	_____	_____
4	_____	_____		4	_____	_____
5	_____	_____		5	_____	_____
6	_____	_____		6	_____	_____
7	_____	_____		7	_____	_____
8	_____	_____		8	_____	_____
9	_____	_____		9	_____	_____
10	_____	_____		10	_____	_____
Total				Total		

APPENDIX B: ROTE SEQUENCING PROGRAM

This program is designed to teach a child to arrange sequentially eight geometric forms in a tray in response to color and number cues.

Entry Behavior. Completion of the Labeling Program.

Terminal Behavior. Upon completion of this program the child will be able to sequence properly any set of appropriately color/number cued geometric forms.

Contingencies. Same as in Labeling Program.

Administration Sequences. The program should be preceded with the pretest. The beginning lesson is then selected (Rote Sequencing Lesson Selection) and the program administered. After completing the program for all lessons, the posttest is administered (same as pretest) and the child is either recycled through parts of the program or moved on to the Subject Selection Program.

Rote Sequencing Program Test (RSPT)

Materials
1. Rote Sequencing Program Test Record Sheet and pencil
2. Form for

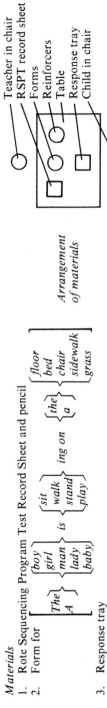

$$\text{The} \atop A \quad \left\{ \begin{matrix} boy \\ girl \\ man \\ lady \\ baby \end{matrix} \right\} \ is \ \left\{ \begin{matrix} sit \\ walk \\ stand \\ play \end{matrix} \right\} ing \ on \ {the \atop a} \left\{ \begin{matrix} floor \\ bed \\ chair \\ sidewalk \\ grass \end{matrix} \right\}$$

Arrangement of materials

— Teacher in chair
— RSPT record sheet
— Forms
— Reinforcers
— Table
— Response tray
— Child in chair

3. Response tray
4. Reinforcers

Before Administering Program
1. Record identifying information (name, date, and so on) on record sheet.
2. Arrange materials as indicated above.

(continued)

401

Rate Sequencing Program Test (continued)

Administering the Program

Step	Evoke the response	Evaluate the response	Provide consequences	Record the response	Select the next step
1	Place forms in front of child for *The boy is sit ing on the floor.*	*Correct:* Child places all forms on tray in their proper order.	*If correct:* Reinforce. *If incorrect:* Do nothing.	*If correct:* Place a √ on record sheet under each word placed correctly. *If incorrect:* Place √s on record sheet for any forms correctly placed and Xs for incorrectly placed forms.	Go to Step 2.
2	Place forms in front of child for *A girl is walk ing on the bed.*	Same as Step 1.	Same as Step 1.	Same as Step 1.	Go to Step 3.
3	Place forms in front of child for *The lady is stand ing on a chair.*	Same as Step 1.	Same as Step 1.	Same as Step 1.	Go to Step 4.

4	Place forms in front of child for *A man is play ing on the side-walk.*	Same as Step 1.	Same as Step 1.	Same as Step 1.	Go to Step 5.
5	Place forms in front of child for *A baby is sit ing on the grass.*	Same as Step 1.	Same as Step 1.	Same as Step 1.	Total √s for all five steps. If child has 40 √s go to Subject Selection Program Test. If child has fewer than 40 √s and has been on Rote Sequencing Program go to Rote Sequencing Lesson Selection; otherwise, go to Rote Sequencing Program and repeat Lesson 8.

Rote Sequencing Program Test Record Sheet

Name _____

Pretest:
Date:

1. The   boy   is   sit   ing   on   the   floor.
   ___   ___   ___   ___   ___   ___   ___   ___

2. A   girl   is   walk   ing   on   the   bed.
   ___   ___   ___   ___   ___   ___   ___   ___

3. The   lady   is   stand   ing   on   a   chair.
   ___   ___   ___   ___   ___   ___   ___   ___

4. A   man   is   play   ing   on   the   sidewalk.
   ___   ___   ___   ___   ___   ___   ___   ___

5. A   baby   is   sit   ing   on   the   grass.
   ___   ___   ___   ___   ___   ___   ___   ___

Posttest:
Date:

1. The   boy   is   sit   ing   on   the   floor.
   ___   ___   ___   ___   ___   ___   ___   ___

2. A   girl   is   walk   ing   on   the   bed.
   ___   ___   ___   ___   ___   ___   ___   ___

3. The   lady   is   stand   ing   on   a   chair.
   ___   ___   ___   ___   ___   ___   ___   ___

4. A   man   is   play   ing   on   the   sidewalk.
   ___   ___   ___   ___   ___   ___   ___   ___

5. A   baby   is   sit   ing   on   the   grass.
   ___   ___   ___   ___   ___   ___   ___   ___

Rote Sequencing Program Lesson Selection

1. If the child has not completed Lesson 1, he is on Lesson 1.
   Construct a pile containing the forms for *floor, chair, bed, grass,* and *sidewalk*.
2. If the child has completed Lesson 1 but not Lesson 2, he is on Lesson 2.
   Construct the pile for Lesson 1 and a pile containing the forms for *the* and *a*, with two red markers.
3. If the child has completed Lesson 2 but not Lesson 3, he is on Lesson 3.
   Construct a pile for Lesson 2 and a pile containing the form for *on*.
4. If the child has completed Lesson 3 but not Lesson 4, he is on Lesson 4.
   Construct a pile from Lesson 3 and a pile containing the form for *ing*.
5. If the child has completed Lesson 4 but not Lesson 5, he is on Lesson 5.
   Construct a pile for Lesson 4 and a pile containing the forms for *sit, stand, walk, lazy,* and *play*.
6. If the child has completed Lesson 5 but not Lesson 6, he is on Lesson 6.
   Construct a pile for Lesson 5 and a pile containing the form for *is*.

7. If the child has completed Lesson 6 but not Lesson 7, he is on Lesson 7. Construct a pile for Lesson 6 and a pile containing the forms for *boy*, *girl*, *man*, *lady*, and *baby*.

8. If the child has completed Lesson 7 but not Lesson 8, he is on Lesson 8. Construct a pile for Lesson 7 and a pile containing the forms for *the* and *a*, with one red marker.

Rote Sequencing Program

Arrangement of materials

Teacher in chair
Reinforcers
Record sheet and pencil
Piles of forms (B)
Blank tray filler
Response tray
Table
Child in chair

Materials
1. Rote Sequencing Program Record Sheet and pencil
2. Forms in piles designated on Rote Sequencing Lesson Selection
3. Tray
4. Blank tray filler
5. Reinforcers

Before Administering Program
1. Fill in identifying information (name and date) on record sheet.
2. Arrange materials as indicated above.
3. For all but Lesson 8, count the number of spaces on the tray, from left to right (right to left for the child) to equal the lesson number (that is, if on Lesson 5, count the last five spaces on the tray).
4. Place the blank tray filler so that it covers all but the spaces you have counted.

406

Administering the Program

Step	Evoke the response	Evaluate the response	Provide consequences	Record the response	Select the next step
1	Part 1: Place 1 form from each of the piles for this lesson between child and tray.	Part 1: *Correct:* Child selects the first form in the sequence and places it in correct slot.	Part 1: If *correct:* Provide verbal praise. If *incorrect:* Provide verbal "no."	Part 1: If *correct:* Record lesson number and a ✓ in appropriate column on record sheet. If *incorrect:* Record lesson number and an X in appropriate column on record sheet.	Part 1: If *correct:* Go to Part 2 of Step 1 in column "*Evaluate the response.*" If *incorrect:* Go to Step 3.
	Part 2: Already presented in Part 1, Step 1.	Part 2: If response is more than one form. *Correct:* Child places each of the rest of the forms in their correct slots in left-to-right sequence. If *incorrect:* Child makes an error in selecting or placing one of the forms. STOP CHILD IMMEDIATELY WHEN ANY ERROR OCCURS.	Part 2: If *correct:* Reinforce. If *incorrect:* Provide verbal "no."	Part 2: If *correct:* Record ✓s in column of record sheet for all elements of response. If *incorrect:* Record X in column of record sheet for this element of the response.	Part 2: If *correct:* Go to Step 2. If *incorrect:* Go to Step 3.

(*continued*)

407

Rote Sequencing Program (continued)

2	Part 1: Same as Part 1, Step 1, but use new forms from same pile where possible. Part 2: Already presented in Part 1, Step 2.	Part 1: Same as Part 1, Step 1. Part 2: Same as Part 2, Step 1.	Same as Part 1, Step 1. Same as Part 2, Step 1.	Same as Part 1, Step 1.	Part 1: If *correct:* Go to Part 2, Step 2. If *incorrect:* Go to Step 3. Part 2: If *correct:* Go to the next lesson of this program. Begin at "*Before Administering Program*" (above).
3	Put form on which error was made back on table and point to correct form.	Part 1: If *correct:* Child places correct form in correct slot. If *incorrect:* Child selects incorrect form or places it in wrong slot.	Part 1: Same as Part 1, Step 1.	If *correct:* Place a √ in column for that element on next row of record sheet and indicate one prompt. If *incorrect:* Place X in column for that element in next row of record sheet and indicate one prompt.	If *correct,* but response from Step 1 or 2 is not complete: Go to Part 2, Step 3. If response is completed without error go to Step 1. If *incorrect:* Go to Step 4.

| 4 | Put form on which error was made back on table and point to correct form, then to tray. | Part 2: If more forms must be placed to fill tray.

Same as Part 2, Step 1. | Part 2: Same as Part 2, Step 1.

Same as Part 2, Step 1. | Part 2: If *correct:* Record √s for all elements correctly placed.

If *incorrect:* Record Xs for the incorrect element. | Part 2: If *correct:* Go back to Step 1.

If *incorrect:* Go back to Step 3, Part 1. |
| | | Part 1: Same as Part 1, Step 3.

Part 2: Same as Part 2, Step 1. | Part 1: Same as Part 1, Step 1.

Part 2: Same as Part 2, Step 1. | If *correct:* Place √ in column for that element in next row on record sheet and indicate two prompts.

If *incorrect:* Place X in column for that element on record sheet and indicate two prompts.

Part 2: Same as Part 2, Step 3. | If *correct,* but response from Step 1 or 2 is not complete: Go to Part 2, Step 4. If response is completed without error go to Step 3.

If *incorrect:* Go to Hand-Shaping Program for this response. Reenter this program at Step 4.

If *correct:* Go to Step 3.

If *incorrect:* Go back to Step 4, Part 1. |

Rote Sequencing Program Record Sheet

Session _____

Name _____   Date _____

Lesson no.	Step no.	Part no.	No. of prompts	Art 1	N	VA	V	ing	Prep	Art 2	N 2
1											
2											
3											
•											
•											
•											
50											

APPENDIX C: SUBJECT SELECTION PROGRAM

This program is designed to teach a child to select subject nouns and place them in context. It is essentially a combination of the behaviors taught in the Labeling Program and the Rote Sequencing Program.

Entry Behavior. Completion of Rote Sequencing Program.

Terminal Behavior. Upon completion of this program the child will be able to select from those nouns taught in the Labeling Program subject nouns appropriate to stimulus pictures and use them in sentence sequences.

Contingencies. Same as in Labeling Program.

Administration Sequences. The program is preceded by a posttest of behavior taught in the Labeling Program, review of that program if necessary, and a pretest of behavior specific to this program. The beginning lesson for the child is then selected and the five steps of the program begun. Following completion of each step in each lesson, a probe test is administered to examine generalization and the child is continued in the program until he has successfully completed the posttest.

Subject Selection Test (SST)

Materials

1. All materials for Labeling Program Test
2. Subject Selection Test Record Sheet and pencil
3. Response tray
4. Symbols for *The* { *boy* / *girl* / *man* / *lady* / *baby* } *is stand ing on the floor*
5. Reinforcers
6. Pictures for *The boy is stand ing on the floor.*
   The girl is stand ing on the floor.
   The man is stand ing on the floor.
   The lady is stand ing on the floor.
   The baby is stand ing on the floor.

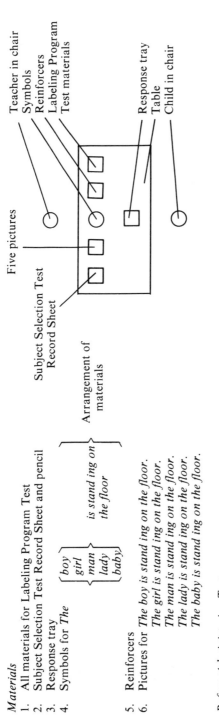

Five pictures

Subject Selection Test
Record Sheet

Arrangement of
materials

Teacher in chair
Symbols
Reinforcers
Labeling Program
Test materials

Response tray
Table
Child in chair

Before Administering Test

1. Administer Labeling Program Test and reteach any items not remembered.
2. Fill in identifying information (name, date, and so on) on record sheet.
3. Arrange materials as indicated above.

(continued)

411

Subject Selection Test (SST) (continued)

Administering the Test

Step	Evoke the response	Evaluate the response	Provide consequences	Record the response	Select the next step
1	Place forms for *The boy girl man lady baby stand ing on the floor* in front of the child and show him the top picture from the pile.	*Correct:* If symbol appropriate to picture is selected and all forms for that sentence are properly placed on the tray. *Incorrect:* If anything else is done.	If *correct:* Reinforce. If *incorrect:* Do nothing.	If *correct:* Record in all blanks on SST record sheet for that response. If *incorrect:* Record on SST record sheet for any correctly placed and selected symbols and record Xs for all others.	Put the picture just used in a new pile, clear the response tray, and repeat Step 1 until all pictures have been used (five sentences). THEN Total the √s and if the total is less than 40 go to the Subject Selection Program Lesson Selection. If the total is 40 go to the Verb Selection Program.

Subject Selection Test Record Sheet

Name _____   Date _____
Posttest _____   Pretest _____

Lesson no.	Part no.	No. of prompts	Art 1	N 1	VA	V	ing	Prep	Art 2	N 2
1										
2										
3										
•										
•										
•										
10										

Subject Selection Program (SSP) Lesson Selection

1. If the child has not completed Lesson 1, he is on Lesson 1.
   Use the symbols for *The (cat, dog) is stand ing on the floor.*
   Use pictures for *The cat is standing on the floor* and *The dog is standing on the floor.*
   Place the dog picture in the A pile and the cat picture in the B pile.
2. If the child has completed Lesson 1 but not Lesson 2, he is on Lesson 2.
   Use all symbols from Lesson 1 plus the symbol for *bird.*
   Use all pictures from Lesson 1 plus a picture of *The bird is standing on the floor.*
   Place the dog and cat pictures in Pile A and the bird picture in Pile B.
3. If the child has completed Lesson 2 but not Lesson 3, he is on Lesson 3.
   Use all symbols from Lesson 2 plus the symbol for *horse.*
   Use all pictures from Lesson 2 plus the picture of *The horse is standing on the floor.*
   Place the dog, cat, and bird pictures in Pile A and the horse picture in Pile B.
4. If the child has completed Lesson 3 but not Lesson 4, he is on Lesson 4.
   Use all symbols from Lesson 3 plus the symbol for *cow.*
   Use all pictures from Lesson 3 plus the picture of *The cow is standing on the floor.*
   Place the dog, cat, bird, and horse pictures in Pile A and the cow picture in Pile B.

When the lesson is selected and materials arranged, go to the Subject Selection Program (Step 1).

If the child has completed Lesson 4 of the SSP and still fails to meet criterion, teach five new nouns with the labeling program and begin the Subject Selection Program at Lesson 1 for those nouns.

Subject Selection Program

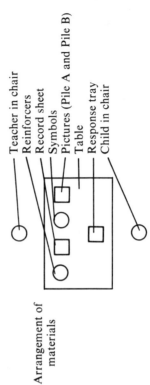

Teacher in chair
Reinforcers
Record sheet
Symbols
Pictures (Pile A and Pile B)
Table
Response tray
Child in chair

Arrangement of materials

Materials
1. Subject Selection Program Record Sheet and pencil
2. Pictures and forms indicated by lesson selection
3. Reinforcers
4. Response tray

Before Administering the Program
1. Fill in identifying information on record sheet.
2. Arrange materials as indicated above.
3. Begin Step 1a with the picture in Pile **B**.

414

Administering the Program

Step	Evoke the response	Evaluate the response	Provide consequences	Record the response	Select the next step
1a	Place symbol for *the* (one red marker) in front of child. Show child the picture.	*Correct:* If symbol is placed in first slot of tray.	If *correct:* Provide verbal praise. If *incorrect:* Provide verbal "no."	If *correct:* Record √ in appropriate slot of record sheet. If *incorrect:* Record X in appropriate slot of record sheet.	If *correct:* Go to Step 1b. If *incorrect:* Go to Step 6.
1b	Place subject noun symbols for this lesson in front of child. Show child the picture.	*Correct:* If symbol matching picture is placed in second slot of tray.	Same as in 1a.	Same as in 1a.	If *correct:* Go to 1c (remove other noun symbols from table). If *incorrect:* Go to Step 6.
1c	Place symbols for rest of sentence in front of child. Show child the picture.	*Correct:* If all forms are placed in proper slots as in Rote Sequencing Program.	If *correct:* Provide verbal praise for each symbol correctly placed and present reinforcer when sentence is complete. If *incorrect* on any symbol: stop and provide verbal "no."	If *correct:* Record √s in appropriate slots of record sheet. If *incorrect:* Record X in slot for symbol not used correctly.	If *correct:* Go to A-B list,[a] choose a picture from the designated pile, and repeat Steps 1a–1c until five consecutive sentences have been produced without error. Then, repeat SNP Test and if child scores less than 100% go to Step 2a.

(continued)

415

Subject Selection Program (continued)

Administering the Program

Step	Evoke the response	Evaluate the response	Provide consequences	Record the response	Select the next step
					If *incorrect* on any symbol: Go to Step 6 for that symbol.
					If *correct:* Go to Step 2b.
2a	Place symbols for *the* (one red marker) and subject nouns for this lesson in front of child.	*Correct:* If article and appropriate noun are placed sequentially in correct slots of tray.	If *correct:* Provide verbal praise after placement of each symbol.	If *correct:* Record √'s in appropriate slots of record sheet.	If *incorrect:* Go to Step 6 for that symbol.
	Select a picture from the A-B list and show that picture to the child.		If *incorrect:* On either symbol stop responding and say "no."	If *incorrect:* Record X in slot for that symbol not used correctly.	
2b	Same as 1c.	Same as 1c.	Same as 1c.	Same as 1c.	If *correct:* Repeat Steps 2a and 2b until five consecutive sentences have been produced correctly. Then, repeat SNP Test and if the child scores less than 100% go to Step 3.
					If *incorrect:* Go to Step 6 for that symbol.

Step				
	in Step 2a in one pile and all symbols from 2b in another pile in front of child. Select a picture from A-B list and show it to child.	priate symbols are placed in proper slots in left-to-right sequence.	after correct placement of each symbol and present a reinforcer when sentence is completed. If *incorrect* on any symbol: Stop responding and say "no."	slots on record sheet for all properly placed symbols. Put X in slot on record sheet for symbol.	3 until five consecutive sentences have been produced correctly. Then repeat SNP Test and if child scores less than 100% go to Step 4. If *incorrect*: Go to Step 6 for that symbol.
4	Place symbols from 2a in one group in front of child. Place symbols from 2b in circle around that group. Select a picture from the A-B list and show that picture to the child.	Same as in Step 3.	Same as in Step 3.	Same as in Step 3.	If *correct*: Repeat Step 4 until five consecutive sentences have been produced correctly. Then, repeat SNP Test and if the child scores less than 100% go to Step 5. If *incorrect*: Go to Step 6 for that symbol.
5	Mix all symbols from Step 4 in front of child. Select picture from A-B list and show it to child.	Same as in Step 3.	Same as in Step 3.	Same as in Step 3.	If *correct*: Repeat Step 5 until five consecutive sentences have been produced correctly. Then, repeat SNP Test and if the child scores less than 100% go to Subject Selection Program (Lesson Selection).

Subject Selection Program (continued)

Administering the Program

Step	Evoke the response	Evaluate the response	Provide consequences	Record the response	Select the next step
6	Present same symbols presented in previous step. Show child same picture. When child gets to response in which he made the error, point to the correct form.	Same as in Step 5.	Same as in Step 5.	Same as in Step 5.	If *correct:* Go back to previous step. If *incorrect:* Go to Step 7.
7	Same as Step 6 but point to both correct symbol and correct slot on tray.	Same as Step 6.	Same as Step 6.	Same as Step 6.	If *correct:* Go back to Step 6. If *incorrect:* Go to Hand-Shaping Program.

[a] Use the same A-B list (Random Selection List) used in the Labeling Program, and use it in the same way.

Subject Selection Program Record Sheet

Name _____ Session _____ Date _____

Lesson no.	No. of prompts Part no.	Art 1	N 1	VA	V	ing	Prep	Art 2	N 2
1									
2									
3									
• •									
50									

chapter

18

Language Intervention Strategies with Manipulable Symbols

Patricia Hodges

Department of Psychology
California State University
Los Angeles, California

Ruth F. Deich

Institute for Research in Human Growth
Claremont, California

contents

Despite the continuous debate over the relationship between language and cognition, it is universally accepted that language communication is a prime requirement for meaningful human interaction. Retarded persons often lack significant language skills, creating frustration for both the retarded and for those with whom they interact. The emphasis in most remedial programs is naturally on the development of oral communication (Berry and Eisenson, 1956; Donovan, 1957; Stevens and Heber, 1964; Schiefelbusch, 1967; Bricker and Bricker, 1970, 1974; Gray and Ryan, 1971; Miller and Yoder, 1972). Programs attempting to teach the nonverbal severely or profoundly retarded population language skills have had minimal success. Carrier (1974) points to three possible factors that may explain this lack of success: 1) most research and training programs have focused on the higher functioning populations, 2) the procedures for training the low functioning group have been based on procedures developed to teach higher functioning populations, and 3) the primary input has been auditory, the primary output, vocal. Before 1970, all language-training programs concentrated on developing auditory and vocal language skills.

In 1970 we became aware of the work of Dr. David Premack (1970 [Chapter 12, this volume], 1971), who successfully taught a chimpanzee (Sarah) to communicate by means of an artificial language system. The literature in comparative psychology contains reports on studies in which chimps were not able to master oral language skills to any meaningful extent (Hayes, 1951; Kellogg, 1933). Premack was not the first to teach a chimp to communicate nonvocally, since the Gardners (1969 [Chapter 9, this volume]) successfully taught a chimp (Washoe) to communicate with American Sign Language. But Premack's work is of major importance because of his revolutionary conceptualization of language.

In examining the function of language from the point of view of the proverbial visitor from outer space, Premack analyzed language not by its grammatical components, but in the step-by-step procedure that would be required to teach communication skills to a nonlinguistic organism. Premack used plastic symbols to represent the units of language (words). For the chimp, the effect of using the symbols was to eliminate the vocal demand and focus on skills occurring in the animal's repertoire (visual discrimination and motor responses). The chimp was not required to create a response (word), but could rather select (discriminate) a prepared response (symbol). For Sarah, language was then based on discrimination, association, and motor response. The impact of Premack's functional analysis of language upon the field of communication is evident. Of equal importance for those dealing with the nonverbal, severely/profoundly retarded population, is his success in breaking language away from its linguistic framework and analyzing it into separate, discrete steps fully within the low functioning retardate's pattern of skills (discrimination, associative learning, motor responses). The rationale for our pilot work then was quite simple. If a nonlinguistic organism (chimpanzee) could learn to communicate in this manner, could a human organism (having no vocal language) learn to use the same system? We hypothesized that the nondeaf, nonverbal, severely to profoundly retarded child could learn to communicate using the Premack system. At that time, the only application of the Premack system known to us was the work of Glass, Gazzaniga, and Premack (1973), who had used the system with adult aphasic patients. These patients had previously had verbal skills, but a stroke had left them language impaired. Glass was able to teach the system with varying degrees of success and competence. Her study, however, did not answer our question because the aphasic patients had previously had language skills.

THE PILOT STUDY[1]

The materials used in the training were the same as those used by Premack: a magnetic board on which the symbols were placed; the plastic geometric shapes (henceforth referred to as symbols) varying in shape, size, and color; the actual objects; and reinforcers. The symbols are the "words" of the system. All the symbols were nonrepresentational, with the exception of those used for "boy" and "girl," which were appropriately shaped. This was done for two reasons. First, if the symbols were representational it would be difficult to demonstrate that any new learning was taking place. And, second, it ensured the child's learning an analog to speech since words constructed from phonemes give no clue to what sound they represent (with the exception of onomatopoeic words such as *buzz*). Therefore, for example, a ▲ represented the word "apple" and ▶◀ represented the word "give." The two symbols which were appropriately shaped, boy and girl, were immediately recognized and correctly used. The symbols were not color coded for word class because supplying additional cues would affect the probability of a successful response for some tasks. For example, in teaching the symbol representing the category food, color coding would have changed the probability of classifying a particular food symbol as belonging to the superordinate category food from a 1 in 39 to a 1 in 16 chance factor.

Three groups of children were subjects, a group of nonverbal retarded children, a group of verbal retarded children, and a group of normal preschool children. The major group under study was the group of eight nonverbal institutionalized retarded children with expressive aphasia caused by physiological or functional disorders. These children

---
[1] The pilot study was supported by research grant MH-21994 from the National Institute of Mental Health.

had not benefited from previous language therapy and had *no* vocalizations. The mean Leiter (1948) Mental Age of the group was 3.8 years, ranging from a low of 2.5 years to a high of 6 years. The mean Peabody (1959) Mental Age for the group was 1.8 years, ranging from a low of unscorable to a high of 3.9 years. The mean chronological age for the group was 11.8 years, ranging from 7.7 years to 20.2 years. Two of the nonverbal group had autistic-like behaviors, and one had cerebral palsy (see Table 1).

A comparison group of eight verbal institutionalized retarded children was matched on chronological and mental age with the nonverbal retarded group. This group had a mean Leiter Mental Age of 3.8 years, ranging from a low of 2.5 years to a high of 5.3 years, with a mean chronological age of 14.1 years, ranging from 8.1 to 16.7 years.

Eight normal preschool children comprised the third group. The preschool group had an average mental age of 4.9 years on the Leiter, ranging from a low of 3.5 years to a high of 5.5 years, with a mean chronological age of 3.8 years, ranging from 3.7 to 4 years. Only the preschool and the nonverbal retarded groups were trained to use the Premack system and tested for their acquisition and retention. The verbal retarded group was not taught the system, but was only a comparison group. The control group permitted comparison with the nonverbal group on pre- and posttest measures (Leiter, 1948; Peabody, 1959; Adaptive Behavior Scale (Revised), 1969). The preschool group was taught the system to provide some index of what would be a normal acquisition rate for the system.

The nonverbal retarded group was initially trained five days a week, twice a day, for 20 to 30 minutes per session. After two months of training, their increased attention span permitted combining the two sessions into one session of 45 to 60 minutes per day. The normal preschool group

Table 1. Pre- and post-training: mean group results: (n = 8 per group) for pilot study

Group		Leiter			PPVT[a]				AAMD[b]	
		CA	MA	IQ	RS	MA	IQ	Concepts	A	B
Nonverbal	Pre-	11.8	3.8	37.4	11.0	1.8	10.5	2.1	278.9	53.0
retarded subjects	Post-	12.3	4.2	37.7	16.1	2.7	17.8	3.5	295.0	58.5
Verbal retarded	Pre-	14.1	3.8	30.0	19.4	2.5	19.8	5.7	316.0	53.2
subjects	Post-	14.4	4.1	32.0	28.8	2.9	24.2	5.9	321.5	54.6
Preschoolers	Pre-	3.8	4.9	131.0	45.7	4.7	112.0	13.8	—	—

[a] Peabody Picture Vocabulary Test (PPVT): RS = raw score.

[b] American Association on Mental Deficiency (AAMD) Adaptive Behavior Scale (Revised): A = positive behaviors (independent functioning, etc.); B = negative behaviors (aggression, tantrums, etc.).

was given the same training schedule: five days a week for 45 to 60 minutes per session. The preschool group completed training within a three-week period.

The basic training procedure consisted of training subjects as follows: to associate the symbols with real objects such as apple, box, and cup, as well as with more abstract concepts such as *different, color of, yellow*, and *give*, and to construct and respond to meaningful sentences (by using the symbols).

Subjects were taught to construct three- to seven-word sentences in which each word was represented by a symbol. The goal was to teach up to 39 such words of which 16 were concrete nouns, five were verbs, and the remainder were connectives, classes, etc. The words (symbols) were presented in sets of two or more except for four words that were presented singly. Following Premack's work (and language usage) the words were always placed on the board in a specific order. In this case, as in normal English writing usage, order was from left to right in the model of a simple sentence (subject, predicate, object, preposition, object).

In the first lesson, the teacher placed three symbols, ▲ (APPLE), ■ (BANANA), and ⌐ (CRACKER), in front of actual objects. The children were taught errorlessly by a series of prompts to tap the symbols against the objects and to then place the symbol on the magnetic board. At first, the child was reinforced for any correct move. Later, reinforcement was given only for complete correct acts. The tapping was used at the initial stage to call attention to the connection between the symbol and what it represented. Tapping was later faded out. At this stage, the child had successfully completed a part of the task. He could successfully pick up the symbol and could, with guidance, tap it against the object and place it upon the board. The children were making no errors and received a reward, and this success was an almost unique experience to many of them. After many of these guided trials, the children were encouraged to enact the same sequence by themselves. Each time there was a new trial, the symbols were placed in a random sequence. To test for learning, the child was required to choose the correct symbol from a group of four symbols, the three food symbols, and an unfamiliar one. This set of symbols, as well as subsequent ones, were considered learned when the child could correctly act upon (and later construct), without prompts, a variety of symbol combinations with eight out of ten trials correctly completed.

There were large individual differences in the learning rates among the nonverbal retarded subjects (see Table 2). For example, one retarded child required 149 trials to learn the symbols for apple, banana, and cracker, while another required only 13 trials to learn the same three

Table 2.   Learning rate of nonverbal retarded subjects in the pilot study

Subject number	Subject						
	1	2[a]	3	4	5[b]	6	7	8[b]
Leiter MA	3.8	2.5	6.0	3.5	2.5	4.5	4.5	3.3
Leiter IQ	38	15	64	26	21	38	53	43
PPVT MA	3.9	2.7	1.0	1.8	0.1	2.2	2.3	0.1

Concept	Number of Trials to Criterion						
Apple, Cracker, Banana	13	40	11	58	76	149	51	95
Subject, Trainer	8	15	8	20	20	20	48	108
Candy, Chip, Cereal	8	20	34	17	8	30	34	—
Eat, Put in	20	34	36	35	270	—	227	—
Ball, Box, Cup, Dish, Spoon, Fork	8	8	11	8	10	12	8	—
Clean, Give	22	10	38	28	108	—	40	—
Same, Different	325	309[c]	673[d]	161[c]	220[c]	—	—	—
Question (?)	36	—	—	—	—	—	—	—
Food	12	40	35	38	36	—	33	—
Red, Blue, Yellow	12	40	69	73	39	—	180	—
Color of	11	—	—	—	—	—	—	—
Numbers 1, 2	—	10	46	18	39	—	120	—
Numbers 1, 2, 3	20	—	—	—	—	—	—	—
Adding (and)	23	—	—	—	—	—	—	—
On, Under (in)	—	170	97	—	17	—	—	—
Boy, Girl	e	e	e	—	—	—	e	—
Small, Large	19	—	—	—	—	—	—	—
Size of	19	—	—	—	—	—	—	—

[a] This subject had cerebral palsy.
[b] Autistic-like behavior.
[c] Not learned.
[d] First taught verbally.
[e] Known by recognition (symbols were appropriately shaped).

symbols. Much learning was of the one-trial learning type, both for the faster retarded children and for the preschool children. All eight of the nonverbal retarded children were able to learn some symbols within our four-month training period, but the total number of symbols, the level of difficulty, and the speed of learning varied. The slowest retarded child learned only five symbols (representing concrete objects) and required a mean rate of 101 trials per set of words, while the fastest learned 36 symbols which included such abstract concepts as *food* (category), *color of*, and *?*. This child learned at a mean rate of 18 trials per set. Six of the eight retarded children learned to construct three- to seven-word sentences. The retarded group (except for the poorest learner who was not given a retention test) had a mean retention score of 88% correct one week after the completion of training. When the retarded group was divided into slow, medium, and fast learners on the basis of the number of trials, it was evident the fast learners also learned more words. The fast group learned 32 words, averaging 31 trials per set, while the slow group learned 8.5 words, averaging 77 trials per set. No statistical analysis was performed because of the low number of subjects in each group. However, neither mental age, chronological age, nor IQ predicted which of the retarded children would be slow, medium, or fast learners (Deich and Hodges, 1975).

At the end of training, the retarded children could furnish missing parts of sentences (CUP SAME AS ?), carry out commands (JOHN PUT BALL ON BOX), write statements (ONE AND TWO IS THREE), write commands to themselves, (JOHN EAT CANDY, JOHN PUT BANANA IN DISH), and write commands to their teachers (TEACHER PUT CEREAL UNDER CUP). The children were also able to generalize. For example, the symbol for food was learned with six foods (apple, banana, cracker, candy, cereal, and potato chip). Later, the children were able to correctly label foods items that had not been taught, such as lemons, pears, and grapes. Some children knew the artificial language quite well and made adaptations where necessary to make sentences meaningful. One child constructed the sentence TEACHER PUT CANDY IN BOX. When the trainer started to eat the candy, the child shook his head and showed the trainer what to do. Another child constructed the sentence CHILD EAT FORK, laughed, put a piece of cereal on the fork, ate the cereal and laughed again.

The results demonstrate that Premack's system can be used to teach nonverbal severely to profoundly retarded children to communicate with a plastic written system. It can be used when speech therapy has been unsuccessful. An unexpected outcome with some of the children was the beginning of spontaneous vocalization (not speech, but vocalization), although baseline data indicated no imitative vocalizations. The teachers were encouraged to use language and to talk to the children while instructing them. By the end of the training, some of the children began to imitate the trainer's speech pattern and intonations (Hodges and Deich, 1978).

The success of this project was very encouraging. However, there were several flaws in the original design:

1. We did not have a matched nonverbal control group receiving the same amount of one-to-one interaction (including verbal interactions), who did not receive training in the system; thus, any conclusion about increasing vocalization is tentative.

2. Data were not systematically collected to determine whether the increase in vocalization was significant.
3. We had no idea what the limits of this system were; i.e., was the system suitable for children who were functioning at a lower level than two years?
4. If the symbols were color coded to represent classes of words (nouns, verbs, prepositions, etc.) would this greatly facilitate language learning for the child?
5. The children came from different wards of the hospital and could not use the system to communicate outside the training situation, so spontaneous interactions and group interactions were limited to the training sessions.

To answer these questions a second study and training program was planned and is currently in progress. Additional work using the system has been carried out by a number of investigators. Blair and Baldwin (1975) used our adaptation of the Premack system for a group of autistic children and concluded that the Premack system was no more effective than was a vocal training program. Munsch and Reichert (1976) used our adaptation of the Premack system to teach four nonverbal autistic children and found that within a five-month training period three of the four learned some words, with varying degrees of abstractness. Again, there were large individual differences in the learning rates, and all subjects showed unexpected increases in spontaneous vocalizations. Munsch and Reichert also reported attention difficulties with two subjects, which caused much interference in training. They concluded the system has limited significance for the autistic child because: 1) there is a lack of specific behavior management techniques, 2) there is an observable boredom factor with the rote-like task, and 3) communication is restricted to the training sessions by the abstract (rather than representational) form of the symbols. Two investigators in England have reported success in using the system. Hughes (1972, personal communication) taught the system to a group of normal intelligence children who had been diagnosed as receptive aphasics. The children were able to use the system and evidenced an understanding of language functions, including negation, modifiers, direct and indirect objects, and questions. Tattersal (1975, personal communication) reported teaching two nonverbal retarded children to use the system within a brief training program (12 weeks). Hodges (1975, personal communication) reported limited success in using the system with an infant of nine months.[2]

---

[2] A study using one infant of age nine months generally supported the view that infants of this age could learn to associate a symbol with an object. Design flaws did not permit any greater generalization.

OTHER SYSTEMS

Carrier (1974 [Chapter 17, this volume]) and Carrier and Peak (1975) made a more extensive study based on the work of Premack. In developing his system, Carrier relied upon the disciplines of logic, linguistics, behavioral analysis, and Premack's functional analysis. This blending produced a systematic program that teaches syntactic rules apart from semantic content. Carrier reports success in teaching a group of 60 retarded children to communicate. The group had no useful language skills, although some did try to imitate one-word utterances. None had responded to conventional language therapy.

Briefly, Carrier divided his program into two separate procedures (labeling and syntactic learning). In the first procedure, the retarded child learns 10 symbols representing 10 nouns (boy, girl, man, baby, lady, dog, cat, bird, horse, and cow). As in our system and the Premack system the "words" are geometric forms, but these forms are marked with colored tape to indicate grammatical class (articles have red tape; nouns, orange tape; auxiliary verbs, green tape; verbs, blue tape; prepositions, black tape). A symbol is placed between the child and the response board, and the child is then shown a picture of what the symbol represents. The child's task is to place the symbol on the response board. In the next step, the child is presented two symbols (for example, a square for boy and a circle for girl), and must choose the correct symbol for the picture. When the child has responded correctly 10 times, a third form is added (for example, a square for boy, a circle for girl, a triangle for man), and pictures of the three are randomly presented until 10 consecutive correct responses are emitted. These procedures are randomized to ensure that 50% of all of the pictures will be of the noun that is being learned at that particular step, and 50% are randomly selected from the previously learned nouns.

Carrier reported the children were able to learn the 10 symbols in a training period of about 2 hours, ranging from a low learning time of 8.18 minutes to a high learning time of 512 minutes. He also reported that some of the children did not attend to the task or show responsiveness, and that these children were placed in a behavior modification program to establish clinical control. These children were then returned to the training program. With this procedure, Carrier reports some progress, although this progress was slow when a comparison was made to the group of 60 children who completed the program.

The second procedure (the syntactic procedure) is a rote learning of syntax through the use of color and number discriminations. The sentence model to be learned is a seven-word declarative sentence. Carrier uses a response board with seven slots (eight in his 1974 ASHA article [see Chapter 17, this volume]) as an analog to the sentence. Thus, a model would be:

Model:	THE	BOY	IS	STANDING	ON	THE	CHAIR
Grammatical class:	article	noun	auxiliary	verb	preposition	article	noun
Response board code:	RED_1	$ORANGE_1$	GREEN	BLUE	BLACK	RED_2	$ORANGE_2$

The response required from the child is a rote sequence of placing a symbol with colored tapes in the slots. The symbols are marked red_1, $orange_1$, green, blue, black, red_2, $orange_2$. One or two stripes of tape are used to indicate sequences. The symbols at this time are not associated with any semantic content. The response is intended only as a model for later operations and does not function as a communication. An unusual feature of this procedure is that the last position ($orange_2$) is taught first. Carrier reports this method was determined empirically to be more efficient (Carrier and Peak, 1975, Non-speech Language Initiation Program—Non-SLIP). The child is first taught to place a symbol with two orange markers in the last slot of the tray. This task is learned quite easily because every other slot is closed. In the next step, however, the last two slots are uncovered and the child is presented with two symbols, one with two orange markers and one with two red markers. The child's task is to place the red marked symbol in the first open slot on the tray and to place the orange marked symbol in the last slot. When this is learned, new geometric symbols of the same color markers are presented to him, and to complete this step the child must demonstrate generalization to the new forms. A black marked symbol is then added and the next slot of the tray is made available. This process of adding forms is continued until the child can take any set of seven appropriately colored numbered symbols and place them from right to left into their correct slots. Carrier reports that most children reach criterion for the first lesson very quickly. However, lesson 2 requires more time, and lesson 3 requires still more time. Most children acquire the concept of sequencing, and the remaining sequencing tasks were learned in approximately 3 hours and 9 minutes of training.

The third procedure in Carrier's program is to combine the two previously learned procedures: the syntactic system (response board position) and the labeling system. The child has learned to select some nouns out of context and has learned to sequence seven symbols (which are designed to produce sentence order). The child is tested on the nouns previously learned in the labeling procedure, and, if the child makes errors in the program, that lesson is repeated until the test criterion is met. In the 1974 ASHA article (see Chapter 17, this volume), only five noun symbols were used. In the Non-SLIP program, however, all 10 noun symbols plus the six symbols for other sentence parts are placed in front of the child. The child selects the symbol for the first slot as taught in the previous procedures. To correctly place the symbol in the second slot, the child must select the correct noun symbol for the picture presented. After filling the second slot correctly, the child fills the remaining five slots by using color/number cues. The same procedure is used until the child can use each of the noun symbols correctly 100% of the time. The mean time required to complete this portion of the training was 1 hour and 10 minutes.

Carrier reports that learning verb symbols, particularly the first two verbs, is a major problem (for five verbs the mean time for learning was 7 hours and one child required 37 hours of training). In his Non-SLIP manual, Carrier mentions a subroutine program to aid the child in attending to the stimulus pictures. Additional sentence parts are learned in the same manner using the same sequencing. To recap the cycle briefly: the first step is to learn the 10 symbol noun names (the labeling procedure without any order); the second step is to learn the rote sequencing; the third step is to combine these procedures by placing the correct noun in the correct sequence to describe a picture. Additionally, Carrier reported that as the children produced these responses and the clinician spoke the words, many of the children began to imitate the words. When clinician's utterances were faded, the children continued to initiate speech responses. (In a personal communication, Carrier indicated that 180 subjects have learned to communicate with this system and have come to verbalize quite fluently.)

THE ONGOING STUDY[3]

We are presently engaged in a study at Pacific State Hospital in which an entire unit of 37 nonverbal retarded children[4] is being taught our version of Premack's system. This study will satisfy many of the demands that were not met by the original pilot design. First, by teaching the entire unit and then allowing the symbols to be available on the unit after they have been taught, we will be able to check for any spontaneous use of symbols between children. In our original pilot study, we had hypothesized that there would be a decrease in negative behaviors as measured by the Adaptive Behavior Scale (Revised), and this decrease was not found. Retrospectively, it was naive of us to hypothesize this, since the subjects were not able to use this communication system outside of the training situation. In the current study, we hope to discover if

---

[3] This study was supported by a research grant from the Office of Education, BEH 6007603152.

[4] The final number of children being taught varies somewhat because the number of children dropped did not equal the number of new replacements on the unit.

availability of the symbols outside the teaching situation will facilitate communication and reduce negative acting-out behaviors. In the ongoing study we have one comparison group of 10 children on the same unit who will not be taught the symbols. Later we will assess how much of the system they spontaneously learn from those exposed to the symbols. The comparison group is being given the same amount of one-to-one interaction and similar exposure to manipulating objects. They are also exposed to the same teacher vocalizations as the training group so that we can later evaluate any differences in vocalizations between the comparison and the training groups. In addition, we have a second comparison group from a different unit being given the same treatment as the on-unit comparison group. An advantage in this ongoing study is that the training period will go on for a longer time (six months) and the children will have more time for learning.

Because of unexpectedly large scale changes that took place in hospital assignment, we now have a much lower functioning population than in our previous study. The children function below the mental age of two and have significant maladaptive behaviors. The children living in the unit fall into two naturally discrete groups. One group, the low functioning group of 30 children, is, in general, nonverbal. Their expressive language skills range from those making grunts, clicking sounds, and speech-like sounds ("ahh," "uuum") to a few who have words. Most could not pass any items on the Leiter or the Peabody Picture Vocabulary Test, and they were therefore given the Kuhlmann-Binet (Shotwell, 1964).

Because of this lower level of functioning most children were unable to pass items on either the nonverbal Leiter scale or the nonverbal Peabody Picture Vocabulary Test. Consequently, the Kuhlmann-Binet was administered, wherein many items also reflect motor functioning. For example, the 12th to 18th month level includes such items as whether the child can drink from a cup, eat with a spoon and fork, and spit out distasteful solids. Only two out of a total of five items query whether the child has speech and whether there is recognition of objects in pictures. (To pass the last item only directed gazing is required.)

In addition to the intelligence tests or developmental tests, the children were rated on language skills. The expressive language test contained ratings for items such as the following:

1. Does the child respond to questions? For example, if the teacher holds up a piece of candy and asks, "Do you want candy?" will the child respond verbally in any appropriate way?
2. Can the child imitate sounds, such as "mm," "pp," "eeh," etc.?
3. Can the child imitate words, such as "ma-ma," "pot," etc.?

Table 3.   Group data on Pretest measures

Group	Leiter MA	Leiter IQ	Kuhlmann-Binet MA	Kuhlmann-Binet IQ	Language skills[a]	Average number of symbols learned as of 12/9/77
Nonverbal N = 22	—	—	1–5	15.4	2	4
Verbal group N = 6	4–6	43.5	—	—	3	14

[a] Expressive Language Scale: 0 = no sounds; 1 = noise; 2 = speech-like sounds; 3 = some words; 4 = meaningful speech.

4.   Does the child spontaneously say anything?
5.   How clear and understandable is the language?

Using this system of rating expressive language, the lower functioning group of 22 children who remained in training included two who had a few words, such as "baby," "candy," "choo-choo train," one who said phrases such as "want my baby," two who babbled, and three who made noises other than grunts. The remaining 14 had no speech or speech-like sounds. The higher functioning group all had some verbal skills ranging from single words to limited sentences.

In the area of receptive language, our groups did not differ as much. The higher functioning group all had some receptive language skills as demonstrated by their responses to our questions, while the lower functioning group varied far more. Eleven of the low functioning group had about the same level of receptive language skills as did the higher functioning group. Five had essentially no receptive language (although none was deaf), and the remaining six had a mixed level of skills, responding only to familiar commands such as "sit" and "come here." The average Kuhlmann-Binet Mental Age for the group was one year five months, ranging from a low of eleven months to a high of two years. The average IQ for the group was 13, ranging from a low of 6 to a high of 30.

The second group of higher functioning individuals were able to respond to the Leiter and the Peabody. The mean Leiter Mental Age for this group was four and a half years, ranging from a low of two years nine months to a high of seven years six months.[5] The average IQ for the group was 43.5, ranging from a low of 36 to a high of 64 (see Table 4).

[5] The child with the highest mental age was a subject in our pilot study and for ethical reasons was assigned to the experimental group. Note that at the time of the pilot, he began making imitative speech sounds, and now has attained a simple vocabulary.

Before beginning the symbol training, it was necessary to determine whether the children had the attentional capacity needed to learn the symbols. Therefore, we developed a behavioral assessment tool which includes ratings for such variables as eye contact, initiating nonverbal interaction with staff and peers, apparent awareness of surroundings, and

Table 4.   Learning rates and pre-test data for the training group

Subject	Kuhlmann-Binet MA	IQ	Expressive language[a]	Number of symbols learned as of 3/1/77
1	1–2	14	0	8
2	1–0	12	0	2
3	1–1	22	0	5
4	1–4	15	0	3
5	1–2	14	0	1[b]
6	2–4[c]	19	0	13
7	1–4	10	0	11
8	0–11	6	0	0[d]
9	1–4	8	3	8
10	1–5	10	0	1
11	1–10	16	0	13
12	1–10	18	0	0
13	1–10	32	2	13
14	1–6	17	1	9
15	1–7	21	1	13
16	1–10	13	0	13
17	1–10	18	3	1
18	1–4	15	0	1
19	1–10	16	0	8
20	1–11	19	3	11
21	1–8	24	3	2
22	1–7	11	1	13
	Higher functioning group Leiter			
23	(3–2)[e]	33	3	13
24	2–5	21	4	13
25	2–9	36	3	13
26	5–9	50	3	10
27	5–0	47	4	38
28	7–6	64	4	33

[a] Expressive Language Scale: 0 = no sound; 1 = noise; 2 = speech-like sounds; 3 = some words; 4 = meaningful speech.

[b] Needed additional work on grasping.

[c] Estimated.

[d] Dropped from training because of medication problems.

[e] Score from Stanford-Binet (1960).

aggressive behavior and self-destructive behaviors. Two raters, one from the unit staff and one of our trainers, independently rated the children. For the retarded children who did not have eye contact or did not display an awareness of surroundings, a training procedure to develop these behaviors has been instituted. Prior to symbol training, these children were trained to establish eye contact, and procedures to control aggressive or self-destructive behaviors were established. Many had very low attention levels, did not attend to the task, and were extremely distractible. A behavior modification program to develop behaviors such as sitting at the table and attending to the lesson was instituted. This included presymbol training in which the child was trained to look at objects, to reach for objects, to follow instructions, to respond to social reinforcement, and to imitate movement. Some children were unable to grasp the symbols, so we developed a grasping program in which they were taught, at first, to grasp larger objects and, later, smaller objects such as symbols. We also found that it was necessary to train some of the children to match-to-sample (i.e., they learned to match an apple symbol to another apple symbol, or a banana symbol with another banana symbol).

RESULTS TO DATE

After four months of training, most children learned some use of the symbol system, but the rate varied widely in trials to criterion, errors, and the time required to learn a lesson. The children with the higher mental ages (over five years) learned the fastest and the greatest amounts. These children are at the stage of writing sentences, including answering questions. Even the nonverbal children are beginning to carry out written commands.

Subjects with mental ages between one and two years show very slow learning rates. They have learned an average of seven symbols ranging from knowing a food name such as apple, to writing phrases such as (CHILD) GIVE APPLE (TEACHER).[6] The children with an MA of above two years have learned an average of 25 symbols ranging from a low of 13 symbols to a high of 40 symbols. It is interesting to note that all the children seemed to learn the symbols for child and teacher faster than other noun symbols.

After four months of training, the teachers are reporting an increase in vocalizations and attention. At this point, all the children continuing in the study, regardless of the level of learning, wish to come to the sessions.

---

[6] Parentheses indicate implied words.

PROBLEMS

Three children out of the original group have been removed from the unit and new children have taken their places. We have also dropped four children from the training program. One was dropped because violent behaviors did not decrease significantly despite behavior modification procedures. Another was dropped because we could find absolutely no reinforcer for the child. The third child was dropped because of extended illness and the fourth was dropped because of medication problems.

Two children remain in the training program who have learned nothing. One child with Down syndrome had great difficulty grasping objects. She was placed in a behavior-shaping program to enhance her grasping abilities and never moved beyond this program. The second child has a mental age of eleven months and is only occasionally responsive because he is generally heavily medicated. The low MA, which at first sight seems to contraindicate teaching, may not be the problem since other low MA children are learning, as we noted above.

The data we have so far suggest the following tentative conclusions. Even the lower functioning developmentally disabled children, that is, below our initial requirement of an MA of two years, can learn the symbol system to some degree. The learning is slow, but it is occurring. Furthermore, as in the pilot study, mental age is not necessarily predictive of learning ability for the lower functioning group. Some children who did not seem to be learning are doing so, as may be seen by the slow drop in their error rate. The staff, too, have been surprised at the unexpected capabilities of some children. This suggests that it may be important to use many trials with these low functioning groups and to break steps down into ministeps whenever necessary before giving up on a particular lesson.

Even for children who had a very low initial attention span, it is worthwhile to attempt training. Three of the children who were most distractible have improved significantly, to the extent of showing their distractibility only between learning trials.

We had predicted that using representational symbols would aid in learning, but, interestingly enough, for two of the children representation actually has been an interference. However, since this number is quite low, it probably remains advantageous to use a representational system wherever possible.

We came upon an unexpected problem with many of our low functioning retardates: Although they had learned to match the symbol to the object, they were unable to match the object to the symbol. We had to train for a shift in learning; that is, after teaching that A goes with B, we also had to teach B goes with A. It was necessary to teach the symbol-object and then the object-symbol sequence for each item the child learned. To illustrate, consider Mary's responses. After many treats Mary learned that the apple symbol, ● , goes with the real (plastic) apple; that is she reliably (over 80% of the time) selected the correct apple symbol from an array of four symbols and placed it in front of the apple. However, when Mary was shown the actual apple and asked to place it next to the apple symbol, ● , she was unable to do so. This step, which we called a shift, was taught separately. Once she learned this shift, she was taught the symbol for banana, ⫘ . Again, Mary reliably learned to select the symbol from an array and place it in front of the real banana. When presented with the banana and required to move the banana to the banana symbol, ⫘ , she was again unable to do this and so had to be taught this shift. The same procedures must be followed, even when the child has learned 11 other symbols and shifts. Shift learning seems to be more rapid than the original pairing but still needs many guided trials.

We have now had many instances in which, for the group with an MA below two years, it is necessary to break lessons into extremely small steps: first, the match-to-sample task for both symbols and objects; next, the association of a symbol with an object; and last, the association of an object with a symbol. This breakdown is necessary because at this level the children do not seem to make even the smallest conceptual leap or deduction. Thus, any procedures requiring an inference or deductive process must be broken into additional training procedures. This group also has great difficulty learning verbs. They were able to master the concrete nouns representing apple, cracker, banana in lesson 1, teacher/subject in lesson 2, box, cup, ball in lesson 3, and candy, chip, cereal in lesson 4. However, when they reached lesson 5, the verbs *clean* and *give* gave them great difficulty. We are presently breaking the teaching of the verb sequences into simpler steps. The question coming to mind is whether the children in this group have merely learned a simple association between two things; that is, that a red symbol goes with a specific object but not that the red symbol represents the object. This higher level of abstraction may be necessary for learning a verb because there is no immediate object with which the symbol can be associated.

Last, although the control group on the same unit is getting equal one-to-one attention, verbalization, and manipulation, the second control group on another unit is not. An outbreak of hepatitis and subsequent quarantine meant that the second control group lost about three weeks of one-to-one interaction in comparison to the training group. Hence, this "hepatitis" control will not be fully comparable to the training group, although the same-unit control group remains comparable.

CONCLUSIONS

The Premack system can be used to some extent with even the low functioning child if taught on a one-to-one basis. We have not analyzed any data on increases in vocalizations, yet reports from the teachers and ward personnel indicate that some of the children are starting to vocalize more often. We will be able to compare the amount of vocalization for this group to the group that received equal interaction and vocalization without any of the symbol training to see if there is a difference. If this system facilitates language or signing, it might be considered a precursor to these behaviors. We will also be able to compare whether the Premack system will act as a facilitator for signing because all the children on this unit are slated to enter a signing program at the end of our training program. Thus, we will be able to compare their learning rates with similar children on the same and other units who have not had such training.

In reviewing the conceptual and perceptual prerequisites for language (Clark, 1974), we noted that our population has the perceptual skills necessary for mastering the Premack system: they can discriminate and respond to shape, size, and movement; none is deaf, and they respond to sound (although hearing is not a requisite for this system); they also respond to taste, having a hierarchy of food preferences; responses to texture and touch have also been observed. Children having perceptual deficits in these areas may not respond to training in the system.

From the Piagetian view of language (1926, 1952) a child must first learn to understand the class of objects before he develops the representation for the object. Premack has commented that in initial training the chimp does not distinguish the referent from the thing to which it refers, and so it smears a piece of apple on the board rather than placing the symbol representing the apple on the board. All of our subjects seemed to distinguish the class of real objects from the class of symbols. None of the children, not even the low functioning group, has attempted to place the object instead of the symbol on the board so, perhaps, they are in some sense preprogrammed for language. Our work has confirmed that symbol systems can be valuable in training nonverbal retardates to communicate, even if such communication remains only partial, as is the case with some of the subjects. We developed match-to-sample tasks, attention-shaping programs, and grasping programs, as Carrier also has done. He has extended his work by developing a grammatical system (by means of placement on the response board). Our present project has not dealt explicitly with grammatical class except to color code for parts of speech. We have taught specific word order, but not specific rules for this order. Our higher functioning children seem to learn syntactic order without any direct teaching. They have progressed from one-symbol labeling to stringing fairly long and complex chains. We therefore are not convinced that Carrier's specific sequencing task requirement is the key to his success. Additional comparative information would be helpful in resolving this question of the need for teaching stringing.

In addition to our own system we had expected to teach Carrier's Non-SLIP method to a small group of children on the second unit in the fourth month of ongoing training. However, hepatitis and the subsequent quarantine eliminated the possibility for a valid teaching and comparison schedule. Further research is needed in comparing the efficacy of different symbol systems.

Carrier's reported learning rate for his subjects seems in some cases to be more rapid than that for ours. Several factors may be involved: First, our large number of low functioning children may have consistently lower mental ages. Data from his reports do not go into sufficient detail to permit clear comparison.

Second, Carrier uses randomization to teach noun symbols. He begins by teaching two such noun symbols, together with pictures of the nouns, and then adds others in a cumulative fashion. Procedures are randomized so that 50% of all pictures are of the noun being learned at a particular step, and 50% are randomly selected from previously learned nouns. This technique provides continuous review and may help prevent perseveration.

Last, we require that the child pass rather stringent tests of retention before learning new symbols. Thus, even when the child learns to criterion, he must still demonstrate symbol knowledge in different contexts and combinations before going on to the next set of symbols.

A point that was consistently emphasized at the Gulf Shores Conference on language intervention (March, 1977) and that should be considered in any future study is the amount of control the child/subject achieves by mastering the symbol system. Our symbols were not chosen to maximize meaningfulness. By individualizing the system and arranging environmental strategies to ensure that the child achieves more control of his reinforcement contingencies, learning rate and motivation to learn may well increase.

Further research is needed to determine if the use of a symbol system does indeed facilitate other communication modalities such as signing or speech. Our results as well as Carrier's seem to support this view. Yet, so far as we know, no other study except our ongoing one has adequately compared the relative facilitative effect of symbols plus one-to-one interaction versus comparable one-to-one interaction without learning symbols. Our program includes two control groups designed for comparison with the training group. If at the end of training, those learning the symbols do better at vocalizing, verbalizing, or signing, then we could show the facilitative effect of a symbol system over one-to-one interaction by itself.

As noted earlier, our second control group unfortunately has been given less interaction time because of their hepatitis quarantine, and so are no longer strictly comparable. However, the control group (on the training group's unit) can and will still be used for comparative purposes at the end of training. Because of this unexpected reduction in the second controls' interaction time, we do not expect to prove or disprove the issue of symbol facilitation on other communication modalities. It would be useful to run another systematic study regarding this issue.

No systematic study has been done to determine why such facilitation should occur at all.[7] This is an empirical question deserving additional investigation.

REFERENCES

Adaptive Behavior Scale (Revised). 1969. Revision of American Association on Mental Deficiency Adaptive Behavior Scale by E. Lu, R. F. Deich, and R. Kingery. (Available from Pacific State Hospital, Pomona, Cal.

Berry, M. F., and Eisenson, J. 1956. Speech Disorders: Principles and Practices of Theory. Appleton-Century-Crofts, New York.

Blair, N., and Baldwin, A. 1975. A comparison of the effects of symbol versus speech training on the behavior of autistic children. Unpublished manuscript.

Bricker, W. A. and Bricker, D. D. 1970. A program of language training for the severely language handicapped child. Except. Child. 37:101–112.

Bricker, W. A., and Bricker, D. D. 1974. An early language training strategy. In R. L. Schiefelbusch and L. L. Lloyd (eds.), Language Perspectives—Acquisition, Retardation, and Intervention, pp. 431–468. University Park Press, Baltimore.

Carrier, J. K., Jr. 1974. Application of functional analysis and a nonspeech response mode to teaching language. In L. V. McReynolds (ed.), Developing systematic procedures for training children's language, ASHA Monogr. No. 18a:47–95.

Carrier, J. K., Jr., and Peak, T. 1975. Non-SLIP: Non-speech Language Initiation Program. H & H Enterprises, Lawrence, Kan.

Clark, E. V. 1974. Some aspects of the conceptual basis for first language acquisition. In R. L. Schiefelbusch and L. L. Lloyd (eds.), Language Perspectives—Acquisition, Retardation, and Intervention, pp. 107–128. University Park Press, Baltimore.

Deich, R. F., and Hodges, P. M. 1975. Learning from Sarah. Hum. Behav. May:40–42.

Donovan, H. 1957. Organization and development of a speech program for the

---

[7] Facilitation of speech with and after signing has also been reported, but again no systematic comparisons with control groups are available.

mentally retarded children in New York City Public Schools. Am. J. Ment. Defic. 67:455–459.

Gardner, R. A., and Gardner, B. J. 1969. Teaching sign language to a chimpanzee. Science 165:664–672.

Glass, S., Gazzaniga, M., and Premack, D. 1973. Artificial language training in global aphasia. Neuropsychologia 11:95–103.

Gray, B. B., and Ryan, B. P. 1971. Programmed Conditioning for Language. Accelerated Achievement Association, Monterey, Cal.

Hayes, C. 1951. The Ape in Our House. Harper & Row, New York.

Hodges, P., and Deich, R. 1978. Teaching an Artificial Language to Nonverbal Retardates. Behav. Mod. 2:489–509.

Hughes, J. Quoted in Cromer, R. F. 1974. Receptive language in the mentally retarded: Process and diagnostic distinctions. In R. L. Schiefelbusch and L. L. Lloyd (eds.), Language Perspectives—Acquisition, Retardation and Intervention, pp. 237–267. University Park Press, Baltimore.

Kellogg, W. N. 1933. The Ape and the Child. McGraw-Hill Book Co., New York. [1967, Hafner, New York.]

Leiter International Performance Scale. 1948. C. H. Stoelting Co., Chicago.

Miller, J., and Yoder, D. 1972. A syntax teaching program. In J. E. McLean, D. E. Yoder, and R. L. Schiefelbusch (eds.), Language Intervention with the Retarded: Developing Strategies, pp. 191–211. University Park Press, Baltimore.

Munsch, K. M., and Reichert, D. 1976. Symbol communication training with autistic and autistic-like children. In preparation.

Peabody Picture Vocabulary Test, Form B. 1959. Minnesota Service, Circle Pines.

Piaget, J. 1926. The Language and Thought of the Child. Harcourt Brace, New York.

Piaget, J. 1952. The Origins of Intelligence in Children. W. W. Norton & Co., New York.

Premack, D. 1970. A functional analysis of language. J. Exp. Anal. Behav. 11:107–125.

Premack, D. 1971. Language in chimpanzee? Science 172:808–822.

Schiefelbusch, R. L. 1967. Language development and language modification. In N. G. Haring and R. L. Schiefelbusch (eds.), Methods in Special Education, pp. 49–73. McGraw-Hill Book Co., New York.

Shotwell, A. M. 1964. Suitability of the Kuhlmann-Binet infant scale for assessment of intelligence in mental retardates. Am. J. Ment. Defic. 68:757–765.

Skinner, B. F. 1957. Verbal Behavior. Appleton-Century-Crofts, New York.

Stanford-Binet Intelligence Scale, Form L-M. 1960. Houghton Mifflin Co., Boston.

Stevens, H. A., and Heber, R. 1964. Mental Retardation: A Review of Research. University of Chicago Press, Chicago.

chapter

Application of Computer-Assisted Language Designs

Dorothy A. Parkel

S. Tom Smith, Jr.

Georgia Retardation Center
Atlanta, Georgia
and
Georgia State University
Atlanta, Georgia

contents

In June, 1975, funds became available for testing the feasibility of using the equipment and procedures developed in the LANguage Analog (LANA) Project (Rumbaugh, 1977) in teaching language skills to severely and profoundly retarded human subjects. The project is being carried out at the Georgia Retardation Center, a small, state-operated residential facility in Atlanta, Georgia. The center serves approximately 440 inpatients with a staff of more than one thousand; thus, its residents enjoy a higher level of programming opportunities than is available in many state-operated facilities.

The work described here is not conceived as an intervention program but as a feasibility study, undertaken to:

1. Test training procedures used with primates of other species
2. Explore, adapt, and expand the uses of the equipment developed with animal subjects
3. Identify and clarify problems of language training in early acquisition stages in a population that does not achieve linguistic facility through normal socialization
4. Amplify and clarify further the emerging body of principles on which language-training programs should be based
5. Pilot alternative designs for language intervention programs

Although we are fortunate to be starting our program at a point when important pioneering efforts have been made (Kent, 1972; Miller and Yoder, 1972, 1974; Bricker and Bricker, 1974; Carrier, 1974 [Chapter 17, this volume]; Guess, Sailor, and Baer, 1974; MacDonald and Blott, 1974; Premack and Premack, 1974; Stremel and Waryas, 1974; Rumbaugh, 1977; Hodges and Deich (Chapter 18, this volume)), many problems remain that must be solved to carry out even a feasibility study. These include:

1. Determining what skills are requisite for language learning
2. Determining the subject's developmental level and performance potential with regard to these skills
3. Selecting and sequencing tasks
4. Determining what experiences have to be built into a training situation to produce the understanding that the tasks being taught in the laboratory are communication functions

As indicated above, the program was begun in an attempt to test the LANA procedures with a retarded population. Two approaches were chosen initially. One of these is similar both to that used with the LANA chimpanzee and to Carrier's Non-SLIP (1974, 1976) in that it involves training several stock sentences. Each sentence is designed to accomplish a particular communication function: requesting, naming, describing, or questioning. Once a sentence is taught, which is done through operant procedures, the subject is trained to substitute first a variety of objects

---

Supported by National Institutes of Health Grant HD-06016-06.

and later agents, actions, and modifiers. Through this process the subject should begin to differentiate the elements of the communication string.

This method, however, places a rather heavy output burden on the subject. Moreover, since it is necessary for the subject to develop a stable response chain, he cannot be allowed to give spontaneous transformations until it is well learned. Because these problems were anticipated at the outset of the project, a second training method was devised paralleling some of the output patterns manifested by normal children. The same communication functions are being taught, but at the first stage of this program only single-word output is required. As with normal children, the subject's intent is inferred from the context. After several communication functions are mastered, the subject is taught to respond with two-word rule-governed structures, and later three-word and longer structures. The strings have been chosen from those found in diary studies of the development of normal children's speech. This program is designed to give attention first to individual elements, then to patterns, cues, and rules for multiword constructions.

INSTRUMENTATION

A computer-controlled keyboard and lexigram display system form the basis of the communication system. The keyboard contains 100 translucent plastic keys with geometric symbols (coined lexigrams, see von Glasersfeld, 1977) printed on their faces. They are arranged in a two by two matrix with 25 keys in each quadrant. The keys can be selectively enabled by a switch panel located outside the training room. When a key is active, it is dimly illuminated; when it is depressed, it is raised to full brightness. The keys can be scrambled by relocating them between sessions or by switching between multiple copies within a session. The PLEASE and QUESTION keys are used to mark requests and questions and appear as the first lexigram in the sequence. The PERIOD key signals the end of a communication and erases the subject's sentence from the lexigram display projectors.

As keys are depressed their lexigrams are displayed in two rows of projectors located directly over the keyboard. Each row contains seven projectors; the bottom row is used by the subject, the top row by the experimenter. The experimenter's display remains active during the subject's response and can either be retained after the subject erases his row or terminated by the subject's completion of his sentence. The display also can be controlled by a keyboard located outside the training room.

A PDP8E computer, using the RTS8 real-time operating system, monitors the keys and controls the lexigram display. The computer concurrently controls several additional devices. Two universal feeders, located outside the room, funnel the reward through a common dispensing tube to a small tray next to the keyboard. A liquid dispenser is located a few feet from the keyboard. A vending window, through which large objects can be passed, is located to the right of the keyboard. A Kodak Carousel random access projector, controlled by the computer, can display any of 80 slides, with a maximum access time of 3.5 seconds, on a screen immediately to the right of the lexigram projectors.

Four calculator type numerical keyboards are monitored by the computer. One functions to provide optional manual control of vending devices and the slide projector. The other three can be used to enter numeric codes for observational data.

We are developing options that will allow some level of independent study by the subjects. Without experimenter intervention, the system can display slides, pose questions about the slides, evaluate the answers, and elaborate on alternative answers. As we learn more about the cognitive and linguistic development of severely and profoundly retarded students, we hope to establish training programs that allow subjects to expand linguistic skills with minimal supervision. This would enable the student to move through training material in a self-paced fashion.

The most valuable option provided by the system is the data acquisition capability. When the subject or experimenter completes a sentence, it is stored with the time of day in seconds. The latency of each key press is recorded and allows us to monitor the rate of responding within subtasks. When any device is activated, either manually or by the computer, the nature of the event is collated with the linguistic data. Additional information concerning the correctness of the performance and the interaction between the subject and experimenter is entered into the computer by observers using numerical data keyboards. Rapid evaluation at the end of the session is possible and provides feedback for planning sessions. Our system transmits the data to a large time-sharing system where it is permanently stored, allowing long term evaluation of our procedures.

ADVANTAGES OF THE SYSTEM FOR THE SUBJECT POPULATION

First, this system provides a very simple output response, i.e., a key press, which is clearly simpler than talking or signing, possibly even than manually arranging cardboard or plastic symbols. Requiring a simpler output response allows the subject to focus more attention on cognitive aspects of the task, such as discriminating input elements and associating them with their referents or functions, evaluating the message, social context, and response requirements, and selecting appropriate output elements. Programs using visual symbols enable the prolongation of the subject's exposure to the linguistic stimuli. In addition this display system gives immediate feedback or confirmation of the subject's responses.

The system makes possible the use of multimodal input, since the English equivalent of each key is spoken by the experimenter as the key is pressed. Thus, specific training is provided for associating the two modalities. Because such stimuli are more easily perceived as individual units, they may aid the subject in delimiting the boundaries of the accompanying auditory stimuli.

The capacity of a computer-based system for extended practice and feedback should be obvious. Also, as with other laboratory-based programs, the stimulus field can be limited, which should aid the subject's focus of attention. Response possibilities can be controlled to maximize the probability of success. And with the automation capacity of the computer, the task can be structured to effect a high degree of consistency of outcomes. (A more detailed discussion can be found in Parkel, White and Warner, 1977.)

SUBJECT SELECTION

The success of the system with chimpanzees suggested that we explore working with a severely and profoundly retarded, nonverbal population, people who are not usually given priority as candidates for language training. Of the five subjects with whom we have attempted to work so far, one had such severe behavior problems that we found ourselves unable to concentrate his attention on language training and had to discontinue work with him. Of the remaining subjects, two had a few "utterances" (less than 10), most of which were unintelligible without clear contextual clues and considerable acquaintance with the subjects, and they were not always consistently used. Although these subjects were attempting to communicate verbally, neither was considered a likely candidate for language training at our center. The higher functioning subject was trying to initiate communication, using gestures and garbled utterances; the other used utterances only in response to other's questions. The fourth and fifth subjects displayed no signs of expressive language. They also used few gestures, and their oral communication consisted of very limited vocalizations.

Although IQ and MA scores with this population have proved to be poor predictors, we have, nonetheless, tried to make estimates in order to communicate with others working in the field. We have limited our selection to subjects with MAs between 18 and 30 months. Although we have included subjects who have behavior problems, it is clear that with limited training time each day such problems must be minimized. Also, at present we are dealing with subjects whose motor and visual abilities are at least sufficient for ready manipulation of the keyboard.

One of the totally nonverbal subjects was discharged from the center before making much progress with the program. The other, who was the lowest level subject chosen, has made little progress and may serve simply to tell us the lower limits to which this program can be applied. We hope, however, to find better methods for providing training for such persons as we better understand the processes of early language acquisition.

RESULTS TO DATE

The procedures, problems, and progress of two subjects who have responded well are discussed in detail below to illustrate the basic organization of each program design.

Stock Sentence Approach

The subject in the program based on the LANA procedures is a Down syndrome male who was 18 years old at the time we began working with him. He had been institutionalized nine years prior to entering the program, five at our center, two at a large custodial care state facility, and two at a small, private institution. He has some self-help skills, e.g., he can dress with help and feed himself. A Cattell administered several months before he entered the program yielded an MA estimate of 25 months. He could do all of the tasks at the two-year level on the Leiter (matching colors, pictures, and forms). He could identify a number of common objects and body parts. He frequently used jargon and occasionally gave verbal approximations for a few words, the most intelligible of which was "yeah," which was used indiscriminately. He was not prone to use vocal means to initiate communication. His vocalizations were mainly given as responses to questions or as imitations. While he is fairly cooperative and often highly motivated, he is equally often frustrated and likely to exhibit behavior problems. His training sessions usually last from 30 to 75 minutes, the average being approximately 50 minutes.

We began his training in early April, 1976 (his program and progress are summarized in Table 1). During his first session (approximately 45 minutes) we began to teach him the stock sentence PLEASE (EXPERIMENTER) GIVE POPCORN PERIOD.[1] These five keys were arranged in order in the top row of the keyboard. We first

---

[1] Words in capital letters are the English translations of the lexigrams in the sentence as it was taught. The word placed in parentheses refers to the class of lexigrams used in that position rather than to the proper name of the experimenter or subject. In subsequent sentences parentheses are used to indicate word classes in which a variety of specific words are being used.

Table 1. Chronology of task introduction for subject in Stock Sentence Approach

Date	Session	Task
4/5/76	1	Introduce request sentence, PLEASE (experimenter) GIVE POPCORN in response to experimenter's question, QUESTION WHAT WANT
5/5/76	20	Introduce first new object, COKE
5/24/76	32	Introduce fifth new object, CRACKER
5/25/76	33	Introduce Naming Sentence, (object-name) NAME-OF THIS in response to experimenter's question, QUESTION WHAT NAME-OF THIS
7/13/76	57	Expand use of Request Sentence to nonedibles
8/10/76	73	Introduce "Reading" Task in response to experimenter's command, TOUCH (object)
9/23/76	98	Introduce Action Sentence, (experimenter) BRUSH/COMB HAIR in response to experimenter's question
9/28/76	100	Introduce Action Sentence, (subject) EAT edible
10/4/76	103	Introduce Alternate Request Sentence, (subject) WANT (object)
10/28/76	118	Introduce slides
11/16/76	129	Introduce Person Identification in response to experimenter question, QUESTION WHO THIS
12/6/76	137	Mesh tasks
12/13/76	142	Introduce Slide Request Sentence, PLEASE SHOW SLIDE TO (subject) in response to experimenter's command, PLEASE (subject) SHOW SLIDE (developed to give subject control over machine)
12/21/76	149	Introduce Slide Erasure Command, (object-name) SLIDE GO in response to experimenter's question, QUESTION (subject) WANT SLIDE GO
1/18/77	182	Introduce color training with sentence, (color) COLOR-OF THIS

taught him to depress the lexigram for "popcorn." Next we interposed the experimenter's question, ? WHAT GIVE (which we later changed to ? WHAT WANT, then to ? WHAT (SUBJECT) WANT). Then we required the sequence POPCORN PERIOD and, finally, PLEASE POPCORN PERIOD. All of these were mastered within the first session. During the next session he mastered the sequence PLEASE GIVE POPCORN PERIOD, but had considerable difficulty in dealing with the sentence when required to give the entire five key sequence. He mastered that by the sixth session, at which time we displaced the POPCORN key to the same column in the third row.

From that point on we continued to move the keys one at a time until the positions of all but the PLEASE and PERIOD keys could be changed as frequently as every trial and be tracked by the subject. This continued for approximately 20 sessions, which ranged in length from 30 to 55 minutes each. We then introduced a symbol for "Coke," which the subject began to substitute in his sentence by the end of the next session. During the next 10 sessions we introduced three other comestibles, COOKIE, WATER, and CRACKER, continuing to shift the positions of the keys.

Because we were not using any irrelevant keys, we could not be sure that the subject really understood what he was asking for, even though he tended to ask much more often for POPCORN, COKE, and COOKIE than for CRACKER and WATER. Therefore, we introduced the naming sentence (OBJECT) NAME-OF THIS to determine whether he could correctly associate these keys with the edibles when held up before him. He mastered this sentence within a single session and was able to identify the edibles more than 70% of the time. We then began to teach him the names of manipulable objects, articles of clothing, body parts, and vehicles.

We had considerable difficulty getting the subject to use his request sentence for nonedibles. We tried to get him to ask for a ball, which he played with during a recreation break. After much modeling by others and cuing and prompting by the experimenter he eventually extended the sentence to this use after 18 sessions.

After 72 sessions we began to test the subject's ability to identify the lexigrams from the projectors, i.e., to "read." Until this time the experimenter had pronounced the English word for each lexigram as it was depressed. For this task the experimenter would project in her row the lexigram for "touch," which she would pronounce, followed by the lexigram for the object to be identified, which she did not pronounce. The subject was then required to identify the object from an array before him. His performance at the first session was slightly above 70%, but improved to the 95% level by the seventh session.

When the subject had been in training for almost 100 sessions, during which he had been labeling, "reading" from the projectors, and requesting edibles and objects from the machine or experimenter, we introduced two action words, BRUSH and COMB, and the sentence (EXPERIMENTER) BRUSH/COMB HAIR. The experimenter acted out each action for the subject and asked the question ? WHAT (EXPERIMENTER) DO. The subject seemed to have no comprehension of the task when both action lexigrams were presented, so we focused for two sessions on BRUSH only, using the same techniques to teach him (EXPERIMENTER) BRUSH HAIR that we had used with his first stock sentence, starting with BRUSH, then BRUSH HAIR, then (EXPERIMENTER) BRUSH HAIR. He performed very steadily even though the keys were dispersed about the keyboard, mastering each step in less than 10 trials. We felt, however, that this action was not particularly salient to the subject so we shifted to the sentence (SUBJECT) EAT (EDIBLE), changing the task to a request task, cuing him with the question ? WHAT (SUBJECT) WANT and allowing him to request either of two highly salient edibles. This string was built up in the same way as (EXPERIMENTER) BRUSH HAIR. The subject seemed very uninterested in this task even though we introduced a more salient edible (ice cream). We also gave him an alternative request sentence, (SUBJECT) WANT (EDIBLE), since we felt this was socially a more appropriate form and since we wanted him to understand that a given communication objective can be accomplished in a variety of ways. His response time for initiating the sentence, however, became longer and longer and was far longer than his initiation time for the labeling task.

Our emphasis by this time had shifted away from actions, which we then tested with pictures from the Peabody Picture Vocabulary Test. Although he could identify 63 of 103 object names from a set of four pictures per trial, he could identify only 12 of 41 common gerunds. We then tried training him to identify actions from still pictures (clearly not the best stimulus material), using five actions during each session. He continued to be very inattentive and to acquire the identifications very slowly. This training involved only his pointing to the picture of the action named by the experimenter. After three sessions we suspended this training, because the subject did not seem to comprehend the task and was becoming more and more restless, and until we could devise better methods for demonstrating the actions and choosing salient ones for initial training.

In late October, 1976, we introduced slides, which he enjoyed very much. Initially he had problems identifying some of the items, probably because of the poor photographic quality of some of the slides. By the end of the fourth session, however, he was performing above the 95% level and handling many exemplars that he had never seen before. Before the introduction of slides, he was able to label eight edibles, five toys, four articles of clothing, five body parts, three people, and three vehicles (his vocabulary is listed in Table 2). After the addition of the slide projector to the system, we were able to show pictures of environmental objects, such as his cottage. Following this he added one edible, one toy, two articles of clothing, one body part, one household fixture (phone) and one eating utensil over a period of 64 sessions.

Our emphasis during this period was not to enrich his vocabulary but rather to improve his motivation, to teach him new concepts (such as

Table 2.   Vocabulary of subject in Stock Sentence Approach showing date and session of introduction

Date	Session	Word(s)	Cumulative total
4/5/76	1	POPCORN, PERIOD, PLEASE	3
4/6/76	2	GIVE, first experimenter's name	5
5/5/76	20	COKE	6
5/18/76	28	COOKIE	7
5/20/76	30	WATER	8
5/24/76	32	CRACKER	9
5/25/76	33	NAME-OF, THIS	11
6/10/76	44	SHOE	12
6/11/76	45	BALL	13
7/8/76	54	CAR	14
7/13/76	57	SHIRT	15
7/20/76	61	HAT	16
8/10/76	73	DOLL, HAIR	18
8/19/76	80	NOSE	19
8/23/76	82	APPLE	20
8/27/76	86	VAN	21
9/7/76	90	HAND	22
9/8/76	91	second experimenter's name	23
9/14/76	94	EYE	24
9/20/76	96	MOUTH	25
9/23/76	98	COMB/BRUSH	27
9/28/76	100	subject's name, EAT	29
10/4/76	103	WANT, ICE CREAM	31
10/13/76	108	CEREAL	32
10/14/76	109	BOOK	33
10/19/76	112	BOX	34
10/20/76	113	BLOCK	35
10/21/76	114	PANTS	36
10/25/76	116	TRUCK	37
11/3/76	122	COTTAGE	38
12/6/76	136	JUICE	39
12/13/76	142	SHOW, SLIDE, TO	42
12/21/76	149	GO	43
1/11/77	173	PURSE, CUP	45
1/14/77	179	EAR, CHAIR	47
1/17/77	181	SOCK	48
1/19/77	184	COLOR-OF	49
1/25/77	191	PHONE, BELL	51

color) and to give him more control over outcomes, teaching him a new sentence to produce a salient display, for example, PLEASE SHOW SLIDE TO (SUBJECT). To reduce his tendency to form a response set and to increase his interest in the session, we meshed the tasks. For the first 136 sessions, tasks were done in blocks with the order of each block being changed from time to time. After this, however, we began to mix the tasks in order to spread throughout the session those tasks that he performed successfully.

Further plans for this subject include training in the identification of modifiers, teaching of locations both with prepositions and adverbs, and, most importantly, training which requires him to make further differentiations of the elements of his stock sentences, by substituting other agents, actions, objects, etc. This last feature of his training is considered critical to his comprehension of the correspondence between sentence elements and their perceptual referents or linguistic functions, a step which we consider a prerequisite to productive language use. It is productive language use that we consider a critical test of the training procedures.

Element Training and Construction Approach

The subject being trained with the element training and construction approach was 16 years old when we began working with her in mid-May, 1976. She was a normal infant who at approximately one year of age suffered brain damage from a gas leak in the furnace of her home. She was admitted to the Georgia Retardation Center at age 12 and has been in residence ever since, going home for holidays and sometimes for weekends. She is very outgoing, has made many friends at the center, but seems to prefer interacting with adults rather than peers. She has some self-help skills, e.g., she can dress with help and can feed herself without help. Her fine motor control is so poor that her performance on the Leiter was difficult to assess. Her receptive language level was considerably greater than that of the subject in the program described above. She could handle two-step commands, identify body parts on herself and on a doll, and identify many common objects and pictures (on the Peabody Picture Vocabulary Test she was scored at the 30-month level).

She is highly motivated but distractible and from time to time has had considerable trouble in controlling her attention to the task. She makes frequent motor errors in using the keyboard, which are obviously frustrating to her, but she seems more upset over errors that we suspect are caused by momentary lapses of attention. Her motivation and social development, however, are such that we switched from primary to token reinforcers after two months and after another six weeks to social reinforcement only.

We began her training with object naming. During the first session she was taught to respond to the keys for "car" and "doll" when presented with the object and the experimenter's question ? WHAT THIS. We were able to add a third lexigram during the third session, and new symbols at the rate of two per week from the second through the fifth weeks.

We introduced each new word by holding up the object, pronouncing the name for it, and then pointing to the key (which was the only key illuminated) and requiring her to depress that key. The projectors were then cleared, and the experimenter asked, ? WHAT THIS, requiring the subject to depress the key for that word. This procedure was repeated, first with cuing and prompting, until she gave five spontaneous responses. The new items were then interspersed with her known words, all of which were presented randomly within blocks. As we continued to introduce new words, we found that she required less and less cuing, and by the time she had a dozen words it was no longer necessary to give more than one trial with the new word nor to disable known keys before going to a random presentation of all her objects.

During the fifth week we began to test her ability to "read" the lexigrams from the experimenter's projectors, by giving her the TOUCH (OBJECT) command. She had to be cued on half the trials on the first day of presentation but was able to identify 90% of the objects on non-cued trials. By the fourth day she was able to perform near the 90% level fairly consistently. She did not like this task until we began allowing her to depress the lexigram after she had pointed to the object. As we have found with all subjects, keyboard manipulation seems to be an engaging activity and a motivating factor in training with this system. (Her program and progress are summarized in Table 3.)

By the time she was using a dozen object names on both tasks, she demonstrated some perceptual confusion with five lexigrams, some of which suggested that she was ignoring the redundant color cue.[2] With a concentrated effort on these items we improved her discrimination to some extent, using both the keyboard and cardboard lexigrams, but never devoting an entire session to such training. We reduced this emphasis after a couple of weeks and found that eventually her confusion with these lexigrams disappeared without continued concentrated focus on the errors, just as normal children eventually sort out auditory and articulatory confusions. This suggests that subjects need to be exposed to a wider range of experience and to develop a greater degree of internal organization for all relevant processing skills to become operative. Therefore, perhaps we should not require too high a level of precision in responding before progressing to new tasks and providing more experience.

By the time she acquired a dozen words it was clear that she had a set for learning new words. Between the 45th and 58th sessions we began to see how quickly she could acquire new words. During this three-week period her vocabulary doubled from 15 to 30 words. By the time she had

---

[2] Lexigram categories (such as action, animate object, edible, etc.) are denoted by the background color on the key face and on the projected facsimile; each geometric symbol is used for one word only and at present is represented in only one color. Hence, the color cue is redundant.

Table 3. Chronology of task introduction and milestones of subject in Element Training and Construction Approach

Date	Session	Task
5/13/76	1	Introduce Object Naming in response to experimenter's question, QUESTION WHAT THIS
6/7/76	15	Introduce "Reading" in response to experimenter's command, TOUCH (OBJECT)
7/14/76	34	Change from primary to token reinforcers
8/20/76	55	Establish permanent keyboard arrangement
8/23/76	56	Introduce Request Task in response to experimenter's question, QUESTION WHAT (SUBJECT) WANT (Subject spontaneously searched for and found new key, APPLE)
8/25/76	58	Introduce Mannequin assembly for request task; switch from token to social reinforcement only
9/23/76	78	Introduce Actions, BRUSH/COMB
9/29/76	81	Try to introduce Word Combination as Description Task, BRUSH/COMB HAIR, in response to question, QUESTION WHAT (EXPERIMENTER) DO.
10/1/76	83	Switch Word Combination to Request Task, EAT/DRINK (OBJECT) in response to experimenter's question, QUESTION WHAT (SUBJECT) WANT
10/28/76	98	Introduce slides
11/12/76	107	Reintroduce two-word combinations
12/16/76	126	Outside lab: Experimenter asked, "What did you do at your Christmas party?" Subject replied, "Eat cookie."
12/20/76	128	Introduce YES/NO as feedback to subject's response, verbally prompt subject's use in answer to experimenter's conversational questions
12/22/76	132	Outside lab: Subject protested experimenter's teasing, uttering, "No, people!"
1/7/77	140	First spontaneous three-word combinations: THIS (EXPERIMENTER) SOCK; (EXPERIMENTER) DRINK WATER; GO (SUBJECT) COTTAGE (at end of session)
1/18/77	154	First spontaneous four-word combination: THIS (SUBJECT) RED SHIRT

learned nearly 30 words, it was clear that she perceived a one-to-one relationship between symbols and things. During session 56 we introduced the request task, placing on a table eight objects for which she already knew the lexigrams and one for which she did not. The ninth item was an apple, which she spotted on entering the room. She went to the table, pointed to the apple, gave a verbal approximation for it (æ ˀ eɪ), turned to the keyboard on which all nine keys were lighted, searched for, quickly found the new lexigram and depressed it, repeating, "æ ˀ eɪ." (Her vocabulary acquisition is summarized in Table 4.)

By the time she had 30 words she was having great difficulty searching all over the keyboard every time we rearranged it, which we were doing every two to five days. After four days of testing (to ensure that she was not responding mainly to position), we organized the keyboard by word categories and have since left the arrangement more or less intact.

Although we introduced the request task by letting her ask for items arranged in her view on a table, after two days we changed the request task to one which would use in a realistic fashion more of the words which she already knew. Using a Peabody Kit mannequin, we required her to identify items of clothing and body parts as they were removed from the mannequin and then ask for each body part or article of clothing so that it could be replaced on the mannequin. She had difficulty with the task on the first day but by the fourth day was able to request the items for assembly even when they were out of her view. This task also meshed the request and labeling activities.

We then tried to get her to ask the experimenter ? WHAT WANT, in hopes of motivating her spontaneous use of a question, and in order to get more equal interchange in the session. She had to be cued and prompted much of the time, but, eventually, during each session in which this was tried, she began to use the question consistently. We abandoned this when we turned to other tasks and have since found that she will not use a question unless cued. Spontaneous interrogation, then, is yet to be taught.

We then introduced her to ? WHO THIS. She mastered her own and two experimenters' names in a single session in preparation for introducing actions and word strings.

As with the other subject described here, the first actions we used were BRUSH and COMB. We tried first the phrase BRUSH/COMB HAIR. Her performance on this task was highly variable; furthermore, we could not tell whether she really understood the action or whether she was merely identifying the objects, brush and comb. We concluded this was a poor choice of action words, so we changed to a new action, requiring EAT (OBJECT) in response to the question ? WHAT (SUBJECT) WANT. We attempted to motivate word combination by giving her the object to eat if she used both words, and showing her a picture of the object if she only identified it. She was very frustrated by the task, possibly because of the reinforcement differences or because she did not understand the relationship of her response and the consequences. It is also possible that she had simply been overprogrammed with one-word

Table 4. Vocabulary of subject in Element Training and Construction
Approach showing date and session of introduction

Date	Session	Word(s)	Cumulative total
5/13/76	1	CAR, DOLL	2
5/18/76	3	PURSE	3
5/21/76	5	SHOE	4
5/25/76	7	SHIRT	5
6/1/76	11	HAIR	6
6/2/76	12	TEETH	7
6/3/76	13	EYE	8
6/4/76	14	EAR	9
6/11/76	19	PHONE	10
6/14/76	20	HAT	11
7/14/76	34	COKE	12
7/20/76	37	POPCORN	13
8/2/76	41	NOSE, BALL	15
8/6/76	45	COOKIE	16
8/10/76	47	PANTS, WATER	18
8/11/76	48	CRACKER	19
8/12/76	49	BOOK, CEREAL	21
8/13/76	50	SOCK	22
8/17/76	52	HAND, BOX	24
8/18/76	53	BALLOON	25
8/19/76	54	TRUCK, CHAIR	27
8/23/76	56	TABLE, APPLE	29
8/25/76	58	MOUTH	30
8/30/76	62	VAN	31
9/3/76	65	FLOOR	32
9/15/76	72	BLOCK	33
9/20/76	75	DOOR	34
9/22/76	77	subject's name, two experimenters' names	37
9/23/76	78	BRUSH, COMB	39
9/29/76	81	EAT	40
10/14/76	90	JUICE	41
10/28/76	98	COTTAGE	42
11/3/76	102	DRINK	43
11/4/76	103	GO	44
11/5/76	104	SHOW	45
11/9/76	106	BIG	46
12/3/76	117	RED	47
12/9/76	121	PICTURE	48
12/17/76	127	THIS	49
12/20/76	128	YES/NO	51
12/20/76	129	EMPTY	52
12/21/76	131	BATHROOM	53
1/3/77	133	friend's name, LITTLE, BLUE	56
1/4/77	134	YELLOW	57
2/4/77	175	DIRTY, COFFEE, ICE CREAM	60

responses and did not understand why the rules had changed. We suspended training with word combinations to try to determine what sort of combinations she could handle most easily, action-object, agent-action, modifier-object, or possessor-object, but results of these tests were ambiguous.

By this time (session 98) the subject was performing very erratically, so we returned to the labeling task and introduced slides, which she enjoys greatly, particularly since many of the slides are pictures of herself. We then again tried two-word combinations, EAT/DRINK (OBJECT) (session 107), and tried to get her to construct the phrases by asking her first, ? WHAT (SUBJECT) WANT, to which she would invariably reply with object names (which, of course, she had been doing for months), then asking her what she wanted to do with it. She would then erase the object name and give only the action EAT or DRINK. We would then ask, ? EAT/DRINK WHAT and found that if we did not inhibit her using the PERIOD key she would erase the action before adding the object. This procedure obviously involves a great deal of redundancy; she probably did not see any point in giving the object name again, since she had just given it. Because such a procedure reduces the communication value of what she has already given, we abandoned this approach.

We meanwhile had begun to model two-word responses following her single-word response. We attempted to get her to imitate, cued a great deal, and verbally prompted her on many responses to "use two buttons." At the same time we were trying to devise a more conversational approach to the task. Thus, we began modeling and accepting a variety of two-word answers as long as they were appropriate answers to the questions ? WHO THIS, ? WHAT THIS, ? WHAT (SUBJECT) WANT, or ? WHAT (SUBJECT) WANT DO. She began very slowly to give more word combinations.

To get her to attend to the keyboard question, we began to concentrate on the questions ? WHO THIS and ? WHAT THIS, using identical slides of persons, getting her to identify the persons or body parts and clothing, using less and less verbal accompaniment to the keyboard. She at first seemed very confused when we did not speak the words as we depressed the experimenter keys, but she slowly began to respond more accurately to these questions whether spoken or not. Also, the proportion of word combinations increased, especially THIS (SO-AND-SO) and THIS (SUCH-AND-SUCH). The information value of these forms, however, is really no greater than for a one-word response, and she often wanted to add other information after these responses. She was therefore told that she could erase what was there and say something else if she wished. She began immediately to give an additional two-word phrase, mostly of the possessor-object type. This form has been modeled a great deal and she has sometimes been cued to use it in response to the question ? WHAT THIS; the frequency of her use of it in this situation is probably a function of the stimuli, which are pictures of people she knows. She makes few informational errors with these responses except for those that seem to be caused by her poor motor control; most such errors she identifies herself, uttering, "No!" as soon as she hears the experimenter say the word, erasing immediately, and trying again.

Approximately two months after we began working on two-word combinations, during which time there were two rather long breaks for holidays, she was spontaneously giving from three to nine such communications per session. In reviewing the data we find that the first occurrence of some of these combinations is not preceded by any previous exposure to that combination, i.e., they have not been modeled by the experimenter nor elicited via cues or prompts; her only experience can be from hearing these words combined in ordinary spoken discourse. We have also found her to utter, outside the laboratory on several occasions, intelligible two-word answers to our questions. When she was asked what she did at her Christmas party, she gave her approximation for "Eat cookie," and once when she was being taken back to her cottage she responded to some teasing from two experimenters with a very emphatic protest, "No, people!" Before our attempts to teach her word combinations we had never been able to get her even to imitate a two-word response.

After 11 months we are still trying to develop a more conversational format with her and to model two-, three- and four-word strings for her, often as elaborations of her responses, sometimes to exchange information with her. Most of her responses are multiword and the proportion of three-word constructions has increased steadily. She also occasionally gives four-word responses spontaneously or in answer to the experimenter's question.

Recently she has shown evidence of incidental learning with a new word. For several weeks we have had most of the keys activated, including a few she did not know. She has, on numerous occasions, depressed one of these keys by mistake, at which time the word has been pronounced for her by the experimenter. On hearing the word she has said, "No," erased it, and gone on immediately in search of the correct key. She had pressed the lexigram STRING in error 16 times during a six-week period. Also, once at the end of a session, the experimenter tied her shoe, then turned to the keyboard and depressed SHOE STRING. Almost a month after SHOE STRING was modeled, when a piece of twine was presented to her for identification, she searched briefly for the appropriate lexigram and depressed it without hesitation.

After two months of systematic training with several modifiers (DIRTY, EMPTY, FULL, BIG, LITTLE, and color names), she has developed consistent use of each lexigram and can apply them to many exemplars in many situations. She still, however, does not always use her verbal approximations for "big" and colors appropriately. At this point it is difficult to determine whether she has a processing problem which affects the accuracy of her verbal output. We have noticed this problem in other contexts. Throughout her training she has been highly consistent in using her lexigrams to identify objects, and she usually accompanies her key depression with an utterance. Phonetic transcriptions of these utterances indicate that they are highly variable. Not only does she have a variety of unintelligible utterances for each key, she also sometimes gives utterances that sound like clear approximations of other words she uses. For example, the experimenter would hold up a doll; she would depress the key for "doll" and say something sounding like "car."

We have also found that she is very inconsistent in many of her uses of "yes" and "no," for which she has clear utterances. Some uses are consistent; for example, when she says, "No," to identify her keyboard errors. In conversations with her, however, we have not been able to determine any reliable use of these words for denial, rejection or negation, or their opposites. We have begun to model the use of "yes" and "no" in response to her answers, and she has begun to use the keys in response to our questions regarding her wishes and to depress NO after keyboard errors and sometimes even to follow NO with the erroneous word. Here, too, she seems to be using the keys more consistently than her utterances.

An earlier attempt to introduce "yes" and "no" was unsuccessful. Because it has proved to be a difficult concept even for higher level subjects in this population, we have decided to phase in its use very slowly, first building receptive skills with the words. Our experience suggests that formidable tasks might best be introduced by providing brief exposure over many sessions, rather than to devote long periods of exclusive attention to them at the outset. We are now trying this method to minimize frustration, to provide some focus of attention to the new material, and to increase receptive skills before a full-scale attack on the problem is made.

It is important to point out that she has not been taught to form word strings in a purely operant fashion. She has not practiced a single word combination trial after trial after trial. She has been verbally prompted to compose word combinations by being asked a specific question and being instructed to use two keys. If she had to be cued or prompted, she was told to erase at the end and, "See if you can do that again faster." On occasion she has dealt with a given combination as many as three times in a row—once to compose, once for cued practice, and once with no cue to practice an uninterrupted sequence. Also she has had a variety of two-word combinations intermingled in each session. We feel that such a method requires more organizing of output cues and commands (i.e., the experimenter question and the experimenter command "use two buttons") than would be involved if she merely practiced a given word string in response to a specific question. The tendency to combine words has not developed quickly with this procedure and the disappearance of erroneous combinations was slow. We are trying this method, however, in hopes of maximizing in the long run her ability to use the linguistic elements we have been teaching her in a productive manner.

Although to those of us working with her in the language project her use of the keyboard is far more impressive than her attempts at utterance, her living unit and program staff report exciting attempts to use language outside the laboratory. They indicate that she is better able to make her needs known and is trying to say many, many more words than previously. We ourselves have found signs of this in walking back and forth with her between her living unit and the training laboratory. Looking at video tapes made last summer, we can also see evidence of less impulsive, more controlled, better organized responses during her current training sessions. She is now receiving articulation training in hopes of reducing the variability of her verbal output, and providing her the skills for transferring what she is learning in the laboratory to the world she must live in and cope with every day.

SUMMARY AND CONCLUSION

No attempt is made to compare these programs at this time because of obvious limitations in the scope of the study to date. In addition to other complications, the subjects are clearly different. The young woman in the Element Training and Construction Approach is highly motivated, had greater receptive language on entering the program, and is more interested in communicating than the young man in the Stock Sentence Approach. The purpose of working with two approaches is mainly to discover the problems and advantages of different methods of training linguistic skills.

In developing any pilot program it is difficult to know where to begin. Although the subject in the Element Training and Construction program was able to handle naming as the first task, a subject must already have a good deal of linguistic experience and motivation to be able to begin language training at this level. Another subject, who was discharged from the institution early in her training, seemed unable to deal with the naming task after several weeks; even though she could identify more objects from standard test pictures than could the young man in the Stock Sentence Approach, she was apparently not ready for the naming task. Requesting seems a far more appropriate initial task, since requesting is a linguistic mode of attempting control over what happens to oneself.

How to sequence tasks is another major problem. For example, when should action concepts be taught? In both approaches, great difficulty was encountered in introducing action words. This is not surprising in view of the literature, but the reasons for the difficulty are little understood. When training is begun with single elements, when and how should the subject be taught to combine words? From our experience with the second program, it appears that a subject can be overtrained in single-element responses and that word combination is very difficult to induce when a more economical output has been consistently effective. We have felt that the answer to this problem lies in making clear to the subject the necessity for more exact communication to control outcomes, exactness being a function of word combinations. However, we have not yet developed a clear test of this hypothesis.

Another major consideration is what to build into the training interaction. It seems likely from our experience that modeling combinations, both through conversation and through expansion of the subject's responses, facilitates combination by the subject. If the subject is expected to express through visual symbols he should also have his receptive capacity built up through exposure to these symbols.

The types of linguistic strings to be used in training should be carefully chosen to provide for maximum substitutions of the elements, particularly if they are introduced early, as in the LANA approach. They should also be such that they can be taught and stabilized quickly so that spontaneous rearrangements and recombinations and unexpected interpretable truncated forms can be accepted. If this is not done, there is a danger in suppressing what little tendency retarded subjects have to give spontaneous responses. Although it is clear that operant strings are learned quickly, we are not yet able to evaluate the extent to which initiating training through this method will facilitate productive language use.

It is clear that motivational factors play a significant role in both the acquisition and use of linguistic tools. With this population it remains both a problem of design and of daily interaction to encourage spontaneity in using and combining symbols to communicate. First, it is important to structure the interaction that occurs in training so that the subject clearly perceives the relationship between his symbol manipulation and the consequences. Second, this relationship should be chosen to enable the subject to realize some new degree of control. Third, it is important to maximize the value of each interpretable attempt to communicate; this is difficult to do in programs involving a high degree of response redundancy. In such programs, it is difficult for subjects to have any comprehension of their behavior as communicating. Fourth, although it should be obvious, it bears repeating that the success rate should be kept high. This can be done by phasing in new difficult tasks through very limited exposure at first, meshing tasks, keeping tasks within the subject's range of competence, and training sufficiently before progressing to a new phase without requiring such a high degree of perfection that the subject never masters the task before he gets bored or frustrated.

A number of problems and principles seem to be emerging as we attempt to develop programs for the retarded and to examine the interplay of our work and primate work (see Savage and Rumbaugh, 1977; Savage-Rumbaugh and Rumbaugh, Chapter 14, this volume). First, we must structure the tasks so that the subject perceives his performance as communication. This is especially important in a laboratory environment where key pressing and automated vending can easily become a sort of mechanical game between the subject and the machine. We must, therefore, be clear in understanding just what sorts of interactions constitute communication and what roles each party must play in carrying out the exchange. Requesting, for instance, can be seen as an attempt to control outcomes by providing information to another party who has greater control.

Second, we must attempt to build programs to maximize the number of communication functions a subject can perform. Even the most basic communication forms involve requesting and information seeking. By providing the subject with a communication vehicle that involves symbols for the transfer of information, we can greatly expand his options for communicating. For this, label learning is essential; with labels, in addition to asking for, he can point to and describe objects, events, and states.

If a subject can be taught to combine and order symbols in normative sequences he can increase both the precision of his communication and the range of information that can be transmitted and thus, presumably, the degree of control over outcomes.

A final but no less important consideration is the problem of structuring a program to facilitate productive language use. While the ability to recognize appropriate conditions for using memorized strings might allow one to communicate, such behavior could not be considered productive language use. For symbol combinations to be used in a fashion that can be called truly linguistic, the user must be able to form novel strings that are normatively ordered and can be interpreted by others.

To teach linguistic skills we must structure our interaction to maximize the subject's understanding of how his use of symbols can control outcomes. It seems critical, therefore, for us to understand how one develops 1) the recognition that symbols stand for things and 2) the understanding that normatively ordered combinations of symbols provide greater precision and thus greater control than symbols used individually. Finally, the test of any language program is whether the client develops the ability to use language productively. Perhaps the test to which language research projects must eventually be put is whether they contribute to our understanding of what training factors facilitate and what cognitive processes underlie the ability to develop productive language use.

REFERENCES

Bricker, W. A., and Bricker, D. D. 1974. An early language training strategy. *In* R. L. Schiefelbush and L. L. Lloyd (eds.), Language Perspectives—Acquisition, Retardation, and Intervention, pp. 431–468. University Park Pres, Baltimore.

Carrier, J. K., Jr. 1976. Application of a nonspeech language system with the severely language handicapped *In* L. L. Lloyd (ed.), Communication Assessment and Intervention Strategies, pp. 523–547. University Park Press, Baltimore.

Carrier, J. K., Jr. 1974. Application of functional analysis and a nonspeech response mode to teaching language. *In* L. V. McReynolds (ed.), Developing systematic procedures for training children's language. ASHA Monogr. 18.

Guess, D., Sailor, W., and Baer, D. M. 1974. To teach language to retarded children. *In* R. L. Schiefelbusch and L. L. Lloyd (eds.), Language Perspectives—Acquisition, Retardation, and Intervention, pp. 529–563. University Park Press, Baltimore.

Kent, L. R. 1972. A language acquisition program for the retarded. *In* J. E. McLean, D. E. Yoder and R. L. Schiefelbusch (eds.), Language Intervention with the Retarded: Developing Strategies, pp. 151–190. University Park Press, Baltimore.

MacDonald, J. D., and Blott, J. P. 1974. Environmental language intervention: The rationale for a diagnostic and training strategy through rules, context, and generalization. J. Speech Hear. Disord. 39:244–256.

Miller, J. F., and Yoder, D. E. 1974. An ontogenetic language teaching strategy for retarded children. *In* R. L. Schiefelbusch and L. L. Lloyd (eds.), Language Perspectives: Acquisition, Retardation, and Intervention, pp. 505–528. University Park Press, Baltimore.

Miller, J. F., and Yoder, D. E. 1972. A syntax teaching program. *In* J. E. McLean, D. E. Yoder, and R. L. Schiefelbusch (eds.), Language Intervention with the Retarded: Developing Strategies, pp. 191–211. University Park Press, Baltimore.

Parkel, D. A., White, R. A., and Warner, H. 1977. Implications of the Yerkes technology for mentally retarded human subjects. *In* D. M. Rumbaugh (ed.), Language Learning by a Chimpanzee: The LANA Project, pp. 273–283. Academic Press, New York.

Premack, D., and Premack, A. J. 1974. Teaching visual language to apes and language-deficient persons. *In* R. L. Schiefelbusch and L. L. Lloyd (eds.), Language Perspectives—Acquisition, Retardation, and Intervention, pp. 347–376. University Park Press, Baltimore.

Rumbaugh, D. M. (ed.). 1977. Language Learning by a Chimpanzee: The LANA Project. Academic Press, New York.

Savage, E. S., and Rumbaugh, D. M. 1977. Communication, language and Lana: A perspective. *In* D. M. Rumbaugh (ed.), Language Learning by a Chimpanzee: The LANA Project, pp. 287–312. Academic Press, New York.

Stremel, K., and Waryas, C. 1974. A behavioral-psycholinguistic approach to language training. *In* L. V. McReynolds (ed.), Developing systematic procedures for training children's language. ASHA Monogr. 18. Interstate Press, Danville, Ill.

von Glasersfeld, E. 1977. The Yerkish language and its automatic parser. *In* D. M. Rumbaugh (ed.), Language Learning by a Chimpanzee: The LANA Project, pp. 91–130. Academic Press, New York.

chapter

20

Application of Manual Signing to the Development of Reading Skills

S. Vanost Wulz

John H. Hollis

Bureau of Child Research
University of Kansas
Lawrence, Kansas
and
Kansas Neurological Institute
Topeka, Kansas

DEVELOPING READING SKILLS

Most of the language studies dealing with nonhuman primates have been limited to a single symbol system. Training has employed spoken English (Kellogg and Kellogg, 1933; Hayes, 1951), American Sign Language (Gardner and Gardner, 1969 [Chapter 9, this volume]), or abstract symbols (Premack, 1970 [Chapter 12, this volume]; Rumbaugh, Gill, and von Glasersfeld, 1973). In this volume, however, two studies have dealt with multiple stimulus input (Fouts, Couch, and O'Neil, Chapter 15; Patterson, 1978 [Chapter 16]). That is, the primates were taught to use, or respond to, both manual signs and speech. This training is similar to total communication programs employed with retarded and hearing-impaired children (see Kopchick and Lloyd, 1976).

The notion of "total communication" assumes the development of an equivalence between two different symbols for the same concept. For example, the child must associate the spoken word "cat" with the sign for cat, and both the sign and the spoken word must be associated with the referent, cat. This is also similar to the behavior required in reading. Reading involves an association among the spoken word "cat," the printed word *cat*, and the referent, cat. In this chapter the language studies involving nonhuman primates and mentally retarded children are analyzed with respect to the skills critical for reading.

Research in reading has demonstrated that some associations can be acquired without direct training. For example, a child may see a cat, and hear the word "cat." Later, he sees a picture of a cat and the word *cat* below it. Without being told, the child should recognize that *cat* means "cat." This phenomenon has been discussed in terms of "triangulation" by Menzel and Johnson (1976 [Chapter 13, this volume]. This chapter analyzes four methods of producing triangulation (or mediated transfer) with respect to reading and language training in primates and retarded children.

There are major gaps in the primate language research dealing with reading. Although the component skills have been established in subjects, integrated reading behavior, as defined herein, has not been demonstrated in nonhuman primates. An example, studying the acquisition of reading using manual signs with mentally retarded children, may have implications for future primate research. This study is discussed in terms of procedures for exceptional children.

Functional Analysis of Reading

Reading involves equivalences among stimuli. An equivalence is demonstrated when one stimulus can be substituted for another. For

This investigation was conducted at the Kansas Neurological Institute, Topeka, Kansas. It was supported by Grants HD-07339 and HD-00870 from the National Institute of Child Health and Human Development to the Bureau of Child Research, University of Kansas, Lawrence, Kansas.

example, a child who can read can employ the spoken word "ball," the printed word *ball*, or the object, ball, to communicate the idea of a ball.

Thus Sidman (1971) defined reading in terms of equivalences among four types of stimuli: (A) auditory labels by the teacher, (B) pictures or referents, (C) printed words (or abstract symbols), and (D) oral labels produced by the child. As Figure 1 shows, the equivalence among these four stimuli results in six tasks. *Receptive tasks* (tasks 1 and 2) demonstrate that the child can select the picture (B) and the printed word (C) when given the auditory label (A). That is, the child can select the picture of a cat and the printed word *cat* when the teacher says, "cat." *Associative tasks* (tasks 3 and 4) demonstrate that the child can match the word (C) to the picture (B), and vice versa. That is, the child can match the word *cat* to a picture of a cat. *Expressive tasks* (Tasks 5 and 6) require the child to produce the oral label (D) when shown the picture (B) or the printed word (C). Thus, the child will say "cat" when he sees the word *cat* or a picture of a cat. According to this definition, a child can read a word when he can perform these six tasks with that word.

Two different responses are required in these six tasks: productive and selective responses. Productive responses require the organism to produce the lexicon by changes in the fine motor musculature. For example, speech requires the coordinated articulation of the larynx, velum, tongue, and lips. Manual signs also involve productive responses, since the lexicon is defined by the placement, configuration, and movement of the hands. The expressive tasks (tasks 5 and 6 in Figure 1)

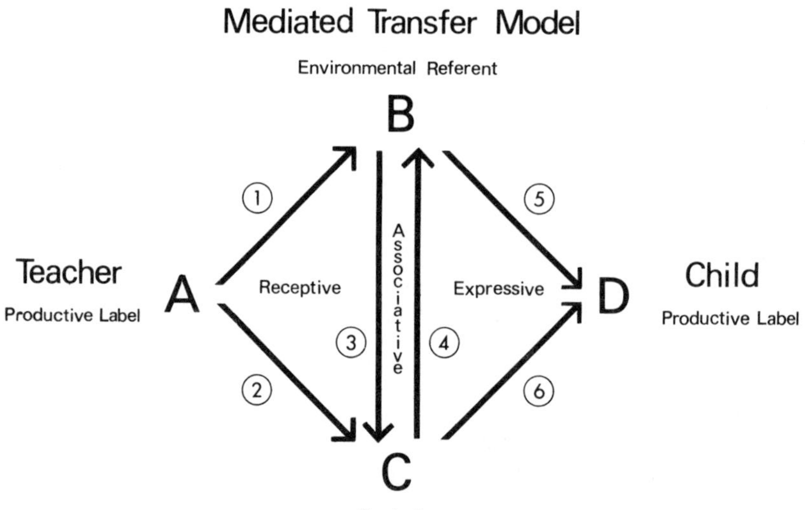

Mediated Transfer Model

Environmental Referent

Figure 1. Mediated transfer model for reading, adapted from Sidman (1971). Numerals in the figure refer to the first six reading tasks presented in Table 1.

involve the productive responses. A normal child responds orally, but other populations, including nonhuman primates, need to be taught a nonspeech productive response, such as manual signs. On the other hand, the inability to produce the lexicon does not preclude comprehension of oral input. For example, although Viki (Hayes, 1951) could produce only three words, she comprehended a large repertoire of spoken words.

Selection responses do not require the fine motor articulations of productive systems because the symbols are prefabricated. Thus, the organism is required to make only as fine a muscle movement as is necessary to indicate which symbol or printed word is chosen. For example, typing is a common selection response. The typist presses the letter to be printed. The receptive and associative tasks in Figure 1 also involve selection responses. The child points to the picture or printed word that is equivalent to the stimulus. He is not required to produce the name of the word or picture.

Productive responses are advantageous because of the speed and flexibility of their transmission (see Hollis and Carrier, 1978). Unfortunately, this also produces a strain on the memory and rate of comprehension of the handicapped. On the other hand, the degree of permanency can be controlled in symbol selection systems. For example, the words can be permanently available to the reader, as on the printed page, or transitory, as in a tachistoscopic presentation. Also, the use of permanent symbols permits the teacher to control the number of response alternatives available to the child and, therefore, to control the probability of error (Premack, 1970 [Chapter 12, this volume]). However, the primary advantage to using a symbol selection system when teaching language is that the child does not need to learn complex motor movements before, or in addition to, learning language (Hollis and Carrier, 1978). On the other hand, it is apparent that most human beings use both types of symbols, since they serve different purposes.

The rapid and flexible transmission of spoken language makes it the dominant mode of communication. However, the permanence of written language is also very important. For example, the written form allows messages to be conveyed among people without requiring their physical presence. In addition, the equivalence between spoken and printed words permits statements, dialogues, or agreements that originate through productive language systems to be preserved in printed form. Thus, it is evident that literacy involves a productive language system in addition to the comprehension of printed words or abstract symbols.

The following section analyzes primate language research in terms of the six tasks demonstrating single-word reading performance. The primate research has neglected the critical equivalence between selection and productive response systems. However, most of the behaviors that comprise this definition of reading have been established.

Analysis of Nonspeech Language Research with Respect to Reading

As previously described, single-word reading competency is demonstrated by the successful performance of the six tasks illustrated in Figure 1. These tasks represent the equivalence among a productive label, printed word, and the referent (or meaning). Table 1 summarizes some of the nonspeech language studies in terms of these six equivalences.

Receptive Comprehension (*task 1, Table 1*)   Receptive comprehension involves the equivalence between a productive label (spoken or signed) produced by the teacher or trainer and an environmental event or referent. For example, the trainer says (or signs) "cookie" and the child points to a cookie. As Table 1 indicates, this equivalence has been established with primates and mentally retarded children using both speech and manual signs. Auditory comprehension has been established in chimps with little or no direct training (Kellogg and Kellogg, 1933). With training, an extensive receptive vocabulary can be established (see Hayes, 1951). A large repertoire of receptive manual signs has also been established with a chimpanzee (Gardner and Gardner, 1969 [Chapter 9, this volume]).

With most studies involving retarded children, and some primate studies, multiple input has been employed. That is, the training has involved two productive systems (speech and signs). These studies and the resulting equivalences are discussed in more detail later.

Reading Comprehension (*tasks 3 and 4, Table 1*)   Reading comprehension tasks involve the equivalence between printed words (or symbols) and environmental events or referents. Premack (1970 [Chapter 12, this volume]) and Rumbaugh, Gill, and von Glasersfeld (1973) have demonstrated that chimps can perform this task with abstract stimuli. Both chimps produced sentences and demonstrated competence with many common oral language structures. Carrier (1974 [Chapter 17, this volume] and Hodges and Deich (Chapter 18, this volume) have extended this research to language training with mentally retarded children.

Picture Naming (*task 5, Table 1*)   Picture naming is the converse of task 1 (receptive comprehension). It involves the equivalence between the environmental event (or referent) and the child's productive label. For example, the child says (or signs) "ball" when shown the object, ball. As Table 1 shows, responses in task 5 may be more limited than input in task 1. For example, Patterson (1978 [Chapter 16, this volume]) presented Koko with both signed and spoken input (see task 1). However, Koko only produced signs (task 5). This is because task 5 requires a productive response, whereas the response in task 1 is selective.

Oral responses have not been successful with nonhuman primates. Gua never produced oral speech (Kellogg and Kellogg, 1933), and Viki produced only three oral responses after intensive training (Hayes, 1951). Signing has been more successful. Washoe quickly learned a large repertoire of single words and spontaneously combined them to form sentences (Gardner and Gardner, 1969 [Chapter 9, this volume]) .When both signed and speech input has been presented to nonhuman primates, the primates produced only manual signed responses (Patterson, 1978 [Chapter 16, this volume]); Fouts, Couch, and O'Neil, Chapter 15,this volume). Kahn (1977) demonstrated that pairing manual signs and speech may increase both forms of communication with mentally retarded children. However, the ability of mentally retarded children to produce speech appears to vary with other confounding conditions.

Productive Reading (*task 6, Table 1*) This task is a reciprocal of receptive reading (task 2). The child or chimp must produce the productive symbol (speech or signs) when shown the printed word (or abstract symbol). As with task 2, this equivalence has been largely neglected in the language research conducted with primates and exceptional children.

This analysis of the equivalences established by language training indicates that primates and retarded children have been taught most of the tasks involved in reading. Both productive and selective systems have been established in response to environmental events (or referents). However, to our knowledge there is no study that has established an equivalence between symbols and productive labels with nonhuman primates. This equivalence has been established by Sidman (1971) and his colleagues with mentally retarded children being taught to read.

Sidman (1971), Sidman and Cresson (1973), and Sidman, Cresson, and Willson-Morris (1974) demonstrated that equivalences among stimuli can be established without direct training. Menzel and Johnson (1976 [Chapter 13, this volume]) have discussed this in terms of "triangulation," that is, the process by which information from various sources and channels becomes integrated.

Mediated Transfer (Triangulation)

Mediated transfer research has shown what elements of a task or situation must be included in the organism's experience in order for triangulation to occur. Triangulation (or mediated transfer) occurs when two stimuli are associated with a common third stimulus. The two stimuli are then equivalent, or interchangeable, given certain conditions. For example, if a child is trying to communicate the idea of a cookie to a person, he might try a variety of methods. He could say the word, write a word, produce the word in another language, perform gestures used when eating or making a cookie, or point to the cookie. Each of these is equivalent in terms of the desired object, cookie.

Table 1. Stimulus and response modes used in ape and child language research

Reading Tasks	Kellogg and Kellogg (1933) Gua	Hayes (1951) Viki	Chimpanzee			
			Gardner and Gardner (1969 [Chapter 9]) Washoe	Premack (1970 [Chapter 12]) Sarah	Fouts, Couch and O'Neil (Chapter 15) Ally	Rumbaugh Gill, and von Glasersfeld (1973) Lana
Receptive						
1. Receptive Comprehension (A–B) (Figure 1, A)	Speech	Speech	Signs		Signs and speech[a]	
2. Receptive Reading (A–C) (Figure 1, A)						
Associative						
3. Reading Comprehension (B–C) (Figure 1, C)				Symbols		Symbols
4. Reading Comprehension (C–B) (Figure 1, C)				Symbols		Symbols
Expressive						
5. Picture Naming (B–D) (Figure 1, D)	No speech	Three words speech	Signs		Signs	
6. Productive Reading (C–D) (Figure 1, D)						

472

	Gorilla	Mentally retarded children					
Reading Tasks	Patterson (1978 [Chapter 16]) Koko	Carrier (1974 [Chapter 17])	Hodges and Deich (Chapter 18)	Kahn (1977)	Van Biervliet (1977)	Sidman (1971)	Present study
Receptive							
1. Receptive Comprehension (A–B) (Figure 1, A)	Signs and speech[b]			Speech and signs[b]	Speech and signs[a]	Speech	Speech and signs[a+b]
2. Receptive Reading (A–C) (Figure 1, A)						Speech	Speech and signs[a+b]
Associative							
3. Reading Comprehension (B–C) (Figure 1, C)		Symbols	Symbols			Printed words	Printed words or symbols
4. Reading Comprehension (C–B) (Figure 1, C)		Symbols	Symbols			Printed words	Printed words or symbols
Expressive							
5. Picture Naming (B–D) (Figure 1, D)	Signs			Speech and signs	Speech and signs	Speech	Speech and signs
6. Productive Reading (C–D) (Figure 1, D)						Speech	Speech and signs

[a] Successive presentation of stimuli.
[b] Simultaneous presentation of stimuli.

473

Table 2 shows four methods of establishing equivalence to produce mediated transfer (or triangulation). *Stimulus equivalence* is a procedure in which a student is trained successively to match two stimuli (A and C) to the same response (B). Equivalence among the stimuli (A and C) is established if A evokes C and vice versa. For example, Van Biervliet (1977) taught mentally retarded children to produce a gesture when presented with an auditory label and then an object (see Table 1). Equivalence was demonstrated when the children selected the object when given the auditory label (task 1, receptive comprehension, Table 1). This task had not been directly trained. To our knowledge, this procedure has not been employed in the primate language research.

Response equivalence is a procedure in which the student is successively trained to respond to stimulus B with response A and then response C. For example, Fouts, Couch, and O'Neil (Chapter 15, this volume) taught Ally to select the object when the trainer said its name (task 1, receptive comprehension, Table 1). Then they taught Ally to produce the manual sign when given the auditory label. Testing demonstrated that Ally had formed the equivalence between the object and the manual sign, although they had never been paired. This procedure has also established integrated reading behavior in retarded children. Sidman (1971) and Sidman and Cresson (1973) trained retarded children to select the picture when given the auditory label (task 1, receptive reading, Table 1). Then the children were taught to select the printed word when given the auditory label (task 2, receptive reading, Table 1). Training these two tasks established correct responses to all six tasks described in the functional analysis of reading.

Fouts, Couch, and O'Neil (Chapter 15, this volume) also employed a *mediated association* procedure. This involves successively matching B

Table 2.   Four procedures for establishing equivalences among stimuli

	Train stimulus-response	Test[a] stimulus-response	Reference
Stimulus equivalence	A–B C–B	A–C C–A	Jenkins and Palermo (1964)
Response equivalence	B–A B–C	A–C C–A	Jenkins and Palermo (1964)
Mediated association	A–B B–C	A–C C–A	Peters (1935)
Contiguity	(A + C)–B	A–B A–C C–B C–A	Estes (1970)

[a] Testing could also involve the reverse of the training condition.

to A and C to B, resulting in the untrained equivalence between A and C. Ally was taught to select the object given an auditory label, as before. Then they trained him to produce the manual sign when shown the object (task 5, picture naming, Table 1). Without training, Ally produced the manual sign when given the auditory label for the object. This is the mediated association procedure. It has also been used by Sidman, Cresson, and Willson-Morris (1974) to teach reading skills to mentally retarded children. When the subjects could select the pictures given the auditory label (task 1, receptive comprehension, Table 1), training them to point to the printed word when shown the picture (task 3, reading comprehension, Table 1) established all six reading behaviors.

The fourth method of establishing mediated transfer (or triangulation) involves *contiguity*. Patterson (1978 [Chapter 16, this volume]) demonstrated this procedure. She presented Koko with auditory and gestural stimuli simultaneously. That is, both the gestures and the oral symbols were presented in response to specific referents or events (task 1, receptive comprehension, Table 1). When Koko was tested, she demonstrated competency with both oral and gestural responses. Wulz and Hollis (1979) also demonstrated that contiguous presentations of oral and visual stimuli resulted in responses to both stimuli when teaching reading.

These examples suggest that the four procedures that establish mediated transfer (or triangulation) in primates and children may facilitate language training. Two symbols (e.g., manual signs and speech) for the same concept (or referent) can be established through stimulus equivalence, response equivalence, mediated association, or contiguity procedures. This result has to be confirmed in respect to the association between productive and selective symbolic responses.

Although Sidman and his colleagues have demonstrated that productive and selective symbolic responses can be associated in mentally retarded children, and that mediated transfer will occur, his work has been limited to spoken expressive responses. The studies with primates and mentally retarded children, however, suggest that signing or signing and speech may be more beneficial to these populations.

The following study was designed to study the effects of teaching reading with gestures using the four mediated transfer procedures just described.

Gesture Reading Experiments

Single-subject experiments were designed to study mediated transfer in teaching simple reading skills with manual signs. Mediated transfer was studied as a function of stimulus equivalence, response equivalence, and contiguity training procedures (Table 2). Training under the stimulus equivalence condition involved varying the stimulus and holding the response constant. In the response equivalence condition, the stimulus was held constant and the response varied. The contiguity training condition involved paired stimuli (e.g., gesture and picture) with a single response (e.g., printed word). A fourth condition involved combined contiguity and stimulus equivalence procedures.

The research was designed to study the effects of these mediated transfer training procedures (Table 2) on untrained tasks (Table 5). That is, which trained tasks were critical for achieving transfer to untrained tasks?

Method

Subjects   The subjects were five young adult retarded residents of Kansas Neurological Institute. Table 3 presents a summary of subject characteristics. Three subjects (B. B., L. D., and S. H.) had mild visual impairments, and G. C. had a high frequency hearing loss. None of the subjects had previous experience with manual signs.

Materials   Two sets of 15 stimuli were each divided into three lists of five words. Lists A, B. and C each consisted of five abstract pictures, consonant-vowel-consonant printed words (Figure 2A) and 15 one-handed Signing Exact English (SEE) signs (Table 4). Lists D, E, and F each consisted of abstract pictures, Non-SLIP symbols, consonant-vowel-consonant syllables (Figure 2B) and 15 two-handed SEE signs (Table 4).

Abstract, rather than meaningful, stimuli were employed to achieve some degree of experimental isolation (control). When a pretest-posttest design is used, experimental isolation is necessary to ensure that extraneous variables do not produce the observed changes.

General Procedure

A single-subject design, counterbalanced for order of training and stimulus lists, was employed. Before training, each subject was probed on all

Table 3. Subject characteristics[a]

Subject	Age (in years)	Measured intelligence[b]	PPVT[c] MA	Sensory deficits		
				Visual	Auditory	Speech
B. B.	19	−3	6–10	20/60	Normal	Interactional
W. S.	18	−3	5–8	Normal	Normal	Interactional
S. H.	19	−4	2–3	Mild	Normal	Single words
G. C.	18	−3	5–5	Normal	Mild	Interactional
L. D.	21	−5	2–11	20/60	Normal	Phrases

[a] At start of experiment.

[b] Heber (1961).

[c] Peabody Picture Vocabulary Test.

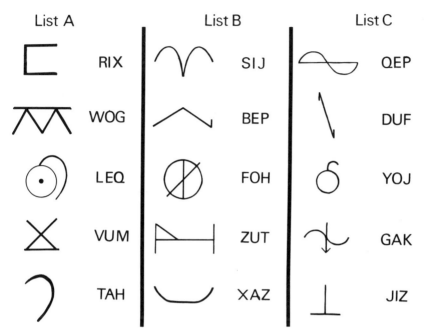

Figure 2A.   Abstract stimuli used in the experiment, lists A–C.

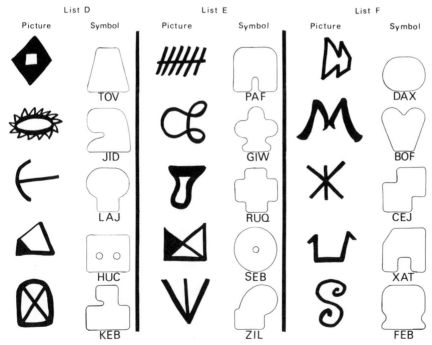

Figure 2B.   Abstract stimuli used in the experiment, lists D–F.

Table 4.   Gestures used in this study

List	Experimental label	SEE sign[a]	Description of sign Right hand	Left hand
A	RIX	adult	"A" thumb on temple; slide down side of face stopping at the chin.	No motion.
	WOG	my	Place palm on chest.	No motion.
	LEQ	never	Open hand in vertical palm out draws question mark in air with tip of fingers.	No motion.
	VUM	Atlanta	Thumb of "A" touches left and then right shoulder.	No motion.
	TAH	mother	Thumb of 5-hand taps jaw near chin once.	No motion.
B	SIJ	rake	Rake with claw-hand several times.	No motion.
	BEP	am	Thumb-tip of "A" starts on lip and moves away.	No motiom
	FOH	mind	Tip of "M" hand taps temple.	No motion.
	ZUT	arm	"A" fist taps arm	Arm held out.
	XAZ	disgust	Claw hand circles at stomach.	No motion.
C	QEP	lip	Index finger draws line under lower lip.	No motion.
	DUF	take	Whole hand open, moves toward body and closes to fist.	No motion.
	YOJ	thing	Palm up, arc hand upward and toward the right.	No motion.
	GAK	above	Palm circles over head once.	No motion.
	JIZ	fish	Flutter hand forward (like fish swimming).	No motion.
D	TOV	elephant	Trace an elephant's trunk beginning at the nose.	No motion.
	JID	apple	"X" hand twisted at cheek.	No motion.
	LAJ	house	Both hands outline the roof and sides of a house with palms facing each other and fingers up.	
	HUC	soup	Ladle thumb out with "H" position; bring to mouth twice.	Hand flat out; palm up.
	KEB	nail	Tap left thumb with right index finger.	Hold in fist.
E	PAF	lamp	Flick middle finger under chin from thumb.	No motion.
	GIW	toothbrush	Point to tooth; brush top of left hand with back of fingers several times.	Hold palm down.
	RUQ	saw	Palm out; thumb up; rub little finger's edge against the back of the left hand.	Hold palm down.

(*continued*)

Table 4—*continued*

List	Experimental label	SEE sign[a]	Description of sign Right hand	Left hand
	SEB	pig	Flap right hand under chin.	No motion.
	ZIL	bike	Both hands pedal up and down in the air with the palms down.	
F	DAX	horse	Flap "H" fingers forward at forehead twice.	No motion.
	BOF	mouse	Flick past the nose with the index finger twice.	No motion.
	CEJ	coat	Both hands move down the lapel in fists with the thumbs out touching the coat.	
	XAT	wagon	"C" behind left hand moves back toward the singer.	"W" holds still in front of the right hand.
	FEB	pencil	Thumb and index finger at mouth; index finger writes on palm.	Left palm held out flat.

[a] Adapted from Gustason, Pfetzing and Zawolkow (1975).

the reading tasks shown in Table 5 and subsequently probed following termination of each training phase.

Pretraining Imitative matching was established for the pictures, printed words/symbols, gestures, and/or auditory labels that were to be used in training. Imitative matching is necessary to demonstrate that any difficulties encountered in training are not caused by the failure to discriminate among the relevant stimuli.

Probes Following imitative matching training, initial probes involving a two-choice match-to-sample procedure were administered to each subject. The probe tasks are outlined in Table 5. Each child was probed for a given task on each of three lists before the next task was probed. The order of the lists was counterbalanced across probes. Probes were repeated on all three lists when a criterion of 93% correct or better was reached in training for two sessions. Final probes were also presented on achieving the same criterion.

Reinforcement All correct responses during training were followed by verbal praise and additional reinforcing stimuli (e.g., food, toys, diet drink, etc.) according to the individual child's preference. Stimuli were removed following incorrect responses. During probes, stimuli were removed following each response. Verbal praise was provided for responding during probes but was not contingent on correctness of responses. Additional backup reinforcers were available after the session.

Training Training utilized a two-choice match-to-sample procedure. In this procedure, two stimuli (response choices) from the same stimulus list were placed in front of the subject. Then the experimenter

Table 5.   Summary of reading tasks and probes

Task	Stimulus[a]	Response
Gestural Receptive Tasks		
1. Gesture comprehension	Gesture (A)	Picture (B)
2. Receptive reading	Gesture (A)	Symbol (C)
Associative Tasks		
3. Reading comprehension	Picture (B)	Symbol (C)
4. Reading comprehension	Symbol (C)	Picture (B)
Gestural Expressive Tasks		
5. Picture naming	Picture (B)	Gesture (D)
6. Expressive reading	Symbol (C)	Gesture (D)
Auditory Receptive Tasks		
7. Auditory comprehension	Auditory label (A)	Picture (B)
8. Auditory receptive reading	Auditory label (A)	Symbol (C)
Oral Expressive Tasks		
9. Picture naming	Picture (B)	Oral label (D)
10. Oral reading	Symbol (C)	Oral label (D)
Receptive-Expressive Tasks		
11. Auditory-gestural	Auditory label (A)	Gesture (D)
12. Gestural-oral	Gesture (A)	Oral label (D)

[a] Stimulus and response notations (A, B, C, D) refer to notations used in Figure 1.

placed another stimulus on a tray or produced a verbal label (sample stimulus). The subject selected the response choice that matched the sample stimulus. Each stimulus in each list served as correct and incorrect response choices in training and during probes. Expressive probes and verbal imitation were slightly different procedures. The experimenter presented the sample stimulus and the subject produced the correct verbal label.

Experimental Procedures

Training phases were classified on the basis of two characteristics: 1) receptive or associative tasks, and 2) successive or simultaneous task training. A task was labeled receptive if the sample stimulus provided a verbal label (gesture or auditory) to be matched by the subject with a picture or symbol (see Table 5). In associative tasks, the subject matches a printed word or symbol to a picture or vice versa. Successive or simultaneous training refers to the number (types) of sample stimuli presented within a training phase. In successive training, one task with one sample stimulus is presented in training phase 1 and another task, changing either the sample or response stimulus, is presented in training phase 2.

Simultaneous training involves the paired presentation of two different sample stimuli. The four types of training used in the gesture reading research are described in the following paragraphs.

Successive Receptive-Associative Training   This training incorporated the stimulus equivalence procedure of Table 2. In the successive receptive-associative training, two tasks (Table 5, tasks 2 and 3) were taught, one in training phase 1 and the other in training phase 2. In the receptive A–C task the gesture (A) was presented with the symbols or printed words (C) as the response stimuli. Associative B–C training consisted of the picture (B) as the sample stimulus and symbols or printed words (C) as the response stimuli. In these tasks, the response stimuli remained the same and the sample stimulus changed.

Successive Receptive Training   This training incorporated the response equivalence procedure of Table 2. In successive receptive training, the two receptive tasks (Table 5, tasks 1 and 2) had the same sample stimulus (A-gesture) but different response stimuli. In training phases 1 and 2 either pictures (B) or printed words (C) served as response stimuli.

Simultaneous Receptive-Associative Training   This training incorporated the contiguity procedure of Table 2. In simultaneous receptive-associative training the subject is presented with paired sample stimuli, a gesture (A) and a picture (B). His task is to select the printed word/symbol (C) that matches the paired sample stimuli (see Table 5, tasks 2 and 3).

Simultaneous Receptive Training—Successive Tasks   This training incorporated the contiguity and response equivalence procedures of Table 1. The simultaneous receptive training involved the simultaneous presentation of an auditory label and gesture as in Total Communication programs. In training phase 1 the response choices were pictures (B) and in training phase 2 they were printed words/symbols (C) or vice versa (Table 5, tasks 1 and 7 and tasks 2 and 3). Mastery of both training tasks is required before mediated transfer could be expected to occur, because all stimuli have to be included at some point in training.

Results

In pretraining all subjects performed at an 85% correct response level or better. Thus, the subjects demonstrated proficiency in discriminating between pictures, printed words/symbols, gestures, and/or auditory labels to be used in training.

For all experimental conditions, the initial probe data (see Table 5) showed a low level of performance for the six probes (Figures 3 through 6). The overall median probe performance level was 31%.

Successive Receptive-Associative Training   Figure 3 presents probe and training data for the successive receptive-associative (A–C/B–C) experimental condition. Training phase 1 resulted in criterion performance being achieved in a range of 105 to 245 trials for associative or gestural-receptive training. The second set of probes (P2) showed an increased proficiency level when compared to P1 but only approximating

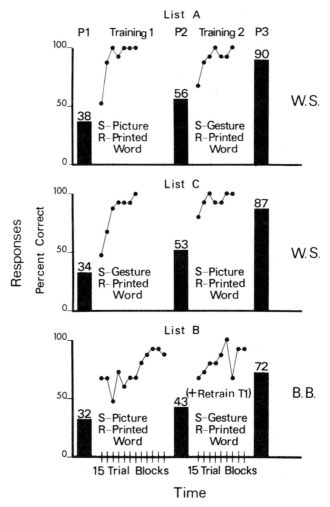

Figure 3.   Successive receptive-associative training (stimulus equivalence). Solid bars indicate mean performance for combined probe tasks 1 through 6 (see Table 5).

a 50% performance level. Training phase 2 resulted in criterion performance being achieved in a range of 105 to 245 trials for the second set of training trials.

The final probe (P3) shows that the second training phase had a significant effect on percent of correct responses. However, the expressive probe tasks showed a lower performance level than the associative and receptive tasks (Table 5). The data from subject W. S. suggest that the order of training tasks (receptive) or associative is not crucial, which is supported by additional data from Wulz and Hollis (1979).

Successive Receptive Training   Figure 4 presents probe and training data for the successive receptive experimental condition (Table 5, tasks 1 and 2). Training phase 1 resulted in criterion performance being achieved in a range of 165 to 345 trials for gesture to symbol/printed word or picture. The second set of probes (P2) showed an increase in proficiency level when compared to P1, but only in the 48%–58% range. Training phase 2 resulted in criterion performance being achieved in a range of 165 to 330 trials.

The final probe (P3) shows that the second training phase had a significant effect on percent of correct responses for subjects G. C. and B.

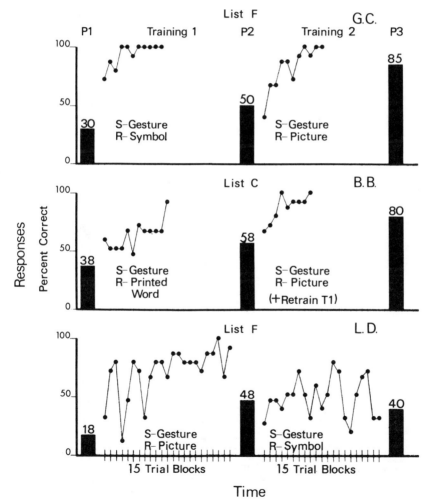

Figure 4.   Successive receptive training (response equivalence). Solid bars indicate mean performance for combined probe tasks 1 through 6 (see Table 5).

B. However, subject L. D. failed to meet criterion in phase 2 and subsequently showed a slight reduction in performance on probe (P3).

Simultaneous Receptive-Associative Training   Figure 5 presents probe and training data for simultaneous receptive-associative training (Table 5, tasks 2 and 3). Training phase 1 resulted in subjects W. S. and B. B. meeting criterion at 105 and 180 trials, respectively. Subject S. H. did not achieve criterion even after 240 trials. The second set of probes (P2) showed an increase in proficiency for subjects W. S. and B. B. but not for S. H. Training phase 2 resulted in criterion performance being

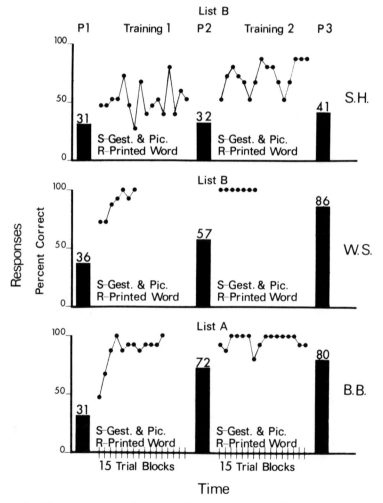

Figure 5. Simultaneous receptive-associative training (contiguity-stimulus equivalence). Solid bars indicate mean performance for combined probe tasks 1 through 6 (see Table 5).

reached rapidly for subjects W. S. and B. B.; however, subject S. H. failed to learn the task after 240 trials.

The final probe (P3) shows that the second training phase resulted in an increase in the percent of correct responses. Under the training procedures used, all subjects should have shown a substantial increase on probe (P3). Although subject S. H. met criterion in training phase 2, she responded proficiently only to the associative probe tasks. There was no indication that she attended to the gestures during the training phases.

Simultaneous Receptive Training—Successive Tasks   Figure 6 presents probe and training data for simultaneous receptive training with successive tasks (Table 5, tasks 1 and 7 and tasks 2 and 8). Training phase 1 resulted in criterion performance being achieved in a range of 165 to 345 trials. The second set of probes (P2) showed an increase in proficiency level when compared to P1, but only in the 38%–63% range. Training in phase 2 resulted in criterion performance being achieved in a range of 150 to 315 trials.

The final probe (P3) shows that the second training phase substantially increased the percent of correct responses for probe (P3). Thus, in the presentation of two verbal labels, auditory and gestural, correct responses to both sets of probes increased. This result suggests that the subjects attended to both stimuli in the multiple-stimulus presentation.

DISCUSSION

These studies demonstrate the effectiveness of the functional analysis of reading in establishing reading behavior with manual signs. All four procedures (stimulus equivalence, response equivalence, mediated association, and contiguity) were successful in producing mediated transfer as a result of reading training with retarded children.

Functional analysis of reading (Sidman, 1971) can be used as a model for teaching language to primates and exceptional children. For example, integration of language training employing two modes (e.g., speech and signs) is demonstrated by successful performance of tasks 1 (receptive comprehension, Figure 1) and 5 (picture naming) with both signs and speech. Furthermore, the use of communication boards is very similar to reading (see Vanderheiden and Grilley, 1976). A child who is fluent with a communication board should be able to perform all six reading tasks with the stimuli on that board. Note that this means that the child also needs a productive symbol system (such as speech or signs). However, he does not need to produce these productive responses. Comprehension is demonstrated by tasks 1 (receptive comprehension, Figure 1) and 2 (receptive reading, Figure 1). If he can perform task 2

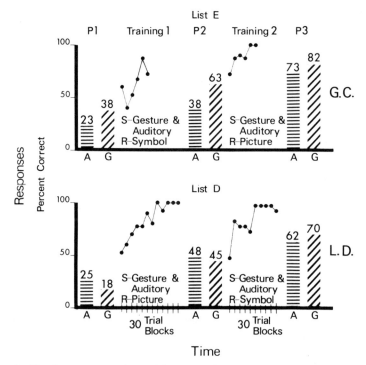

Figure 6. Simultaneous receptive training–successive tasks (contiguity-response equivalence). Bars labelled A (Auditory) indicate mean performance for combined probe tasks 7 through 10, and bars labelled G (Gesture) show performance for tasks 1, 2, 5, and 6 (see Table 5).

with the symbols on the communication board and a productive stimulus presented by someone in his environment, he has developed the equivalence between the productive and symbol selection systems. The same is true of children or primates being trained with other symbol selection systems (e.g., Carrier and Peak, 1975; Hodges and Deich, Chapter 18, this volume). Keeping the functional analysis of reading in mind, the gaps in the primate language research can easily be filled.

Triangulation, or mediated transfer, is an adaptive skill that allows generalization of a fact learned at one time or place to a fact learned at another time or place. However, in the cases where mediated transfer has occurred, there has always been a common stimulus (see Table 2). For example, in stimulus equivalence, the response remains the same in training phase 1 and training phase 2. Conversely, in response equivalence the stimulus remains the same. The mediated association procedure indicates that the common stimulus need not remain either a receptive or expressive stimulus. It is only essential that there is a common stimulus in training phases 1 and 2.

On the other hand, it cannot be assumed that mediated transfer will occur. Figures 3 through 6 indicate some intersubject variability in transfer, even when the tasks have been learned to criterion. However, additional training or applying consequences (reinforcers) during testing should establish the behavior.

The primary advantage of mediated transfer or triangulation is that very little training time needs to be invested to develop a complex behavior. For example, a primate or child being taught a less common communication mode (e.g., manual signing or use of a communication board) can learn to comprehend receptive speech with little additional teaching time through the contiguity procedure (see Table 2). In addition, the chimp or child can learn to read orthographic symbols while learning manual signs and/or receptive speech. There is no indication of a decrement in learning as a result of teaching two language stimuli simultaneously. Wulz and Hollis (1979) present data that suggest that simultaneous presentation actually facilitates learning. Therefore, the current concept of language training can be modified to include two or more input stimuli. This is especially relevant to the research with nonhuman primates in which training has involved only one response mode.

The procedures for producing mediated transfer that have been described in this chapter can be applied to a variety of educational problems. For example, Spradlin, Cotter, and Baxley (1973) demonstrated that classifications can be taught by a procedure involving mediated transfer. Spradlin and Dixon (1976) and Dixon and Spradlin (1976) demonstrated that mediated transfer can also occur in learning to assign labels to categories. Ongoing research in our laboratories is combining Spradlin and Dixon's research with Sidman's work on reading to demonstrate how concepts and reading can be taught simultaneously.

Those involved in research with nonhuman primates should find the mediated transfer research a fruitful area of investigation. Mediated transfer may provide a basis for concept development (Spradlin and Dixon, 1976) as well as establishing dual communication systems.

Our study and the studies analyzed herein indicate that researchers need to be more aware of mediated transfer and its application to language training. Many of the probes to test for mediated transfer have been neglected when the phenomenon might have occurred.

REFERENCES

Carrier, J. K., Jr. 1974. Application of functional analysis and a nonspeech response mode to teaching language. In L. V. McReynolds (ed.), Developing systematic procedures for training children's language. ASHA Monogr. 18.

Carrier, J. K., Jr., and Peak T. 1975. Non-speech Language Initiation Program. H & H Enterprises, Lawrence, Kan.

Dixon, M., and Spradlin, J. 1976. Establishing stimulus equivalences among retarded adolescents. J. Exp. Child Psychol. 21:144–164.

Estes, W. K. 1970. Learning Theory and Mental Development. Academic Press, New York.

Gardner, R. A., and Gardner, B. T. 1969. Teaching sign language to a chimpanzee. Science 167:664–672.

Gustason, G., Pfetzing, D., and Zawolkow, E. 1975. Signing Exact English. Modern Signs Press.

Hayes, C. 1951. The Ape in Our House. Harper & Brothers, New York.

Heber, R. A. 1961. Adaptive behavior: A manual on terminology and classification in mental retardation (2nd ed.). Am. J. Ment. Defic. (Monogr. Suppl.).

Hollis, J. H., and Carrier, J. K., Jr. 1978. Intervention strategies for nonspeech children. In R. L. Schiefelbusch (ed.), Language Intervention Strategies, pp. 57–100. University Park Press, Baltimore.

Jenkins, J. J., and Palermo, D. 1964. Mediation processes and the acquisition of linguistic structure. In U. Bellugi and R. Brown (eds.), The Acquisition of Language. University of Chicago Press, Chicago.

Kahn, J. V. 1977. A comparison of manual and oral language training with mute retarded chidren. Ment. Retard. 15:21–23.

Kellogg, W. N., and Kellogg, L. A. 1933. The Ape and the Child: A Study of Environmental Influence on Early Behavior. McGraw-Hill Book Co., New York.

Kopchick, G. A., and Lloyd, L. L. 1976. Total communication for the severely language impaired: A 24-hour approach. In L. L. Lloyd (ed.), Communication Assessment and Intervention Strategies, pp. 501–521. University Park Press, Baltimore.

Menzel, E. W., and Johnson, M. K. 1976. Communication and cognitive organization in humans and other animals. Ann. N.Y. Acad. Sci. 280:131–142.

Patterson, F. 1978. Linguistic capabilities of a lowland gorilla. In F. C. C. Peng (ed.), Sign Language and Language Acquisition—New Dimensions in Comparative Pedolinguistics, pp. 161–201. Westview Press, Boulder, Col.

Peters, H. N. 1935. Mediate association. J. Exp. Psychol. 18:20–48.

Premack, D. 1970. A functional analysis of language. J. Exp. Anal. Behav. 14:107–125.

Rachlin, H. 1970. Introduction to Modern Behaviorism. W. H. Freeman & Co., San Francisco.

Rumbaugh, D. M., Gill T., and von Glasersfeld, E. 1973. Reading and sentence completion by a chimpanzee (Pan). Science 182:731–733.

Sidman, M. 1971. Reading and auditory-visual equivalences. J. Speech Hear. Res. 14:5–13.

Sidman, M., and Cresson, O., Jr. 1973. Reading and crossmodal transfer of stimulus equivalences in severe retardation. Am. J. Ment. Defic. 77:515–523.

Sidman, M., Cresson, O., and Willson-Morris, M. 1974. Acquisition of matching to sample via mediated transfer. J. Exp. Anal. Behav. 22:261–273.

Spradlin, J. E., Cotter, V. W., and Baxley, N. 1973. Establishing a conditional discrimination without direct training: A study of transfer with retarded adolescents. Am. J. Ment. Defic. 77:556–566.

Spradlin, J. E., and Dixon, M. H. 1976. Establishing conditional discrimination: Without direct training. Am. J. Ment. Defic. 80:555–561.

Van Biervliet, A. 1977. Establishing words and objects as functionally equivalent through manual sign training. Am. J. Ment. Defic. 82:178–186.

Vanderheiden, G. C., and Grilley, K. 1976. Non-vocal Communication Techniques and Aids for the Severely Physically Handicapped. University Park Press, Baltimore.

Wulz, S. V., and Hollis, J. H. 1979. Reading skill development in severe retardation: An analysis of cross-modal transfer. *In* R. L. Schiefelbusch (ed.), Nonspeech Language and Communication: Analysis and Intervention. University Park Press, Baltimore. In press.

Section

Epilogue

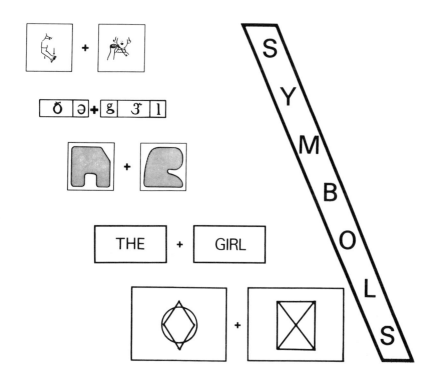

chapter

21

Perspectives on Nonspeech Symbol Systems

Joseph K. Carrier, Jr.*

Bureau of Child Research
University of Kansas
Lawrence, Kansas

The purpose of this chapter is to provide a perspective on nonspeech symbol systems to facilitate constructive explanation and future application. Nonspeech systems, as components of communication training strategies, are a relatively recent development. It should be clear from the earlier chapters in this book that the art is still in its early formative stages. There is a need for intensive study of several issues if nonspeech systems are to achieve their potential as powerful teaching tools.

This chapter is divided into three sections. The first is a general statement of what we now know about applications of nonspeech symbols in teaching communication. Preceding chapters have provided details on applications. This section of this chapter provides an overview to help the reader gain a perspective for the second part of the chapter, which is a presentation of a variety of issues seen by this author as directly related to the ultimate incorporation of nonspeech symbol components into viable communication training strategies. Several areas of research and development must be dealt with if nonspeech symbols are to play a meaningful, lasting role in communication training. The final section of the chapter presents a series of issues less directly related to communication training but quite relevant to responsible, professional treatment of nonverbal, handicapped individuals. These issues are presented because they are the issues that are most important in using nonspeech symbols.

STATUS OF NONSPEECH SYMBOL SYSTEMS

Other chapters in this volume present details on recent work with nonspeech symbol systems. The discussion here presents an overview of what has been done in order to provide a meaningful perspective on where future efforts might best be directed.

Until recently, most efforts to use nonspeech systems with the handicapped were limited to teaching manual symbol systems to the deaf. Since the early 1970s, some researchers and teachers have been exploring applications of various symbol system types with a variety of impaired individuals. Manual symbol systems have received attention from both the scientific and the teaching communities, and efforts have been directed toward using a large number of different systems with special groups of noncommunicative humans. In addition, some researchers and teachers have begun working with systems individually tailored to the needs of persons with severe, limiting handicaps. These promise to add many nonspeech system types to those already in common use.

In addition to interest in a growing number of nonspeech symbol systems types, there have been (in the past few years) increased efforts to apply such systems with nondeaf, handicapped individuals. Data are now available for severely and profoundly retarded individuals (Carrier and Peak, 1975) and for autistic children (McLean and McLean, 1974; Car-

---

* Affiliation given reflects author's former affiliation.

rier, 1974a, 1974b), and data are currently being collected from deaf-blind individuals and aphasic adults. Nonspeech symbol systems have potential benefits for nearly every subgroup of severely communicatively impaired individuals.

A few years ago there was concern about transfer from one symbol system to another. Educators of the deaf dichotomized themselves into "oral schools" and "manual schools" because of a generally accepted hypothesis that individuals who learned manual systems would then have no need to learn speech. They believed that the mastery of a manual system would interfere with learning spoken symbols. However, recent research has shown that this assumption was not based on observations. There are now data to show transfer from manual systems to speech (Moores, 1979; Schaeffer, 1979), from manipulable symbol systems to speech (Carrier and Peak, 1975), and from manipulable systems to written systems (Kuntz, 1974). Furthermore, based upon learning theory, performance data, and inferences about human motivation, there is now a strong rationale that the most expedient teaching strategies should begin with the system most easily mastered by the learner. That system should then be used to establish another symbol system that will have maximal utility in the individual's everyday environment. The nonspeech symbol system research of the past few years indicates that it is important to begin teaching a communication system that is easily learned by the individual involved.

Finally, research in the past few years indicates that nonspeech symbol systems can be applied to teaching in an effective, efficient, and replicable manner. For example, manipulable symbols can be used to teach language and (ultimately) spoken communication to many severely and profoundly retarded individuals who were previously considered unable to learn linguistic communication. These procedures are efficient. Data (Carrier and Peak, 1975) show a mean time of less than 15 hours of formal training for learning to generate original, seven-word responses. Data from this same training program (Non-SLIP) also has shown that more than 180 severely handicapped children in over 20 different centers with different trainers have demonstrated remarkably similar results, indicating that programmed work with manipulable symbols is clearly replicable. Nonspeech symbol systems offer both theoretical and data-based advantages as potentially powerful teaching tools.

ISSUES RELATED TO
NONSPEECH SYSTEMS FOR TEACHING COMMUNICATION

The recent surge in effort and interest in nonspeech symbol systems for teaching communication to severely impaired persons has created a corpus of data-based information and has provided significant improvements in teaching strategies. However, only the surface has been scratched. There is much that is still unclear, much for which data are still unavailable, and much that has not yet received serious consideration. In this section issues related to the use of nonspeech systems for teaching communications, issues that are appropriate subjects for research in the near future, are identified.

Figure 1 maps some of the more general, critical components of an effort to incorporate nonspeech systems into a viable treatment strategy or strategies. The bottom row on the lattice (areas for study) consists of a series of issues for which current knowledge is seriously lacking. Each of these, when appropriate information is made available, will contribute to more effective teaching study and planning and will facilitate the development of viable training programs. The study of stimulus control and continuing management should improve our training technology and greatly enhance our efforts to develop effective prelanguage training programs. Language systems (areas for study) need careful examination if the functions of the various symbol systems are to permit a nonspeculative understanding of appropriate application of emerging teaching strategies. This understanding, combined with the prelanguage training programs, will permit development of effective individual appropriate symbolic language training programs. The study of post-nonspeech training and of transfer from one symbol type to another will form the rationale for appropriate transfer and post-nonspeech training. The addition of explicit criteria for functional communication will lead to a viable communication training program in which nonverbal humans are taught to use effective communication.

The end product would ideally be a training program or a series of well coordinated programs in which any nonverbal human would acquire:

1. Skills prerequisite to learning linguistic communication
2. Language using an appropriate symbol type
3. Appropriate transfer and follow-up training

Training would be completed when functional communication was optimally intact. The lattice represents only one form of an ideal. It is intended primarily as a framework for this chapter but could serve as a map for professionals interested in further pursuit of applications of nonspeech symbol systems.

Improving Initial Training Procedures

Available data indicate that, once a child has learned a few basic symbols and sequencing skills, that child will progress through subsequent training at a reasonably high rate (Carrier and Peak, 1975). However,

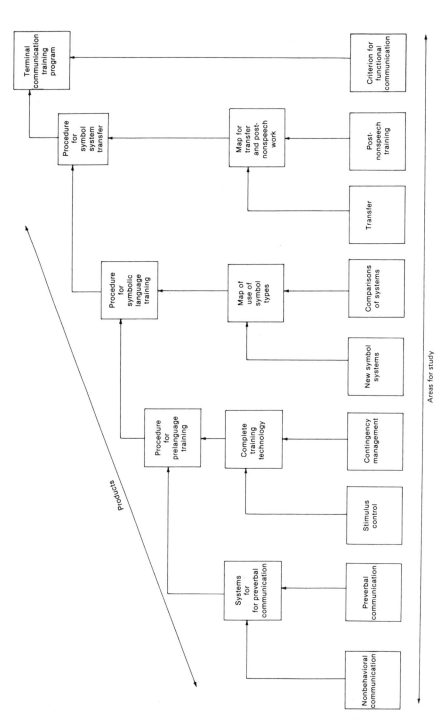

Figure 1. Critical components of an effort to incorporate nonspeech systems into a variable treatment strategy or strategies.

establishing the first few skills to be trained is frequently quite difficult and is not always possible. This suggests that more research is needed to develop viable programs for the initial phases of training. There are several distinct study areas that may contribute significantly to solving those problems.

Stimulus Control   One of the first steps in any training endeavor is to establish "stimulus control" or to reach a point at which the trainer can consistently evoke from the child a response of some specific class when a stimulus of a specific class is presented. This could be putting a toy in the trainer's extended hand, pressing a button when a light appears, or responding with some other behavior easily emitted by the child when the trainer presents a stimulus. Stimulus control is not often a major problem in a well controlled laboratory setting, nor is it often a problem to the highly skilled trainer, but the simple fact is that most children are trained out of the laboratory by persons who do not always have extensive skills. That is why one of the most perplexing problems to teachers of the severely handicapped is one of establishing stimulus control.

Many problems encountered by teachers attempting to get children started in training could be eliminated by a formal training program consisting of a set of explicit instructions for teachers. This program should be flexible in terms of the children with whom it would be effective, thus allowing for a broad spectrum of individual differences. There should be a variety of possible stimuli and responses, and there should be mechanisms for selecting stimuli and responses most appropriate to each child. Such a program should have, as a terminal goal, conditioned behaviors that indicate when the child is indeed operating under stimulus control.

In addition to a need for a formal program that can be used by trainers in establishing stimulus control, there is a need for further understanding of the dynamics of stimulus control among the severely handicapped. Some children exhibit excellent stimulus control when left alone in a room to interact with a teaching machine. Those same children may show no real control when interacting with a human trainer (Carrier and Peak, 1975). Others come under stimulus control during the early phases of training and then suddenly appear to be completely incapable of learning any more or remembering what they just learned (Carrier and Peak, 1975). (Sometimes the child appears to be deliberately refusing to learn.) The reasons behind such problems are not known, nor are the solutions. However, it should be possible to study these issues and determine the dynamics of stimulus control and suggest viable prerequisites to stimulus control. (Stimulus control is generally presumed to be one of the lowest order concepts basic to learning, but there may well be more basic skills that could facilitate learning stimulus control.)

Contingency Management   The issues related to the selection, use, and maintenance of effective reinforcers constitute another area in need of additional effort. The nonspeech symbol systems are reaching children never before seriously considered suitable for formal training. The result has been a growing awareness of technological problems never before considered to be significant. It is clear that, as strategies improve and continue to improve, technological problems that were once of no serious concern are now vital issues. Contingency management is one such issue. Defining a reinforcer as a stimulus following a response (Holland and Skinner, 1961) is helpful when a reinforcer can be found that is both effective and consistent. However, when either effectiveness or consistency with one child may change from moment to moment, there is a need for deeper understanding. Many severely communicatively handicapped persons are difficult children who do not respond to things commonly known as effective "reinforcers" (Carrier and Peak, 1975). Many will accept a consequent event as a reinforcer for a while but later will want nothing to do with it. Other children will accept reinforcers as positive reinforcers for part of training and then later react to them as negative reinforcers. (Response rate increases and then decreases with the same reinforcer.)

Such observations are common and are serious problems to any trainer of the severely impaired. Again, there is a need for greater understanding of the dynamics of these processes, and there is a need, ultimately, for a simple set of step-by-step procedures that a trainer at any level of experience can follow. It is only by clearing up these technological issues, both stimulus control and contingency management, that it will be possible to learn the true potentials of nonspeech symbol systems and of many of the individuals who are currently the most difficult to teach.

UNDERSTANDING APPLICATIONS OF VARIOUS SYMBOL TYPES

One conclusion to be drawn from previous chapters of this book is that there are now in use (and under study) a variety of nonspeech-oriented strategies for teaching communication skills. Specific symbol types being used include numerous manual symbol systems (Moores, 1979), manipulable symbols (Hodges and Deich, Chapter 18, this volume), written symbols (Kuntz, 1974), computer-assisted symbols (Parkel and Smith, Chapter 19, this volume), and individually tailored symbol sets to be used in communication boards (McDonald, 1979). These symbols are used to teach linguistic communication, but the language rules being taught vary greatly. Several different language systems are used with the various manual symbol systems (Moores, 1979). Some teachers have chosen limited but functional language as their goals (Hodges and Deich, Chapter 18, this volume; Schaeffer, 1979). Others strive to master Standard American English. At least one program (Non-SLIP) teaches only a small set of language rules as a means of facilitating individual teaching efforts on the part of the child. Thus, although the ultimate goals of all efforts may be to teach children to communicate, the symbol systems and the languages taught vary greatly.

There is some value in independent explanations of various symbol types and language systems, but the need for coordinated efforts is critical. The current trends toward individual development of "ideal language models" and toward study of some "pet symbol systems" create a danger of producing so many completely different sets of strategies that coordinating them into appropriate training mechanisms for all children may be impossible. The issue of how to best teach a particular child could become one of making arbitrary decisions about numerous, quite different strategies. There is a need for careful coordination of various efforts to objectively determine the advantages and disadvantages of different symbol types and languages for each individual handicapped person.

Coordinating the linguistic rules, stimuli, and vocabularies to be taught is not a simple matter. There are sound rationales for various strategies. However, of the languages and rationales available, some may serve unique contributive roles, whereas others may be little more than attempts by teachers and researchers to meet their own needs independently of what has already been done. There is a danger that several centers across the country may create separate, complete systems that will successfully teach some form of communication, but that will be incompatible with all other systems. It is unlikely that there will be for some time any one model of language that works for all, but it seems that there is a definite need for standardization efforts in this direction.

The tremendous variety of emerging nonspeech symbol systems is another problem of the same ilk. Researchers and teachers tend to choose and create symbol sets and to study and apply them without careful consideration of others. There is not one study, in this book, of comparisons among symbol types. Each symbol type has a theory-based rationale, but there are no data showing which symbol types work best for which children or which is most conclusive to transfer to other types. Chapter 1, by Hollis and Schiefelbusch, defines variables that should be studied in relation to various symbol types. Each has advantages and disadvantages that can be defined in terms of child characteristics, but there are no data to support objective statements.

When the individual characterization of the various language models and symbol types are understood, the matter of developing appropriate training programs will be considerably easier. The language symbol types to be used for any given child should be determined by the child's needs rather than by what is available in the child's training environment.

Development of Training Programs

The development of effective, efficient, and replicable training programs is another area in need of considerable additional study. The work reported in the earlier chapters of this book represents numerous creative efforts to teach children, and it points out similarities among findings of independent investigations as one form of evidence of potentially powerful strategies. However, there is a dearth of carefully defined training procedures. Not only is replicability an impossible task, but it is still quite impossible to conclude that the nonspeech symbols were any more related to success than was a good teacher or an intensive training effort. It will be necessary to define precise teaching strategies before it will be possible to define the function of symbol types. Specified procedures and carefully collected data will facilitate comparisons among symbol types, languages, different diagnostic groups, and acquisition rates of different skills. All this information is basic to effective, efficient, and replicable training procedures that are suited to the needs of each individual nonverbal human.

FACILITATING TRANSFER
FROM ONE SYMBOL SYSTEM TO ANOTHER

The ultimate goal of communication training is the establishment of skills that allow the learner to communicate effectively in any circumstance. Even though most trainers would agree that spoken linguistic communication is probably the most desirable goal, there should be options for those individuals without adequate physiological mechanisms for speech. Experience with nonspeech systems suggests that training should begin with whichever symbol system is most conducive to the individual's initial success in training and should evolve to the system that is most conducive to satisfactory communication in the individual's everyday environment. This suggests that the issue of transfer from one system to another is basic to a meaningful, productive use of nonspeech symbol systems.

Although the concept of *transfer* has begun to receive special attention in the past few years, there are several issues (perhaps peculiar to transfer from one communication symbol system to another) that remain unresolved. Although transfer from one symbol system to another can indeed be accomplished, and the data clearly show that many severely impaired individuals can learn to use spoken symbols, attempts to develop formal training programs for facilitating transfer in this special case have not been fruitful. The following paragraphs speculate about some of the issues that may be relevant and suggest (at least indirectly) some of the areas in which exploratory efforts might profitably be channeled.

The development of the Non-speech Language Initiation Program (Non-SLIP, Carrier and Peak, 1975) included attempts to facilitate transfer from manipulable to spoken symbols. Although this did not yield a finalized formal transfer training program, it illuminated several issues that need to be resolved. First, it is unclear when transfer training should begin, and it is unclear what variables best tell the trainer when to begin transfer training. Different children with apparently similar imitative abilities respond to transfer training in different ways. The level of progress through the nonspeech training in Non-SLIP is also a poor predictor of progress in transfer training. At this time it is clear only that there are undefined individual differences that must be identified if transfer training is to be introduced at appropriate times.

A second set of issues related to transfer from one symbol set to another is the procedures used to effect transfer. The protocols used in Non-SLIP are effective with many children, but, because they are contingent on voluntary child responses, they are nonfunctional for others. Furthermore, the procedures outlined in Non-SLIP are sometimes dependent (in their final stages) upon a trainer who has some background in speech pathology. The point is that current procedures are less than ideal and there is a clear need for formal programs for transfer training that can be administered reliably by paraprofessionals.

A third set of transfer issues relates to deciding if a child has made the transfer or if some alternative target or transfer program is needed. These issues (success/failure criterion levels) have been dealt with only in a subjective sense. There is a need for objective criteria defining successful transfer.

In conclusion, the entire transfer problem is critical to further developments in study and application of nonspeech symbol systems. It is possible to teach language with nonspeech symbols. Programs have been or are being developed to provide systematic efforts to do that. It is equally clear that transfer from one symbol system to another can be accomplished in most cases, but there is little effort being devoted to the study of transfer and the development of viable formal transfer training programs. The ultimate viability of nonspeech symbol system strategies may well depend upon the manner in which the issues of transfer are managed.

Determining Post-Nonspeech Training Strategies

As more and more viable programs become available for teaching children to use nonspeech symbol systems, the issues related to post-nonspeech training will become more and more important. It is likely that some programs will teach a terminal set of skills as does the Bliss system (McNaughton, 1979), i.e., the nonspeech system will become the child's communication system. In many cases, however, it may be desirable to begin training with a symbol set most easily learned by the child and then transfer linguistic concepts from that symbol set to speech or some other more generally applied symbols. Furthermore, even after a child has completed nonspeech training and made a transfer to speech, it is unlikely that training is complete. There is a series of issues relating to what becomes of a child after completion of nonspeech training. The solutions to these issues will be critical to the ultimate viability of nonspeech symbol strategies.

Defining Terminal Training Goals

Even with the emphasis the helping professions have placed upon communication and language, we remain in the dark about precisely what we should teach and precisely when our job is done. What grammar must be present in a child's repertoire? What vocabulary will render a child an acceptable communicating individual? Skinner's attempt to define verbal behavior (Skinner, 1957), Premack's functional analysis of language (Premack, 1970, 1976), linguistic literature, and recent research into the structure and dynamics of language offer suggestions of what is needed and come close to defining training goals. The first chapter in this book represents some of the analyses that might lead to appropriate definitions and Carroll (Carroll, 1979) offers great promise in this direction, but the work is all far from complete. It is only when such parameters are clearly defined that communication training programs will be maximally effective and efficient.

CONCLUSION REGARDING
NONSPEECH SYSTEMS FOR COMMUNICATION TRAINING

The issues presented above are not intended to be all-inclusive. They serve as a map for future goal-oriented research efforts. There are any number of issues worthy of study that were not discussed here because they are not critical or directly related to the use of nonspeech symbols for teaching functional communication to handicapped humans. If the issues discussed above are satisfactorily resolved, it should be possible to develop a viable, totally programmed, highly efficient training program.

Such a program might begin by systematically determining which of various possible symbol systems have the highest probability of succeeding with a specific child. The child might then proceed through the most appropriate of numerous training programs, make transfers from one symbol system to another, be channeled into an appropriate follow-up program, and dismissed at a point at which functional communication is intact. The nonspeech systems appear to have their own appropriate place in communication training, and the task at hand is to strengthen the knowledge of nonspeech systems and to coordinate that knowledge with other treatment strategies.

ISSUES RELATED TO
OTHER APPLICATIONS OF NONSPEECH SYMBOL SYSTEMS

The previous section of this chapter concerned efforts directed at developing effective communication training strategies using nonspeech symbols. This section is an attempt to expand that perspective to include other issues that may have not received serious consideration in the past, and that may not have such immediate direct application to communication training.

The past few years have witnessed a marked increase in successful efforts to teach various skills to children who were previously considered too seriously impaired to learn. A by-product of this work has been an increasing awareness that nonverbal humans are barely understood by the scientific teaching community. Our strategies have consistently been to change the handicapped to become more like us. We have made little if any real effort to explore their world. They are different because they do not learn to talk. They are different because they violate some of the principles of our teaching technologies. We have failed to understand these differences on their terms.

Nonspeech symbols are symbols, and symbols are basic to communication. Therefore, any study of nonspeech symbol systems is related to communication. However, as in any area of research, once a goal orientation has been established, some specific research projects are more directly relevant than others, and a goal-oriented plan for investigation must be restricted (at least in its early phases) to the most relevant issues. The previous section of this chapter discussed issues seen by this author as most directly relevant to the problem of developing the most effective and efficient programs (using nonspeech strategies) for teaching communication skills to certain handicapped individuals. This section departs slightly from the communication training goal to present a few additional, potentially constructive applications of nonspeech systems. This distinction is made not so much to isolate different areas of study as it is to suggest research strategies so that efforts can be devoted to meaning-ful projects that should ultimately be united into one body of knowledge. The issues presented in the previous section are those most directly rele-vant to the rapid development of communication training programs based on nonspeech strategies. The issues presented in this section are also relevant to that same goal but are not (at this time) as critical or as clear. This section contains issues that might be viewed as speculative, just as the viability of nonspeech systems was speculative only a few years ago. The purpose is to begin to deal with issues not directly related to communication training goals at this time, but with a potential for yielding invaluable information in the future.

In the early 1970s, communication training efforts with nondeaf humans were limited almost exclusively to spoken symbol system train-ing. Nonspeech systems were not "new." They were simply not considered for teaching humans. Then, as results from another, somewhat different area of research became available, some persons speculated that the nonspeech systems being used to study intellectual functioning in chimpanzees might serve as training strategies for non-verbal humans (Carrier, 1974a; Hodges and Deich, 1975). As clinical research efforts in this new direction began there was some criticism and opposition. "Nonspeech systems are not linguistic." "Nonspeech systems cannot be functional." "Nonspeech systems will interfere with speech development." "Nonspeech systems cannot be transferred to spoken systems."

Perhaps it is a necessary part of the process for new ideas to be criticized before being accepted, but it seems that it is also part of the process for new ideas to be considered objectively rather than to be rejected because they are unconventional or because they conflict with commonly accepted notions. The experience with nonspeech systems for teaching communication clearly illustrates that significant progress can be generated by exploration of new, and perhaps rather unconventional, directions.

Study of Preverbal Cognition

The concept of nonspeech symbol systems for teaching communication skills has evolved (at least in part) from the use of symbols to study cognition. Long before nonspeech symbols were used to teach human communication (manual systems for the deaf being one exception) they were being used by scientists studying intellectual functioning of both human and subhuman primates (Premack, 1970). They provided a mechanism by which linguistic-like functions could be studied inde-pendent of the physiological mechanisms for speech and, to some extent, independent of prior spoken language history (see Yerkes and Nissen,

Chapter 7, this volume). The thrust of the work with communicatively impaired humans has been a significant change in the application of nonspeech symbol systems, but it does not preclude the need for beginning more traditional areas of study with various handicapped populations.

The central issue is what the prelanguage child perceives in his environment and what such a child makes of those perceptions. There are arguments that concept formation is largely a function of language development—the label is based upon the identifying characteristics of a concept and thus permits an individual to develop a concept that can be communicated meaningfully. However, there are questions about such hypotheses that are suggested by work with certain preverbal individuals, particularly the severely communicatively handicapped. The fact that nonverbal, institutionalized retarded persons are able to emit any nonreflexive behavior that is functional would suggest that such a child, in spite of the lack of "words," must have developed some functional concepts (see Menzel and Johnson, Chapter 13, this volume). To go to the sink or fountain to get a drink suggests some concepts related to drinking water, the source for water, movement to that source, and proper manipulation of the drinking source to obtain the desired result. To indicate pain or hunger to an attendant, to eat food, to use the toilet, and to change clothes all require concepts. Nonverbal children do learn to emit a variety of behaviors. They learn to respond to stimuli of specific classes by using responses of specific classes. These actions indicate that these children must have certain preverbal concepts.

The data available from Non-SLIP, a program designed to teach communication skills with manipulable symbols, also contain some indication that preverbal concepts do exist (see Carrier, 1974a [Chapter 17, this volume]; Carrier and Peak, 1975). For example, many children (when learning noun symbols) learn to discriminatively use two different symbols to represent two different pictures and then, when a third picture and symbol are added, to immediately make an association between the two new items. It is not clear what parameters of pictures and symbols are used by the child, but it is clear that the child sees the new picture and the new stimulus as different from the old ones. Indications are that (at least in the case of nouns) children have some pretraining concepts that are readily generalized to the training environment. Such data are compatible with the fact that when a nonverbal child in an institutional cottage is hungry or in need of help, that child will generally go to an attendant rather than wander aimlessly from one person to another until the need is met. Such a child must have some conceptional base that permits consistent discrimination among various persons and objects in the environment.

Assuming that prelanguage concepts do exist, the real issues are clearly ones of identifying the nature and functions of these concepts. Viable communication training programs can be developed without a thorough understanding of preverbal concepts, but it is unlikely that such programs will ever be truly effective or efficient if such information is not obtained. Such information could contribute to a better understanding of the processes of normal language development.

The nonspeech strategies employed by researchers studying chimpanzees have also assumed that cognitive functioning does exist in a way that is functional for the nonverbal organism (Premack, 1970, 1976; Rumbaugh et al., Chapter 3, this volume; Stahlke et al., Chapter 4, this volume; Savage-Rumbaugh and Rumbaugh, Chapter 14, this volume; Fouts, Couch, and O'Neil, Chapter 15, this volume). The problem is one of finding ways for the organism to communicate this cognitive functioning to the researcher. Nonspeech symbol systems, as they provide successful strategies for studying chimpanzees and language-using humans, may provide strategies that add to the understanding of preverbal human cognition.

Studies such as those reported by Premack and other experimental psychologists might all be replicated with nonverbal humans to add to an understanding of preverbal cognition. There is another related type of research strategy that might prove equally beneficial. The common strategy is to begin by teaching a subject a language designed by the researcher and then using training data, generalization data, and subsequent verbal problem solving as evidence of various types of cognitive functions. An alternative to such a strategy might be to teach a child to teach language to the researcher. The child could then use nonspeech symbols to map his world for the researcher just as the researcher or clinician currently maps the verbal adult's linguistic world for children. Such a proposal may at first seem impractical. But there is evidence to suggest that such exploration would not be so difficult to begin. For example, a training situation could be easily established in which one nonverbal child and two trainers were present. One trainer would be inactive and the other would follow procedures already known to be effective, to teach the child a small number of nonspeech nouns. When the child indicated the mastery of the noun concept the active trainer would then proceed to teach the child how to teach the trained nouns to the inactive trainer. This would simply involve shaping the training behavior and teaching the child to present stimuli, to assess responses, and to provide contingencies. The child would then be given a new set of symbols and stimuli and taught to assign symbols to stimuli and to teach those labels to the inactive trainer. Finally, when the child learned to take a neutral symbol, assign a meaning to it, and teach this symbol to the inactive trainer, the child would be given a collection of neutral symbols and provided with a variety of environmental stimuli to label and teach to the inactive trainer. The inactive trainer would keep data on apparent identifying characteristics of child-labeled concepts and would use these data to form hypotheses about the nature of the child's concepts. These hypotheses could then be tested by presenting them back to the child for labeling. In this way a child could show his concepts to a researcher and tell the researcher when the concept was correctly perceived. Interestingly enough, most of the child behaviors necessary for such a project are behaviors that have already been taught to such children in a slightly different context and for different purposes. Such a project would be informative even in its very early stages. It would provide the basis for further studies of non-noun concepts and would perhaps eventually lead to verbal description by the child of his nonverbal conceptual world.

As information about the nonverbal child's conceptual world becomes available, and as strategies are developed for efficiently exploring each individual child's concepts, it should be simple to incorporate such strategies and findings into productive language-training efforts. For example, if it becomes possible to predetermine certain concepts a nonverbal child is likely to have, it would then be possible to teach labels for these concepts without teaching concepts and labels simultaneously. This is only one of several ways the training process could be improved by information about prelanguage cognition.

Study of Preverbal Communication

Current strategies for teaching communication skills to the severely impaired usually begin with an assumption that the nonspeaking child is a noncommunicating child. Since no semblance of spoken language exists, the child must begin at the beginning, learn discrimination among objects and symbols, learn to produce or manipulate symbols, learn to apply linguistic rules, and learn to use all this knowledge for functional communication. It seems appropriate, in this regard, to consider at least two possibilities:

1. First, it is an implicit assumption, and only an implicit assumption, that nonspeaking humans are also noncommunicators. Such an assumption is not even believed by most individuals experienced in working with non-speech-using humans. It is merely an assumption that is implicit in current training strategies because there is, as yet, no functional understanding of preverbal communication systems, what they are, or how they function.

2. Second, although the study of preverbal communication in the past has been primarily descriptive, nonspeech symbol systems appear to

offer a vehicle for studying such phenomena experimentally. If nonspeech symbol systems can be used to either translate or validate nonverbal communication events, they may help open the door to better scientific understanding of preverbal communication.

The concept of preverbal communication, like its antithesis, must be viewed as an assumption at this time, but it is hardly an assumption without attraction. If such a concept exists, it may be possible for spoken language users to systematically learn communication systems to allow them to communicate both deliberately and functionally with preverbal individuals. This could open the door to untold possibilities for communication with handicapped children and adults and with normal functioning infants. It could form the basis for unforseeable advances in teaching spoken language systems and it could obviously offer possibilities for improving all modes of teaching nonverbal humans.

The evidence for preverbal communication systems is unquestionably less than it might be, but it does exist. Gestures have been considered important to communication among and by nonverbal retardates for many years. Facial expressions, body postures, vocal patterns, and eye movements have long been accepted parameters of communication, and they are all used profusely by nonverbal humans. Babies in their cribs, as any parent can report, emit cries indicating certain specific needs that can be discriminated by the mother. Such systems are not necessarily linguistic in nature, but that does not mean they are not communication. The assumed value of language itself is something that may someday be evaluated. It is not the only communication system, nor is it necessarily the most desirable.

Observable behaviors that are traditionally linked with communication processes constitute one primary area for exploration. The communication functions of gestures, eyes, facial expressions, body postures, and nonverbal vocal behavior are all issues that remain unclear. These behaviors, however, can be observed, quantified, and used as the bases for hypotheses about various communication functions. Once these functions and systems have been hypothesized, it should be an easy matter to design analog systems using experimenter-chosen symbols as appropriate units. Transfer from the child's system to the analog system could then be taught and appropriate probe tests and generalization tests used to assess the similarity between the two. Once the analog system is taught, its various parameters as well as those of the child's system and appropriate communication circumstances could be manipulated as variables in numerous experiments designed to define the child's system. The nonspeech systems designed by the experimenter might act as translators from the child's communication system to that of the experimenter.

The possible findings from such research could be both extremely productive and extremely challenging. They could suggest ever-improving strategies for communicating with preverbal individuals. They might also help many severely nonverbal persons during the extensive period before they learn to communicate with organized symbol systems.

REFERENCES

Carrier, J. K., Jr. 1974a. Application of functional analysis and a nonspeech response mode to teaching language. *In* L. V. McReynolds (ed.), Developing systematic procedures for training children's language. ASHA Monogr. 18.

Carrier, J. K., Jr. 1974b. Non-speech noun usage training with severely and profoundly retarded children. J. Speech Hear. Res. 17:510–512.

Carrier, J. K., Jr. and Peak, T. 1975. Non-speech Language Initiation Program. H & H Enterprises, Lawrence, Kan.

Carroll, J. B. 1979. A performance grammar approach to language teaching. *In* R. L. Schiefelbusch (ed.), Nonspeech Language and Communication: Analysis and Intervention. University Park Press, Baltimore. In press.

Hodges, P., and Deich, R. 1975. Teaching an artifical language to nonverbal retardates. Unpublished manuscript, California State College, Los Angeles, and California Department of Mental Hygiene, Pacific State Hospital, Los Angeles.

Holland, J. G., and Skinner, B. F. 1961. The Analysis of Behavior. McGraw-Hill Book Co., New York.

Kuntz, J. B. 1974. A nonvocal communication development program for severely retarded children. Unpublished doctoral dissertation. Kansas State University, Manhattan, Kan.

McDonald, E. 1979. Children at risk in the development of intelligible speech. *In* R. L. Schiefelbusch (ed.), Nonspeech Language and Communication: Analysis and Intervention. University Park Press, Baltimore. In press.

McLean, L., and McLean, J. 1974. A language training program for nonverbal autistic children. J. Speech Hear. Res. 35:186–193.

McNaughton, S., and Kates, B. 1979. The application of Blissymbolics. *In* R. L. Schiefelbusch (ed.), Nonspeech Language and Communication: Analysis and Intervention. University Park Press, Baltimore. In press.

Moores, D. F. 1979. Alternative communication modes: Visual-motor systems. *In* R. L. Schiefelbusch (ed.), Nonspeech Language and Communication: Analysis and Intervention. University Park Press, Baltimore. In press.

Premack, D. 1970. A functional analysis of language. J. Exp. Anal. Behav. 148:107–125.

Premack, D. 1976. Intelligence in Ape and Man. John Wiley & Sons, New York.

Schaeffer, B. 1979. Spontaneous language through signed speech. *In* R. L. Schiefelbusch (ed.), Nonspeech Language and Communication: Analysis and Intervention. University Park Press, Baltimore. In press.

Skinner, B. F. 1957. Verbal Behavior. Appleton-Century-Crofts, New York.

Section VII

Appendix

Additional Readings and Films

ADDITIONAL READINGS

Aitchison, J. 1976. The Articulate Mammal. Universe Books, New York.

DeVore, I. (ed.) 1965. Primate Behavior: Field Studies of Monkeys and Apes. Holt, Rinehart & Winston, New York.

Harnad, S. R., Steklis, H. D., and Lancaster, J. 1976. Origins and Evolution of Language and Speech. The New York Academy of Sciences, New York.

Hayes, C. 1951. The Ape in Our House. Harper & Brothers, New York.

Kellogg, W. N., and Kellogg, L. A. 1933. The Ape and the Child: A Study of Environmental Influence on Early Behavior. McGraw-Hill Book Co., New York. [1967, Hafner, New York].

Köhler, W. 1959. The Mentality of Apes. Vintage Books, New York.

Linden, E. 1974. Apes, Men, and Language. Penguin Books, New York.

Premack, A. J. 1976. Why Chimps Can Read. Harper & Row, New York.

Premack, D. 1976. Intelligence in Ape and Man. John Wiley & Sons, New York.

Rumbaugh, D. M. 1977. Language Learning by a Chimpanzee: The LANA Project. Academic Press, New York.

Van Lawick-Goodall, J. 1971. In the Shadow of Man. Houghton Mifflin Publishing Co., Boston.

Yerkes, R. M. 1943. Chimpanzees: A Laboratory Colony. Yale University Press, New Haven, Conn.

Yerkes, R. M., and Yerkes, A. W. 1945. The Great Apes. Yale University Press, New Haven, Conn.

FILMS

Gardner, R. A., and Gardner, B. T. 1973. Teaching sign language to the chimpanzee Washoe (16-mm sound film). Psychological Cinema Register, State College, Pa. (Transcript of the sound track available from the authors on request.)

Hayes, K. J., and Hayes, C. 1950. Vocalization and speech in chimpanzees (16-mm sound film). Psychological Cinema Register, State College, Pa.

Hayes, K. J., and Hayes, C. 1952. Imitation in a home-raised chimpanzee (16-mm silent film). Psychological Cinema Register, State College, Pa.

Hayes, K. J., and Hayes, C. 1953. The mechanical interest and ability of a home-raised chimpanzee (16-mm silent film). Psychological Cinema Register, State College, Pa.

Kellogg, W. N., and Kellogg, L. A. 1932. Comparative tests on a human and a chimpanzee infant of approximately the same age (16-mm silent film). Psychological Cinema Register, University Park, Pa.

Kellogg, W. N., and Kellogg, L. A. 1932. Experiments upon a human and a chimpanzee infant after six months in the same environment (16-mm silent film). Psychological Cinema Register, University Park, Pa.

Kellogg, W. N., and Kellogg, L. A. 1933. Some behavior characteristics of a human and a chimpanzee infant in the same environment (16-mm silent film). Psychological Cinema Register, University Park, Pa.

Kellogg, W. N., and Kellogg, L. A. 1933. Some general reactions of a human and a chimpanzee infant after six months in the same environment (16-mm silent film). Psychological Cinema Register, University Park, Pa.

Kellogg, W. N., and Kellogg, L. A. 1945. Facial expressions of a human and a chimpanzee infant following taste stimuli (16-mm silent film). Psychological Cinema Register, University Park, Pa.

Time-Life Multimedia. The first signs of Washoe. (59-min color sound film). WGBH, Time-Life Multimedia, Time and Life Building, New York, New York.

Recent Research on the Non-speech Language Initiation Program (Non-SLIP)

RECOMMENDED USE OF PROGRAM

The Non-speech Language Initiation Program (Non-SLIP) has been field-tested in several different clinics with several different trainers. The data have been carefully monitored to determine whether they are consistent with the laboratory data generated during earlier phases of program development and consistent from trainer to trainer and center to center. The data have been consistent, with two exceptions. The laboratory work, including speech, was conducted by research assistants with no experience with speech training, and the field work has been conducted primarily by professional speech pathologists. The speech pathologists have been more successful in training speech production, i.e., have accomplished speech training in less time. The other exception was the data from a center in which the trainers did not follow the program instructions. These deviations from the specified training routines increased training times, increased error rates, and frequently required that the child be taken back to repeat portions of the program.

Non-SLIP is ready for general clinical application. It is an effective means of getting a large percentage (over 90% in available data) of children, with previously low likelihood of success, started in the process of learning communication skills.

These conclusions are further validated by the work of Hodges and Deich (1975; Chapter 18, this volume) in which similar procedures were used successfully. Their data are quite similar.

Non-SLIP has been tested with a variety of individuals with different etiologies and with different behavioral symptoms. Most children with primary emotional problems do quite well in Non-SLIP. In fact, some of the most remarkable success cases have been children diagnosed as autistic. McLean and McLean (1974) reported success using a similar approach with autistic children. Only a small number of children with

---

This material is provided as an addendum to Chapter 17, "Application of Functional Analysis and a Nonspeech Response Mode to Teaching Language." The following text is taken substantially from Carrier (1976), with appropriate updating provided by John Hollis.

primary diagnosis of hearing impairment have been run through Non-SLIP, but these children have been quite successful. This indicates that this program is appropriate for them.

Similar procedures used by Maison (1975) suggest that deaf children are viable candidates for such training. The reported success with hearing-impaired children is no great surprise because many of the concepts basic to Non-SLIP are similar to those used in education of the hearing impaired for many years (e.g., the Fitzgerald key, discussed in Davis and Silverman, 1965, pp. 446–447). Concurrent training on Non-SLIP and on manual communication has produced very rapid learning of syntax by a small number of deaf children. Children with a primary diagnosis of retardation (measured intelligence levels of IV and V and adaptive behavior levels of IV—Heber, 1961) have been successful in Non-SLIP, and the degree of success is not related to the measured degree of retardation. The programs have been conducted with individuals in nearly every age group from two- to three-year-olds to retarded adults in their 50s. The data on children under eight years of age are not comprehensive enough to conclude much about the rate of learning, but such children are able to complete Non-SLIP successfully. The data on adults, although also somewhat limited, indicate that they learn much more slowly than children.

Carrier has used Non-SLIP successfully with a small number of adult aphasics. Others (Velletri-Glass, Gazzaniga, and Premack, 1973; Gardner et al., 1975) also have found a nonspeech symbol system to be a viable approach for teaching adult aphasics.

The children with whom Non-SLIP is least successful fall into three groups. Children with motor problems that interfere with the required responses have learned very slowly and in some cases have not been able to go beyond training of motor responses. This problem may be reduced by using some of the techniques and devices described by Vanderheiden and Harris-Vanderheiden (1976). Children with frequent and severe seizures have been a problem as far as retaining behavior learned before a seizure, but a set of specially developed procedures called the Retention Program (Carrier and Peak, 1975) has largely eliminated this problem. The most troublesome children are those with a primary diagnosis of severe or profound retardation and with clear emotional overlay. At least two such subjects have shown resistance to learning. One was on the Labeling Program at a step where criterion levels were 15 consecutive correct responses. He began running 14 consecutive correct responses, then missing one, running 14 more, missing one, etc. The other child was working on the SMP and was supposed to select from two symbols the one matching the one on the tray. She would perform correctly to the preset criterion on some days but would never repeat the behavior for the next session, even if it were only a few minutes later. These two children gave continued indications of being able to learn the necessary tasks but were unwilling to cooperate long enough to meet criterion and move from step to step. Children showing such patterns over a large number of sessions have a very low likelihood of succeeding in Non-SLIP.

Areas in Need of Additional Study

Although Non-SLIP is currently ready for clinical application, it is still in need of further research. The teaching of the first two verbs and the first two prepositions is particularly difficult. The programs and the actual processes of teaching verbs and prepositions might be further studied and improved. Speech training is another major area in need of additional work. Recently, Horrocks and Hollis (1978) obtained some evidence indicating that learning semantic and syntactic rules in a nonspeech response mode facilitates the development of speech in some nonspeaking children.

The dynamics of the nonspeech language approach are quite similar to those involved in reading and writing. Kuntz, Carrier, and Hollis (1978) studied the transfer of nonspeech training to printed words and reported a high degree of success with severely retarded children. In another study Peach (1978), working with severely and moderately retarded people, compared the learning of semantic and syntactic rules using nonspeech plastic chips and printed words. He found that the nonspeech program was applicable to both types of stimulus materials. Furthermore, there may be an advantage with respect to training time in using only printed words.

Another general area in which Non-SLIP might be further studied is in training children with severe motor problems and/or children with severe sensory problems. In some cases, alternative stimuli should be developed. In others, alternative symbol sets should be studied. The basic procedures used in Non-SLIP could function as a starting point in such work and could possibly expedite development of effective procedures for such special children.

In addition to the clinically oriented issues mentioned above, a variety of research questions remain about why children are as successful as they are with the nonspeech program. It might be profitable, for example, to compare processing of auditory versus visual stimuli. This problem, in part, has been approached in a study by Wulz and Hollis (Chapter 20, this volume) on the development of reading skills. It is this type of research that may lead to further improvement in training and to new ways to deal more effectively with children who have difficulty with nonspeech programs.

REFERENCES

Carrier, J. K., Jr. 1976. Application of nonspeech language system with the severely language handicapped. *In* L. L. Lloyd (ed.), Communication Assessment and Intervention Strategies, pp. 523–547. University Park Press, Baltimore.

Carrier, J. K., Jr., and Peak, T. 1975. Non-speech language initiation program. H & H Enterprises, Lawrence, Kan.

Davis, H., and Silverman, S. R. 1965. Hearing and Deafness. Holt, Rinehart & Winston, New York.

Gardner, H., Zurif, E., Berry, T., and Baker, E. 1975. Visual communication in aphasia. Unpublished manuscript, Aphasia Research Center, Boston University School of Medicine and Psychology Service, Boston Veterans Administration Hospital, Boston.

Heber, R. 1961. Adaptive behavior: A manual on terminology and classification in mental retardation (2nd ed.). Am. J. Ment. Defic. (Monogr. Suppl.).

Hodges, P., and Deich, R. 1975. Teaching an artificial language to nonverbal retardates. Unpublished manuscript, California State College, Los Angeles, and California Department of Mental Hygiene, Pacific State Hospital, Los Angeles.

Horrocks, B. L., and Hollis, J. H. 1978. Non-speech language training. *In* N. Haring (ed.), Teaching the Severely Handicapped, Vol. 4.

Kuntz, J. B., Carrier, J. K., and Hollis, J. H. 1978. A nonvocal system for teaching retarded children to read and write. *In* C. E. Meyers (ed.), Quality of Life in Severely and Profoundly Mentally Retarded People: Research Foundations for Improvement. American Association on Mental Deficiency, Washington, D. C.

McLean, L., and McLean, J. 1974. A language training program for nonverbal autistic children. J. Speech Hear. Res. 35:186–193.

Maison, E. P. 1975. Teaching preschool deaf children to use written language: A pilot study of a new approach. Unpublished manuscript, Oral Education Center of Southern California, Los Angeles.

Peach, R. V. 1978. A reading and writing initiation program administered in the homes of moderately and severely retarded illiterates. Unpublished doctoral dissertation, Kansas State University, Manhattan, Kan.

Vanderheiden, G. C., and Harris-Vanderheiden, D. 1976. Communication techniques and aids for the nonvocal severely handicapped. *In* L. L. Lloyd (ed.), Communication Assessment and Intervention Strategies, pp. 607–652. University Park Press, Baltimore.

Velletri-Glass, A., Gazzaniga, M., and Premack, D. 1973. Artificial language training in global asphasics. Neuropsychologia 11:95–104.

index

Ally
language comprehension in,
300–301, 474
reading skills, 472
syntactic competence in, 301–303
teaching language to, 300–303
translating English into signing,
300–301, 475
use of mediated association,
474–475
use of prepositions, 302
use of response equivalence, 474
Ambiguity, semantic, and
communication process,
60–61
American Sign Language (ASL,
Ameslan), 175–176, 307–309
see also Manual signing
Ape
in behavioral research, effect of
environment on, 134–135,
142
biological relation to human, 85,
113, 140–141, 297
general system for language analysis
in, 3–48
human speech in, 6–7, 76, 138–139,
163–164, 166, 209–211
humanizing of, 6–7, 122–124, 127,
129–144, 215
intelligence in, versus human,
161–162
in language research
general overview of, 3–17, 27–40,
121–127
use as model, 47–48, 87
proposed rearing in human
environment, 137–139,
142–143
teaching language to, see Language
acquisition; Language
training
see also Chimpanzee; Gorilla
Aphasic adult
use of nonspeech symbol systems,
518

use of plastic word symbols, 422
see also Child, receptive aphasic
Association, mediated, 474–475, 486
Associative tasks, in testing reading
skills, 480, 481–482, 484
Attention, selective, definition, 124
Autistic child, see under Child

Babbling, 163–164, 182–183, 207, 209,
308
Back-channel responses, in
conversations, 68–70
Behavior
communicative, behavior models
and, 49–72
motor
as linguistic expressive function,
25–26
symbolic significance of, 274
"symbolic," 147
Behavior modification, use in teaching
language, 314
Behavioral development, nature versus
nurture, 131–144
Behavioral properties
of humans versus animals, 133–134,
297
importance in research, 5, 175, 221,
313–314
Behavioral research
animal models in, 75
criticisms of, 134–135, 142
Booee, teaching language to, 298–299
Bruno
ability to distinguish chimpanzee
calls, 303–304
comprehension of same/different,
303–304
teaching language to, 11, 12,
298–299

Child
autistic
speech development in, 309, 310,
311, 312

521